The Media at War

DA

By the same author

Winning Hearts and Minds: British Governments, the Media and Colonial Counter-Insurgency, 1944–60

War, Culture and the Media: Representations of the Military in Twentieth Century Britain (edited, with Ian Stewart)

The Media at War

**Communication and Conflict
in the Twentieth Century**

Susan L. Carruthers

Published by
PALGRAVE MACMILLAN
Houndmills, Basingstoke, Hampshire RG21 6XS and
175 Fifth Avenue, New York, N. Y. 10010
Companies and representatives throughout the world

PALGRAVE MACMILLAN is the global academic imprint of the Palgrave
Macmillan division of St. Martin's Press, LLC and of Palgrave Macmillan Ltd.
Macmillan® is a registered trademark in the United States, United Kingdom
and other countries. Palgrave is a registered trademark in the European
Union and other countries.

Outside North America
ISBN 0–333–69142–3 hardback
ISBN 0–333–69143–1 paperback

Inside North America
ISBN 0–312–22800–7 hardback
ISBN 0–312–22801–5 paperback

This book is printed on paper suitable for recycling and made from fully
managed and sustained forest sources.

A catalogue record for this book is available
from the British Library.

A catalogue record for this book is available
from the Library of Congress.

ISBN 0–312–22800–7 hardback
ISBN 0–312–22801–5 paperback

10   9   8   7   6   5   4
10   09   08   07   06   05   04

Printed in China

For John Hardie Carruthers

Contents

Contents

Acknowledgements

Many people have helped me write this book, some of them – I'm quite sure – without their realising it. The following list of thanks represents partial repayment to only a few of those to whom I'm most heavily indebted.

I would never have had an opportunity to write this book without the provision of two semesters of sabbatical leave from the Department of International Politics, in the University of Wales, Aberystwyth. I would therefore like to thank my colleagues and the University for providing me with time in which to reflect and write. And I should also express my thanks to the staff of both the Hugh Owen Library and the National Library of Wales for helping me get hold of materials I needed.

Friends in the Department have also played a critical role in supporting me through the writing process, though I regret that I did not see them as often as I might have wished due to prolonged periods spent hunched over my computer in the attic. Special thanks are due to Steve Hobden and Lucy Taylor for both supporting and distracting me, and to Nick Wheeler, who attentively read part of the manuscript, and kept me straight on UN resolutions. I am also grateful to five generations of students to whom the code IP35920 will mean something, and to Masters students who have taken my option. Teaching these courses has stimulated me to consider not only what I think but how best to communicate what I think about war and the media in an accessible way, and I hope that future students will benefit from insights I gleaned from their predecessors.

My intellectual and personal debts extend far beyond 'Interpol', however. A number of colleagues whom I also value as friends have stimulated my thinking and sustained my spirits over the years. Phil Taylor, who first introduced me to the study of war and the media as an undergraduate, has my ongoing gratitude. But also particular thanks to Nick Cull, Tom Doherty and Ian Stewart, who in different ways have cheered me through *The Media at War*. Deferred dead-lines notwithstanding, my publisher Steven Kennedy provided timely advice, support and encouragement.

Finally, I must thank – and apologise to – those closest, who have borne the brunt of my long lapses into silence and retreats to the study. *I Elwyn–diolch am bopeth a chariad anf erthol, fel arfer.* And to my parents, heartfelt thanks for nurturing a love of books, and for constantly encouraging me in everything I do. This book is dedicated to my father, John Hardie Carruthers, a belated present for a significant birthday, in long overdue thanks for fruitless hours spent trying to instil some algebraic sense into an unreceptive pupil all those years ago, and so much more.

SUSAN L. CARRUTHERS

Abbreviations

BBC	British Broadcasting Corporation
BBFC	British Board of Film Censors
BMP	Bureau of Motion Pictures (US, Second World War)
CIA	Central Intelligence Agency
CNN	Cable News Network
CNNI	Cable News Network International
DORA	Defence of the Realm Act (UK)
ETA	*Euzkadi Ta Akatasuma* (Basque Homeland and Liberty)
FTU	Forward Transmission Unit (attached to the Coalition military during the 1991 Gulf War)
IGO	Inter-governmental Organisation
INLA	Irish National Liberation Army
IRA	Irish Republican Army
ITN	Independent Television News
ITV	Independent Television
JIB	Joint Information Bureau (of the UN Coalition during the 1991 Gulf War)
MIA	Missing in Action
MOD	Ministry of Defence
MOI	Ministry of Information (UK, Second World War)
MRT	media reporting team (in the 1991 Gulf War)
NGO	Non-Governmental Organisation
OKW	*Oberkommand das Wehrmacht* (Army High Command, Germany, 1933–45)
OWI	Office of War Information (US, Second World War)
PAO	public affairs officer
PK	*Propaganda Kompanien* (Propaganda Companies, attached to the Nazi Wehrmacht)
PRO	public relations officer
RFK	*Reichsfilmkammer* (Reich Chamber of Film, Germany, 1933–45)

RKK	*Reichskulturkammer* (Reich Chamber of Culture, Germany, 1933–45)
RPF	Rwanda Patriotic Front
RMVP	*Reichsministerum Für Volksaufklarung und Propaganda* (Reich Ministry for Popular Enlightenment and Propaganda, Germany, 1933–45)
RTLM	*Radio Television Libre des Milles Collines* (radio station in Rwanda)
RTS	Serbian Radio Television
SD	*Sicherheitsdienst* (Nazi Security Service)
SS	*Schutzstaffeln* (Nazi Blackshirts)
UFA	*Universum Film Aktiengesellschaft* (Universal Film Studio, Germany)
UNITAF	United Task Force (in Somalia)
UNOSOM	United Nations Operation in Somalia
UNPROFOR	United Nations Protection Force (in Former Yugoslavia)
WTB	Wolff Telegraphic Bureau (Germany, First World War)

Introduction

Sighting the Enemy in a Century of War

How can we make sense of the twentieth century without war? Historian Eric Hobsbawm insists we cannot. The century 'was marked by war. It lived and thought in terms of world war, even when the guns were silent and the bombs were not exploding' (1995, 22). Its first half – an 'Age of Catastrophe' – was marked by the two most destructive wars in human history (or, as Hobsbawm proposes, by a single world war 'thirty one years' long). The First World War is estimated to have left 10 million people dead, with a further 20 million maimed, 9 million children orphaned and 5 million women widowed. The casualty figures for the Second World War are similarly hard to gauge with any degree of accuracy – and equally beyond the imagination's capacity to conjure – at a conservatively estimated 55 million. Some 20 million Soviet citizens perished in the war. Six million Jews, most of Central Europe's Jewish population, were exterminated in Nazi concentration camps. China lost possibly 15 million lives in its long war with Japan from 1937 to 1947 (Dower, 1986, 295). And in a uniquely destructive century, not only did more people die in and as a result of war than during any other period of human history, but many experienced death as victims of mass extermination, not just as isolated casualties. Modern science, harnessed to the purposes of mass destruction, generated such horrors as the Nazi gas chambers and the atomic bomb, although the genocide in Rwanda of 1994 provided a chilling reminder that simple metal blades can serve as ruthless an exterminationist project as anything in the technological military arsenal.

Some historians point out that many features of 'total war' had already characterised conflict before 1914: the targeting of both civilians and an enemy's economic capacity, for instance (Beckett, 1988). Nevertheless, only in the twentieth century did war become a truly mass phenomenon. Both world wars ensnared civilians on several different continents in ways and to a degree unprecedented hitherto. War now required sweeping mobilisations of civilians into armed forces. It also demanded the wholesale conscription of citizens into auxiliary roles on the 'home front', binding them more closely with those engaged in combat. Now a collective endeavour, total war, as anthropologist Margaret Mead observed, 'stretch[ed] out the human beings who form a nation into a great straggling chain, as strong as their ability to join hands rapidly again if one drops out' (cited by Sherry, 1995, 89). What had once been an activity participated in by the select armed and uniformed few had now – in the age of 'mass society' – become a phenomenon which touched all.

The technological progress which mechanised and industrialised warfare drew civilians into twentieth-century war in other ways too. Mass media afforded people different, and more widely accessible, ways of 'witnessing' combat. Increased popular literacy in the nineteenth century, along with the emergence of transportation networks and superior printing mechanisms, permitted the emergence of a mass press in many industrialised countries. New media also emerged which made no requirement of literacy. Radio broadcasts blanketed much of Europe and North America by the 1930s, with some states, such as Nazi Germany and the USSR, deliberately fostering radio-listening to inculcate ideological unity on the home front, and transmit propaganda beyond (radio waves being no great respecters of territorial boundaries). And while the bakelite 'wireless' set became a feature of many homes in the industrialised world, visual media were also evolving apace. The equipment for still photography became less cumbersome; film less volatile and easier to develop. Meanwhile 'picture palaces' sprang up to exhibit footage in which the images moved, rapidly progressing from black and white silence to 'talkies' and soon to full-colour, stereo-sound 'motion pictures'. These advances in cinematography, and the subsequent development of television and video, have conferred special status upon twentieth-century civilians as spectators to wars' on-screen representation.

Both mass warfare and mass media owe their modern forms to a particularly fertile period of 'invention' towards the end of the nineteenth century. In some cases, the technology which has enabled civilians to learn of, or even 'see', events in a war zone has derived, more or less directly, from military research. 'The history of battle', Paul Virilio suggests, 'is primarily the history of radically changing fields of perception' (1989, 7). Modern warfare, in which destruction has become more distanced, relies on the accurate location of targets, human or otherwise: literally and fig-uratively, it is necessary to have the enemy in one's sights. The term 'shooting war' is aptly suggestive of both soldiers' and photojourn-alists' professions, as the camera owes its sighting mechanisms to those developed for artillery. Likewise, many means of transmission by which news from war zones reaches those at home evolved from technologies originally pioneered to allow soldiers to communicate with one another (telegraphy and radio broadcasting), or secretly to ascertain their enemy's military capabilities (the satellite: see Flichy, 1995).

Given their shared genesis, it is perhaps scarcely surprising that mass media throughout the century should have been drawn to the subject of war. War, it has often been noted, sells. Certainly, almost as soon as cinema was born it showed a proclivity towards screening violence. The first fight on film was apparently Thomas Edison's 'Bar-room Scene' in 1894, while the opening year of the new century offered what was probably the first scene of war on film in a British production, *Attack on a China Mission*, about the Boxer Rebellion (Basinger, 1986, 341). Ever since, violence and war have remained staple cinematic themes, as reflected in a number of the century's most critically acclaimed, and/or most lucrative, films: some depict-ing war with a view to exposing its inhumanity, others serving to ennoble combat as a field of human endeavour.

Cinema's enthralment has been scarcely less pronounced than that of the news media. One British observer commented after the First World War: 'War not only creates a supply of news but a demand for it. So deep-rooted is the fascination in war and all things appertaining to it that...a paper has only to be able to put up on its placard "A Great Battle" for its sales to mount up' (cited by Lasswell, 1927, 192). The sentiment, if not its precise formula-tion, would not be out of place, however, coming from the lips of a Ted Turner or a Rupert Murdoch, the Gulf War of 1991 seeming to prove the pertinence of an adage coined in 1919. Twenty of Amer-ica's twenty-five largest circulation newspapers enjoyed circulation gains during that conflict, while Cable News Network (CNN) experienced a ten-fold increase of its audience (Hallin and Gitlin, 1994, 149).

   The degree to which a 'war sells' of course depends on whose war it is, and the degree to which civilian media 'consumers' feel involved therein. War may be, as Hallin and Gitlin propose, 'genuinely a part of popular culture in a way that politics rarely is' in contemporary America (Hallin and Gitlin 1994, 149). But this sense of shared participation, not just in America, is more likely to hold true for 'our' wars than 'other people's'. 'Other people's wars' – unless they involve 'us' too somehow – may not grip the attention of distant media, which often presume a lack of interest on their audience's part in remote conflict. The words of Evelyn Waugh's fictional press baron, Lord Copper, proprietor of *The Beast*, still resonate: 'The British public has no interest in a war which drags on indecisively. A few sharp victories, some conspicuous acts of personal bravery on the Patriot side, and a colourful entry into the capital. That is *The Beast* policy for the war' (1943, 42). Here too experience from the early part of the century has found an echo in events towards its close. The Gulf War provided dramatic action by the side with the suggestively named 'Patriot' missiles, not to mention a colourful entry into Kuwait City, spearheaded by journalists in advance of the UN Coalition's advancing forces. But it also vividly demonstrated the Pentagon's fear that, without a hasty victory, American public enthusiasm for war would indeed evaporate in the fashion Lord Copper suggested.

   In the 1990s, this anxiety was fuelled by a long-standing belief amongst the military (and others) that television is capable of 'losing' a war; a notion that was grounded in a particular interpretation of the Vietnam War. America's long, uphill struggle to contain communism on the Indo-Chinese peninsula was the first extensively televised war and, as it was also the first war in which victory eluded the USA, many 'believed that the first feature was the cause of the second' (Mandelbaum, 1982, 157). But long before that, even dating back to the nineteenth century's Crimean and Boer wars, militaries have resented the civilian beneficiaries of the (sometimes military-led) communications revolution, exhibiting deep-seated mistrust of mass media in wartime (Knightley, 1989). Both journalists and soldiers take a certain professional pride in seeing themselves as locked in a mutually antagonistic relationship, each bound by irreconcilable working practices and codes of honour. As the accreditation papers with which Britain's Ministry of Defence provided journalists sailing to the Falklands/Malvinas islands in 1982 put it:

'The essence of successful warfare is secrecy; the essence of successful journalism is publicity.' In military eyes, journalists' overweening desire for a 'scoop' at any price makes them prone to spilling operational secrets with scant regard to the military casualties which might ensue from their careless talk. Such mistrust (and, arguably, such a limited understanding of whose interests mass media broadly serve) aside, grudgingly or more enthusiastically, the military in many twentieth-century wars have come to recognise potentially positive applications of media power in wartime. Mass media – too influential to be left to their own devices – have thus been harnessed to military purposes in the pursuit of victory.

Forging the bonds of sentiment

Recognising that media can forge bonds between the home front and the fighting front – increasing civilian commitment to the war effort, while raising the morale of combatants – militaries sometimes encourage or cajole journalists into providing what veteran British correspondent Martin Bell calls 'military mood music' (1995, 13). Even if the military do not believe that civilians have an unfettered 'right to know' where news of military operations is concerned (and they almost invariably do not), they may well regard civilian support as essential to the war effort. A feature of many twentieth-century wars has been their greater involvement of civilians, whether as spectators, victims or active participants; and a feature of most twentieth-century states has been greater concern with their own popular legitimacy. Thus governments, mindful of their own popularity, generally seek to harness mass media in wartime to persuade citizens of a war's justness and the enemy's implacability: a concern with public attitudes which transcends any narrow pursuit of post-war *electoral* success as such. (The Soviet regimes of the 1980s, for example, were so concerned to stem any haemorrhaging of popular support for the war in Afghanistan that they insisted the dead were returned to the USSR in sealed zinc coffins, encased against any possible media intrusion.) Media thus serve as the vital conduit between those fighting and those more distantly participating in – or vicariously experiencing – war. But the flow of news and images which filters through media channels is likely to be as strictly regulated by the state as conditions permit. News and images become strategic commodities in wartime, as subject to rationing as other essential items, and sometimes as scarce (Roeder, 1993, 7).

Hallin and Gitlin maintain that 'the primary role of the media in wartime in the Anglo-American world has long been to maintain the ties of sentiment between the soldiers in the field and the home front' (1994, 161). Maintaining morale – both civilian and military – is, however, by no means the only task which the military allots the media in wartime, though 'cheerleading' is often the one which certain media most enthusiastically espouse if they perceive their public as willing participants in a 'war culture'. The British reporter Max Hastings famously wrote during the Falklands/Malvinas conflict in 1982 that no British reporter could be neutral when his own country was fighting: objectivity was a peacetime luxury, and reporting became 'an extension of the war effort' (cited by Foster, 1992, 158). Of course, not all correspondents align themselves so dutifully with the military (or not so publicly and self-consciously, at any rate). Journalists often protest loudly at the state's withholding of information, as at its attempts to use media as channels of misinformation, designed to confuse or deceive the enemy. Such protests often occur after the event, once reporters discover that wartime information fed to them by military briefers was inaccurate, misleading, or downright false, although on some occasions, as during the 1991 Gulf War, certain journalists have actively connived in the deception of the enemy: in this case over the direction of the imminent Allied assault on Kuwait, and whether it would be land- or sea-borne.

To serve the same tactical objective of deceiving the enemy and to other demoralising ends, armed forces often establish their own media outlets in wartime. Such efforts fall beyond the central scope of this book (which deals primarily with *mass* communications), but the proliferation of media by the military in wartime should certainly be noted. Radio in particular, during the Second World War and thereafter, has played a major role in military psychological operations, with the true source of such clandestine broadcasts frequently disguised, to delude enemy listeners into assuming that the station is run by disgruntled elements from their own side. Such radio stations are a classic form of what is known as 'black propaganda': propaganda which wilfully mystifies its own provenance. 'Black' broadcasting was a notable feature of propaganda during the Second World War, with both the Allied and German militaries establishing clandestine radio stations in order to spread disillusion and defeatism amongst the forces of the other side (Cruikshank, 1977; Howe, 1982; Bergmeier and Lotz, 1997). Forty years later, similar aspirations inspired the 'black broadcasting' undertaken by the Coalition forces during Operation Desert Shield in the Persian Gulf (P. Taylor, 1997).

News and entertainment media, as this brief outline of some of their roles in wartime should suggest, undoubtedly matter to the military in wartime. For different reasons, media are equally important to civilians: as sources from which information, interpretations and images of war are acquired, either a supplement to, or substitute for, first-hand experience. For many citizens of the developed world, television, since the 1960s, is likely to have been the primary provider of news (though those who watch television news may, of course, also listen to broadcast radio news, read press reports, and log on to Internet news services). Whether television, for all its millions of viewers and its technological capacity to deliver images almost simultaneously with the events filmed, is capable of providing genuinely informative news remains much debated, as does the medium's capacity for doing more than offering a 'cruel mime of immediacy' when screening others' suffering (Ignatieff, 1998, 11). Television news is often lambasted for being sensational, driven by entertainment considerations (news as 'infotainment'), and led by images to the detriment of analysis and context (Postman, 1987; Tester, 1994; Bourdieu, 1998). Rather than aiding our understanding of what war is 'really like', television arguably diminishes its reality. As American cultural critic, Michael Arlen, observed of US networks' coverage of Vietnam, television made events 'less "real" – diminished, in part, by the physical size of the television screen, which, for all the industry's advances, still shows a picture of men three inches tall shooting at other men three inches tall' (cited by Hallin, 1989, 103).

Despite, and partially because of, its inadequacies as a vehicle for understanding, television has undoubtedly been perceived by policy-makers and the military as the most *influential* medium, however. Television's power is generally attributed to a combination of sheer audience size, visual impact and immediacy. But precisely what influence television (or other mass media) has on the audience – how far, and in what ways, media shape rather than reflect public opinion – remains the subject of much academic discussion. Studies of 'media effects' have reached divergent conclusions, though very few hold that all-powerful media, acting in a uni-directional, 'hypodermic' fashion, simply inject audiences with certain messages. To the extent that early researchers in mass communication ever really advanced such simplistic notions as this 'magic bullet' theory of communication, their theories have certainly long been modified – if not abandoned outright – by later generations of scholars (Curran, 1990). Some, for example, prefer to see the media's main function as one of 'agenda-setting'. Bernard Cohen's formulation that the press 'may not be successful in telling its readers what to think, but ... is stunningly successful in telling its readers what to think about' has been widely echoed (cited by Van Ginneken, 1998, 87). Others suggest a modification: that the real, a priori, agenda-setting is in fact done by the media's primary sources. Consequently political elites, fond of representing themselves as led by powerful mass media, actually tend to play a determining role in the communication process, as routine initiators of news stories and often as primary 'definers' or 'framers' of those stories (Tuchman, 1978; Gans, 1979; Bennett, 1990).

A different tradition of media scholarship, influenced by post-structural theory, has focused not on the pivotal role of elite sources but on reversing the traditional conception of media 'consumers' as essentially passive. Postmodernism problematises the very notion that media content contains unambiguous 'messages', let alone messages which irresistibly influence the viewer/reader/listener in a direction intended by the communicator. Rather than inhering in a newspaper column or television programme, meaning is constructed and extracted by the individual. Audiences (in so far as individuals do coalesce into homogeneous 'audiences') are thus not passively absorbent sponges but active 'negotiators' of meaning in media 'texts'. Moreover, they can resist intended, surface meanings and find instead subversive interpretations, uses or 'gratifications' from the media they consume (Fiske, 1987; Ang, 1991).

Where early scholars tended to attribute considerable power to media to shape popular attitudes and beliefs, many scholars now regard media effects as much more complex and, in many ways, less overwhelming. But amongst 'lay people' – notably politicians and soldiers in wartime – such scepticism about media effects is less evident. Television, especially since America's débâcle in the

Vietnam War, is still frequently credited with a tremendous capacity to sway and remodel public opinion. The media therefore matter in wartime, to no little degree, because of their perceived power over their 'consumers'. And this power has often been construed, by the state at least, as innately negative: the very act of representing war has been taken as anti-war in effect, if not in intent.

The Fog of Falsehood

Partly on account of the resilient belief that untrammelled media may stab the military in the back – that unregulated images generate intrinsically anti-war effects – states have often taken considerable pains to manipulate the presentation of war. If, as senator Hiram Johnson remarked in 1917, 'in war, truth is the first casualty', the reason is as likely to be state obstruction and obfuscation as the inherent difficulties, dilemmas and dangers war poses for reporters. States frequently expect high degrees of compliance from their media in wartime, usually rationalised on grounds of 'operational security' and the protection of militarily sensitive information demanded by the war effort. By identifying the ends for which war is waged as indivisible from the national interest, states have also made considerable use of patriotism as a mechanism for disciplining mass media. Criticism of the war – its ends or means – consequently becomes an act of treachery.

Once patriotism is mobilised in this way, critical voices are rapidly silenced. As Arthur Ponsonby pointed out presciently in 1928: 'War is fought in this fog of falsehood, a great deal of it uncovered and accepted as truth. The fog arises from fear and is fed by panic. Any attempt to doubt or deny even the most fantastic story has to be condemned at once as unpatriotic, if not traitorous' (1928, 26). Given that war seems to require the projection of all responsibility on to 'a menacing, murderous aggressor' (as Harold Lasswell observed in 1927), periods of hostility have tended to generate 'fantastic stories' in profusion (1927, 51, 77). Indeed many atrocity stories about the enemy's barbarity have shown remarkable resilience – in at least generic form, if not precise details – from the First World War to the present day. As we will see, mass media are often willing participants in, if not always initiators of, this process of demonisation. Perhaps more surprisingly, sections of the media also sometimes prove remarkably eager to discipline dissident voices within their own profession. Condemnation of those 'traitors' attempting to dispel the 'fog of falsehood' is not enacted by the state alone but often by rival media who shoulder up squarely with government and military, branding as unpatriotic any outlet which sets broader limits on the expression of critical, or merely sceptical, viewpoints. John Simpson, for example, noted with dismay during the 1991 Gulf War that many of his colleagues were loudly 'demanding a curb on free reporting', in headlines that sounded as though they came from the Nazi newspaper '*Volkischer Beobachter*, sniffing out traitors' (1991a, 12). Media in wartime sometimes appear to be at war with each other as much as with the state, or with the enemy.

Battlefield conditions also make it difficult for journalists (should they be so minded) to disperse the 'fog of war'. The war correspondent must piece together often confused reports from a wide geographical area, though he or she is confined to a particular location. With regard to the Gulf War, British Broadcasting Corporation (BBC) reporter John Simpson likened his position to that of the football spectator seated near one of the goal-mouths: 'Whenever the play was down at my end I had a superb view of it. But when it moved to the far end of the pitch I only knew what was happening when I heard the crowd roar' (1991b, xv–xvi). Having assembled a story, reporters must then find a means of transmitting their copy from the battlefield back to their base, which may be easier said than done. Television journalists with the British Task Force, sailing to the Falklands islands in 1982, had to be winched by helicopter on to ships equipped with the satellite telephone system which would enable them to send 'voice pieces' (but not pictures) back to London (R. Harris, 1983; Morrison and Tumber, 1988).

War reporting, then, presents journalists and news-organisations with the possibility for additional sales but also with a battery of professional dilemmas and personal dangers. The Gulf War of 1991 was unusual in modern experience as a war almost bereft of journalistic casualties, not even facing reporters (unless going it alone without the Coalition military) with any severe personal danger, despite the ostentatious donning of gas masks and flak jackets by journalists in the safety of Dhahran (A. Thomson, 1992). Some wars, on the other hand, may be too dangerous for many 'outside' news organisations to consider covering them, the civil war in 1990s

Algeria being a notable case in point. Practical considerations as to whether particular wars offer journalists sufficient 'immunity' that they may report from the battle zone with reasonable assurance of personal safety jostle with professional (part political, part ethical) dilemmas regarding the degree to which journalists self-consciously suspend peacetime practices. Should they accede to the state's demands for 'patriotic' conformity in wartime, or attempt to retain peacetime standards, such as 'objectivity', 'neutrality', 'balance'? In a democracy, how far does the public's 'right to know' – and the media's function as watchdog on the state, its 'Fourth Estate' – extend in wartime?

Since war throws troubling issues into stark relief – as well as forming a perennial preoccupation of news and entertainment media – the relationship between 'war and the media' has been the subject of considerable scholarship. This work falls, broadly speaking, into a number of different categories: studies of the media's performance in single, specific conflicts; participant accounts and memoirs by war correspondents; analyses of the military-media relationship; and thematic treatments of particular branches of media activity in wartime, such as propaganda, war photography, or wartime cinema. However, there remain few academic overviews of the field as a whole, a deficiency to which Daniel Hallin has recently pointed (Hallin, 1997, 206). *The Media at War* is thus intended to serve as a synoptic introductory study, offering a synthesis of existing scholarship, but also adopting a fresh approach, based on an examination of media before, during and after conflicts of varying kinds throughout the twentieth century.

Sliding State Control

One of the book's central contentions is that no clear demarcations distinguish different types of conflict. States' expectations of media compliance therefore tend to blur, as do journalistic routines in war and peacetime. Normative theory holds that there *ought* to be a gradation in the democratic state's practice *vis-à-vis* media as war escalates in magnitude. In other words, while there may be a place during 'limited war' for measures to protect operational secrecy, conflict over limited (sometimes politically contentious) objectives does not legitimise sweeping censorship which a war of 'national survival' may necessitate (Young and Jesser, 1997). Some observers suggest that state attempts to control media do indeed offer evidence of a gradated response. Thus Phillip Schlesinger observes (with particular reference to Britain):

> The extent to which the state can effectively censor broadcasting and other media during an armed conflict varies considerably. It is important to distinguish what has happened during a total war (World War II), limited engagements (the Suez crisis, the Falklands adventure) and a counterinsurgency campaign within the national territory (Northern Ireland). Each of these has occupied a distinct position on the sliding scale of control. (Schlesinger, Murdock and Elliott, 1983, 111)

However, in practice much state intervention has sought a similar position on the scale, with a generalised notion of 'war' presented as justification for special measures. The paradigmatic wartime experience most commonly evoked since 1945, in Britain and elsewhere, has been the Second World War, upon which many states continue to base their expectations of media compliance (Hallin, 1997, 209). Berating a BBC radio interviewer for his scepticism over the likely success of NATO's bombing raids in Kosovo in March 1999, British Defence Secretary, George Robertson, demanded of his interlocutor: 'Look, can you imagine if during the Second World War you had the opportunity, day after day, of questioning the Ministers in that Government and asking, what if we are defeated at D-Day?' (reported in *The Observer*, 28 March 1999, 2). Even in campaigns of terrorism (though they fall into a legalistic grey area between war and peace), total war is sometimes offered as a relevant analogy, by states and supportive media alike. Thus, for example, the chairman of Britain's Independent Broadcasting Authority, Lord Aylestone, insisted during a period of intense Irish Republican Army (IRA) activity in the 1970s that since Britain was 'at war with the IRA', Republicans would 'get no more coverage than the Nazis would have done in the last war' (Schlesinger, Murdock and Elliott, 1983, 122). Clearly, though, even if states do exhibit an almost reflexive impulse to censor their media in wartime, practical circumstances (if not political considerations) may keep this urge more or less in check. 'The question, then', Gadi Wolfsfeld proposes, 'is not so much whether governments *should*

restrict information in the midst of a conflict but whether they *can*'
(1997, 28).

War presents special challenges to media organisations and states
alike. Wartime's distinctive features have been much studied in
those volumes which scrutinise media performance in specific conflicts. They include military/governmental censorship; other forms
of interference such as denial of access to the war zone, and/or to
communications equipment; 'news management' systems for briefing and 'propagandising' journalists; and the dilemmas (or seeming
dilemmas) confronting journalists: the tension between 'loyalty' and
'objectivity', and the incommensurability of the public's unfettered
'right to know' with the military's requirement for secrecy. All of
these issues are aired in *The Media at War*. But this book also
suggests, as others have done, that 'war should not be seen as a
special case of how the media works' but rather as a magnifying
glass which 'highlights and intensifies many of the things that happen in peacetime', albeit revealing them in exaggerated form (Williams, 1992, 158). Extreme cases may thus help us reflect more
critically on everyday practices.

At many levels, it is misleading to treat war as wholly aberrational
and utterly distinct from peace, just as it is to regard 'total war',
'limited war' and 'terrorism' as governed by distinct rules of engagement determining how combatants fight each other, and how
states constrain their media. Even the boundary between 'our'
wars and 'other peoples'' may be blurred. Distinctions between
'ours' and 'theirs', 'peace' and 'war', 'total' and 'limited' conflict
often appear rather arbitrary. For those engaged in fighting (or
indeed for civilians whose lives are dislocated and endangered by)
any war, the epithet 'limited' could scarcely be less appropriate.
Reflecting on the wars in the Former Yugoslavia in the 1990s, the
British correspondent Martin Bell concluded: 'All war is local.
For the individual soldier it is the wood where he bivouacs and
the ditch or trench where he fights and maybe dies. Nothing
else matters. The war may begin as a fight for his country, but it
ends as a fight for his life' (1995, 237). All war, one might suggest,
is both local and total; both like and unlike peacetime (Hynes,
1998). Certainly wars labelled 'limited' by one of their combatants
– such as America's in Vietnam (fought for the 'limited', if open-
ended, objective of containing communism, and with 'limited'
deployment of America's military arsenal) – may feel very much

like 'total war' to those under bombardment from a better endowed military's 'limited' firepower.

Similarly, it may be hard to tell precisely when a war begins. Parties to a conflict often date its origins quite differently. And media operations in war and peacetime are more continuous than often imagined. It would certainly be misleading to imagine that media in Western democracies are subject to state interference and regulation *only* in wartime, and clearly many of the 'special conditions' war imposes for media in pluralistic systems obtain constantly for media in more authoritarian regimes where they are forcibly subservient to (and often owned by) the state, and fulfil transparently ideological purposes. Since the rise of mass media in the late nineteenth century, states – of all political hues – have routinely regulated the activities of the press, radio, cinema, television and, in so far as they can, the Internet. In democratic states, media are generally subject to legislation governing ownership (particularly 'cross-ownership' of different media outlets), to prevent undue concentration in the hands of one individual or corporation, and ensure plurality of output. Many states (democratic or otherwise) also try, by various national and international legal mechanisms, to guard against excessive penetration by foreign media, in the attempt to preserve cultural and linguistic integrity in the face of media 'imperialism' from beyond. Such measures may also aim to prevent the dissemination of politically undesirable material (as Rupert Murdoch's difficulties in penetrating the Chinese media market in the 1990s testify). Internally, media in democratic systems are likely to be bound by various strictures governing how they report domestic politics, in pursuit of news free from 'bias' and partiality, especially during election campaigns.

Most states also enact legislation to protect the privacy of the individual, to prohibit libel, and to shelter their publics from immoral or obscene material: whether printed, filmed, or merely uttered. Freedom of speech, even in a country with a strong libertarian tradition such as the USA, is rarely absolute, though where the boundaries are drawn around the illicit terrain of indecency, treason or blasphemy obviously differs from one state to another (as the dispute over Salman Rushdie's *The Satanic Verses* clearly showed), and over time, as social values change. That censorship exists in peacetime should be obvious to anyone, certainly in Britain or America, who visits the cinema, or hires a film on videotape. The fact that films are given a certain classification, aimed at preventing children and young people from viewing inappropriately explicit material, indicates the operation of censorship, though it may not reveal quite how far-reaching such scrutiny is. British film censorship in the inter-war years, for example, was so stringent that the onset of war actually saw a liberalisation of permissible film content, not further restriction.

It is, then, a mistake to regard 'censorship' or state intrusion into media activity as the critical difference between media reporting in wartime and in peace, though of course the controls in war may be much more apparent to journalists, if not necessarily to the public. But it is equally misleading to take the study of war and the media as coterminous with examination of war correspondents' activities. In reporting war, the procedures and decisions of those far from the 'front line' may be as important as the actions of those correspondents who observe it first hand (or as close as they are permitted to come).

Making War, Making News

Long before our current age of 'celebrity journalism', war reporters have liked to portray themselves as exceptional individuals operating in exceptional circumstances: 'soldiers without the means of self-defence', who court danger in order to bring back 'news from hell' (Bell, 1995, 10; Pedelty, 1995, 29). But we should beware journalistic mythographers. War correspondents belong to larger news organisations which discipline their work, sometimes in such routinised and subliminal ways that individuals may be largely unaware of the forces constraining them, and determining not only which stories are covered but how they are framed (Van Ginneken, 1998, 65–75). Likewise, news organisations do not float detached from their society's political, cultural and economic structures. The 'news values' that determine what passes muster as news in different polities are the product of these broad 'invisible' influences, as well as more specific, institutionalised practices. Although news-people often claim otherwise, 'news values' do not inhere in stories; the news agenda is therefore not self-selecting. News editors sometimes suggest that their job is rather like judging a beauty pageant: potential stories parade their easily-evaluated assets under the trained

gaze of the judge, waiting to be plucked from the crowd of contestants and elevated to a place in the press columns or broadcast
bulletin (Berkowitz, 1997, xi). But like notions of beauty, newsworthiness is also in the eye of the beholder, not an inherent
property, and where the eye beholds either one is shaped by cultural
norms as much as by idiosyncratic, individual preferences. In other
words, news editors set out with engrained (but often unacknow-
ledged) assumptions about what makes a 'good story', and indeed
about what constitutes a 'story' in the first place.

Whatever war reporters might egocentrically claim, news production is best not regarded as an individualistic business. Reporters,
with very few exceptions, do not blithely set out on their own
initiative for a combat zone, risking all to hold their journalistic
mirror to the atrocities of war (and even if they do, they cannot rely
on a ready market for their wares). Rather, news organisations
determine which wars constitute news, who will cover them and
for how long, though not necessarily always as a result of conscious
decision-making. Particularly for television companies, where the
costs of news-gathering are greatest, priorities are partly rooted
in commercial considerations. In the current age of increasingly
cheap and miniaturised communications technology, covering
foreign news (which war often is) still remains the most expensive
form of news, and news itself is one of the most costly forms of
programming. But it should also be noted that much coverage of
war is not the work of war correspondents at all, just as most news-
reporting derives from secondary sources, not first-hand observation (Van Ginneken, 1998, 86). Reporting of distant conflict is
often based largely on agency reports and footage shot by less
glamorous (and less well paid) local 'stringers' in trouble-spots.
Moreover, coverage of wars in which the media's own state is
involved is likely to depend, in large part, on domestic elite sources
within government and the military. In the most heavily televised
war to date, that in the Persian Gulf in 1991, much news relayed by
the US networks and press was gathered from regular 'newsbeats' –
the 'golden triangle' of Pentagon, White House and State Department – rather than from the frontline in Saudi Arabia and Kuwait
(Cook, 1994). Indeed, the presence of journalists at a site of conflict
may well result from their state's having led them there in the first
place. Even in wartime – battlefield confusion notwithstanding –
much news may nevertheless be 'routine', in Molotch and Lester's

typology, with those who enjoy 'habitual access' to the media packaging stories for the journalists' ease of consumption (1997, 193–209).

To look at which wars media cover, for how long, and in what ways, is less to see a recognisable reflection of the 'world as it is' – as journalists are wont to claim – than a map of the broad preoccupations, interests and values of their particular society (or at least of its dominant groups). While this book shares with Gadi Wolfsfeld a belief that no single theory can explain how all media behave in all wars (not least in the course of a century which has seen such transformative changes in the nature of war, the state and mass media), it does espouse certain underlying conceptions about how media operate (Wolfsfeld, 1997, 4). It rejects the naive premise that media simply mirror a world 'out there', and dispenses with the idea that it is possible for journalists to cover stories – as Richard Salant of the American CBS network famously proclaimed – 'from nobody's point of view' (Shoemaker and Reese, 1996, 35). Such notions form articles of faith for many journalists schooled in certain traditions of 'objectivity' where the separation of 'fact' from 'comment' is held up not just as journalistic grail but as workable practice. Journalists, however, are 'not innocent', as Paletz and Entmann remind us (cited in Wolfsfeld, 1997, 40). Regarding themselves often as mere 'mirrors' to reality, journalists deny what invariably distorts their reflections. They belong to socio-economic classes and ethnic groups; they are male or female; they have certain predispositions and views (even if they think they successfully suppress them), and they breathe a particular 'cultural air', which as Richard Hoggart put it, infuses 'the whole ideological atmosphere' of any given society, telling its members 'that some things can be said and others had best not be said' (cited by Schudson, 1997, 19).

This does not mean that reporters wilfully 'make up' the news, as they sometimes misconstrue academic critiques. But it does mean that they – their sources, their organisations and the broader structures in which they are embedded – 'manufacture' news and, in so doing, 'invent reality', in Michael Parenti's phrase (1993). Accordingly, news can never be 'value-free', from 'nobody's point of view', in the way its 'manufacturers' like to claim. Indeed, the very attempt to separate 'news' from 'comment' mystifies the epistemological impossibility of pristine, value-free 'facts', and obscures the underlying assumptions and preferences which news content will unavoidably contain, irrespective of the 'professionalism' (or otherwise) of the reporter in trying to avoid 'bias'. Certainly many Western news organisations have striven, during at least some of the twentieth century, for 'objectivity', but this should not be taken as synonymous with 'truthfulness'. Although reports may duly 'balance' different viewpoints, above which the journalist hovers seemingly detached, the practices of 'objectivity' often reproduce dominant understandings and values, while simultaneously professing the ideological innocence of news so manufactured (Pedelty, 1995, 9). Openly avowed partisanship may therefore be more honest – more 'truthful' in its willingness to make explicit judgements on the relative merits of competing truth-claims – but likely to attract damaging charges of 'bias' (thus journalists' adoption of self-protective codes of 'objectivity' in the first place).

Precisely what generates 'bias' (if one wishes to call it that) in news is the subject of much scholarly debate, and the answer partly depends on what level of analysis one adopts, and what feature of news content one wishes to explain. Some early studies tended to regard the 'mirror' analogy as flawed because news is made by individual, and inescapably subjective, humans. In selecting which stories become news, and how they are reported, news editors and journalists inevitably bring their own predispositions, beliefs, cultural norms and ethnocentric stereotypes to bear (Breed, 1955). Arguably, however, human subjectivity only takes us so far in understanding news content: the individual news-maker is not the only relevant unit of decision-making, or even perhaps the most appropriate level of analysis. Even before individual 'gate-keepers' set to work, broader forces influence the constitution of 'news' and 'newsworthiness' (for example, shaping preferences for stories centred on individuals, or on short-term 'events' rather than long-term processes). These may be so pervasive – and 'invisible' – that individual news-makers, almost irrespective of personal subjectivities, will function in much the same way, and not simply as a result of professional socialisation which renders much decision-making routine (Tuchman, 1997, 173–92).

What determines these fundamental dispositions? The political economy approach posits that news organisations at root reflect the interests and needs of their commercial sponsors, or broader economic systems and their supporting ideologies as a whole (Herman and Chomsky, 1988). In this respect, then, there may be little difference between the role of media in communist states and their 'propagandist' function in capitalist liberal democracies, except that the media's ideological purpose is veiled (and frequently denied) in the latter, whereas it was openly espoused in the former. Some such studies suggest that media consciously weed out material which may, in discomforting the viewer/consumer, displease corporate advertisers and sponsors: a process of filtration which is perhaps most noticeable in wartime, when profound disturbance looms (Kellner, 1992). But it is also possible that news and entertainment media alike may serve the interests of the status quo in more complex, subliminal ways, reflecting 'dominant ideology' without *conscious* deference to the impositions of particular corporate sponsors, owners or advertisers.

Different (but not necessarily incompatible) approaches emphasise the relationship of media with political elites, often the routine sources of news who may deliberately package 'events', or actually stage them, precisely to appeal to journalistic norms of 'newsworthiness' (Molotch and Lester, 1997, 193–209). As early as 1961, American sociologist Daniel Boorstin remarked on the prevalence of made-for-the-press news, or 'pseudo-events' in his coinage. Others have also demonstrated that news gathering (in America, though similar patterns are observable elsewhere) follows very closely the structures of state bureaucracy. The 'beats' to which correspondents are assigned tend to mirror important departments of state: trade and industry, welfare, health, education, and so on (Fishman, 1980; Cook, 1994).

Emphasis on the media's preponderant relationship with the state may, however, overlook another important variable: the less easily traced flows of influence between media and audience. Where some research has asserted explicitly that the audience is unimportant in shaping content (as news organisations proceed largely on the basis of what they think people either *want* or *ought* to know about the world, without much regard for their consumers' actual preferences), others insist that a more reciprocal relationship exists (Schlesinger, 1987, 116). Even if journalistic judgements are sometimes made on the basis of intuition, concern with the consumer is nevertheless a real determinant of news form and content, regardless of whether the editorial instinct accurately registers public sentiment (assuming it *could* be properly 'measured'). Thus

Hallin and Gitlin suggest that media, in wartime most particularly, aspire to reflect their publics: by celebrating consensual values and emphasising their own responsiveness to the popular mood (1994). Certainly, decisions about how much of war to reveal – where to draw boundaries around the showable and sayable – are often rationalised with reference to public sensibilities, not state sensitivity. Self-censorship is thus undertaken, at least ostensibly, in the interests of ordinary viewers or readers, not to protect the state from potentially embarrassing or damaging images, opinions or disclosures. And in this respect, too, a common feature of the media's behaviour in wartime is also apparent in peacetime. As a matter of course, decisions are taken regarding 'taste and tone' in news, especially with respect to the depiction of dead or injured bodies, and similarly about acceptable representations of violence in fictional films (J. Taylor, 1998).

The Media at War draws, then, on a number of different sociological and 'culturological' approaches to the media, foregrounding, at times, particular theories to explain precise aspects of media behaviour in wartime which have been much disputed. Different chapters accordingly highlight distinct issues concerning media performance, and the shifting relationships between mass media and political elites, the military, and their viewers, readers, and listeners.

Chapter 1, *Media Before War*, illustrates the continuity between peace- and war-time practice, centring on the relationship of mass media with the state. In particular, it examines the way in which entertainment and news media – by following the 'cues' of dominant policy makers or elites – may favour particular policy outcomes, and, in so doing, privilege military options over other possible outcomes to international disputes. Exploring the media's projection of 'enemy images', it also assesses the way in which media, prior to conflict, may be overtly compelled by states to carry bellicose messages, moulding exclusive ethnic and national identities as a precursor to war.

Chapter 2, *Media and 'Total War'*, traces the development of state techniques of control over mass media from the First to the Second World War. While assessing a 'totalitarian' model of media control in Nazi Germany, the chapter also reveals the ways in which Allied news and entertainment organisations often enthusiastically enlisted for service in wartime. Although mechanisms to limit the flow of news, to constrain journalists' movements on the battlefield, and over-see home-front film production were in many respects far-reaching, the state in Britain and America could rely to a considerable extent on 'gentlemen's agreements' with journalists, broadcasters and film-makers. Such arrangements had the added advantage of public 'deniability', such that citizens were often ignorant of quite how far their media were censored or shackled in wartime.

Chapter 3, *Media and 'Limited War'*, on the other hand, places greater stress on media effects, and the impact of television especially on viewers. Here, the debate over the American media's role in the Vietnam War is scrutinised, along with its consequences for subsequent 'limited wars'. A pervasive belief that uncensored media reportage destroyed public support for the war, thus stabbing the US military in the back, has informed later attempts to rein in the media more tightly during 'limited' conflicts. State controls over the media during the Falklands/Malvinas conflict in 1982 and the Persian Gulf War of 1991 bear ample witness to the prevalence of certain 'lessons of Vietnam'. However, whether the media really did 'lose the war' in Vietnam – and whether television footage of war unavoidably has such a unilinear, negative impact on public opinion – is open to question, as is the insistence, often proclaimed by both professions, that military-media relations are invariably hostile.

Chapter 4, *Media and Terrorism*, is devoted to a relationship which has particularly vexed a number of Western states in the latter part of the twentieth century: that between 'terrorist' groups and mass media. A number of scholars and policy-makers alike assert that terrorist campaigns demonstrate the ease with which the usual hierarchies of access to media can be overturned by challengers. Terrorists thus seize the news agenda by creating unquestionably newsworthy 'spectacles': in Molotch and Lester's typology, they may be considered 'event promoters' who gain 'disruptive access' by 'somehow crashing through the ongoing arrangements of newsmaking, generating surprise, shock, or some more violent forms of "trouble"' (1997, 201–2). This chapter examines the way in which such notions of 'symbiosis' between terrorists and mass media have become an orthodoxy, with Western states often attempting to curb media reporting of terrorism as a key plank of counter-terrorist strategy. But the chapter also suggests that the framing of news stories of such disruptive hijackers of the news agenda may not be as functional to their cause as policy-makers and some academics frequently insist.

Chapter 5 turns to *Media, Globalisation and Other People's Wars*. Here, the central proposition under examination is the notion that 'real-time' television, and 'globalised' international media, are increasingly driving foreign-policy making: the so-called 'CNN effect'. While some commentators welcome the constitution of global 'macro-publics' – increasingly sensitised to distant suffering and conscious of themselves as world citizens in which 'humanity' is the most meaningful shared identity – others have decried a per-ceived loss of prerogative from policy-makers to fickle media. Examining media performance in a number of conflicts and human-itarian emergencies of the 1990s (Kurdistan, Former Yugoslavia, Somalia and Rwanda, especially), this chapter suggests that many conceptions of 'globalised media' are exaggerated; that official sources may still routinely shape the news agenda, resisting calls to action where they feel little inclined to act. Why only *some* distant wars and humanitarian crises become headline news is also addressed here, leading us back to questions of 'news values', and whose values determine the agenda.

Chapter 6, *Media After War*, brings the study full circle. How do the media represent past wars? In what ways do they serve to annihilate or reanimate memory, to bury past wars or exhume and refight them? Does the media's fascination with war furnish us with enduring images of 'war-in-the-head' which not only shape (and possibly obscure) our understanding of what war means but also dull our capacity to think beyond war as a means of settling dis-putes? In endlessly recycling past wars, perhaps media representa-tions serve to prepare us for future war, luring us into the easy assumption – unsettling in its implications – that war 'isn't just something that humans *make*, it *is*' (Gray, 1997, 1).

1
Media Before War

It is a truism that when war comes truth is the 'first casualty'. Senator Hiram Johnson's utterance in 1917 has been much repeated, lending itself as title to Phillip Knightley's influential history of war correspondence. Johnson's maxim seems to capture an essential truth about truth's very elusiveness in wartime. Taken too literally, however, the aphorism may be misleading. Applied to the realm of journalism, it might suggest that peace and war constitute two quite distinct spheres, in which reporters necessarily operate differently: in peacetime, they convey truth, while in wartime, half-truths, propaganda and lies. But where truth slides into half-truth or outright falsehood may be difficult to determine, and whether journalists can ever hope to convey 'the truth' – whether there is indeed *a* truth to be told – is a moot point, both at the level of philosophical abstraction and of professional practice.

The boundary between war and peace is often every bit as elusive. Terrorism's status – unorthodox war, or crime? – is particularly contested. 'Total war', on the other hand, is relatively easy to define, though unlikely to recur in the nuclear age, according to many strategists (Mueller, 1989). But its apparent obsolescence has not necessarily made 'total peace' any more likely a proposition (indeed, the very presence of nuclear arsenals renders peace latently perilous to all but the most convinced proponents of deterrence theory). Peace is rarely absolute, if defined not simply as the absence of war but something more akin to Johan Galtung's formulation 'positive peace', which entails 'patterns of co-operation and integration between major human groups' (Roach, 1993, 2). For much of the twentieth century, citizens of many countries have felt their security threatened, as often by their own state as by external pressures, or others' armed forces. (Since 1900 almost as many people, an estimated 90 million, have been victims of the exterminationism of the regime under which they live – and die – as of the two total wars, which together claimed approximately 100 million lives: Ponting, 1998, 537.) The insecurity of 'negative peace' may shade almost incrementally into war. Many twentieth-century conflicts have not been heralded with formal announcements after decisive opening shots. (At what point, for example, did America's undeclared war in Vietnam begin?) Even when wars have been 'declared', these formalities are unlikely to mark the real start of hostilities: would Czechs, whose country was overrun by the Nazis in 1938, agree that the Second World War started in September 1939? And when did war begin for Jews in the Third Reich?

A state of war is frequently acknowledged only after protracted hostilities. Wars result from long-term planning and germination during the 'negative peace', more often than from spontaneous implosions of violence between states, or groups within states. This is not to say that every war is the result of a carefully laid blueprint, followed with clockwork precision. The outbreak of war (or the particular form it takes) may surprise even the engineers of aggression, who – while often being prepared for conflict as a last resort – may have believed that a certain amount of territorial expansion could be accomplished without general war. (This case has been made by students of both Hitler's foreign policy in the 1930s and of Saddam Hussein's in 1990.) But war certainly requires both military and psychological mobilisation if we accept, as the preamble to the UN Educational, Scientific, and Cultural Organization charter insists, that 'wars begin in the minds of men'.

Some scholars of the media and peace researchers contend that mass media form an integral part of the 'war system'. If war does indeed begin in the mind, then the media keep minds constantly primed. Popular culture's fascination with violence and the priorities of the news media legitimise, even glorify, war, permitting the unthinkable – the wholesale destruction of human life – to be thinkable. War, according to this reasoning, is not a 'natural' outgrowth of some essential human nature but rather a learnt form of (anti-)social behaviour. By repeatedly showing war as a necessary, perhaps even desirable, form of conflict-resolution or pre-emptive 'self-defence', media serve generally to perpetuate the institution of war.

In more specific instances, media also play a central role in the projection of enemy images, a vital pre-requisite to war. 'In the beginning', suggests Sam Keen, 'we create the enemy. Before the weapon comes the image. We *think* others to death and then invent the battle-axe or the ballistic missiles with which to actually kill them. Propaganda precedes technology' (1986, 10). Films, television and radio broadcasts, newspaper reports and cartoons may serve to sanction the inhumane treatment of those no longer regarded as fully human, though simultaneously obscuring how weapons injure flesh (Scarry, 1987, 63–81). Christopher Coker argues that a 'pernicious divorce of language and meaning' came of age in the nuclear era: 'Nuclear missiles soon became "weapons of mass destruction". War became "conflict". Winning was too loaded a term. Nations preferred not to win, but to "prevail". "First strikes" and "second strikes" masked the full impact of a provoked or unprovoked attack' (1994, 51). In fact, the view that mass media predispose societies towards war – by stripping meaning from language – far predates the nuclear age. Thus, for example, the German playwright and philosopher, Karl Kraus, held the print press primarily responsible for the First World War. According to Coker,

> [Kraus] saw the journalist not as a messenger of bad news so much as a producer of it. He hated journalistic clichés, the jingoism of newspaper editors which encouraged men to join up, the references in newspapers to 'groups forming' and armies 'massing' when they meant that armies were on the march. A newspaper, he once insisted, was as much a weapon of war as a grenade . . . Journalism, he maintained, had so impoverished the imagination that humanity was now prepared to fight a war of annihilation against itself. Deprived of the capacity to experience life, man now relied on the newspapers to implant the courage to join up. 'The abuse of language embellishes the abuse of life', he complained. (1994, 52)

Unable to visualise the horrors war would entail through the fog of ennobling and obscuring euphemism, men eagerly joined up. Media made the unthinkable possible without its actually being imaginable. Visualisation was short-circuited by language which 'name[d] things without calling up mental images of them', as Orwell later put it in his influential essay, 'Politics and the English Language' (Orwell, 1995, 432). And war was the result.

In the age of visual media, images can also fulfil this obfuscatory role. They may do so by showing the horror of war too repeatedly, so desensitising viewers to suffering, or by failing to reveal enough. Susan Sontag diagnosed in the 1970s symptoms of a 'syndrome' which by the 1990s had been dubbed 'compassion fatigue': 'The quality of feeling, including moral outrage, that people can muster in response to photographs of the oppressed, the exploited, the starving, and the massacred ... depends on the degree of familiarity with these images ... Photographs shock insofar as they show something novel. Unfortunately, the ante keeps getting raised' (1979, 19). But if, as Sontag insists, graphic photographs evoke ever less response from anaesthetised viewers, television footage can conversely be indicted for omitting too much. Thus while television holds the promise of immediacy, its selective footage (calculated not overly to offend the viewer's sensibilities), and inevitable reduction in scale enfeebles our capacity to conjure the consequences of warfare, and to empathise fully with its victims. Moving images do not necessarily move audiences. No wonder, then, that in the aftermath of the Gulf War in 1991, critics of American network news (in particular) lambasted not only the latter's faithful replication of military euphemism – 'collateral damage' for civilian casualties, 'surgical strikes' for bombing raids – but also their use of Pentagon video footage, which projected a sanitised impression of bloodless 'techno-war' free from human casualties (Cumings, 1992; Kellner, 1992; Mowlana, Gerbner and Schiller, 1992; Norris, 1994).

Having aired the argument that communications media are supportive of a 'war system' in the most general terms, the bulk of this chapter deals with more specific aspects of media performance in periods of tension, focusing particularly on the ways in which media may serve to narrow the options towards war. That the output of news organisations and entertainment media alike may have this mobilisational and legitimatory effect is widely agreed. However, the autonomy of media operations is open to question. In the case studies that follow, we examine debates surrounding the extent to which media have initiated a drift – or more precipitate rush – to war, or have themselves been acted upon by other agencies, from without or within the state.

The chapter begins by exploring how a neutral country's media may be targeted by foreign propaganda, aimed at encouraging the 'target' state to abandon its neutrality and enter a war already under way elsewhere. American opinion-formers (journalists, in particular) were singled out for such treatment before, and in the early stages of, both world wars. Afterwards, critics twice claimed that clandestine British propaganda had played a significant role in re-orienting American media, and consequently in bringing a hitherto neutral USA into the war effort against Germany. Worse, some isolationist politicians charged, in the late 1930s, that native media – Hollywood most especially – were actually *leading* the country into another war: 'interventionist propaganda' was, in this view, less the machination of a foreign power than the subversive doing of un-American Americans.

The latter half of the chapter turns to instances of national media being led – or compelled – by their own state into adopting 'pro-war' positions. This supportiveness may result from standard journalistic news-gathering and framing practices rather than intentional 'partisanship'. The behaviour of American press and television networks in the period after Saddam Hussein's invasion of Kuwait in August 1990 and prior to 'Operation Desert Storm' in January 1991 provides a telling illustration. But it is certainly by no means always the case that media simply attune themselves to cues provided by official sources. The complicity of media in projecting enemy images and in catalysing conflict may result from an ample measure of state coercion, as an examination of media in Former Yugoslavia prior to the outbreak of war in the early 1990s, and in Rwanda before the genocide of 1994, suggests.

Following a Foreign Lead? American Media and Intervention in Two World Wars

When both the First and Second World Wars broke out in Europe, the US Government initially adopted a position of neutrality. Non-involvement in these 'Old World' wars enjoyed considerable popular support in the 'New World'. Geographical distance from Europe was reinforced by a deeply ingrained habit of mental detachment, or isolationism. And as consumers of a press which was largely dominated by domestic stories, many Americans in both 1914 and 1939 had very little understanding of why war in Europe was being fought. Parochial distaste for foreign news and isolationism were thus mutually reinforcing. As we might consequently expect, newspaper editors began both wars largely opposed to American involvement, even if they hoped for Germany's defeat. However, on both occasions, before the US government had formally declared war on Germany and its partners, significant sectors of the American media shifted decisively away from isolationism towards a position of support for Britain and its allies. And in both wars, the re-alignment of influential organs of the media was encouraged by British propaganda organisations and influential individuals working in America. Indeed, by the late 1930s, when history appeared to be repeating itself – and two-thirds of Americans were convinced their entry into the First World War had been mistaken (according to a Gallup poll of 1937) – prominent isolationists frequently asserted that British propaganda had 'duped' America into joining the war (Toplin, 1996, 83). Americans were consequently warned to be vigilant against renewed interventionist propaganda purveyed by a Fifth Column of pro-British agents, intent on undermining US neutrality once again.

It is easy to see why conspiracist theories of foreign subversion were popular in inter-war America, especially as a second – equally distant, equally ill-understood – world war loomed. Isolationists derived evidence concerning manipulative techniques from a series of academic studies published in the 1920s and 1930s (such as H. C. Peterson's judiciously timed, *Propaganda for War: The Campaign Against American Neutrality, 1914–17*, appearing in 1939), some with an explicit view to inoculating Americans against a new propaganda epidemic (Taylor, 1983, 22). Practitioners' memoirs – including an account published in 1918 by Sir Gilbert Parker, the architect of British efforts to undermine US neutrality – also contributed to Anglophobic fear of subversion by Britons and aligned Anglophiles. So too did more general historical or journalistic accounts of the origins of American involvement in the war, notably Walter Millis' 'damning bestseller', *Road to War: America, 1914–17* (Cull, 1995, 9; Sherry, 1995, 25). The notion that insidious British propaganda was responsible for America's entry into the Great War in 1917 even received something like an official stamp of approval with the Neutrality Acts of 1935 and 1936, designed to ensure both that America remained unentangled in distant wars through its own acts, and that other powers did not covertly entrap America by theirs. But how much persuasive power ought one to attribute to British efforts prior to American entry into the First World War in 1917, and the Second World War in 1941?

The First World War was the first war in which propaganda was a vital, and thoroughly organised, instrument. All major combatants established institutions specifically dedicated to carrying out propaganda on the home front, and towards enemies, neutral and Allied states alike. After the outbreak of war in 1914, both sides sedulously courted American opinion, hoping to persuade the US government at the very least to maintain its neutrality, but preferably to intervene on their own behalf. To attain the desired effect, however, the message was best disguised, for, as one British observer remarked in October 1914, 'Undue effort to influence public opinion, and more quickly in America than elsewhere, generally reacts unfavourably. The American press and people are suspicious of so-called publicity work, no matter what may be its object' (James Davenport Whelpley, cited by Squires, 1935, 49; see also Viereck, 1931, 136). Partly because German efforts lacked such subtlety in the early months of the First World War, they were largely judged a failure, by their practitioners as much as by other observers. German propagandists, one chided with hindsight, were 'far too open about their activity; far too obvious in their appeals; far too negligent of tact and finesse in spreading their message' (Viereck, 1931, 45). British propaganda organisation in America during the First World War was better concealed: so well camouflaged, in fact, that for much of the war the British government insisted that *no* official propaganda was being carried out there (Squires, 1935, 48). The Prime Minister was reticent about the very existence of Wellington House, a secret propaganda bureau charged with shaping attitudes towards the war in Allied and neutral countries, but in fact its covert activities were extensive.

In the Second World War, British propaganda was impeded by the mystique surrounding its Great War efforts, which were widely believed to have successfully elicited American entry into the war, and decisively undermined German civilian and military morale. Consequently, British propaganda technique was grudgingly admired in Germany (nowhere more so than in Hitler's *Mein Kampf*) and legislated against in America. When war broke out in September 1939, the British government was obliged to maintain a policy of 'No Propaganda', adopted in 1924 to assuage American suspicions about British information work (Cull, 1995, 10).

However, in practice, British propagandists – through a string of Foreign Office-funded offices – were as active in clandestine attempts to remould American opinion as their 'unofficial' counterparts had been at the start of the First World War.

Influencing the American Press: British Propaganda Techniques

In both wars, British propaganda techniques were similar in essence, though communications technology progressed considerably between 1919 and 1939. During the First World War, newspapers constituted the main organ of mass communication, with silent black and white film gradually being drafted into propaganda work. Radio broadcasting was as yet unavailable for civilian purposes. By 1939 both radio and film were firmly established in everyday patterns of American life. Consequently during the Second World War, British propaganda had to work through considerably more channels but the fundamental approach remained unchanged: namely to reach the American public via – not over the heads of – American opinion-formers (Lasswell, 1927, 157, 212–13). Americans would be nudged towards interventionism more easily by their own kinsfolk than by Britons whose motives were liable to be mistrusted.

In wooing indigenous opinion-formers, British propagandists played on certain innate advantages. The War of Independence bequeathed a legacy of anti-British sentiment in some American quarters but this was offset by an enduring Anglophilia in others. Moreover, 'the basic patterns of American life were more English than German', observed Harold Lasswell in the 1920s (1927, 187). Deep networks of family contacts and friendships connected America and Britain, and while there had been substantial German emigration to America in the late nineteenth century, and in flight from Hitler's Germany in the 1930s, common German-American bonds were less pronounced. As Viereck observed, the British had 'one inestimable advantage in the battle of propaganda': they spoke the same language. Differences of idiom and inflection notwithstanding, they 'merged with the crowd. They "passed" as Americans. In every newspaper office, in every great industrial concern there were Englishmen whose national origin no one suspected or questioned' (1931, 119).

Mastery of language was undoubtedly important in propaganda campaigns where camouflage was of the essence, but control over information – the raw stuff of news – was yet more vital. In the Second World War, news was dubbed the 'shocktroops of propaganda'; it was also allotted a vanguard role in the First World War. Both sides therefore attempted to manipulate the news carried by the American press. However, in the First World War British propagandists faced little competition from Germany, having severed the latter's cable communication links with America almost as soon as the war began. Accordingly a British version of the news, as circulated by the London-based Reuters telegraphic agency, formed the basis of American press reports (Peterson, 1939, 13). At a stroke, 'England [had] the ear of the world' (Viereck, 1931, 38). And even American correspondents working behind German lines relied on these direct British-controlled cables, as indirect cables running through neutral Scandinavia and Portugal were slower and therefore costlier (P. Taylor, 1995, 178). Much American war reporting in the First World War was, in any case, done from London, which had strong links with America's most influential East Coast daily papers (notably the *New York Times*). In some cases, reporters for the US press were themselves British. These ties helped to ensure that, in Peterson's words, 'the American view of Europe was normally and unavoidably coloured very deeply by the British attitude' (1939, 7). And if this was true of peacetime, how much more so in wartime, when American correspondents in London, or those eventually permitted at the Front with the Allies, had to clear their reports with British censors?

In both world wars, British propagandists recognised that their task of courting American journalists would be easier if more lenient arrangements for censorship were introduced, and if reporters were provided with easier access to the physical location of dramatic stories. But propagandists' desiderata frequently ran into opposition from the service departments of the armed forces. In September 1914, the military permitted a British officer to serve as 'official eye-witness' at the front, in an unsatisfactory bid to 'make the stifling of news more acceptable to the dissatisfied correspondents' (Peterson, 1939, 25–6). But his reports were no substitute for American correspondents being allowed to witness the front for themselves, and gradually the military relented sufficiently to offer British – and then overseas – reporters tours of the battlefield. However, lessons concerning censorship had to be relearnt in the Second World War. British propagandists liaising with American journalists again had to press the military (and sometimes senior propaganda officials) for less draconian censorship, playing on their superiors' knowledge that American assistance in the war was vital. During the Blitz, for example, the BBC's chief censor, who had befriended star American radio reporter, Ed Murrow, urged the Home Office to permit American journalists greater latitude to report on bomb damage to civilian areas. The cultivation of US reporters was, he urged, 'the finest form of propaganda of which we can avail ourselves' (Cull, 1995, 101). If American audiences were exposed to the suffering, and resilience, of ordinary Londoners under bombardment, they might come to believe that their country had a duty to help the plucky Brits who were doing their best to help themselves (Cull, 1995, 97–125).

British campaigns against American neutrality in both wars combined both positive and negative themes. A positive effort had to be made to increase American identification with the Allies: to encourage Americans to believe that the war in Europe concerned them, and that the values and peoples threatened by German aggression deserved American support. But at the same time American antagonism towards the Allies' enemies had to be heightened, and this called for negative propaganda, demonising Germany. The intention was to effect a change in attitudes whereby Americans would believe they had chosen intervention unprompted, and on the basis of the 'factual' evidence available to them. However, behind the scenes this evidence – whether in the form of American media output, or of pamphlets, public lectures, or sermons – was heavily manipulated by British propagandists.

The factual accuracy of the mass of ready-written features (as well as cartoons and photographs) passed via British channels to American journalists was sometimes far from scrupulous. Unsurprisingly, British propagandists slanted news to suit their own purposes, particularly to emphasise Allied heroism, but in the First World War, their eagerness to demonise Germany far exceeded selective presentation of serviceable 'facts'. The war spawned perhaps the most notorious epidemic of atrocity propaganda of the modern age. 'There must have been more deliberate lying in the world from 1914 to 1918 than in any other period of the world's history', wrote one of its first systematic analysts (Ponsonby, 1928, 19). Within Britain, atrocity propaganda played an important role in military and civilian mobilisation, forming one of the most effective means of arousing soldiers' 'blood-lust', according to General Crozier, and generating 'the brute-like bestiality which is so necessary for victory' (cited by Reid, 1941, 6). Beyond Britain, stories of German atrocities visited on 'Poor Little Belgium' – babies speared and carried aloft on German bayonets, and women mass-raped (to name but two of the most widespread variants) – helped instil interventionist ire (Reid, 1941; Squires, 1935, 65–8; Peterson, 1939, *passim*; Viereck, 1931, 146–53).

Students of propaganda often claim that it manipulates emotion more readily than reason, and that hatred is most easily aroused when propagandists sow their seeds in soil already fertilised with ingrained prejudice. Germans in America, because their 'speech and group feeling were different from those of their neighbors', were an easily recognisable 'out-group' (Peterson, 1939, 36). And if many Americans mistrusted German 'foreignness', it was a relatively small step for propaganda to persuade them that 'the Hun' – racially distinct and distinctly inferior – was capable of appalling brutality. Once people were minded to believe the worst of the Germans, the actual veracity and provenance of individual atrocity stories became insignificant. Even the wildly implausible, such as stories of poor little Belgian babies whose hands had been severed by 'the Bosche', gained credence as the sort of thing Germans *might* do, to the extent that rumours of Belgian nurseries filled with handless infants were greeted not with scepticism but parcels of baby-clothes and adoption offers (Ponsonby, 1928, 78–82; P. Taylor, 1995, 181).

Not all such stories were manufactured, and certainly they did not all originate in the febrile imaginations of British propagandists. Some activities – notably submarine warfare and aerial bombardment – deemed 'atrocities' in the First World War not only *had* occurred but would resurface in later wars as accepted forms of warfare (Reid, 1941, 4). Other atrocities attributed to 'the Hun' were neither unique to the First World War nor to Germans: the familiar litany of wartime barbarism included the rape of women, mutilation of the dead, and brutality towards prisoners of war (Lasswell, 1927, 82). Some stories were probably battlefield exaggerations of behaviour which Allied soldiers had themselves witnessed. Others, including one tale of a crucified Canadian soldier, were popular soldiers' rumours, though civilians could manufacture equally bloodthirsty tales, such as those of Germans slicing off women's breasts (Ponsonby, 1928, 67–9, 91–3; Reid, 1941, 37).

Although it is difficult to judge how many they themselves actually invented, British propagandists were unquestionably enthusiastic peddlers of second-hand atrocities. The most notorious story of the war – that of the German corpse factory which melted down German soldiers' bodies for glycerine – was, it appears, deliberately circulated in 1917 by British officials, with an explicit intent to mobilise anti-German feeling in China, where the dead were especially venerated (Ponsonby, 1928, 111; Squires, 1935, 32; Reid, 1941, 38). This much-discussed example should make us cautious in accepting the claim, stressed retrospectively by both Charles Masterman and Sir Campbell Stuart (two important practitioners), that British propaganda rested on a strategy of truthfulness (Lasswell, 1927, 206; Ponsonby, 1928, 108). Even if British propagandists themselves concocted very few stories, the government undeniably gave extensive currency to battlefield exaggerations, distortions and outright fabrications with the publication in 1915 of the Bryce Report (the *Report of the Committee on Alleged German Outrages*). This document was the result of an official investigation into German conduct in occupied Belgium. Its 60 pages were accompanied by bulky appendices carrying eye-witness testimonies of German atrocities. But its authors avoided any attempt to evaluate the veracity of these accounts, such as endeavouring to distinguish between rumour and half-truth, or to ensure that testimony had not been given in response to leading questions (Peterson, 1939, 53–61; Reid, 1941, 202–8; Wilson, 1979, 369–83). Simply by virtue of their reproduction in a government report, the stories were no doubt assumed by more credulous readers to be true, as the government probably hoped. Thus the report itself was, according to one's perspective, either 'one of the worst atrocities of the war' or Britain's 'stroke of genius' (Lasswell, 1927, 88; Peterson, 1939, 58).

Bryce's report, authored by a man whom Americans trusted, helped to quell initial scepticism concerning German atrocities in Belgium. American journalists who visited Belgium in September 1914 were inclined to disbelieve anti-German atrocity stories, having personally found no corroborating evidence (Reid, 1941, 29–30; Knightley, 1989, 120–1). However, on publication of the Bryce report, Wellington House reported that: 'Even in papers hostile to the Allies, there is not the slightest attempt to impugn the correctness of the facts alleged. Lord Bryce's prestige in America put scepticism out of the question, and many leading articles begin on this note' (American Press Résumé, 27 May 1915, cited by Peterson, 1939, 58). The *New York Times* greeted the publication with the headline 'GERMAN ATROCITIES ARE PROVED' (Ross, 1996, 53). Thanks not only to the efforts of British propaganda but to the actions of Germans themselves (providing 'real' atrocities by torpedoing the passenger ship, the *Lusitania*, in May 1915, and executing Nurse Edith Cavell), anti-Germanism soon swept America.

In both wars, important organs of the American media largely behaved in ways which gratified British propagandists. While it is impossible to quantify how far media endorsement of interventionism resulted from British encouragement, it is still necessary to sound a note of caution before concluding that American media, almost solely at the behest of British propaganda, initiated US entry into two world wars. That the British government succeeded, on both occasions, in bringing America into the war while Germany failed to keep the USA out, was not purely a measure of the former's skill and the latter's ineptitude. Had there been no British propaganda, it is likely that America would still have entered both wars on the Allied side, and that American media would have facilitated this abandonment of isolationism.

In the First World War, President Woodrow Wilson, despite having fought an election on the slogan 'He Kept Us Out of the War' ticket, came to provide a firm lead in manoeuvring America towards war, even when the country was still officially neutral (Ross, 1996, 145–213). For Wilson, Europe's war jeopardised values crucial to American democracy – respect for international law, state sovereignty and the rights of national groups to govern themselves – which, if universally respected, would form the basis for a lasting peace. While American banks made ever larger loans to the Allies, Wilson sought direct American involvement in the war. His cause was aided by a number of incidents which appeared (admittedly with magnification by British and other interventionist propagandists) as direct provocations by Germany: notably, the sinking of the American passenger ship, the *Lusitania*, by German submarines, and the publication of the Zimmermann telegram (which British intelligence had intercepted and deciphered) from the German foreign minister to his ambassador in Washington, proposing unrestricted submarine warfare against the USA, and a German alliance with Mexico should America intervene (P. Taylor, 1995, 182).

Given the re-orientation of the policy-making elite in Washington, fuelled by the stringent anti-Germanism of many of Wilson's key advisers (not least US Ambassadors in many European capitals) and the President's own *volte-face*, it seems either rash or politically-motivated for scholars to insist that American media were in the very vanguard of interventionism, ahead of policy-makers and public alike. Those hostile to American entry in the Second World War were keen to assert that, between August 1914 and February 1916, American newspapers initiated the shift, acting in effect as agents of British propaganda. Thus Peterson avows that:

> In almost all cases the American press accepted the British views as conceived by Wellington House and as released by the British censor. As a result American newspapers of those years should be viewed not as a mirror reflecting American reactions to the war, but as the principal medium through which the British influenced the Americans. (Peterson, 1939, 159)

It was doubtless a mistake to read the prestige East coast dailies – notably the *New York Times* – which were strongly pro-war, as representative of American opinion *en masse*, at a time when the West coast and mid-West were still firmly isolationist or simply apathetic. Yet it is equally plausible that, rather than being simply a cipher for British propaganda, the interventionist press reflected a particular strain of American reaction to the war, gathering force amongst the elite. The *World*, for example, the *New York Times*'s closest rival, took its lead squarely from President Wilson (as Peterson himself acknowledges: 1939, 162). It thus seems fair to conclude that the American press, presented initially with a vacuum in which the policy-making establishment and public opinion were squarely divided over the issue of war, gave free rein to partisanship in one direction or another. (The Hearst press, for example, exhibited profound scepticism – or outright hostility – towards British propaganda.) But as the Presidential direction became firmer, and the elite consolidated around interventionism, so too did the East coast prestige press.

As for the Second World War, an even clearer case can be made that American entry into the war was not simply the work of a manipulated press. Nazi policies – at home and abroad – found few admirers in America. If Allied propaganda over-stated German barbarity during the First World War, Nazi atrocities needed no exaggeration (although some sceptics, remembering discredited Great War stories of corpse factories, mistrusted reports of Nazi concentration camps, still suspecting that 'atrocity' was synonymous with 'falsehood': P. Taylor, 1995, 197). Where the US squarely divided over the First World War, a 1939 Gallup poll found, by contrast, most Americans wanting the Allies to win: even if 96.5 per cent thought the USA should stay out of the war, 84 per cent hoped for Germany's defeat (Shindler, 1979, 12). President Roosevelt's relaxations of neutrality legislation led inexorably towards American military commitment to an Allied cause that Americans overwhelmingly supported (at least passively). In June 1940, the President announced that America would take further measures of rearmament. Three months later, he gave Churchill 50 old US destroyers in return for the lease of naval bases in British colonies, a move which prefigured the introduction of Lend-Lease in January 1941. A peace-time call-up was initiated in October 1940 and, by August 1941, Churchill and Roosevelt were drafting a joint statement of something akin to war aims, in the *Atlantic Charter*. November saw the amendment of the neutrality laws to allow US merchant vessels to carry arms and fire in self-defence. When Japan sent bombers to destroy the US fleet at Pearl Harbor in December 1941 its 'sneak attack' simultaneously shattered America's residual isolationism. This galvanizing blow ensured that what already looked a near inevitability – American entry into the war on the Allied side – became a wholeheartedly national endeavour, not just a preference of the interventionist elite.

American journalists, as Nicholas Cull has shown, were firmly in favour of such a declaration, and although he attributes considerable skill and determination to British propagandists in campaigning against American neutrality, he concedes that their efforts did not so much 'change the course of history' as 'accelerate the process' (1995, 201–2). Their task had been, in Isaiah Berlin's words, to 'make friends friendlier', not to win converts outright (Cull, 1995, 199). This friendliness had been exhibited in Ed Murrow's radio dispatches on the London Blitz, and in the tolerant spirit which he and fellow print and broadcast journalists exhibited towards the vexations of official British censorship (Knightley, 1989, 235). We should be wary, then, of concluding that the US media, manipulated by foreign propagandists, led the country in a direction which either contradicted the journalists' own inclinations or those of their government.

That such charges have frequently been made against overseas propagandists and their American dupes is perhaps, in part, a result of media folklore's reiterated stories of wars 'created' by magnates themselves. (William Randolph Hearst frequently boasted that he had personally 'furnished' a war between Spain and America in 1898 over the fate of Cuba – then struggling for independence – by printing such a flood of impassioned reports on the islanders' plight that America's isolationist President was forced to intervene: Seib, 1997, 1–13.) Such tales played straight into the hands of isolationist politicians, for whom exposing the machinations of 'un-American' propagandists became standard practice. Most notably, prior to the Second World War, Senators Nye and Clark instigated a Senatorial subcommittee to conduct hearings into Hollywood's allegedly 'vicious' interventionist propaganda, in the form of such films as Anatole Litvak's *Confessions of a Nazi Spy* (1939), Charlie Chaplin's *The Great Dictator* (1940), Frank Borzage's *The Mortal Storm* (1940) and Howard Hawks's *Sergeant York* (1941). It soon emerged, as the Senators wilted under questioning, that they had not actually seen the arraigned movies or, if they had, salient points of offensive plotting and characterisation mysteriously eluded them (Koppes and Black, 1987, 44–5; Culbert, 1990). The films, it transpired, were rather beside the point. Motivated by an unappetising blend of isolationism and anti-Semitism (slyly insinuating that Jewish émigré studio bosses were insufficiently American), the Senators' underlying purpose was to rally like-minded isolationist sentiment by making a sacrificial slaughter of the highest profile scapegoat to hand. It mattered little, then, that Hollywood's treatment of Nazism had actually been rather muted, with studios reluctant to tackle Hitler or Mussolini head-on for fear of alienating apolitical home-grown audiences and lucrative European markets. It was the Nazis who ultimately debarred Hollywood from these markets, rather than the studio bosses' own anti-fascist scruples (Shindler, 1979; Koppes and Black, 1987; Doherty, 1993). When the hearings were stalled by Japan's attack on Pearl Harbor, Hollywood was able to proclaim that the films which it had strenuously defended from charges of propaganda were in fact highly prescient; but only at that point did the film industry whole-heartedly join up for a war effort in which it had hesitated to enlist hitherto.

Following the Lead? Media Espousal of Military Options

Those who oppose their country's involvement in war often present mass media as the culprit for unwanted entanglements: easier to blame a foreign power – or unassimilated 'foreign' elements – for duping media into interventionism than to criticise one's own government for choosing to enter or make war. However, in many cases, media endorsement of military solutions to diplomatic crises is occasioned by their following a governmental lead, rather than by their setting a 'war-mongering' agenda. As has already been argued, American media prior to 1917 and to 1941 shifted from isolationism to interventionism at least as much in response to a strong Presidential steer as from British manipulation. But this process of media serving to narrow options – in favour of military solutions – has more vivid and recent illustrations, as an examination of US media performance prior to the Gulf War of 1991 suggests.

'The quality of news coverage is never more important that when a society is pondering whether to wage war'; so say Dorman and Livingston, as would any liberal proponent of the press's democratic function: to apprise citizens fully on matters of foreign and domestic significance, thereby encouraging informed deliberation of policy options (Dorman and Livingston, 1994, 63; Peer and Chestnut, 1995, 84). But far from encouraging vigorous debate on the courses open to America following Iraq's invasion of Kuwait in August 1990, mainstream US media appeared to favour the use of force above continued economic sanctions against Iraq, or UN-brokered diplomatic negotiations, during the crucial months of Operation Desert Shield (when the USA mustered in Saudi Arabia the largest coalition of forces deployed since the Second World War). In so doing, the media moved behind a President who, despite public attempts to continue exploring diplomatic options during 1990, in fact had privately come to believe in war's necessity at a very early stage in the crisis, or so insiders have averred (Woodward, 1992).

In what ways did American media limit debate over – or even positively favour a military 'solution' to – the Gulf region crisis? Various sins of omission and commission have been laid at the media's door. With regard to ellipses, news media (television most notably) were reticent about the relationship between the US administration and Iraq during the 1980s, largely failing to explore the way in which America had favoured Saddam Hussein at the expense of the White House's *bête noire*, Iran (Dorman and Livingston, 1994, 66–7). Despite repeated violations of sovereignty by both protagonists during the decade-long Iran–Iraq war of the 1980s, and irrespective of Saddam Hussein's record of human rights violations (particularly with respect to Iraq's Kurdish minority), mainstream US media chose to represent Iraq as a significant threat to international stability only *after* August 1990. Lang and Lang speculate that a more attentive American media would have alerted Americans to the nature of the Iraqi regime at an earlier stage, and that this vigilant public might not accordingly have tolerated the 'appeasement' of Iraq by both Reagan and Bush (Lang and Lang, 1994, 59–60).

As it was, however, media attention to the Iraqi-American relationship in the 1980s had been sporadic at best, with the White House successfully managing to keep its support for Iraq under wraps. Even when transcripts of the controversial 25 July 1990 meeting between US ambassador April Glaspie and Saddam Hussein were published in September 1990 – showing that she had not strenuously warned Hussein against an invasion of Kuwait – most media were reluctant to suggest that the US administration might itself have encouraged Iraq's adventurism by transmitting unclear signals, if not a clear green light (Dorman and Livingston, 1994, 68). Missing an opportunity to rework the ubiquitous analogy with the 1930s, mainstream media merely echoed President Bush's warnings against appeasement of dictators. The print media, with few exceptions, failed to suggest that 'if Saddam Hussein was Adolf Hitler, up until August 2 George Bush had played the role of Neville Chamberlain, not Winston Churchill' (Dorman and Livingston, 1994, 71).

Instead, from a very early stage, mainstream media framed the story of Iraq's invasion of Kuwait and its ramifications using the same rhetorical and interpretative template as the Bush administration (Peer and Chestnut, 1995). The White House repeatedly explained Saddam Hussein's behaviour by reference to Hitler's aggression in 1930s Europe, with television and press reports voraciously seizing upon Bush's preferred analogy. Indeed, so frequently did he liken Saddam to Hitler some newspapers saw fit to comment on occasions when the President failed to do so (Dorman and Livingston, 1994, 71). The importance of this framing of the Gulf Crisis was not 'merely semantic'. After all, the analogy dictated clear policy prescriptions. The catechismal 'lesson of Munich', finally grasped by Chamberlain in September 1939, was that dictators' territorial appetites are never satisfied by swallowing only one country. Conquest and concessions merely whet the dictatorial palate, and such rapaciousness can only be halted by war. If Americans were persuaded to see events in the Gulf as closely echoing those in Europe 50 years earlier, they were thereby encouraged to see war as the fitting response to Iraqi aggression: 'With Saddam-as-Hitler, "compromise", or any other alternative policy option, was effectively eliminated from debate well before the actual debate got under way' (Dorman and Livingston, 1994, 74).

Thus by the time that Congress came to debate America's response to the Iraqi invasion of Kuwait, the dominant interpretation of the crisis had already taken hold. This is not to say that US media failed to report the range of viewpoints within Congress, particularly as aired at the Armed Service Committee hearings which began on 28 November. With 'objectivity' taken to lie in the replication of divergent elite viewpoints, and media reluctant to be seen as *instigating* criticism of the President, journalists sought to 'balance' the Administration's preferred policy against other options debated on the Capitol (Cook, 1994, 108). But such balancing mechanisms did not ensure that the scales reached equilibrium. On the contrary, they tipped against those whose viewpoints, conflicting with the President's, were heard but marginalised (Entman and Page, 1994, 91–2). This was not an isolated instance of asymmetrical 'balance' but the standard outcome of American journalistic routines where the President forms the apex of the media's hierarchy of sources.

Consequently, not only did the White House manage to place Iraqi aggression firmly within the 'sphere of consensus' from the outset (aided by the Congressional recess which limited expression of elite oppositional views from August to November), but the President continually benefited from his cardinal position (Peer and Chestnut, 1995, 90). Indeed, in general, Entman and Page conclude, the US media calibrate their attention to the power of their source. The President, Pentagon and State Department (which constitute the key 'newsbeats' for reporters covering foreign policy stories) are routinely accorded greater attention – and respect – than those with less institutional influence over the policy-making process. Whilst this over-reliance on official sources is common to the news-gathering process in many (but not all) countries, the American deference to those in high office is not merely the outcome of routinised newsroom procedures but 'a definition of the news in terms of helping audiences predict future events by focusing on actions, plans and statements of the powerful' (Entman and Page, 1994, 93–4). The media – particularly television, where controversy is especially eschewed – thus abjure a role as initiator of public participation and debate, preferring to act as barometer of the Capitol's micro-climate.

By privileging elite sources, news organisations thus favoured a president who himself favoured war. Moreover, by following Bush's rhetorical lead in 'Hitlerising' Saddam Hussein, the news media also laid themselves open to abuse from professional public relations consultants who were energetically working on Kuwait's behalf. That the emir of Kuwait and his exiled regime hired the services of US-based public relations firm Hill & Knowlton, at a cost of some $10.8 million, is now well known (see, for example, Kellner, 1992; MacArthur, 1993; Manheim, 1994). Hill & Knowlton's brief was, in essence, to massage the image of the al Sabah regime, persuading Americans that Kuwait was a country worthy of their sacrifices. However, initial attempts to work on 'positive' themes – that Kuwaiti women could drive (even if they could not vote), that the regime was amongst the freest in the Gulf region – fell on unreceptive ears, as Hill & Knowlton's polling subcontractors found in their telephone surveys and 'focus groups' (Manheim, 1994, 142–3).

Many Americans were not moved to sympathy for Kuwait because it was, in however limited a way, like America. What inspired them, rather, was dislike of Saddam Hussein and an acquired eagerness to punish the 'butcher of Baghdad'. Hill & Knowlton therefore concentrated their efforts on demonising the Iraqi leader, just as Bush was doing. Accordingly, Kuwait's exiled leaders were (reluctantly) persuaded that their best chances of winning US military support lay in portraying themselves as Saddam's passive victims. To foster hatred of Hussein and pity for his victim, Hill & Knowlton sought to publicise Iraqi atrocities in occupied Kuwait. Their work in this respect recalls First World War atrocity propaganda, for the principal stories centred on Iraqi troops' abuses of Kuwaiti babies (MacArthur, 1993, 51–2, though he also offers a comparison with Hearst's machinations in 1898,

237–9). The best-known story of this kind – that plundering Iraqis had thrown Kuwaiti babies out of their hospital incubators – was tearfully repeated on 10 October 1990 to the US Congressional Caucus on Human Rights by a fifteen-year-old Kuwaiti girl, known only as Nayirah (MacArthur, 1993, 57–9). Her testimony, and that of others both at that hearing and later ones, moved Bush to the extent that he retold the story five times in the next five weeks (MacArthur, 1993, 65). The credibility of Nayirah's account was enhanced by the respected human rights watchdog, Amnesty International, which repeated allegations that over 300 babies had died in this way in their own report on Iraqi violations of human rights in Kuwait published on 19 December (MacArthur, 1993, 66). Bush could now claim to be citing Amnesty – an almost unimpeachable source – rather than an unknown Kuwaiti girl. The incubator story was tremendously resonant, becoming one of the key 'facts' to support the 'Saddam-as-Hitler' analogy. However, its status as 'fact' was questionable indeed.

Although the Iraqi regime undoubtedly did violate human rights in Kuwait, verifying these was immensely difficult, given Iraq's sealing of the border. Those who tried to research the story on the ground – which was easier after rather than during the conflict – found no incontrovertible first-hand evidence for it (MacArthur, 1993, 62). After the war, Amnesty International distanced themselves from this story: but by then, and by the time it was revealed that Nayirah was in fact the daughter of the Kuwaiti ambassador to the US, and that her tearful testimony was not that of a traumatised witness but of a well-coached accessory to Hill & Knowlton, the repudiation was too late (MacArthur, 1993, 59). Her story, and others like it, had done their work in helping mobilise Americans for war. In the impassioned climate wrought by tales of dead Kuwaiti babies, it was perhaps easier to persuade people that American lives might need to be sacrificed to halt Saddam. Or as John Mueller argues in his study of opinion polls and the Gulf War, 'Bush's emotional state helped him to bring off the war' (1994, 53). Even those who did not positively wish for war came to see it as inescapable, and the media, by narrowing the scope of debate and taking their cue so clearly from the White House, encouraged this sense of 'helpless fatalism' amongst an electorate offered only, in Elaine Scarry's phrase, a 'mimesis of deliberation' (Mueller, 1994, 56–7; Scarry, 1993, 59).

State Compulsion and the Creation of 'Enemy Images'

In the build-up to war, the media may play an important legitimatory role in sanctioning the resort to organised violence by not only suggesting the inefficacy of other options but also by presenting an enemy so threatening that it requires to be 'self-defensively' engaged (Keen, 1986). MacArthur suggests a high degree of purposefulness in American policy-makers' use of news media to exaggerate the threat posed by Saddam in the tense transition from Desert Shield to Desert Storm (MacArthur, 1993, 37). But though the White House may have sought to co-opt the media, the latter's complicity in narrowing the debate (or in 'starting a war' if one accepts MacArthur's interpretation) resulted from long-standing news routines, not any measure of *direct* Presidential compulsion. However, under different circumstances mass media are sometimes compelled by their state to fulfil vital 'mobilisational' roles prior to war and, on occasion, genocide. The final section of this chapter therefore examines instances of state intervention to ensure that media lay the psychological preparations for the physical assault of enemies systematically represented as less-human beings. Media have accordingly been used to animate hatreds both between and within states, castigating one or more groups as 'foreign' and 'Other', even though they may share (or have shared) the same nationality and a common (though denied) ethnicity. In so doing, media in Former Yugoslavia and Rwanda helped prepare the ground for mass participation in war and genocide, their 'enemy images' serving to diminish personal responsibility, conscience and ethical norms towards enemies no longer regarded as fellow humans (Spillmann and Spillmann, 1991, 71).

In struggling to make sense of these conflicts (somewhat reductively depicted as Hutus versus Tutsis in Rwanda, Serbs versus Slovenes, Serbs versus Croats, Croats versus Bosnians, and Serbs and Bosnian Serbs versus Bosnian 'Muslims'), Western media and policy-makers have often concluded that these are essentially nonsensical, 'tribal' wars between peoples drenched in ethnic hatred (Glenny, 1993, 183; Magaš, 1993, 317; Cigar, 1995, 5–6, 11–12; Allen and Seaton, 1999). As frequently represented, atavistic bloodletting lacks rational explanation but perpetually simmers, occasionally boiling over, in 'the Balkans' or 'darkest' Africa. Besides removing any further obligation to understand the roots of conflict, explaining violence as inexplicable may also be conveniently self-serving: if 'ethnic violence' is age-old and engrained, then there is little that onlooking states or international organisations can do, other than apply humanitarian band-aids to its consequences, or else retreat into 'shallow misanthropy' from a world 'too crazy to deserve serious reflection' (Ignatieff, 1998, 24). However, the 'tribalist' paradigm obscures the intentionality of violence in both cases. In neither Rwanda nor Former Yugoslavia was violence a spontaneous eruption of age-old hatreds, but rather it was deliberately planned and launched to advance particular political agendas.

In Rwanda, a Hutu elite from the north of the country sought to consolidate its power, stave off popular Hutu discontent (in the face of rising unemployment and straitened economic circumstances), and avoid making concessions to the Tutsi Rwanda Patriotic Front (RPF), which from 1990 had been launching ever more successful incursions into Rwanda from Uganda. Hutu extremists, who ultimately arranged the killing of their own Hutu President Habyarimana (for having ceded too much ground to the RPF in the 1993 Arusha Accords) wrapped their power-building aims in the cloak of exclusive nationalism, persuading Hutus that only they were true Rwandans, and that others must be exterminated before the Tutsis robbed Hutus of their patrimony.

In a more politically complex situation in the Former Yugoslavia, the end of Tito's rule in 1980 led to a period of instability during which the Federal Republic of Yugoslav States broke down into its constituent parts, gradually recognised by the EU as sovereign states in their own right. Regretting the break-up of a Federation which had privileged Serbia, and having failed to preserve a Serb-dominated Federation, Communists in Belgrade, led by President Milošević, also donned nationalist garb. Presenting Serbia as threatened by its neighbours, and Serbs as disenfranchised minorities within these successor states, Milošević sought to enhance Serbia's position within Former Yugoslavia by building – or 'reconstituting', as Serb nationalists insisted – an enlarged Serbia. As the 'lost' Serbian lands lying in Kosovo, Slovenia, Croatia and Bosnia-Hercegovina were in fact ethnically mixed, a 'pure' 'greater Serbia' could only be built by expunging non-Serbs, either by killing them outright, or by driving them from their homes and obliterating all traces of their existence; this dual process was euphemistically termed 'ethnic cleansing' (Cigar, 1995).

In both Rwanda and Serbia, violence was preceded by months of propaganda, encouraging its recipients to hate and fear enemies portrayed as ethnically distinct. The media played analogous preparatory roles, albeit through different channels: Rwanda's main mass medium was radio, while in Serbia, anti-Croat and anti-Bosnian propaganda was carried by a full range of television, press and radio outlets. In both, media came under increasing state scrutiny. Purges of 'disloyal' journalists occurred, and new ultra-nationalist media mushroomed. Pre-war propaganda themes in Serbia and Rwanda were also thematically interchangeable, and thoroughly familiar, following a long-standing pattern whereby violent intent is disowned and projected as a 'war of defence against a menacing, murderous aggressor' (Lasswell, 1927, 51).

Accounts of the wars in the Balkans and the Rwandan genocide which reject the 'ancient hatreds' interpretation have emphasised the role played by the media in creating killers from one-time neighbours who had managed to co-exist peaceably for lengthy periods, if not perpetually. Misha Glenny, a British journalist, revisiting the Serbian population of the Krajina region (in Croatia, but claimed by Serbia) in the early 1990s, was astonished at the difference which the 18 months since his earlier visit had made: 'It was as though the whole town had suffered the fate of the American... town featured in Don Siegal's film, *Invasion of the Body Snatchers*: some alien virus had consumed their minds and individual consciences' (1993, 20). The main agent of this virus was *Srpski Radio Knin*, a Serb-run station pouring out anti-Croat propaganda, and a 'vital accomplice in the dissemination of falsehoods and the perpetuation of divisive myth' (Glenny, 1993, 21). Similarly, historian Noel Malcolm rejected the notion that Yugoslavia was 'forever seething with ethnic hatreds'. Having watched RTS (Serbian Radio-Television) in the period 1991–92, however, he came to understand why Bosnian Serbs believed themselves threatened, and found persuasive a parallel drawn by Belgrade journalist Milos Vašić: 'You must imagine a United States with every little TV station everywhere taking exactly the same editorial line – a line dictated by David Duke [of the Ku Klux Klan]. You too would have war in 5 years' (1996, 252).

In short, if Milošević's plans for territorial aggrandisement were to be realised then 'a campaign of intense propaganda was needed to mobilise the population, to make war thinkable in Yugoslavia'

(Thompson, 1994, 1). In the 'preparatory phase', the Serbian mass media were used by the political leadership to 'change the value system of an entire generation of Serbs', persuading them that the Serbs of Croatia and Bosnia were dispersed members of a Serb 'national entity' (Thompson, 1994, 51–2; Cigar, 1995, 21). This exclusive national identity was built at the expense of Croats and Muslims, whom the media verbally assaulted prior to any physical attack. As one Sarajevo-based journalist put it, 'Every person killed in this war was first killed in the newsrooms' (Borden, 1993).

In Former Yugoslavia, the propaganda of ethnic chauvinism was more easily spread thanks to the 'Balkanisation' of the media. The citizens of the Communist Republics had long relied primarily on their individual republic's media. Some pan-Yugoslav broadcasts and newspapers found a nationwide audience, but perhaps not enough to cement a strong sense of Yugoslav identity (Ramet, 1992, 81–5). Indeed, the severing of programme-sharing arrangements between the various republics' media outlets in the late 1980s prefigured the dissolution of the Federation itself (Thompson, 1994, 17–21). In the successor states, the final vestiges of pan-Yugoslav media quickly withered in the early 1990s. The populations of the newly independent republics failed to listen to or read the media of their neighbours. And tellingly, as media also fragmented along ethnic lines *within* Croatia and Bosnia, Serbs in those states increasingly relied on their own regional Serbian services rather than Croatian or Bosnian national outlets. While media addressed themselves to ever narrower audiences, so too did nationalistic content become more ethnically intolerant: a heightened politicisation which was furthered by state purges of media personnel in Belgrade. In the late 1980s and early 1990s, Milošević's government ousted a number of key personnel from Serbia's leading press group and from RTS for their oppositional stance (Thompson, 1994). Rid of dissenting voices from the mainstream media, with press freedoms still constitutionally enshrined but with law enforcement agencies turning a blind eye to state repression (or worse, police officers themselves harassing journalists), the Serbian media stridently articulated a 'language of war before war was even conceivable in Yugoslavia'; this was 'a language of menacing ultimatums, of infinite self-pity, of immense accusations backed by no evidence or investigation; of conspiracy-mongering, paranoia and brazen incitement to violence' (Thompson, 1994, 55).

In Rwanda the media have also been described as a 'tool of genocide' (Destexhe, 1995, 29). Journalist Feargal Keane observed that, for several years before the genocide of 1994, 'Hutus were exposed to an ongoing and virulent campaign of anti-Tutsi brainwashing', as a result of which tens of thousands became convinced that the Tutsis were 'going to turn them into beasts of the field once again' (1996, 8–9). Radio (known as *ibitega*, or 'magical means to act upon someone else at a distance') was a particularly potent channel of propaganda, its impact intensified by the absence of alternative sources of news and Rwanda's isolation from all international media other than the BBC World Service (Destexhe, 1995, 30). The national service, Radio Rwanda, was active in promoting anti-Tutsi feeling in the early 1990s, while agitators simultaneously toured the country establishing the *interahamwe* militias which would later carry out the genocide. According to the human rights organisation, African Rights, it was Radio Rwanda that gave the signal for an earlier massacre of Tutsis at Bugusera in 1990 (1994, 71). But even this station found itself eclipsed by the more virulently anti-Tutsi *Radio Television Libre des Milles Collines* (RTLM). The latter was established with the approbation of President Habyarimana, who refused to urge moderation on its broadcasters even after RTLM transmitted a speech by Dr Leon Mugesera (a prominent Hutu extremist), calling for the Tutsi to be sent back to Ethiopia – whence they allegedly came – via the Nyabarongo river (African Rights, 1994, 71). In other words, Hutus should slaughter their Tutsi neighbours, disposing of their bodies in the river which feeds into Lake Victoria. So blatant was its incitement of racial hatred that, after the genocide, the international press watchdog, *Reporteurs sans Frontières* successfully urged the UN Commission on Human Rights to bring journalists and sponsors of RTLM to justice (African Rights, 1994, 127–8). As in Serbia, journalists who had questioned the prevailing mood of ultra-nationalism found their working lives made impossible. In Rwanda, many found themselves silenced in the most drastic fashion, themselves targeted by the militias. As one Rwandan journalist pointed out: 'the most sensitive issue of all was the ethnic chauvinism of extremists. A journalist who challenged their ideology did so at his peril...Whether you were Hutu or Tutsi did not matter. If you pointed out the dangers of ethnic politics, you were automatically labelled an RPF accomplice' (African Rights, 1994, 152).

The Propaganda of Racial Hatred

The propaganda themes carried by the media in Rwanda and Serbia prior to war bear distinct resemblances, the key technique lying in manipulation of history to serve the ends of an ethnically-exclusive nationalism. Some commentators have taken the Serbs' lengthy, and frequently regurgitated, catechism of historical grievances as evidence that 'ancient hatreds' did indeed constitute the root cause of conflict in Former Yugoslavia. But perhaps distant events themselves had less bearing on the outbreak of conflict than the wilful resurrection of historical ghosts by politicians and propagandists (Brough-Williams, 1996, 23). History was presented as a series of atrocities perpetrated against Serbs: the quest for a Greater Serbia as a self-defensive search for security (Magaš, 1993, 322). Serbian nationalists repeatedly raised the spectre of the Ottoman Muslim victory over Serbs at the Battle of Kosovo in 1389 and, even more resonantly, of Second World War concentration camps established by the pro-Nazi Croatian *Ustase*, in which thousands of Serbs died. Serbian media, echoing Milošević, both before the war and during it, constantly referred to Serbia's enemies as Croatian or Muslim *Ustase*. Stjepan Meštrović considers this manipulation of the past a manifestation of 'postemotionalism': 'a neo-Orwellian mechanism found in Western societies in which the culture industry markets and manipulates dead emotions from history that are selectively and synthetically attached to current events' (1996, 11). This is not to deny that many Serbs harboured residual fears built on historical memories but to suggest that such anxieties had lain relatively dormant until the 1980s, and resulted in violence only with the catalysis of virulent nationalist propaganda.

   Through constant reiteration of *Ustase* atrocities of the Second World War, Serbian nationalists portrayed Serbs as history's victims, and projected their own intentions on to Croats and non-Serbian Bosnians, who were depicted as planning new onslaughts against the Serbs. Not only did such scenarios have considerable resonance for Serbs within the states comprising the Former Yugoslavia but they were also accepted, to varying degrees, by many beyond. For example, the analogy (drawn by Milošević and others) between Serbs and Jews – fellow victims of Second World War genocide – encouraged the Israeli government to adopt a pro-Serbian stance during the wars in Croatia and Bosnia, despite Serbia's own 'ethnic cleansing' and evidence of Serb-run 'concentration camps' (Primoratz, 1996, 195–206).

Similarly, Serbia's political leadership, the Orthodox Church and the media repeatedly warned that Bosnian Muslims were launching an 'Islamic jihad' against Serbia with international pan-Islamic backing (Cigar, 1995, 28–30, 62–3, 65–6). Serbian media distorted Koranic texts as proof that Islam mandated the killing of non-Muslims, and Karadžić, the Bosnian Serb leader, warned that the 'Muslim' Sarajevo government would force Bosnian Serb women to wear the veil (Cigar, 1995, 65–6). In Serbian nationalist rhetoric, Muslims were not only *Ustase* but also 'Islamic fundamentalists'. To bolster this assertion, history was once again deployed: Bosnian Muslims were projected as the descendants of Serbs who had betrayed their country by converting to the Ottoman invader's religion (and who, by implication, had no legitimate claim to 'Serbian' soil in Bosnia). Atrocities which the Ottomans had allegedly visited on the Serbs were re-cycled in fresh horror stories of Bosnian Muslim plans to castrate and otherwise disfigure Serbian men (Gutman, 1993). Like the evocation of Second World War atrocities, the notion of an 'Islamic threat' was equally useful overseas, reinforcing Israeli identification with beleaguered Serbs, and chiming with the post-Cold War assertions of some Western academics and journalists that 'Islamic fundamentalism' and 'civilizational conflict' were the greatest challenges to security in the 1990s (Huntington, 1996).

Extremist Hutu propaganda bore many of the same traits. Tutsis were consistently dehumanised in both state and privately-funded media as *inyenzi* (cockroaches) to be stamped upon. Radio broadcasts also encouraged Hutus not only to believe themselves ethnically distinct from the Tutsis but also to regard the latter as 'foreigners': lighter-skinned, Nilotic Africans who had arrived in Rwanda centuries after the indigenous Hutu. In fact, centuries of intermarriage make a nonsense of the myth of racial purity, though it had been serviceable to Rwanda's European colonisers to treat Hutus and Tutsis differently. Thus they attempted to co-opt the latter through preferential treatment, rationalised on the grounds that Tutsis were 'proto-Europeans, pastoralists who had come down from the north, possibly Ethiopia, into the dark and savage lands in the heart of Africa to impose their superior civilization' (F. Keane, 1996, 13; see also Destexhe, 1995, 36). The higher status and greater wealth Tutsis achieved under colonial rule left a lingering sense of grievance amongst Hutus, which extremist propaganda exploited. Anti-Tutsi propaganda presented them as a 'minority, well-off and foreign', and attempted to elevate a 'historical outcome into a primordial difference' (Destexhe, 1995, 28; Mamdani, 1996, 6).

As in Yugoslavia, then, the past provided a fertile source of propaganda themes and myths. Consequently, despite the fact that Hutus had ruled Rwanda since independence, and it was under a Hutu government that many Rwandans had seen their living standards fall in the 1980s and early 1990s, peasants were encouraged to see Tutsis as the root of their problems and to believe that the RPF was coming to steal their land (F. Keane, 1996, 22–3). Here too the Hutu extremists' own genocidal intent was transferred on to its future victims. Tutsis were compared with Hitler and Pol Pot (African Rights, 1994, 38). And like the Bosnian 'Muslim fundamentalists' of Serbian propaganda, the Tutsis were presented as part of an international conspiracy: here with President Museveni of Uganda (whose country had sheltered the RPF) in an alleged plot to establish a 'Hima-Tutsi kingdom in the Bantu [i.e. Hutu] area of the great lakes region' (African Rights, 1994, 38).

Conclusion

Allowing for the occasional difficulty of determining precisely when a war begins, it is nevertheless clear that media can play important preparatory and legitimatory roles prior to direct violent confrontation, whether or not it later culminates in a formal declaration of war. As the case studies suggest, the pre-war roles media espouse, and the reasons for their adoption, vary considerably. Media endorsement of military options may conceivably stem, at least in part, from foreign encouragement. More commonly, *de facto* media approval for the resort to war derives from a bias in news-gathering towards powerful elite sources who themselves sanction war (arguably reinforced by the symbiosis between US television networks and the defence industry: Kellner, 1992). Sometimes, as in Serbia and Rwanda, media are directly compelled to transmit the war-mongering propaganda of their state through much less subtle means.

It is also clear, though, that despite differences in how media may come to assume a mobilisatory function, the themes of state and media 'pre-propaganda' are often notably similar: an insistence that the Other began hostilities, or is intent upon launching them (thus making a pre-emptive, 'defensive' attack necessary); a return to history for evidence to justify (and perhaps nurture) this sense of victimisation; and a corresponding focus on enemy 'atrocities' (verified, rumoured or invented). Such atrocity stories may justify retaliatory attack, and, in testifying to the Other's lesser humanity, also sanction treatment otherwise considered inhumane, even within wartime's extended parameters of the morally acceptable (Keen, 1986).

Finally, an examination of media–state relations before war suggests that governments often expect unquestioning compliance from news media during periods of tension, behaving during pre-war hostilities in much the same way as during war itself. This was certainly the case in Serbia and Rwanda during the early 1990s, but the pattern is familiar (albeit to differing degrees). In 1982, for example, the British government under Margaret Thatcher – having despatched a naval 'Task Force' to the South Atlantic to reclaim the Falklands/Malvinas from the Argentinians – brooked no questioning of government policy by British media. Even before fire had been exchanged at sea and while UN resolutions were still being tabled, the BBC found itself under severe attack for allowing critical viewpoints to be aired on a discussion programme (R. Harris, 1983; Morrison and Tumber, 1988). Its behaviour was branded 'unpatriotic' by Conservative MPs and vocal elements of the Fleet Street press, who lined up behind the government to berate both the Corporation and the *Daily Mirror* (the sole tabloid to condemn the dispatch of the Task Force). Support for government policy and loyalty to one's country became blurred. In this, as in many other instances, patriotism – or the charge of being insufficiently 'patriotic' – became a powerful disciplinary weapon at the government's (and its media allies') disposal.

The Falklands episode illustrates the difficulty that journalists face in questioning the efficacy or morality of military solutions to diplomatic crises once mobilisation is under way; this phenomenon was also observed during the months of Operation Desert Shield in 1990. To demur is to open oneself to charges of 'treachery', 'defeatism' and 'back-stabbing'. Paradoxically, dissidents (or those branded as such) are treated as though their very doubts about military action endanger the lives of their country's armed forces, even though diplomatic alternatives aim to forestall loss of military life and are sometimes endorsed by strategists themselves. (General Colin Powell, for example, supported lengthier UN sanctions against Iraq.) Consequently, in much the same way that a military mobilisation often increases the likelihood of war – troop deployments are expensive to mount, and once forces and munitions are in place momentum easily gathers behind their precipitate use – the weight of governmental and journalistic 'jingoism' may steam-roller potential opposition from the very outset.

2
Media and 'Total War'

'There is no question but that government management of opinion is an unescapable corollary of large-scale modern war', wrote Harold Lasswell in a pioneering academic study of propaganda (1927, 15). His judgement was based on recent experience of what was then called the 'Great War' – the most destructive conflict in human history to date – in which all sides had made intensive use of propaganda at home and abroad. Doubtless, like many of his contemporaries, Lasswell hoped that the truth of his dictum would not be subjected to future testing. With hindsight, however, his words seem all the more apt. Many of the techniques of state propaganda pioneered between 1914 and 1918 were adopted and adapted during the second 'large-scale modern war' of 1939–45, though 'government management of opinion' had already proved to be a peacetime feature of Europe's emergent authoritarian regimes, notably in the USSR and Nazi Germany.

The 'totality' of the First and Second World Wars took many different forms. Both wars were global in a way no previous conflict had been. In 1914–18, the war not only entangled the European rivals' colonies but also drew in the USA. In 1939–45, two distinct conflicts in Europe and Asia meshed, with Nazi Germany and Imperial Japan forging an Axis. Their alignment ensured that America's declaration of war against Japan after the attack at Pearl Harbor also marked America's wholehearted commitment to the European war against Hitler. These wars, then, encompassed more countries than hitherto, but they also dented civilian life more profoundly than any previous conflict. Industrialisation and mechanisation ensured that twentieth-century warfare ceased, in many respects, to resemble the cavalry-dependent nineteenth-century wars fought by professional soldiers. Vast military 'machines'

54

deployed new weapons of mass destruction: submarines, torpedoes, tanks, zeppelins, bombers, shells, rockets, and ultimately atomic bombs. Maintaining such forces required the mass call-up of men to fight, and their mental and professional re-orientation from civilian to soldier. Equipping them further necessitated re-structuring national economies to war production, and the consequent 'conscription' – or something like it – of women to 'man' the factories.

In different ways, total war blurred boundaries: between traditional gender roles certainly, but also between previously upheld distinctions in warfare between 'combatants' (war's legitimate protagonists and targets) and 'non-combatants' (those properly beyond its sights: Walzer, 1992). If the whole of society was mobilised for war, then society as a whole became a 'legitimate target' for bombing, though the precise targets were often mystified in military pronouncements. The rationale for bombing civilian areas, as publicly presented at the time, was primarily to incapacitate an enemy's productive infrastructure by destroying the factories which produced the munitions of war, and the communications networks which distributed them. But 'strategic bombing' – as the aerial destruction of urban areas came to be termed in the Second World War – served another function, psychological not material: to strike enemy morale, undermining civilian will to participate in the war effort, and miring society in defeatism. For in total war, achieving 'total victory' was held to consist of both demonstrating one's military supremacy and effecting the enemy's mental surrender. Consequently, to marshal and maintain morale on one's own side, and attack the opponent's, 'munitions of the mind' were an integral part of total war. Mass media received their call-up along with other vital wartime industries.

In many respects, the roles allotted to mass media and state techniques for regulating the flow of news and shaping its presentation in the First World War prefigure those of the Second. An examination of the First World War serves as a point of departure for comparison with its yet more destructive and far-reaching successor. The story is not simply one of continuity, however. Much changed in the inter-war years. The technology for fighting war, and reporting it, evolved; the nature of the combatant states was transformed. Europe saw the emergence of regimes in which the peacetime management of public opinion was central to the functioning of the 'total' – or totalitarian – state. Film, a nascent propaganda weapon during the Great War, was used intensively in the 1920s and 1930s as an instrument of 'revolutionary consolidation' in both Nazi Germany and the USSR (R. Taylor, 1998). By 1939, cinema-going was a deeply rooted social habit throughout industrialised Europe and North America, with the result that in the Second World War, 'motion pictures' – alongside newsreels and documentary 'shorts' – were as much weapons of war as the press. Likewise radio, still in its infancy as a military communications system in the First World War, grew into a mass medium between the wars, being variously (sometimes simultaneously) used for the broadcast of propaganda, news and entertainment.

The states which confronted each other in the First World War were, in many respects, not so very dissimilar; indeed, that many were competing over the same fruits of imperialism was one major cause of war. (Likewise, Germany, America, Britain and France all had parliamentary systems with such restricted franchises – excluding women, some poorer citizens and certainly 'ethnic minorities' – that the designation 'liberal democracy' scarcely looks appropriate.) The Second World War, on the other hand, affords an opportunity to compare how quite different states used national media in wartime. This chapter highlights Nazi Germany and Britain, in particular, as their respective state approaches to news are often taken to be antithetical: the 'Big Lie' versus the 'Strategy of Truth'. Is it possible, though, that British 'truthfulness' has been exaggerated in post-war mythologising, and that total war necessarily entailed – for all combatants (if perhaps to different degrees) – erosion of press freedom? Whether or not that was so remains to be assessed. But certainly understanding how, and on what grounds, media were managed in democracies as well as dictatorships in the Second World War serves another important comparative function.

A fundamental corollary of total war was the prospect of 'total defeat', or 'unconditional surrender', as the Allies termed their objective *vis-à-vis* Nazi Germany and Imperial Japan. Total war was conflict in which 'self-determination' itself was jeopardised. The severity of the stakes legitimised far-reaching official media-management and censorship. Moreover, where state and *national* survival were identical (or could be made to appear thus), governments could invoke the patriotism of 'responsible' journalists, entertainment and news media, and so inspire even greater self-censorship. None of the wars prosecuted by Western states since 1945 has replicated 'total war' conditions (within their borders at least). And yet, argues Kevin Williams, the boundary between total and limited war has been wilfully blurred by governments seeking similar powers over (and co-operation from) mass media in limited conflict as those they exercised in the Second World War. Thus he contends, 'Those seeking to stress the war correspondent's patriotic duty have used the experience of the Second World War to recast these modern conflicts as wars of national survival' (Williams, 1992, 156). Likewise, Daniel Hallin asserts that 'many of the conflicts over wartime communication arise from the clash between expectations based in the culture of total war and the political reality of limited war' (1997, 209). Familiarity with total war thus allows us to assess practice in limited war more critically.

News Media and the State in the First World War

When the assassination of Austro-Hungarian Archduke Franz Ferdinand in Sarajevo set a global war in motion in August 1914, combatants on both sides (Austria-Hungary and Germany ranged against Britain, France and Tsarist Russia) quickly assigned to their national media the task of raising and sustaining morale. As millions of young male civilians were hastily enlisted into swollen military ranks, 'the mobilisation of the civilian mind' (in Lasswell's phrase) was an endeavour of utmost urgency (1927, 10). Ideally, states hoped that their media would provide both a positive projection of war aims while crystallising public animosity towards the enemy. As the predominant medium of the day, the press was to become in effect an arm of official propaganda: one of its many tentacles. Both Britain and Germany (and in due course the USA, when it entered the war in 1917) also undertook considerable 'publicity' work overseas to influence neutral and allied opinion, in part by targeting foreign journalists. Additionally, though these efforts fall beyond the scope of this book, enemy morale was assaulted by various specially devised means of communication, such as mass pamphlet-drops from aeroplanes and Zeppelins, which encouraged disaffection amongst the enemy ranks and provided instruction on how the severely demoralised should surrender (Sanders and Taylor, 1982; Messinger, 1992).

The Release and Censorship of News

Germany's arrangements for managing news in the First World War have received considerably less attention (from English-language academics at least) than have Anglo-American initiatives. If it is true that the victors of history determine its writing then small wonder, perhaps, that they should have exhibited such little interest in a propaganda campaign which manifestly failed. The German government's efforts have been widely berated. Lasswell's seminal study set the tone when he bemoaned the undue influence of the military over proceedings (1927, 198). Phillip Knightley's classic *The First Casualty* is equally dismissive, asserting that the Germans were 'never able to efface the impression that they were the aggressors' (1989, 82), and Philip Taylor also states that from the outset German propaganda was 'poorly organised and co-ordinated' (1995, 190). But Germany's defeat (despite subsequent stab-in-the-back myths) was primarily effected on the battlefield, and, at the start of the war, it was no more apparent that Germany's propaganda would prove deficient than it was that the Prussian military would be outgunned by the Anglo-Franco-Russian *entente*. In fact, Wilhelmine Germany arguably entered war with better developed arrangements for press management than did Britain.

Germany was, after all, a more militarised society than pre-war Britain, with a tradition of government news management established under Bismarck and Wilhelm II (Messinger, 1992, 16). When, on 31 July 1914, a State of Siege was declared, which entailed suspension of 'the right to express opinion freely by word, print or picture', Chancellor Bethmann-Hollweg simultaneously issued the press with 26 prohibitions 'to prevent unreliable information from reaching the public' (Marquis, 1978, 470–1). And to drive the point home, on 8 August General von Kessel (Chief Commander of the Berlin military district) reminded the press that 'the printing of news regarding military affairs is prohibited'. While this attitude might strike civilians as peculiarly ostrich-like, it was not exclusive to the German military, or confined to the First World War. The British military were similarly reluctant, especially in the war's early days, to release any news at all (a position repeated over the years by many other militaries at the onset of hostilities). In this instance, as others, the untenability of such a position – not least in the absence of anticipated lightning victories – slowly dawned, with civilian encouragement.

In Germany – as in Britain – the likelihood of national media actually possessing any potentially damaging military news in 1914 was slim indeed. Dire warnings against publication were thus largely symbolic. Until 1921, the only wire service in Germany was the 'semi-official' Wolff Telegraph Bureau (WTB), through which all official news was transmitted, any 'politically sensitive material' having already passed through Foreign Office clearance (Marquis, 1978, 472). Once Germany was at war, the German press was completely reliant on the censored-at-source WTB for front-line news. Should a newspaper manage to send one of its correspondents into the field, or otherwise acquire war news – such as soldiers' letters – these too were subject to censorship by the local military command (Marquis, 1978, 476). Moreover, although the purpose of censorship was ostensibly – as it invariably is – to prevent damaging information reaching the enemy, its remit in practice was much broader: governing the tone of news presentation and the expression of criticism, not simply excluding 'security'-sensitive material.

In addition to politically-motivated allocation of newsprint, the German government exercised news-management primarily through the *Kriegspresseamt* (War Press Office, formed on 7 September 1915), which both suppressed and released news. It disseminated its own publications aimed largely at troops (*Deutsche Kriegsnachrichten, Nachrichten der Auslandpresse* and *Deutsche Kriegswochenschau*), held regular press briefings, and twice or thrice weekly conferences at which editors were hectored and showered with a welter of 'recommendations'. In Marquis's account: 'The tenor of government dealings with the press generally was that of a long-suffering and kindly – but stern – parent dealing with a wilful, malicious, unruly – and potentially murderous child' (1978, 480). Newspapers were strictly warned, amidst a deluge of other repressive instructions, to desist from informing their readership of the censorship measures. But it is hard to imagine that the more astute reader could have remained ignorant of their existence, given the closure of seditious titles which refused to conform, and the uniformity of press content and presentation, with its avoidance of bad news and defensive presentation of Germany's war aims.

So why did repression fail? One might conclude – as many disquisitions on propaganda have subsequently done – that *any* system based primarily on suppression is destined to long-term demise. Whether that is so or not, the German First World War apparatus was afflicted by another serious, and worsening, condition: civil-military strife. The military assumed an increasingly prominent role in the whole news-management system. This was a serious impediment as the military men had 'little contact or experience in dealing with ordinary people, whilst those who had such experience – the publishers and the journalists – were systematically excluded from information policy-making' (Marquis, 1978, 489). Indeed, in Lasswell's opinion, the explanation for German maladroitness in propaganda lay in 'the influence which the military mind had upon it' (1927, 198).

Moreover, as matters worsened for Germany on the battlefield, the military tried to press home their advantage on the domestic propaganda front by establishing their own press service, the *Deutsche Kriegsnachrichtendienst*, under Chief of Staff General Ludendorff's personal direction. This move predictably angered politicians who, not unreasonably, feared that the growing battalion of uniformed press officers was inspiring political stories to serve its own agenda: refusal to sue for peace, and determination (in the face of civilian opposition) to achieve a complete German victory (Messinger, 1992, 18). Although the army had little notion of the state of German public opinion, Ludendorff believed it had become pessimistic and desperate, and ought consequently to receive a more direct drilling: thus the employment of writers, painters and caricaturists under the rubric of *Vaterländischer Unterricht* (patriotic instruction: Demm, 1993, 165). But as one German propagandist later pointed out, while his country's propaganda may always have been logical, it was 'not psychological' (Viereck, 1931, 114). Created behind a veil of ignorance regarding its likely public reception, German propaganda reflected a gulf between its initiators and its audience which, by 1917, was probably unbridgeable.

Germany's propaganda record seems thus to be one of progressive deterioration. According to many accounts, this downwards curve was reversed in Britain. Analogous stories are in fact told about the emergence of British propaganda organisations in both world wars: namely, that a British sense of 'fair play' made the very notion of propaganda distasteful except as a defensive countermeasure thrust upon reluctant Westminster by the enemy's tendentious activities. Where Germany had assembled a well-oiled machinery for media management in both 1914 and 1939, the hapless Britons belatedly mounted an amateurish mobilisation on the propaganda front. Having evolving successful machinery only at the eleventh hour, Parliament then hastily demobilised its propagandists immediately following the war's end, lapsing back into its customary state of peacetime squeamishness; or so the stories go.

It is true that Britain lacked a centralised propaganda agency at the outset of war in August 1914. It is equally true that a Department (subsequently Ministry) of Information was not founded until 1917, though most certainly not the case, as Beaverbrook (its first minister) asserted, that nothing had been done properly till his arrival (Messinger, 1992, 123). Not only was there a great deal of, admittedly de-centralised, activity prior to 1917 but there had also been a fair amount of thought devoted to future wartime censorship arrangements before 1914, as rivalry between Britain and Germany intensified (Towle, 1975, 103–16). Germany might have been a more militarised society than the UK but any shortfall in British militarisation was more than compensated for by an excess of official secrecy. The growing public appetite for news, served by what has been described as a 'system of newspapers that was unequalled in the world', was met by an increasing official reluctance to offer the press appropriate fodder (McEwen, 1982, 461). An Official Secrets Act in 1910 determined that the press would not be told anything deemed contrary to a – diffusely defined – public interest (T. Rose, 1995, 7). Already in 1904, a draft Bill had been placed before Parliament to 'provide for the control of the publication of Naval and Military Information in Cases of Emergency', and in 1911, representatives from the War Office and Admiralty, with five press delegates, formed a committee to determine what information could reasonably be withheld from the public at times of military emergency (T. Rose, 1995, 11). The question of state control over the press had therefore received some attention prior to 1914, confounding the assertion of chief censor, Edward Cook, that wartime press censorship was 'as unfamiliar as it was unwelcome' (1920, xiv).

When war began, this committee was superseded as the main basis of censorship or news-release machinery. The early months were marked by confusion and extreme military sensitivity, but not by an unfettered press. Remembering the Crimean War (in which it was believed that British correspondents had disclosed information useful to the Russians), the military hoped – like their German counterparts – to thwart the press's 'bias in favour of publicity' by simply suppressing war news (Cook, 1920, 18). Two immediate steps were taken with regard to censorship which had far-reaching consequences.

First, the government used powers reserved in the International Telegraph Convention to suspend telegraph and radio services throughout the empire. A telegraph service would continue but all incoming or outgoing traffic had to pass through a Press Bureau, whose existence was announced by Churchill (the First Lord of the Admiralty) on 7 August 1914, with the promise that it would ensure a 'steady stream of trustworthy information' (Haste, 1977, 30). Germany's own transatlantic cables were also severed, thus resulting in a British monopoly of the cable services. Second, under the Defence of the Realm Act (DORA), wide-ranging prohibitions were imposed against the collection or publication of information about the war, or any material which might, directly or indirectly, be useful to the enemy. False statements or utterances 'likely to cause disaffection to His Majesty' were also proscribed (Cook, 1920, 25). These sweeping powers somewhat undermine Cate Haste's argument that the slow evolution of the official Press Bureau and other home front propaganda agencies resulted from government confidence that a patriotic press could be left to its own devices (Haste, 1977, 21). DORA's terms, and the penalties attached to infringing them – with editors initially facing the prospect of Court Martial and a possible life sentence for severe infractions – suggest less than complete certainty (Cook, 1920, 27–8).

DORA's terms were as broad as they were vague. For example, they forbade the publication of information that might be useful to the enemy but omitted any definition how utility might be gauged. The most charitable explanation for this elasticity is that no one in Whitehall knew exactly what *would* aid the enemy in this new type of warfare, and consequently they preferred to err on the side of caution. Less generously, one might suggest that the very open-endedness of DORA's provisions (whether calculatedly so or not) pushed the press towards self-censorship for fear of transgressing a boundary whose precise location was unspecified. Tiptoeing through DORA's minefield was not an activity the press particularly enjoyed. Subjects such as German air raids on Britain were, understandably, particularly vexed. But while most editors could probably appreciate the sensitivity here (and agree to wait until after an official communiqué had been released, at which point air raids could be written up according to individual editors' taste), other suppressions – such as weather forecasts – were 'never understood' and 'much sarcasm was expended on us', the Press Bureau's chief censor later moaned (Cook, 1920, 142).

Many editors sought Press Bureau guidance on stories (acquired from sources other than the official wire service) which they feared might contain an infringement of the nebulous rules. This was 'voluntary' self-censorship in operation. And in this way, as Cook points out, the Bureau 'became a shield for the Press. It was no offence not to submit an article or an item of news to the Press Bureau, but to do so was a sure defence ... Submission thus relieved one of responsibility' (1920, 43). 'If in doubt, ask the censors', became the editors' unwritten rule at a time when the margin for doubt was extremely wide, and penalties for miscalculation potentially severe. But there was another reason besides editorial wariness why prosecutions of editors were fairly rare, with only 12 referrals to the Director of Public Prosecutions in 1915 (Haste, 1977, 31). Some editors did in fact infringe DORA and, to the chagrin of their scooped rivals, got away with it. This happened on occasions when the Director of Public Prosecutions judged that a prosecution would only compound the initial damage, by drawing greater public – or enemy – attention to the offending article. As Cook observed, the system engendered the 'anomaly that the more serious the indiscretion was, the more reason there might be for letting it go unpunished' (1920, 83–4; T. Rose, 1995, 19).

The Press Bureau also issued, but did not originate, news as this was largely a function of the military in wartime. However, as a frequent scapegoat for military reticence, it formed the butt of much press criticism. The Bureau – its employees were keen to maintain – was the mere conduit through which official news flowed. It took no responsibility as regards vouching for the accuracy of the military's 'steady stream', or sometimes slow trickle, of information; and given that the most experienced censor could only process around 110 incoming telegram messages in an eight-hour shift, 'slow trickle' was more likely (Cook, 1920, 53). However, much as Cook might deny that the Bureau's job was to colour news, undoubtedly the military attempted to slant information. Thus Brownrigg, the Naval censor, later recalled that Churchill at the Admiralty would 'hold on to a bit of bad news for a time on the chance of getting a bit of good news to publish as an offset', a technique evident in many subsequent wars (cited by Lasswell, 1927, 203). Moreover, the Bureau itself offered (admittedly non-binding) advice on the presentation of news, sometimes damping down press over-optimism, 'in order to prepare the British public for a prolonged war' (Hopkin, 1970, 155).

Although the British state's approach to the release of news was more open than Germany's, information was nevertheless heavily circumscribed, leading the press baron Lord Northcliffe to complain that newspapers were being made 'part and parcel of a foolish conspiracy to hide bad news', when in fact 'English people do not mind bad news' (cited by Messinger, 1992, 151). One source of particular contemporary criticism lay in the utter secrecy initially surrounding events at the front, and the refusal of the War Office, once Kitchener became Secretary of State, to accredit any press correspondents. Some British reporters made their way to France regardless, but they were liable to arrest and expulsion. Lord Burnham reputedly stated that 'the men who at first went abroad for the Press were treated as if they were criminals let loose; war correspondents were locked up in stalls by a corporal's guard' (cited by Cook, 1920, 178). From August 1914 to May 1915, correspondents and photographers were officially excluded from the war zone. Journalistic infiltrators were treated as 'alien enemies', in the words of Lord Derby, former Chief Censor during the Boer War, and an advocate of greater lenience towards the press (cited by Farrar, 1998, 67). Indeed, criticism mounted – in Parliament as in the press itself – of a policy of such secrecy that British newspapers were forbidden from reporting the despatch of a British Expeditionary Force to France, even though an event of this scale could scarcely be kept hidden. But in return for having loyally remained mute – and having proved that they could be 'potent war auxiliaries' – editors increasingly demanded greater co-operation from the military. After all, British correspondents who made their way to allied French or Belgian units received co-operation in sending back copy: an anomaly which not only mocked the War Office's parsimonious attitude to news, but also raised the danger that British civilians would under-estimate the role their own troops were playing, and ignore the need for further civilian exertions and the calls for more military recruits (Farrar, 1998, 37–8).

Gradually, Kitchener relented. His first grudging concession, however, was not an unadulterated success. In September 1914, he appointed a uniformed 'Eye Witness' to report on the war. Until July 1915, Lieutenant Colonel Sir Ernest Swinton was attached to the Commander-in-Chief's staff and his reports (already censored by General Headquarters) were then submitted to Kitchener for approval. Not surprisingly, as an officer, he was quite clear that his primary responsibility was to 'avoid helping the enemy' rather than 'the purveyance of news to our own people'. Accordingly he would only 'tell as much of the truth as was compatible with safety', his function in reporting from the Front being both 'to guard against depression and pessimism, and to check unjustified optimism which might lead to a relaxation of effort' (Swinton cited by Haste, 1977, 32; Farrar, 1998, 24). In Haste's view 'not much truth got through those barriers', which was presumably exactly as Kitchener intended, given his legendary 'contempt for the "public" in all its moods and manifestations', not to say for journalists as 'drunken swabs' (Asquith cited by Haste, 1977, 33). Small wonder then that one editor proposed, on the basis of Swinton's mollifying reports, that ' "Eyewash" would have been a better pseudonym' (Knightley, 1989, 86).

Eye Witness entered an early retirement, and a further concession on the War Office's part in the spring of 1915 saw four renowned British correspondents being accommodated by the military at the Front. This tour soon evolved into a wider scheme of official accreditation of journalists, incorporating American reporters. Indeed, the need to persuade America to abandon its neutrality constituted a compelling argument for greater press freedom, not least when former US President Theodore Roosevelt (now an active champion of US intervention) himself insisted that there was a 'very striking contrast between the lavish attention showered on war correspondents by the German military authorities and the point-blank refusal to have anything to do with them by the British and French governments' (cited by Knightley, 1989, 95). His criticism chimed with one made by British newspapers: namely, that Britain lagged behind the enemy in the propaganda war. 'By brilliant war correspondents and constantly changing kinematograph films and photographs', editorialised the *Daily Mail* in April 1915, 'every man, woman, and child [in Germany] knows what the war means and how the nation is fighting' (cited by Farrar, 1998, 66). Britain consequently suffered in comparison with not only its more open allies but also its better organised, and more persuasive, enemy; or so critics claimed.

The system of accreditation which emerged forged a mutually beneficial relationship between press and military, although it hardly amounted to a policy of great openness. Permitted to report from the front, newspapers revealed the extent to which, as editors had long insisted, they construed their wartime role as patriotic chroniclers of 'the splendid deeds of our heroes' (as the *Daily Mail* put it). What the military thereby discovered, suggested H.C. Peterson in 1939, was that 'the news writers could be pacified and at the same time be made to serve as propagandists. By stationing the reporters at the various army headquarters, and by making them personal friends, they became apologists for the British cause' (1939, 26).

The reporters were, after all, given the notional status as officers – resplendent in the appropriate uniforms – and billeted in luxurious accommodation. No wonder, then, that Philip Taylor refers to these privileged war correspondents as 'chateaux warriors', prototypes for the Gulf War's 'hotel warriors', comfortably encamped in Dhahran and entrusted with embargoed military secrets (1997, 104). The parallels are striking: journalists in France (as in Saudi Arabia) had to be escorted everywhere by military minders who not only 'lived with them, ate with them, read their dispatches' but had also been 'discreetly instructed to waste the correspondents' time as much as possible' (Knightley, 1989, 96; Farrar, 1998, 73). The British military learnt – though it quickly forgot – that those hitherto viewed as latent enemies could be transformed into docile friends (accomplices, even) through a process of 'domestication'. The 'writing chappies' were accordingly rendered as harmless as the military's belittling moniker implied, from free will as much as formal curbs. 'There was no need of censorship of our dispatches', wrote Sir Philip Gibbs, one such 'chappy', in 1933, 'We were our own censors' (cited by Knightley, 1989, 97). The reporters, after all, were well aware of their debt to the Army in whose regalia they were uniformed, and shared an identity of interest which left the formal mechanisms of control almost redundant.

The discovery, since re-learnt many times, of journalists' 'co-optability' marked one military 'victory' of the First World War. Indeed, British propaganda organisations successfully managed to enlist all sorts of willing proselytisers, not least key figures in the Edwardian literary establishment, including H.G. Wells, John Buchan, Rudyard Kipling, J.M. Barrie, John Galsworthy and G.K. Chesterton, who enthusiastically evangelised, 'unofficially' or as paid appointees of the state (Buitenhuis, 1989; Messinger, 1992). But perhaps the most indispensable recruits were the great press barons of the day, who themselves were elevated to the very highest positions within propaganda organisations: a stark contrast with the military-dominated German arrangements. Thus Lord Beaverbrook (the Canadian-born owner of the *Daily Express*) was appointed Minister of Propaganda in 1918, when the complex web of home and overseas propaganda agencies was fused into a new Ministry. Under its auspices, the work of addressing the enemy – hitherto undertaken by covert operatives domiciled at Crewe House – became the province of Lord Northcliffe (owner of *The Times* and the *Daily Mail*), whose brother, Lord Rothermere, directed propaganda to neutral countries (Messinger, 1992). As Lasswell approvingly remarked, such individuals were used to telling their tales in 'terse, vivid style' and were not hampered by 'needless scrupulosity' (1927, 32). They were adept at putting a patriotic spin on good news, even though some of these same individuals had earlier criticised the government's suppression of depressing events. For those at the political helm, recruiting the most powerful press magnates was therefore an astute manoeuvre to contain such criticism, and gain the pressmen's expertise, though the 'incestuous union' of Fleet Street and Downing Street was a matter of controversy among politicians who feared that Beaverbrook *et al*. might offer assistance to particular political parties in peacetime (Marquis, 1978, 467).

Besides its ability to secure the services of prominent opinion-formers from within and beyond the press, the British system of propaganda held a number of other benefits, some of which were duplicated in the Second World War. Overall, the news-management system was less detectable than its German counterpart. Thus the censorship of cables at source, also enacted in Germany, was probably less noticeable to the British newspaper reading public because it was not combined with such didactic prescriptiveness concerning how released material ought to be written up. The Bureau was not, however, averse to issuing reams of helpful hints, and editors also had to abide by Defence (or D-) notices, outlining items of sensitive information that could not be published (T. Rose, 1995, 22).

Additionally the system of 'voluntary' censorship had the advantage, for the state, of what in Intelligence parlance is known as 'plausible deniability'. In other words, the government could boast a remarkably free press, as the decision to refer material to the Bureau lay with editors (overlooking, that is, the long shadow which DORA cast over them). Thus Cook was able to claim that 'the most remarkable feature of our newspapers during that time was that they bore no palpable trace of having been censored at all. An outside observer, if he chanced to miss the occasional tirades against the Press Bureau, might reasonably have concluded that there was no censorship in force' (1920, 164). 'Facts' might be rationed but views were presented with a 'highly spiced vocabulary'. This arrangement – replicated in the Second World War – preserved the appearance of plurality while masking the extent to which the British public remained 'fog bound' concerning many aspects of the war. Under this system, journals expressing pacifist sentiments continued to appear throughout, only courting judicial danger if they buttressed their moral arguments with 'facts' concerning the war which contravened DORA's regulations (Hopkin, 1970, 159–63).

Film and the First World War

Censorship and news management had existed prior to the First World War in various forms. But the use of moving images for propaganda purposes was more novel, and perhaps the First World War's most significant propaganda innovation. By 1918, all the major belligerents had not only committed scarce resources to film production but also 'recognised the apparent potential of the medium of cinema for powerful, mass, political propaganda' (Reeves, 1993, 181). Some combatant states did so more tentatively than others, most notably the tottering Tsarist regime in Russia, which showed little inclination to explain the war to the public through any medium, let alone through film. As a result, patriotic film-making in Russia remained largely in private hands (Kenez, 1995, 36–42).

Russia may have been an extreme – certainly unique – case, but other belligerents also harboured ambivalent feelings about this new medium. In Germany, conflicts between government and military over the value of film propaganda, and who should control it, resulted in severe organisational delay. Only in January 1917 did the military establish the *Bild- und Filmamt* (BUFA) to produce and distribute such material (Curry, 1995, 140). Making up for lost time, in July 1917, Ludendorff integrated commercial film-makers – eager to lend a patriotic hand – more directly into official propaganda through the creation of UFA (*Universum Film Aktiengesellschaft*). And in recognition of film's central role in the maintenance of civilian morale, through entertainment as much as exhortation, the state conceded cinemas priority in receiving electricity and coal as rationing worsened in 1917 (Curry, 1995, 142).

In the area of film propaganda, German officials believed their own efforts, where they existed at all, inferior to those of the Entente powers, whose instructional films and patriotic dramas were consequently to be imitated (Röther, 1996, 185–91). But it had taken considerable time for the potential of film to be realised by propaganda personnel in London, despite the cinema's popularity: some 20 million visits were recorded in 1914 (Messinger, 1992, 42). And Fleet Street was wont to believe that Britain should be copying Germany in this regard, as in its access permitted war reporters. Many of those vested with prosecuting the military and propaganda wars were ignorant of the new medium, and this ignorance was often compounded with snobbish disdain. Cinema-going was, broadly speaking, a class-specific recreation, and along with music halls and pubs, the picture palace was a preserve of the working class. 'Vulgar and without serious importance' was how Lucy Masterman (wife of the head of Wellington House, Britain's proto-propaganda ministry) characterised her peers' attitude towards cinema (cited by Reeves, 1993, 188; see also Haste, 1977, 45). This aristocratic hauteur doubtless concealed a good deal of fear as well, concerning the visual image's emotive power. Still photographic images were likewise the subject of considerable anxiety: hence Kitchener's banishment of photographers from the front until 1915. Indeed, images of war – moving or still – have often formed the sorest point in state-media relations in wars throughout the twentieth century, and the First World War highlights many of the reasons for the state's ambivalence towards visual media.

Any medium capable of winning millions of devotees – intelligible to all irrespective of literacy, and evoking emotional responses – was (and is) bound to attract state attention, in total or more limited war. Film offered itself as a more authentic and memorable mode of witnessing war, as the press baron, Lord Northcliffe, somewhat reluctantly avowed: 'Not everyone reads the newspapers, and those who do forget what they have read, but no one can forget what he has seen happen on the screen' (cited by Haste, 1977, 45). Charles Masterman at Wellington House consequently determined to hitch the power of the silver screen to the *entente* cause, even in the face of considerable military opposition. So although the first official British film, *Britain Prepared*, did not appear until 1915, it was subsequently screened in 'practically every country which possesses cinematograph facilities', Wellington House boasted, and was followed in the next six months by 27 short films (cited by Reeves, 1986, 15).

The following year, probably the best known (certainly the most widely discussed) film of the First World War, *Battle of the Somme*, was released, to widespread acclaim from British audiences unaccustomed to seeing realistic representations of war on film. In fact, some of the most famous sequences of that film were reconstructed: most notably one in which a soldier is depicted going 'over the top' and appears to collapse back dead in the trench, under the camera's watchful gaze (Smither, 1993, 149–68). The *post hoc* staging of certain scenes alerts us to insurmountable obstacles for film-makers and photographers in shooting war as it actually occurs. Real battle may be too dangerous for cameramen to capture, its action (and inaction) spanning vast, stunted landscapes, with its most 'dramatic' moments frequently unobservable. Thus 'only deliberate deception...could restore the whole truth to the films' (Badsey, 1983, 106). Fakery was necessary to make war footage compelling and to convey a sense of emotional, if not literal, realism, a conclusion also reached by still photographers (Hüppauf, 1995, 102). At the time, contemporary audiences seem to have accepted at face value the visual evidence's verisimilitude. (After all, 'faking' was also used to make trench-warfare conform to pre-existing notions of what battle looked like.) But perhaps more tellingly, viewers were not unanimously in favour of being shown so much of what they assumed was the reality of war. Thus, for example, *The Star* reported after *Battle of the Somme*'s theatrical release in London: 'There is no doubt that the Somme pictures have stirred London more passionately than anything has since the war. Everybody is talking about them. Everybody is discussing them. Everybody is discussing whether they are too painful for public exhibition' (cited by Reeves, 1997, 17). Private individuals' scruples about the film's 'realism' sprang from different sources. Some felt that images of the dead and wounded – which, unprecedentedly, *Battle of the Somme* showed – trespassed on private grief. Some believed that it was simply wrong to turn soldiers' suffering into 'a spectacle for the pleasure of those who like to gloat, in perfect safety themselves, over the agonies of others' (letter to the *Manchester Guardian*, 15 August 1916, cited by Reeves, 1997, 17). But others welcomed the film for making tangible what had previously, on the cold and none-too-revealing page, seemed unreal.

And there lay the propagandists' dilemma. Still and moving photography lends itself to interpretation in different – sometimes utterly incompatible – ways. By some viewers, images of war are read in a straight-forwardly anti-war fashion, as necessary testimony to war's inhumanity. But others will regard war footage as evidence of the enemy's barbarity and affirmation of the necessity of fighting the good fight: 'Praise God, from whom all blessing [sic] flow, A few more Germans gone below', chorused one viewer, after watching *Battle of the Somme* (cited by Reeves, 1997, 19). The impact of film on the audience is consequently immensely hard to predict, and even some who themselves regard 'graphic' imagery as galvanising may fear that less patriotic and more squeamish individuals will be adversely affected by exposure to it. Consequently film, despite – and conversely because of – its recognised potency and reach, is also the most double-edged of propaganda weapons.

In the case of *Battle of the Somme*, patchy data on audience responses suggests that the film did largely fulfil its intended aim of increasing identification between the home and fighting fronts: 'showing', as Lloyd George extolled, what 'our men at the Front are doing and suffering for us, and how their achievements have been made possible by the sacrifices made at home' (cited by Badsey, 1983, 99). But, as Nicholas Reeves points out, that the film did not have an unintended boomerang effect – depressing morale – was largely due to the backdrop against which it was projected: one of reasonable public contentment. A few months later this would change. As civilians wearied of enforced conscription, price rises and the uneven burden of rationing, a wave of strikes swept Britain from the spring of 1917 through to early 1918 (Reeves, 1993, 185). It does not seem coincidental, then, that later official British

propaganda films – playing to a more war-weary and restive audience – avoided repetition of the starker sequences of *Battle of the
Somme* (Reeves, 1997, 21). Beaverbrook, then Chairman of the War
Office Cinematograph Office, noted in November 1916 that a
'jaded' public needed something 'a little more dramatic' to 'tickle
its palate' (Reeves, 1993, 194).

It is impossible to quantify film's impact on its audience. How to
disentangle the influence of film from off-screen determinants of
morale, and individual beliefs and predispositions which bear on
viewers' appreciation of what unspools before them? But though
precise calibrations of cinematic effects may be impossible, film was
certainly *believed* important at the time, as evidenced by its ubiquity
in propaganda arsenals on all sides. Here too, although British
filmic efforts have perhaps attracted the most (and most favourable)
scholarly attention, some assert that Germany's newsreel propaganda was in fact superior to that of Britain (Messinger, 1992,
251). This was not the verdict of the German film industry itself,
whose journal *Kinematograph* wrote, damningly, after the war that
German newsreels had been 'not only a burden on the film programme...[but] also an annoyance...often pieced together from
old material rather than portraying the war' (cited by Mühl-
Benninghaus, 1996, 184). But aided as it was by the state, the German film industry overall 'won from the social and economic conditions that war had created' (Curry, 1995, 144).

Hollywood, however, was undoubtedly the greatest Great War
profiteer. Even before the war, Hollywood was poised for victory
over the world movie market, with a weekly domestic audience of 80
million. But war certainly helped open overseas markets and establish the movie industry as a patriotic institution, with a broadened
appeal to more middle-class audiences attracted to the auditoriums
by newsreels and more 'high-minded' wartime fare. In many
respects, Hollywood, in the nineteen months of America's formal
involvement in the war, rehearsed the role which it would play with
yet more aplomb in the Second World War. Hooking up with the
government Committee on Public Information (or Creel Committee, after its chairman), Hollywood's own Committee of the Motion
Picture Industry (chaired by D.W. Griffith, celebrated director of
one of cinema's earliest classics, *Birth of a Nation* (1915)) urged the
studios to manufacture such enthusiastically anti-German fare as
The Hun Within (1918), *The Kaiser, Beast of Berlin* (1918) and *The*

Claws of the Hun (1918). With cinema lobbies doubling as bazaars for war bonds, the stars of the silver screen helped simultaneously sell *and* finance the war effort, while also raising Hollywood's own stock. By personal example, on- and off-screen, film stars encouraged Americans to emulate them in new roles, as soldiers, nurses, production-line workers or simply as committed supporters of the war (DeBauche, 1997). And though Hollywood later defended itself from charges of interventionism prior to the Second World War with the cherished nostrum that propaganda was inimical to entertainment – 'propaganda disguised as entertainment would be neither honest salesmanship nor honest showmanship' – one did not have to delve very far into movie industry history to uncover persuasive evidence that Hollywood had not been as abstemious in this respect as the Hays Report insisted (cited by Shindler, 1979, 5).

State and Media in the Second World War

Rationales for State Control

It is impossible to assess the Third Reich's use of media in the Second World War without considering the Nazi regime's extension of state power over all aspects of the public and private spheres after assuming power in 1933. Central to the very functioning of the Nazi state, control over the media stretched far beyond those purposes which wartime measures generally further. Hitler assumed power convinced that propaganda was largely responsible for his National Socialist party's success. His views on the potency of mass persuasion, set out at length in *Mein Kampf*, derived in no small measure from an insistence that *British* propaganda had similarly been largely responsible for Germany's defeat in the First World War, which was effected not on the battlefield but on the home front: a *'Dolchstoß Legende'* (stab-in-the-back myth) widely shared by many embittered Germans in the 1920s and 1930s (1992, 161–9).

Given Hitler's enthusiasm for propaganda, it is scarcely surprising that control over mass media was crucial in the 'Nazification' of German political, social and cultural life, a process known as *Gleichschaltung*. Although it took some contemporary non-German observers a good while (too long) to realise it, the Nazi regime was not akin to democratic governments of the day, for Hitler assumed power intent on effecting what his Propaganda Minister, Josef Goebbels, termed a 'spiritual mobilisation in Germany'. The Third Reich had no place for waverers: to be a 'good German' was to be a devout Nazi. This uniformity of belief would be achieved by compulsion and terror if necessary but preferably, in the regime's eyes, because the Aryan *Volk* would see how perfectly 'State' and 'Party' represented their interests: an organic unity Rudolph Hess captured in his slogan 'The Party is Hitler, but Hitler is Germany, just as Germany is Hitler!'. 'It is not enough to reconcile people more or less to our regime, to move them towards a position of neutrality towards us', Goebbels further elaborated before press representatives on 15 March 1933, 'we want rather to work on people until they are addicted to us' (cited by Welch, 1983a, 5).

In the Third Reich, power over media was intrinsic to the 'total state'. The press, Goebbels informed journalists, was to 'instruct' not merely 'inform'; to amplify state ideology and explain policy, as bridge between government and people, and not to criticise with lofty detachment (Taylor, 1983a, 34–7). Media were required to legitimise and mobilise popular enthusiasm (far beyond mere 'consensus') for the various planks of Nazi policy at home and abroad: anti-Semitism, anti-Bolshevism, social eugenics, and Germany's pursuit of *Lebensraum* (living space) in the East at the expense of 'racially degenerate' Slav *Untermenschen*. None of these themes disappeared in wartime but they were augmented by heightened expectations of the media, most particularly to inspire enthusiasm for a new war which, remembering the suffering of 1914–18, many Germans did not relish (Kershaw, 1987, 122–3).

The objectives allotted to propaganda were too all-encompassing to be left to mass media alone, however. The Nazis aimed to colonise the imaginative life of Germans, to eliminate private mental space for critical reflection or dissent: as Goebbels put it, 'winning people over to an idea so sincerely, so vitally, that in the end they succumb to it utterly and can never again escape from it' (cited by Welch, 1983, 216). 'All that matters is propaganda', Hitler once remarked, and consequently it imbued all aspects of life in the Third Reich. Nazi visual symbolism was insistent and pervasive: flags, banners and uniforms bearing the swastika insignia; parades and rallies choreographed to impress onlookers and participants with the formidable unity of the mass, in much the same way as architecture, under the direction of Albert Speer, was designed to awe the individual with the transcendent power of the Reich (Hoffmann, 1995; Thies, 1983, 45–64). Corresponding with Hitler's views on propaganda, great reliance in effecting the 'spiritual mobilisation' was placed on appeals to the emotions and senses of Germans, not to their capacity for rational argument. (For one who professed himself 'of the people', Hitler showed considerable disdain for the intelligence of the mass, which he thought could never be over-estimated.) Impressed by theorists of crowd behaviour, such as Gustav le Bon, Hitler similarly believed that the mass was much more manipulable than the isolated individual, who descended 'several rungs on the ladder of civilization' as part of a crowd (le Bon, cited by Hoffmann, 1996, 83). Such notions also help explain why great importance was attached to film, viewed (as films invari-ably were) in a darkened and thronged auditorium. Where better to observe le Bon's dictum that 'the improbable does not exist for a crowd' (cited by Baird, 1974, 12)?

The transformative ambition which impelled the Nazis' seizure of power over German media was, needless to say, not replicated in Britain, where official propaganda served more modest, war-related aims. Where Hitler had undertaken propaganda on behalf of the National Socialist movement since the 1920s, the British govern-ment began thinking – in a rather leisurely fashion – about a possible wartime propaganda agency only in July 1935, two years after Goebbels had assumed stewardship of his Ministry for Popular Enlightenment and Propaganda (RMVP). Thus what emerged in 1939 as Britain's Ministry of Information (or MOI, the very title reflecting squeamishness about the business of propaganda, quite unlike the Nazi RMVP which was proud to proclaim its function openly) owed its immediate genesis to a government decision in July 1935 to establish a Sub-Committee of the Committee of Imper-ial Defence, charged with examining the question of censorship in wartime (Balfour, 1979, 53). With no great urgency, the committee produced a report twelve months later, after only three meetings. It advocated a centralised propaganda ministry with five broad func-tions: the release of official news; security censorship of the press, films and the BBC; maintenance of morale; the conduct of publicity campaigns for other government departments; and the dissemina-tion of propaganda to enemy, neutral, allied and empire countries (McLaine, 1979, 3). The decision to establish a single Ministry seems to have been a foregone conclusion, based on the presumed

– but not carefully documented – success of the First World War's Ministry of Information. Moreover, as Balfour points out: 'there was a widespread view that, if we were going to fight the Germans again, we ought to have exactly the same weapons as they did – though there was not an equal recognition, particularly in the Services, as to what exactly those weapons were'. Ironically, then, 'the British imagined they were copying from the Germans something which the Germans imagined they had copied from the British' (1979, 54). As during the First World War, both Britain and Germany characterised their opponent as possessing superior propaganda skill and organisation.

Repetition of past precedent (though without any clear institutional memory) was not the only questionable premise on which British propaganda planning proceeded. The planners also assumed that war – in the unlikely event of its occurrence – would be short but intense, with victory belonging to the side which delivered the most decisive aerial knockout blow. In such a confrontation, it was imperative for the state to maintain civilian morale, for it was widely feared that this new style of aerial warfare would quickly shatter British nerves (McLaine, 1979, 26). Maintaining morale was at a premium, but no one quite knew what it was nor how to sustain it, although many planners assumed that working-class Britons did not possess 'high morale' in natural abundance. Much pre-war planning was shrouded in unreality: desperate anxiety to avoid war, coupled with fundamental misapprehension as to the shape future conflict would assume. And although it was recognised that high morale would partly hinge on careful rationing of news, plans for the putative Ministry's relations with the BBC and newsreel companies – early recognised as being of 'no little importance' – were still extremely fluid as the 'Phoney War' began, and British officials awaited the drone of German bombers overhead.

Mechanisms of Control

That German media occupied central ideological ground in the 'spiritual' re-orientation of the nation was evident from the sheer volume of machinery dedicated to controlling the personnel, content and increasingly the very ownership of newspapers, film studios and radio networks in the Third Reich. Responsible for 'the spiritual direction of the nation', Goebbels headed three distinct organisations. He is primarily remembered as head of the Reich Propaganda Ministry (an organisation largely staffed by fanatical Nazi graduates and PhDs which grew from some 350 to over 1900 in 1941). But he was simultaneously President of the Reich Chamber of Culture (*Reichskulturkammer*, or RKK) and Director of the Central Propaganda Office of the Party; Nazi rule resting on duplication of Party and state functions to ensure that no area of life fell beyond the purview of the state, and that state, Party and nation became thoroughly synonymous.

To ensure that press, radio and film fulfilled their designated task of popular 'enlightenment', all branches were subjected to the rigours of *Gleichschaltung*, or 'co-ordinating the political will of the nation with the aims of the state' (Taylor in Welch, 1983, 36). Applied to the media, this entailed the compulsory oversight of its various subsidiaries by the RKK. Seven distinct branches of the Chamber presided over all spheres of media, culture and the arts. The Chambers, headed by a Party/state functionary, acted as 'guilds' for their specialist field of endeavour, regulating conditions of employment and the personnel employed therein. To operate as a print journalist in Nazi Germany one therefore had to belong to the Reich Press Chamber, but as the gate-keeper of this organisation was a fervent Nazi, potential members with racial or political 'impurities' were screened out. Through this purgative mechanism, the Nazi state immediately removed potential dissidents, without making Party membership itself a *sine qua non* of professional activity. David Welch suggests that the RKK's activities allowed the regime largely to dispense with formal censorship since the remaining personnel needed little coercion (1993, 27). But the media were not in fact free from further scrutiny, despite their likely docility. The very ownership of production was increasingly taken into state hands, and each branch of the media found itself with particular responsibilities both in the Nazification of German life, and latterly in the war effort.

Radio was ripe for *Gleichschaltung*, the German network having been state-owned since 1925. But whereas the Weimar government had exercised relatively little say over programme content, Goebbels had an altogether different vision of the radio, which he lauded as 'the most modern instrument in existence for influencing the masses', though not his personal favourite (Welch, 1993, 30). By a decree of June 1933, the network's nine former regional stations were brought under the control of the RMVP. The next step was to bring this 'magnetic' medium closer to the people, and to boost listenership the state set about producing cheap radio sets: the 'people's receiver' (the radio equivalent of the *Volkswagen*, or 'people's car'). These sets were heavily subsidised so workers could afford what was still a relatively new innovation, and were manufactured to pick up frequencies only from a limited range; no design fault but an intentional impediment to the reception of foreign broadcasts (Welch, 1993, 32–3). Consequently the 70 per cent of German homes which owned a set by the outbreak of war – the highest percentage anywhere in the world – were almost obliged to listen to home-grown fare, whether they liked it or not (and Goebbels found plenty of evidence, as the war progressed, to sug-gest that they did not). For those 30 per cent without, and even for some of the radio-owning majority, the state also encouraged 'community listening', complete with local party functionary – the *Gau* radio warden – to monitor audience reaction.

The German press posed a rather more complex problem for state control, not least as Germany in the 1930s probably had more newspapers per capita than any other state. Mirroring the federal nature of German institutions, the press was largely decentralised, unlike in Britain where – regional and local papers notwithstanding – London's Fleet Street had emerged as the pre-eminent producer of newspapers read throughout the UK (Hale, 1964, 2). The frag-mented nature of Germany's press therefore rendered it in some respects a less easy target for *Gleichschaltung* than either the radio or film industry (though its very fragmentation meant that there could be little collective resistance to Nazification). Gradually, the National Socialist party in power set about acquiring ownership of German newspapers through its own publishing house, *Eher Verlag*, headed by Max Amann, an important party functionary and pres-ident of the Reich Press Chamber.

Amann's underlings screened out unsuitable personnel, while undesirable press content was increasingly filtered out by the state, thanks to the work of the state-controlled press agency, the *Deutsches Nachrichtenburo*, which issued daily press briefings and directives. From October 1933 onwards, German editors were com-pelled to excise anything 'calculated to weaken the strength of the Reich abroad or at home' (Welch, 1993, 37). Editors who disobeyed were likely to find their newspapers shut down or bought out by the

Party. Indeed, by the outbreak of war, *Eher Verlag* controlled – directly or indirectly – two-thirds of the German press, whereas in 1933 the Party owned only 59 papers (with a fairly paltry circulation of 782 121) in a country with 4700 titles (Welch, 1993, 38). But it was the war which really enabled the state to consolidate its hold over the press. Wartime privations meant that press circulation would have fallen irrespective of state policy, as paper, print and personnel shortages bit (Hale, 1964, 275). However, the Nazi regime exploited these practical difficulties for political purposes, rationing the wherewithal of the print media in such a way as to reward Nazi papers at the expense of the last remnants of an independent press. As more and more newspapers were shut down (most casualties being non-Nazi titles, including the prestigious *Frankfürter Zeitung*), Amann could at last proclaim in 1943, 'The Party Commands the Press' (cited by Hale, 1964, 289). But by February 1945 newspapers scarcely existed, reduced to little more than a handbill on which was printed the daily military communiqué and desperate appeals of the party elite.

As for newsreels and documentaries, these too were subjected to rigorous state intervention. The function of both was more to inspire 'mass intoxication' than to inform, or, when shown abroad, to intimidate audiences with the invincible might of Germany's armed forces (Sakmyster, 1996, 485–514). Notionally independent until wartime, Germany's four newsreel companies were merged into one directly state-owned and run newsreel, the *Deutsche Wochenschauen*, filmed by special military film units (*Propaganda Kompanien*, or PK). German newsreel cameramen, unlike their British or American counterparts, were trained soldiers who, armed with cameras, were expected to throw themselves whole-heartedly into battle, an innovation which the propaganda minister boastfully extolled (Welch, 1983, 206). Certainly, the German news-reels – with exhilarating, close-up footage (carefully edited to elim-inate bloodshed and death) and commentaries supervised by Goebbels himself – seem to have been popular with the Third Reich's cinema-goers in the early months of the war (Welch, 1983, 208–12). But of course this initial popularity was bought at some cost: partly met by the expendable PK cameramen, since a higher premium was placed on dramatic footage than on their lives – over 1000 PK men were killed or missing in action by October 1943 (Hoffmann, 1996, 95). The regime ultimately suffered too, however, as public rapture with the newsreels curdled into bitter disillusion in the war's latter stages, after the *Blitzkrieg* victories of 1939–40 gave way to frozen stalemate (and a never wholly acknowledged defeat) at Stalingrad, losses in North Africa, and then in Europe itself. And crucially, as the defeats mounted, the Führer himself – a once popular newsreel subject – went 'missing in action' from the screen and public sphere alike, making only three addresses in the final ten months of war (Balfour, 1979, 123; Rentschler, 1996, 172).

It is clear, then, that although war heightened the Nazi state's ability to achieve compulsion over German media, much had already been done to eliminate press freedom well before 1939. In this respect, putative British propagandists were not wrong to regard themselves as under-prepared when they found themselves at war with Germany for, despite some pre-planning, the MOI remained in a state of disarray in September 1939. Chamberlain, hoping as he did that Hitler could be appeased, had not accorded a wartime propaganda ministry high priority, and no one in government appeared entirely sure how to recruit experts in the nebulous sphere of propaganda. As McLaine points out, 'experience in, say, psychology and journalism seems almost to have been a positive disqualification for employment' (1979, 6).

The new Ministry consequently underwent a bewildering series of organisational and personnel shake-ups, which left one of its Ministers wondering what Goebbels would have made of the mess, could he have 'believed a tenth of what was happening here' (Reith cited by Balfour, 1979, 109). Of course, Goebbels might well have had every sympathy for an organisation beset with intra-Departmental and civil–military strife, had it not belonged to the enemy. Ignorant of the fissures within what appeared to be a monolithic German propaganda apparatus, detractors ridiculed the MOI as a 'behemoth, greatly overstaffed and swallowing great quantities of taxpayers' money to little apparent effect'. This 'monster' – described by one of its Ministers as 'so large, so amorphous that a single man could not cope with it' – devoured three different incumbents before July 1941, and most historians agree that it was not until the appointment of Brendan Bracken as Minister of Information in July 1941 that the Ministry found its feet (Duff Cooper, cited by Chapman, 1998, 14). Meanwhile in the first eighteen months of war, the Ministry lost, but then regained, responsibility for news and censorship.

British newspapers vigorously berated the MOI for its early, heavy-handed suppressions, though not all were directly the Ministry's fault. For example, in an echo of 1914, the Services' reflexive secrecy was such that a total news blackout was imposed on the dispatch of the British Expeditionary Force to France in 1939, only lifted after it had actually arrived, but reimposed once the newspapers had gone to press. This resulted, as Philip Taylor puts it, in 'a farce which saw Fleet Street offices occupied by Scotland Yard and the offending newspapers seized from startled early morning commuters before the ban was lifted again shortly afterwards' (1995, 212). Meanwhile, on the outbreak of war, the BBC cranked out hours of organ music, an unedifying diet which listeners could not escape by seeking refuge in the cinemas. These had all been closed down for the duration, in anticipation of a short aerial war during which urban-dwellers' safety would be jeopardised by their herding together in close proximity to flammable film stock: a decision soon reversed as the war confounded all expectations (Aldgate and Richards, 1995, 1).

The most critical relationship which the MOI had to forge was arguably that with the BBC, for although the British press had one of the highest readerships of any country, it was radio, not newspapers, which assumed greatest prominence as purveyor of wartime news. By 1944, the BBC's nine o'clock evening news bulletin was estimated to reach 43–50 per cent of the entire British population (Briggs, 1995, 43). The BBC itself estimated its audience at 34 million but, given the scale of licence evasion, others have estimated that 40 million (in a population of 48 million) might be more accurate (Nicholas, 1996, 12). Britons first heard war news breaking from the radio, and stories broadcast at night would then be re-read in different forms in daily papers the following morning (Pronay, 1982, 178). Pluralism was thus maintained: the factual consistency of press and BBC stories acted as mutual confirmation of their veracity, while diversity in presentational styles suggested considerable press freedom. Significantly, and unprecedently, the BBC's evening bulletin actually scooped the print media. Prior to 1939, the BBC had been forbidden to make news broadcasts before 6 p.m. This arrangement, designed to protect the position of the print media, was jettisoned in wartime for good (Nicholas, 1996, 13; 220–1).

The BBC's central role in wartime had been foreseen, and encouraged, by pre-war planners, who included the BBC's founding father, Sir John Reith (later, briefly, Minister of Information). Indeed, Nicholas Pronay argues that the BBC originated the concepts, central to the MOI's ethos, of 'propaganda with truth' and 'news as the shocktroops of propaganda'. Reith fully recognised that in total war, total truthfulness could only be an aspiration (Pronay, in Pronay and Spring, 1982, 182; Nicholas, 1996, 18). But the BBC was nevertheless insistent that purposeful lying was poor strategy: the Corporation's 1941 handbook insisted that 'no permanent propaganda policy can in the modern world be based on untruthfulness' (cited by Briggs, 1995, 10).

Close to the point of symbiosis, the MOI's relationship with the BBC was not always harmonious. A residual tension underlay the BBC's attitude towards government, from which it was quasi-autonomous, although it was financially dependent on a state-collected licence fee, and editorially bound by a state-formulated Charter. Not without reason, the BBC feared that politicians would seek total control over the Corporation in wartime, and this was duly mooted on many occasions (Balfour, 1979, 82–3). However, the BBC persuasively argued that it could perform a better task as a propagandist (raising morale at home, and providing authoritative and seemingly independent news to Britons and Overseas Services listeners alike) by remaining free from direct governmental compulsion. In fact, the MOI's assistance was required to win the argument in the face of Churchill's recurrent preference for an outright take-over of an organisation which he branded 'an enemy within the gates, doing more harm than good', though the BBC perhaps did not always fully recognise the Ministry as ally rather than oppressor (Briggs, 1995, 32). The 'silken cords' which bound broadcasters to the MOI could feel like 'chains of iron' (Briggs, 1995, 31). Constitutionally, the BBC's position did alter somewhat during the war. Its Board of Governors was temporarily disbanded but then reinstated in a bureaucratic fudge whereby the government assumed, on paper, complete power over the BBC, but chose not to exercise it (Balfour, 1979, 85). Instead, liaison between the MOI and BBC was undertaken by two new Governors, for Home and Foreign Affairs respectively, lest the BBC simply overlook MOI 'advice', for as far as the MOI was concerned the sometimes combative Corporation did not sufficiently recognise the Ministry as the best guarantor of BBC independence (McLaine, 1979, 231).

In its news output the BBC drew, as we will see, from the same pool of MOI-filtered information as its print media counterparts. By 1941, the BBC was further permitted nine accredited 'observers' (accompanied by somewhat inaptly named 'mobile reporting units') with British forces, another innovation inspired by the apparent success of German frontline radio broadcasts transmitted by the PK (Nicholas, 1996, 208). But these special 'War Reports' aside, as Chief Censor Thomson pointed out, the BBC 'depended for their news bulletins on the agency tape machines. And this news had, of course, already been submitted to and passed by the censorship' (1949, 165). MOI influence over broadcast content extended even further than this pre-censorship of information. Scripts of all manner of broadcasts – from seemingly innocuous children's programmes to more polemical talks of popular radio 'demagogues', such as J.B. Priestley – were subjected to prior scrutiny, and speakers whom the government feared were dangerously radical for the British public, Communists in particular, were kept from the airwaves altogether (Calder, 1969, 246–7). Yet despite intrusive supervision, BBC studios still contained a 'switch censor' as live programmes were transmitted, to guard against the fearful possibility that a speaker might depart from the approved script. In the horrifying event of 'hysterical outbursts either by announcers or artists', the transmission could be instantaneously blocked (Nicholas, 1996, 19).

Only newsreels were subjected to more invasive state scrutiny. By August 1940, the MOI had determined that the newsreel – above feature films or documentaries – was the most important vehicle of film propaganda. But official propaganda planners grasped the potentialities of film slowly. Not only had they reckoned on cinemas being shut for the duration of a lightning aerial war, but they appeared as hamstrung by upper-class scruples about an essentially proletarian medium (with a weekly audience of some 20 million) as their First World War forebears (Pronay, 1982, 175–6, 184). And for their part, the military in 1939 were as sensitive as their Great War counterparts to the power of the visual image; hence the War Office's initial order banning all photography of military subjects.

Regarded as more popular than documentaries, and as compelling overseas ambassadors for the British cause, the newsreels suffered the sharp end of the film propaganda war, enduring vigorous pre- and post-censorship, unlike other media. Like the press and BBC, they were subject to reams of censorship 'stops'. While these eased somewhat after the first few months of war, they remained fairly detailed, and more so for the newsreels than for other media. For example, the newsreels were given precise instructions as to how much bomb damage they could display, as evidenced by a note of 13 September 1940 that each 'pan must start from an undamaged building and must conclude on an undamaged building, and it must not linger over the damaged building' (Pronay, 1982, 193). But censorship did not press in a uniformly restrictive direction as far as war's costs were concerned. On occasion, the MOI positively encouraged the filming of bomb damage, so long as the commentary emphasised British resolve in dealing with such misfortunes – no doubt with the American audience uppermost (Cull, 1995, 107). In this respect the MOI's attitude can be compared with shifting American official policy towards war photography, which became less restrictive towards photographing war's human casualties as American involvement lengthened, in the hope that complaisant civilians would be jolted into awareness of their uniformed counterparts' sacrifices, and readied to receive injured men home (Roeder, 1985, 1993).

For British newsreel companies, there was little 'voluntarism' about the censorship system. MOI censors visited their offices to view all footage proposed for inclusion in any single issue. They also scrutinised proposed commentaries, and once a newsreel was complete, it was brought to Malet Street for a final Scrutiny Viewing (Pronay, 1982, 193). Faced with this overwhelming state oversight, the newsreel companies rapidly fell into line. The MOI in practice removed relatively little: of 1500 stories produced by Paramount between 1940 and 1944, the Ministry made only 166 cuts. This reflects both the companies' patriotic willingness to get 'on-side' and a more hard-headed recognition that it was futile wasting precious film-stock shooting stories likely to arouse Ministry objections (Pronay, 1982, 198).

News Policy

By the middle of the war, if not before, all branches of the German media had been brought thoroughly under state control and, in many cases, into state ownership. The flow of information which ran through the media conduits was every bit as regulated. News was a commodity to be strategically dispensed, withheld or manipulated in the interests of victory. As Goebbels informed his diary in May 1942: 'News policy is a weapon of war. Its purpose is to wage war and not to give out information' (Goebbels, cited by Doob, 1995, 203). But obviously *some* information had to be released, for in wartime the Minister also recognised that the public's 'hunger for news must somehow be satisfied' or Germans would be 'compel[ed] to listen to foreign and enemy broadcasts' (Doob, 1995, 203). But questions of how much news should be reported, by whom, and with what degree of openness, proved contentious and divisive ones for the wartime Nazi elite.

In wartime, Goebbels' power over news and propaganda waned. It had never been total, thanks to Hitler's insistence on dividing his elite, duplicating their functions the better to rule over them, in 'calculated chaos' as Michael Balfour characterises it (1979, 35). War ensured that the military acquired greater prominence in the release of news, and so Goebbels found himself warring with Major Hasso von Wedel, head of the *Wehrmacht* high command's propaganda division (OKW/Wpr), General Alfred Jodl at the Führer Head-Quarters, and the Reich Press Chief, Otto Dietrich, who accompanied Hitler on his peregrinations to the various Fronts. The OKW controlled military information, and its press releases were referred to Hitler as their final arbiter, bypassing Goebbels and his machinery altogether. If the OKW communiqués met with the Führer's approval, they were released through the state News Agency in time for the two o'clock radio bulletin (Balfour, 1979, 105). If they did not, they were amended accordingly, often privileging the fantastical at the expense of the factual, with Hitler frequently insisting on altering whole passages, particularly if they contained news of German failures. Typically, on one occasion, reading that the Army had taken 3000 Prisoners of War, Hitler insisted that an extra zero be added to the total: 'Don't put 30,000 but 30,723 and everyone will believe an exact count has been made' (cited by Balfour, 1979, 122).

In this matter of news policy, Hitler and Goebbels differed, despite popular mythology which casts the latter as a mere sounding-box for the former. Their relationship was considerably more complex, as was Goebbels' relationship with lying, despite his name having become synonymous with that activity. Not simply a megaphone for the Führer's views, Goebbels on occasion vigorously challenged them, tending to caution against incredible exaggerations and blatant propaganda. More paradoxically yet, having done so much to create the 'Hitler myth', Goebbels increasingly had to assume the Führer's role himself. In the wake of the Stalingrad disaster, Hitler – the 'representative individual' who had predicted victory – shunned the public spotlight, leaving Goebbels to encourage and exhort, promise and threaten the German people (Balfour, 1979; Kershaw, 1987). Consequently, even as he lost power over the news media to the OKW – which Balfour dates to early 1942 – Goebbels assumed a yet more significant role as ersatz Führer. While the increasingly reclusive Hitler tightened his grip on the press further in the wake of Stalingrad, even censoring Goebbels's own column in *Das Reich*, the propaganda minister adopted a position of somewhat greater realism in at least some of his public appearances, playing the Führer in a way which doubtless failed always to meet Adolf's approval.

Goebbels offered much suggestive testimony to those who regard him as history's 'greatest liar', not least in his notorious dictum that 'propaganda does not have anything to do with truth! We serve truth by serving a German victory' (cited by Welch, 1983a, 5). But the less-quoted preceding sentence – 'There must be absolute certainty that words are followed up by corresponding events' – suggests his simultaneous appreciation of the need for credibility. In fact, as Balfour comments, 'Goebbels all along kept a firmer grip on reality than many of his colleagues', though not unwaveringly so (1979, 116). He was infuriated when the OKW erroneously boasted German successes at Salerno in September 1943, regarding this as both flawed propaganda strategy and a blow to his own personal reputation: 'The whole pack of enemy propagandists attacks me and makes me responsible for this totally faulty news policy!', he fumed (cited by Baird, 1974, 35). When the 'corresponding events' to Nazi propaganda constituted a string of undeniable defeats, Goebbels proposed that something more akin to the British approach – 'Total Frankness' in owning up to short-term failure, in his estimation – might be appropriate, and certainly preferable to a repeat of Hitler's premature announcement of victory over Russia (Balfour, 1979, 125, 321–31). In the most significant speech of his career, at the Berlin *Sportspalast* on 18 February 1943, Goebbels accordingly intimated that Germany could lose the war if the *Volk* did not respond, in the fervent affirmative, to his call for a war effort 'more total and radical than ever imagined' (Balfour, 1979, 321). But even at this stage of the war, Goebbels was not entirely consistent with another of his *obiter dicta*: that propaganda's function was 'not to make predictions but to report facts' (Balfour, 1979, 287). As Germany spiralled towards defeat, Goebbels's vaunted new 'frankness' was diluted by flights of fancy and wild promises, such as the deliverance of victory (or vengeance at the very least) by the secret V2 rocket. In his favourite arena of film propaganda, Goebbels retreated into 'the mythical and irrational elements of National Socialist doctrine' (Welch, 1983, 6).

What, then, of British news policy with which Goebbels claimed to be so impressed? The MOI's role as both conduit of news and suppressor of information had received some pre-war attention, but its precise functioning in these spheres, as in so many others, remained cloaked in ambiguity in 1939. Indeed so controversial was the MOI's news-giving and withholding role that the Ministry temporarily lost these functions altogether, after its disastrously draconian start, when they were hived off in October 1939 to a new Press and Censorship Bureau under Home Office control (Balfour, 1979, 59). Different operating principles vied for supremacy. The military's habitual preference for non-disclosure, limited journalistic access to the front, and a reactivated, all-encompassing D-notice system conflicted with the advice of various 'experts' that national morale would be better served by having people 'feel they are being told the truth'. A report received by the MOI in September 1939 advised: 'Distrust breeds fear much more than knowledge of reverses. The all-important thing for publicity to achieve is the conviction that the worst is known' (cited by McLaine, 1979, 28). To adopt such an approach required the Ministry to jettison its class-bound assumptions about the need for the 'lower orders' to be wheedled and cajoled into playing their part in the war effort, but it also depended on greater liberalism in the armed services.

No-one was unaware of the importance of news to overall propaganda strategy: Lord Reith had dubbed news 'the shocktroops of propaganda'. But the problem lay in marshalling the shocktroops in a fashion acceptable to the various parties concerned: press, public, politicians and military. The system which finally evolved in the MOI (which regained censorship and news release functions after six months) was far more akin to Britain's First World War system than the Nazis' supposed replica. Once again, censorship rested on a somewhat euphemistic 'voluntarism'. Newspaper editors were issued with a battery of D-Notices, which 'covered just about every conceivable human activity', in the words of the retired Rear-Admiral elevated to Chief Censor in 1940 (Thomson, 1947, 6).

As at the start of the First World War, the Notices erred wildly on the side of security-minded caution, with editors encouraged to submit to the censors any material which might contain an infringement (again transferring responsibility for violations on to officialdom). The editors' job, compromised in so far as complete editorial control over content passed out of their hands, was perhaps more enviable than that of the censors, who had to second-guess what information might assist the enemy. Most censors were retired military men, often with little or no press experience. Rear-Admiral Thomson freely admitted that his prior knowledge of the press 'had hitherto been limited to reading my newspaper at the breakfast table' (1947, 1). The censors' job was to provide a workable interpretation of D-Notices so far-reaching that censors found themselves adjudicating stories as trivial as one concerning a football match played by Battersea power station workers, whose only connection with national security was their employment in an industry of wartime importance. In the war's early months, the censorship system collapsed under an avalanche of such trivia. A more coherent news strategy was required to guide individual censors' decisions and streamline the Notices. This was evolved under Cyril Radcliffe at the MOI, who laid down the policy (again echoing First World War practice) that while 'facts' could be censored if they threatened to aid the enemy's military campaign, opinion and comment should be free from regulation (Balfour, 1979, 66).

The MOI's *modus operandi* thus contained a judicious mixture of pragmatism and principle. It has often been repeated that the MOI's News Division aspired, in the words of Ivone Kirkpatrick, to 'tell the truth, nothing but the truth and, as near as possible, the whole truth' (cited by P. Taylor, 1995, 213). This was a suitably ambiguous aphorism, for in the nature of total war (not least as prosecuted by a military which would have preferred a policy of complete secrecy) the disclosure of information was perhaps more often 'as near as possible' than 'nothing but' the truth (McLaine, 1979, 36; Nicholas, 1996, 16). Nevertheless, British propagandists self-consciously occupied the moral high ground, the aim of the

MOI on the home front being 'by the dissemination of truth to attack the enemy in the minds of the public' (cited by McLaine, 1979, 137). In comparison with its Nazi counterparts, undoubtedly the MOI possessed a more scrupulous attitude towards veracity, but the Ministry's 'truthfulness' was grounded in pragmatic calculation and not just morality, its policy tellingly deemed a *'strategy* of truth'. The aim after all was to enhance the home front's sense of parti-cipation. Greater openness resulted from a growing sense (aided by research into the 'national character' conducted in 1941) that the English – though not necessarily the Scots and Welsh – delighted in knowing the worst, and became disgruntled to the degree that they believed the worst was being kept from them (Balfour, 1979, 74–5). A nation of grumblers should thus be given sufficient to grumble about.

Undoubtedly, however, the very worst was neither always told openly nor without delay. Siân Nicholas suggests that bad news was generally released slowly, 'in driblets', over a protracted period. The worst casualty statistics from the Battle of the Atlantic were never surrendered, and the Air Ministry later confessed that it had ex-aggerated German losses by some 55 per cent, even though its 'cricket score' was generally believed to be accurate (1996, 199). Certainly, then, the 'whole truth' was sometimes lacking, but on occasion sins of omission and of approximation (as 'near as possible the whole truth') were surpassed by 'stretching the truth to the threshold of lying', as McLaine suggests the MOI and Service departments did in characterising the RAF's bombing strategy in Germany as essentially 'strategic' (1979, 137).

That the system for censorship and news release ultimately came to operate so smoothly, with journalists generally so uncomplaining, was not simply a product of their support for the war effort but also a reflection of popular ignorance as to precisely how much informa-tion was pre-censored. Shared commitment to a war 'in which the wickedness of the enemy did not have to be invented' had not, after all, stifled press criticism of early MOI misjudgements in 1939 and 1940 (Knightley, 1989, 319). But, gaining sophistication and subtlety, the MOI did enjoy one advantage of which the British public was utterly unaware. Happily for the Ministry, the cables of both the Press Association and Reuters were routed into the same London building. Here the MOI's censors could excise damaging material arriving on the wire services before media subscribers received the tickertape messages. Thereafter, newspapers and the BBC were free to present this pre-censored information in their own inimitable house styles (Pronay, 1982, 177–8). The system's toleration of dissenting opinion sometimes irked the Prime Minister, Churchill, who had to be dissuaded (on several occasions) by the MOI and Home Office from suppressing the *Daily Mirror* outright. But it did at least leave newspaper editors some latitude, unlike their German counterparts who became mere conduits for official communiqués, with freedom over neither the lay-out of dictated stories on the page, nor the size and wording of headlines.

Feature Films and the Second World War

Relations with the State

Nowhere was newsreel the most magnetic attraction of cinema. Feature films, 'movies', were the biggest box office draw, and, consequently, whatever importance state propagandists attached to documentaries and newsreels, they could hardly afford to ignore the most popular filmic form. Indeed, the feature film offered very particular benefits to propagandists which were well recognised on all sides. Compare the following assertions:

> The easiest way to inject a propaganda idea into most people's minds, is to let it go in through the medium of an entertainment picture when they do not realise that they are being propagandised.

> The film being a popular medium must be good entertainment if it is to be good propaganda.

> The best propaganda is that which as it were works invisibly, penetrates the whole of life without the public having any knowledge of the propagandist initiative.

The words, respectively, belong to Elmer Davies, Head of America's Office of War Information (OWI); the MOI Film Division's Programme for Film Propaganda, and Goebbels (cited by Koppes and Black, 1987, 88; Chapman, 1998, 41; Kaes, 1989, 5). The sentiments, however, are clearly interchangeable. Feature films appealed to state propagandists because movies appeared to their audiences as the antithesis of propaganda: entertainment. But in practice there was no dichotomy. Far from being mutually exclusive, propaganda was regarded by officialdom (on all sides) as more compelling when it masqueraded as entertainment. 'Film propaganda will be most effective when it is least recognisable as such', cautioned the MOI's Programme for Film Propaganda in 1940, and Goebbels likewise wrote that 'propaganda becomes ineffective the moment we are aware of it' (cited by Taylor, 1983, 230). The 'picture palace' was consequently the ideal venue for catching audiences unawares.

If contemporary audiences unwittingly swallowed the pill, we should exhibit more scepticism. Goebbels liked to claim that under Hitler very few 'political films' were made. One can however argue, as Erwin Leiser does, that there was in fact no such thing as a '"non-political" film' in the Third Reich (Leiser, 1975, 17). The majority may not have contained *overt* ideological messages: only an estimated 15 per cent of the UFA studios' total output during the *Hitlerzeit* did (Hull, 1969, 100; Herzstein, 1979, 272; Reuth, 1993, 284). But this was because Goebbels, a subtler propagandist than the Führer, recognised that 'conveyor-belt brownshirt epics were box-office poison', insisting, not always successfully, that 'ideology must never be allowed to become obtrusive bias' (Grünberger, cited by Rentschler, 1996, 9; Welch, 1983b, 23). Goebbels's 'cinema of pleasure' was no less propaganda for that: in Rentschler's words, 'lighthearted shapes and innocuous forms contained political meanings and served ideological purposes' (1996, 12; Herzstein, 1979, 272). That this disappearing trick was generally pulled off is attested to by one German, who noted in 1938: 'A really clever person might claim that even if there are no propaganda films, there is still propaganda tucked away beneath film's surface details. This person, though, will have a hard time finding examples to prove his point' (Rentschler, 1996, 19).

In Britain, America and Germany alike, although levels of state supervision over the film industry diverged, no feature film could be theatrically released without having acquired at least some prior official approval. Nazi Germany, unsurprisingly, exerted the tightest control. 'From the script to the final print – every single filmmaking process must be disciplined', proclaimed RMVP film impresario, Fritz Hippler (cited by Rentschler, 1996, 16). To ensure that this was so, the Nazis established the *Reichsfilmkammer* (RFK) in July 1933, with ten separate branches encompassing every aspect of film-making, and a *Reichsfilmsdramaturg* in February 1934 to act as an official censor for scripts and administer a ratings system for films in distribution (Welch, 1983b, 6–38). Goebbels enthusiastically adopted the task of script censorship, brandishing his 'Minister's pencil' with the relish befitting a keen *cinéaste*, who additionally boasted an intimate knowledge of several stars of the German screen, not all of pure Aryan stock (Reuth, 1993, 195). Even if fewer than 10 per cent of the films made during the Nazi era were directly commissioned by the RMVP, Herzstein reminds us that 'no film appeared on the German screens without intense analysis of its contents by the censorship people of the ministry and the RFK' (1979, 273). That most films also relied on the state film bank for finance left film-makers doubly beholden to a regime whose values and beliefs many film personnel internalised (Weinberg, 1984, 121). If some segments of the German audience read the resultant films in subversive ways (as admirers of the aesthetic merits of German cinema during the *Hitlerzeit* have subsequently insisted), certainly as far as the state was concerned, nothing damaging to the Nazi enterprise could reach the screen.

In Britain and America, the film industries were considerably freer. However, in Britain, the MOI's influence over commercial film production was more extensive than its powers on paper (mainly relating to the sponsorship or production of information films) might imply. Arrangements for film propaganda had not received priority consideration before September 1939, probably (as Pronay and Croft point out) because 'film producers were entirely accustomed to working under conditions of practically total censorship', so war 'made little difference' (Pronay and Croft, 1983, 146). Pre-war planners anticipated that the British Board of Film Censors (BBFC), which scrutinised films on grounds of both 'public decency' and political seemliness, issuing the certificates necessary for theatrical release, would assume a 'security' dimension in wartime. Ten categories of sensitive topics (including bomb disposal incidents and treatment of prisoners of war) would supplement its excisions of indecorous female attire, undue displays of passion, offensive expletives, irreverent portrayals of the Royals, and matters likely to aggravate labour relations (Chapman, 1998, 16–17). In practice, however, while the BBFC did continue to be mindful of wartime bad language and loose morals, the MOI assumed greater supervision over the broad contours of wartime film-making than tentative plans envisaged. Indeed, while the BBFC reviewed films in the long-cut on grounds of 'morality' (rather like Hollywood's Hays Office) the MOI usurped the BBFC's former role of liaison with film companies at the pre-production stage. The MOI, not the censors, deliberated over appropriate themes for wartime cinema and how best to project 'the positive virtues of British national characteristics and the democratic way of life' (MOI, cited by Aldgate and Richards, 1995, 11–12).

Reserving the ultimate right to ban a film *in extremis*, the MOI never actually exercised its prerogative. Its control was pervasive enough that no film could even enter production without some prior sanction. In 1940, the Board of Trade reached an agreement with the MOI's Films Division that the distribution of film stock – a strategic commodity – to commercial film production companies would be carried out only in consultation with the MOI (Aldgate and Richards, 1995, 11–12). Prior to allocation, the Board of Trade required a film scenario, which it then passed to the MOI for vetting. In practice, production companies learnt that the speediest way of proceeding was to submit film treatments to the MOI in the first place, and also engage a script consultant, or even writer, appointed by its Films Division (Pronay and Croft, 1983, 152). Thus British film-makers, like their radio-broadcasting counterparts, were bound to the state by at least 'silken cords' if not 'iron chains', though many feature film producers and documentarists appeared keen to collaborate with the state in the hour of need, generously lending their creative talents to the MOI's 'Ideas Committee' (Aldgate and Richards, 1995, 10).

As for Hollywood, the American motion picture industry also co-operated more closely with government and the military than was its peacetime practice. Having made a strong case to Washington that film could variously distract Americans from the war and educate them about it, while providing morale-boosting fodder to celluloid-starved allies, Hollywood was rewarded by having its business declared an 'Essential War Industry'. Impressed by the argument that 'a Gary Cooper in the heroic screen role of a Sergeant York can contribute more to the success of America's war effort than this same Gary Cooper as a member of the American Army', the US government agreed that Hollywood's least dispensable 1 per cent of personnel would be exempt from conscription, and that studios would be guaranteed pre-war quantities of film stock (Short, 1985a, 99). This special dispensation enabled Hollywood to continue producing movies at a rate almost undiminished by war: approximately 440 features per annum compared with some 500 annually in the 1930s (Sklar, 1975, 250).

In return, the Office of War Information expected, and generally received, Hollywood's willing participation in the war effort. The price for the studios' freedom from burdensome OWI control was that Hollywood shackle itself more closely to the state from patriotic preference: a practice the industry termed 'voluntary self-discipline' (Short, 1985, 91). Hollywood did, after all, owe considerable debts to the US government. In allowing Hollywood to continue operating 'business as normal' during wartime, Washington effectively perpetuated the monopoly status of the big studios, for whom war would bring new markets and increased trade: soldiers to be instructed and entertained, civilians looking for diversion, and allies with ailing film industries (Sklar, 1975, 250–1; Doherty, 1993).

The wartime marriage of convenience between Washington and Hollywood was not without its strains, however. In particular, film-makers bridled at the temerity of the OWI's Hollywood outpost, the Bureau of Motion Pictures (BMP) in pushing propaganda themes which were obviously dictated far more by the exigencies of policy than an informed knowledge of the film industry. Nelson Poynter, who fronted the BMP's Hollywood office, had 'no previous film experience', as unimpressed producer Walter Wanger pointed out (Doherty, 1993, 47). Even a cursory perusal of the Information Manual for Hollywood (circulated just prior to the OWI's formal constitution, in June 1942) illustrates why film-makers might have felt aggrieved, stuffed as it was with high-minded defences of American democracy and injunctions to show the Allies in a positive light – 'the Chinese are not little people who run laundries, they are a great nation, cultured and liberal' – and to avoid fanning the flames of racism in portraying the enemy (Short, 1983b). Couched in language, and covering issues, not easily translatable on to the big screen, injunctions such as 'Picture and dramatise the tax programme' were unlikely to cut much ice in Los Angeles. Little wonder, then, that Hollywood had, as Thomas Doherty relates, a sardonic name for 'pushy cues' emanating from the BMP: 'poynters' (1993, 47). When the maligned individual suggested that his office receive preliminary screenplays of all prospective Hollywood features, he received a predictably hostile response, and eventually the OWI and the industry reached a compromise whereby only military-themed films were subject to compulsory pre-production review, while the rest continued to be the subject of voluntary collaboration.

Functions and Genres

To some extent, feature films discharged comparable propaganda functions in Britain, America and Germany. Universally valued for their ability to entertain, films offered audiences 'vacations from the present', an opportunity to forget their tribulations beyond the darkened auditorium (Rentschler, 1996, 216). But since official propagandists often had other instructional purposes in mind for film, their recognition of the 'pleasure principle' did not always override this latent didacticism. Where Hollywood scorned the 'high-falutin' OWI guidelines, others similarly charged that the MOI's Programme for Film Propaganda failed to value humour sufficiently (Aldgate and Richards, 1995, 27).

The specific propaganda messages which officials sought to smuggle into various film genres naturally varied according to the state in question and its overall objectives. In Nazi Germany, where propaganda was charged with effecting a complete 'spiritual mobilisation', film directly contributed to this fundamental reshaping of values and beliefs. The Nazis thus deployed film to lay the ideological groundwork for particular – and particularly noxious – outgrowths of state policy, such as the euthanasia campaign (promoted in films such as *Ich Klage An*, 1941), and the 'Final Solution' (Herzstein, 1979, 259–321; Welch, 1983b, 121–31, 280–304; Rentschler, 1996). In very different modes, respectively typifying Hitler's and Goebbels's divergent preferences in film propaganda, both quasi-documentaries such as *Der Ewige Jude* (*The Eternal Jew*) and features, most notoriously the costume melodrama *Jud Süß* (both released in 1940), demonised and dehumanised Jews, paving the way for ordinary Germans to become what Daniel Goldhagen terms their 'willing executioners' (1996). In Nazi Germany, as Rentschler points out, 'mass culture also became a crucial precondition for mass murder. The media enabled Germans to withstand awful truths and ignore hideous presentiments, serving as a shield and a blindfold, audiovisual instruments that ensured uplifting fictions no matter how bitter the realities' (1996, 222). With all *Schutzstaffeln* (SS) guards ordered to view *Jud Süß*, no wonder Omer Bartov concludes that 'the emotions factory of Nazi propaganda was essential for the technological factory of death' (1996, 186).

The Nazis uniquely abused national cinema for genocidal ends. In all states, however, films served to define war aims, and in so doing to sharpen a sense of nation and national identity: to show audiences who they collectively were, what they were fighting to preserve, and from what depredations. The task of informing people about why they fought was particularly pressing in America. Where Britons had been at war since 1939, and palpably experienced the Nazi threat, Americans tended to be somewhat ill-informed regarding the whys and wherefores of the war in Europe, and were liable (the OWI feared) to see US entry into the war as simply a defensive response to Japan's raid on Pearl Harbor. Alarmingly, as many as a third of respondents to an OWI poll in summer 1942 affirmed willingness to sign a separate peace with Germany, while many acknowledged ignorance as to why America was fighting or expressed hostility towards America's new Allies (Weinberg, 1968, 78). Especially for Americans in uniform – who, unlike their civilian kin, stood to lose their lives in this conflict – film had to explain the war. The OWI encouraged film to project both the nature of the enemies and the necessity for America's combating them alongside Allies who were reliable and worthy partners, their Bolshevism or imperialism notwithstanding. The most significant set of 'instructional' propaganda films of this kind was undoubtedly Frank Capra's *Why We Fight* series, which skilfully spliced animation, graphics, and archive footage (from Riefenstahl's *Triumph of the Will* amongst other sources) to expose and indict the enemy (Culbert, 1983, 173–91). In turn, American servicemen's contribution to the war effort was impressed upon civilian America through the documentary record of many of Hollywood's most celebrated and popular directors, such as John Ford, William Wyler and John Huston, who temporarily enlisted with the armed forces' photographic units (Meyerson, 1995, 225–59).

Explaining the war was, then, in part a matter of self-representation. 'In total war, nations in their entirety confront each other, and all expressions of national life become weapons of war', opined Fritz

Hippler (cited by Rentschler, 1996, 202). But this broad attitude was not confined to Germany for, in defining nationhood, wartime cinemas generally sharpened the contours of national identity by projecting it in opposition to enemy 'Others', though strikingly less so in Japanese cinema than elsewhere (Dower, 1996, 39). In British and American films, this 'Other' was usually an Axis national, or occasionally a treacherous Fifth Columnist, working to subvert his or her own state from within. The OWI, however, was insistent that Hollywood refrain from undue racial stereotyping of the enemy. Given the ethnic heterogeneity of America itself, and Washington's bid for the moral high ground on matters of race, the OWI preferred to instil a 'properly directed hatred' of 'militarism' – the essence of enemy *ideology* – rather than of the enemy peoples as such (Short, 1983b; Doherty, 1993, 122–48). Acutely sensitive to the portrayal of race relations within America, and keen to tarnish Nazi Germany for its racist policies, the OWI struggled to mitigate Hollywood's lurid post-Pearl Harbor depictions of the Japanese (Dower, 1986; Koppes and Black, 1987, 60–3).

In Germany, where a scientifically nonsensical biological determinism under-pinned Nazi ideology, the Aryan *Volk* was defined not only in opposition to foreign foes – barbaric Bolshevik subhumans and sadistic English imperialists – but also to racial enemies within, who were subjected to the state's genocidal exterminationism (Welch, 1983b, 238–79). Nazi propaganda, as Hannah Arendt recognised, made anti-Semitism 'a principle of self-definition': Germans would recognise themselves as everything the Jew was not, their own negative characteristics having been disowned and projected on to this odious Other (1958, 355–6; Rentschler, 1996, 159–64).

Where German films promoted an exclusive Aryan identity, British and American cinema, on the other hand, strove to foster an inclusive sense of domestic belonging. This extended notably to women, whose contribution to the home front in both Allied countries was lauded and championed in such films as *Millions Like Us* (1943) and *Swing Shift Maisie* (1943: Harper, 1988, 168–202; Lant, 1991; Doherty, 1993, 149–79; Chapman, 1998, 201–15). Ethnic inclusiveness was another prominent theme of Hollywood's wartime output. In the USA, the OWI encouraged Hollywood films to exemplify the 'melting pot' ideal: 'a nation of many races and creeds, who have demonstrated that they can live together and progress' (cited by Short, 1983, 175). Similarly, though with considerable circumspection (at a time when white Americans still overwhelmingly endorsed segregation), Army films attempted to demonstrate the contribution of what was then called the 'Negro soldier' in combat (Cripps, 1983, 125–45; Doherty, 1993, 205–26).

In Britain, the emphasis was less on racial unity of purpose than on the distinct national and regional components of the UK, and its stratified social classes, pulling together in the war effort (Gledhill and Swanson, 1996). Films dealing with the development of an *esprit de corps* amongst disparate recruits to the armed forces were particularly well suited to the task, such as Noel Coward's *In Which We Serve* (1942) and Carol Reed's *The Way Ahead* (1944). The notion of a *British* 'national character' was thus perpetuated through film, and the commendable qualities with which this character was identified – the MOI singling out 'sense of humour', 'tolerance', and 'stoicism' – threw into stark relief the enemy's contrasting traits. But besides emphasising (by implication, if nothing more overt) the odiousness of the antithetical enemy, 'national' propaganda also offered a positive sense of what was being fought for. Wartime British films projected a peculiarly rural, and distinctly English, version of what Britain represented, though it is questionable what viewers in Scotland or Wales (or even factory-working city-dwellers in industrial northern England) made of the British 'nation' imagined as Ruritanian demi-paradise. One such film, *This England* (1941), required a tactful name-change to *Our Heritage* before release in Scotland, and as Jeffrey Richards notes, films exemplifying the 'rural myth', such as Powell and Pressburger's *A Canterbury Tale* (1944), did not always prosper at the box office (Richards, 1988, 50; Richards, 1997). But British cinema increasingly combined its fanciful depiction of 'olde England' with a more controversial vision of a remodelled Britain that ordinary people were fighting to realise, and with more realistic portraits of present-day working-class life (Stead, 1988, 62–83).

In constructing national characters, myths and archetypes, all national cinemas plundered the past. Nazi cinema was especially wedded to the historical epic (Taylor, 1979, 164; Welch, 1983b, 164–85). German films of the era made very little attempt to transfer ordinary life in the Third Reich on to the screen, perhaps because ordinary life was itself so suffused with Nazi propaganda as to frustrate Goebbels' preferences (Rentschler, 1996, 19). Instead, film-makers furthered the Nazi project by displaying the historical greatness of Germany, depicting situations and characters from the past which audiences would, correctly, read as analogues for the present. Consequently, cinematic 'biographies' of legendary Germans, such as Frederick the Great and Bismarck, were less concerned with eulogising their eponymous heroes than, as Hippler acknowledged, with lauding the Führer himself (Weinberg, 1984, 115). As fictional films were forbidden from representing Hitler's likeness, and as he showed an increasing distaste for public display, these hagiographic portraits played a necessary role in filling the void where the Führer's face should have been (Rentschler, 1996, 172).

Historical films thus generated unmistakably contemporary messages. But as film-makers could mask any propagandist intent by trumpeting their films' 'facticity', such fare, along with other escapist oeuvre (musicals, comedies, romances and so on) remained popular as people tired of war, and its on-screen cinematic reflection. One of the paradoxes of British wartime cinema, in particular, was that thanks to a relaxation of the BBFC's forbidden topics, films could deal unprecedently with the 'burning questions of the day', but increasingly the quotidian realities of ordinary citizens' or soldiers' lives in this 'People's War' were not what audiences themselves most enjoyed watching (perhaps understandably). A trip to the cinema offered a chance to escape the grind of a war which lasted far longer than anyone had expected. Although some war-themed films – such as Noel Coward's *In Which We Serve* and Anthony Asquith's *The Way to the Stars* (1945) – were also contemporary box office hits, evidence (patchy and impressionistic though it is) points towards a growing preference for more lighthearted fare and 'fewer war films' (Richards and Sheridan, 1987; Aldgate and Richards, 1995, 11).

If this was the view on the home front, it is even less surprising that those actually fighting should have preferred entertainment to combat movies: 'tinsel' to 'realism'. According to a 1944 *Time* poll, American GIs rated 'musical comedies best, comedies next best, then adventure films and melodramas' (cited by Costello, 1986, 180). Soldiers purportedly craved ' "the three L's" – laughs, lookers, and letters'. As Thomas Doherty points out, the movies could deliver two and 'make kith and kin feel mighty guilty about not mailing off the third' (1993, 180). Movies, then, served as uplifting distraction, alleviating soldiers' immediate burdens while reconnecting them with those back home. As one Marine Private observed, after six months' active service in the Pacific, entertainment movies 'stop us from thinking of ourselves and our surroundings...[and] remind us that there are such things as pretty girls, gay music, and a civilization worth living for', a sentiment almost indistinguishable from Hollywood's tagline for *China Girl*: 'An American will fight for only three things – for a woman, for himself, and for a better world' (Costello, 1986, 181). Perhaps the greatest contribution of Hollywood movies to the war effort lay in reminding their viewers that the Allies were not just fighting for abstract ideals but those tangible things that made life worth living for.

Lessons of Total War

Famously, Goebbels once confided to his diary: 'In propaganda as in love, anything is permissible which is successful' (cited by Welch, 1995, 17). How far, then, did success validate the draconian management of media and public opinion in the Third Reich? Some scholars have suggested that to infer failure on the propaganda front from Germany's military defeat is a false syllogism. Robert Herzstein goes so far as to assert that propaganda was the 'war that Hitler won'. For him, the 'continuation of the struggle by the German people into 1945 until practically every *Gau* was in Soviet or Western Allied hands' represents the 'greatest success of Goebbels' propaganda apparatus', not least as most Germans were unenthusiastic about war in 1939 (Herzstein, 1979, 22). But perhaps his seductive logic is flawed. For one thing, as Ian Kershaw has argued, not every *Gau* resisted the Allies' advances as resolutely as Herzstein implies. For another, the reasons why Germans did struggle on – despite the low morale and defeatism which *Sicherheitsdienst* (SD) reports increasingly exposed – may have owed much to factors other than Goebbels's promises of deliverance by V2 rockets and threats of destruction (including castration) by Bolshevik hordes (1987, 169–225; in Welch, 1983a, 180–205). Kershaw concludes that 'terroristic repression' became the predominant currency of the regime as the war lengthened and the 'Hitler myth' finally crumbled (in Welch, 1983, 201). But whatever complex reasons explain the Third Reich's survival into 1945, there are clearly grounds for claiming that the Nazi system of media management was less than successful, despite – but more probably because of – its totality.

Every branch of the German media suffered from excessive state control, and public confidence eroded as Germans compared the erroneous or fantastic accounts of war offered by the press and newsreels with first-hand evidence, and testimony of loved ones at the Front. That the press was gagged to the point of suffocation was recognised by the journalist in Goebbels: 'No decent journalist with any feeling of honour in his bones can stand the way he is handled by the press department of the Reich government' (Welch, 1993, 39). Likewise Max Amann mused, too late: 'How could an editor publish a good paper when he sat with one foot in jail and the other in the editorial room?' (Hale, 1964, 323). Under state dictation newspapers became uniform and, in their collective singing from the state hymn sheet, uniformly mistrusted, as the satirical slogan *Ein Volk, ein Reich, eine Zeitung* (One people, one state, one news-paper) attests (Balfour, 1979, 35). This was not entirely what Goeb-bels had intended, realising that too visible and prescriptive state control over form and content could be counter-productive. His ideal was a press 'monoform in will but polyform in the trappings of that will', though he rationalised his own failure to promote pluralism on the grounds that Germans – unlike the British – had not yet reached a sufficient level of 'maturity' (Zeman, 1973, 43–4; Balfour, 1979, 34).

Whether with greater personal direction over the wartime press Goebbels would have avoided the mistakes of his rivals is, however, a moot point, as indeed is the degree to which the failings lay in his own actions, which often vitiated his precepts. Balfour suggests not only that 'a press which had the function of producing a uniform outlook could hardly avoid being uniform itself' but also that greater 'realism' about German losses might only have had a depressant effect (1979, 35, 130). Certainly the newsreels, over which Goebbels enjoyed most control, lost their initial popularity (Hoffmann, 1996, 193). In May 1940, the length of the newsreel was increased to 40 minutes, and the number of prints of each issue doubled to 2000 (Welch, 1983, 209). However, the early triumph of the newsreels probably owed more to military victory than consum-mate propaganda technique (Welch, 1993, 94). If, as Z.A.B. Zeman suggests, 'military success is the best propaganda in a war', then correspondingly by its final months 'the failure of German arms was too apparent to be obliterated by propaganda' (1973, 172). Even though cinema attendances themselves doubled, the newsreels squandered their popularity as the war lengthened and popular hopes of German victory receded. Goebbels's policy veered between what Hippler called 'optimistic propaganda that exuded confidence in victory' – making much of the V2 rocket – and graphic depictions of Bolshevik atrocities, designed to frighten Germans into staunch resistance against the Red Army, though evidence suggested that audiences simply revolted at such scenes (Hoffmann, 1996, 234–7).

Receiving intelligence from local SD reports that patrons were dawdling in cinema foyers rather than watching the newsreels, Goebbels initiated legislation in 1943 obliging proprietors to lock their audiences into the auditorium before the programme commenced. In this way, cinema-goers whose dilatory habits derived from a desire to avoid the newsreel found themselves also debarred from the main feature. But if they could no longer vote with their feet, disgruntled German cinema-goers could still vote 'with their voices...by laughing and jeering at the newsreels they had once applauded', observes Richard Taylor (1998, 148–9). As radio listeners could not be ensnared quite so readily, Goebbels resorted to other means of trapping listeners, having realised that endless hectoring speeches were literally a turn-off. A decree of 1942 compelled radio stations to devote 70 per cent of their airtime to light music, a move which Goebbels hoped would deliver an audience for the important political broadcasts (Welch, 1993, 34).

Paradoxically, the system of media management which Goebbels himself did much to institute inevitably suffocated the variety which he purportedly wished to maintain. According to Goebbels' 'orchestra principle', the regime did not 'expect everyone to play the same instrument, we only expect that people play according to a plan'. But not fully trusting the players to follow the score unless taken into increasing state ownership and under legislative compulsion, the Nazis ensured that precisely the same notes were played by the various media instruments. The result, however, was a cacophony of noise in which the conductor's directing hand was all too evident. To achieve 'polyformity' it was necessary to allow the 'musicians' more latitude for interpretation than the Nazis could possibly sanction, given the degree of popular addiction which they craved.

The Ministry of Information better approximated the 'uniformity of purpose' and 'polyformity of expression' which was Goebbels's unrealised (and unrealisable) ideal. For, as Nicholas Pronay points out, British news media 'managed to maintain the trust of the British public at home and gained a reputation for Britain abroad for having even in wartime an honest, free and truthful media' (Pronay and Spring, 1982, 174). At the same time, however, British media 'gave practically nothing of significance away to an ever-vigilant enemy', although this did not stop the military from carping, on more than one occasion (prefiguring clashes during the Falklands conflict), that the BBC had let slip classified information, and been too accurate in speculation over future operations (Nicholas, 1996, 214–15).

Was the much-vaunted British 'truthfulness' a sham? Might the ultimate testimony to the success of British propaganda be that its own veracity should have been so widely acclaimed? Certainly, irrespective of its proximity to the MOI, the BBC won plaudits from many (and some unlikely) quarters. In occupied Europe, and Germany itself, BBC broadcasts were eagerly tuned into, despite severe penalties attached to listening (Balfour, 1979, 96). At home, even left-wing commentators such as George Orwell, who loathed the inter-war BBC's stuffiness and 'the unbearable voices of its announcers', noted its 'truthfulness' and remarked that the BBC was 'generally regarded here as more reliable than the press' (Orwell in West, 1987, 16). A number of policy-decisions enhanced the BBC's reputation: notably its principled refusal to jam enemy broadcasts, and the organisational separation of 'black' and 'white' radio propaganda activity, which kept covert 'black' stations well removed from the BBC (Balfour, 1979, 91–102; Briggs, 1995, 60). But nevertheless, the BBC's kudos is remarkable, as Siân Nicholas comments, when one considers that the 'British people were only told what their war leaders wanted them to know, were told much that was deliberately false, and were denied knowledge of much more that they may have wished to know' (1996, 220).

Undoubtedly much was omitted from British news but, despite the MOI's withholding and slanting of information, and unprecedented oversight of news and entertainment media, the war was still a boom-time for some British media, as it was for their American counterparts. This expansion was reflected in enlarged workforces, audiences and budgets. The BBC grew from a staff of 4800 in September 1939 to some 11 663 in March 1944, while its output trebled in hours and quintupled in transmitter power, 10 foreign language services in 1939 rising to 45 in 1943 (Briggs, 1995, 18). Meanwhile, America acquired an international radio broadcasting network for the first time during the war. Although the Voice of America was intended as a wartime expedient, its utility to American post-war foreign policy objectives was quickly recognised as the Cold War froze. For its part, Hollywood generated 'unprecedented profits', despite the OWI exerting an influence 'never equalled before or since by a government agency' over an American medium (Koppes and Black, 1977, 103). As an Essential War Industry, the movies in fact did better business than usual. And even the British film industry – which saw its studios dwindle from 22 to 9, its film stock rationed, two-thirds of its technicians called up, and tax-inflated ticket prices – experienced a wartime boom in attendance and boost in critical reputation. With average weekly audiences increasing from 19 million in 1939 to over 30 million in 1945, the war, conclude Aldgate and Richards, 'was definitely to prove a "golden age" as far as domestic films were concerned' (1995, 3).

Wartime conditions, however, did not just result in expanded audiences but also, arguably, in 'better' films and radio broadcasts. Defining 'better' is a slippery business, but if we mean more accessible, then certainly the war allowed the BBC to descend somewhat from its Reithian pedestal. Programme makers, recognising the importance of maintaining morale, realised that the BBC might have to abandon (or at least scale down) some of Reith's improving ambitions towards the audience, and be more responsive to what listeners actually wanted. After all, the price for misreading the audience was high: they might be tempted to tune into Lord Haw Haw's pro-Nazi broadcasts instead, for amusement if not from sympathy (Nicholas, 1996, 40–1). Under the impetus of war, the BBC began conducting audience research – via a new Listener Research Department – to monitor response to its output. Accordingly, its programming incorporated more comedy and light entertainment, and a greater diversity of regional accents and political opinions. The BBC consciously encouraged political debate, though stimulating controversy made the Corporation itself controversial, prompting Conservative critics to charge that it had been a Trojan horse for the socialist landslide in 1945's General Election. Some politicians were bound to disapprove of views they disliked being given such public airing, but at least the BBC was now capable of dealing with gripping political issues rather than tiptoeing around them, as during its more deferential youth. And as far as the BBC was concerned, it never violated its Charter obligation to be impartial: the Corporation would not take political sides within Britain, though in wartime it saw no contradiction between impartiality and taking the British side (Balfour, 1979, 87).

In British film-making a greater degree of liberalism in content did not emerge *despite* the heavy degree of state influence over production, but to a considerable extent *because* of the MOI's vision of film's function in total war. Whereas in the past British film-makers had been constrained by a censorship system which made a boast of keeping the 'burning issues of the day' well out of frame, in wartime films invariably had to deal with matters previously considered dangerously 'political'. The war itself was the most burning issue of 1939–45, and the MOI clearly wanted to see it reflected on film. The wartime government therefore had every reason to lift strictures such as the ban on 'representations of living persons', which the BBFC previously policed, especially to permit depictions of 'enemy aliens'. Indeed, Pronay and Croft suggest that the Ministry was keen now to 'mobilise people's minds, to politicize ordinary people, rather than dull them into passivity' (Pronay and Croft, 1983, 150–1).

In fact, the only British medium to suffer a serious blow to its popularity or reputation in wartime was the newsreel, and even here the evidence is somewhat contradictory, demonstrating again (as popular responses to film in the First World War did) how divergently audience members read film. The organisation Mass Observation – which produced fascinating but impressionistic analyses of public opinion on various topics – found audiences divided. Some viewers were no keener to see graphic representations of war in the newsreels than they were to watch combat movies for entertainment. 'Cannot the censor prevent the issue of these pictures which only bring pain and suffering to those with loved ones on active service?', inquired one cinema-goer, after witnessing bomb damage in Belgium, 'After all we go to the cinema to be carried away from our troubles' (cited in Richards and Sheridan, 1987, 405–6). But while such sentiments appear fairly widespread, the reason why the newsreels' popularity dipped in the first year of war was that they did not contain enough news (though obviously 'news' and 'graphic imagery' should not necessarily be conflated). Mass Observation found that while two-thirds of respondents expressed a liking for the newsreels in 1939, only a quarter did so in 1940, with the number of critics spontaneously berating them for an absence of news rising from 12 to 35 per cent (Richards and Sheridan, 1987, 212). However, Mass-Observation also found a decline in critics attacking the newsreels for heavy-handed propaganda, observing instead only some praise for the newsreel as good propaganda. It would seem, then, that the newsreel suffered from the Service Departments' initial parsimony with news, but was thereafter held in esteem to a degree which varied depending on how much vivid footage audiences actually wanted, or felt they ought, to see.

In conclusion, then, the systems of 'media management' evolved in Britain and America, although unprecedented in their scope, were also relatively free in their operation. As Daniel Hallin points out: 'a wartime relation between the state and civil society developed which involved not primarily the suppression of civil society by the state, but co-operation, co-optation and blurring of the lines, in which state functions were often taken on by institutions like the press, and vice versa' (1997, 209). As in the First World War, certainly there was considerable interchange of personnel: a radio broadcaster (Elmer Davies) headed the OWI; a Director-General of the BBC served briefly as Minister of Information; and numerous broadcasters, journalists, advertising agents and film-makers lent their services to official and non-official wartime propaganda, as they had in the First World War.

This intimacy between state and civil society sometimes frayed. The OWI, for example, antagonised a group of liberal writers drafted into its early operations, who thought that its efforts borrowed too much from vulgar advertising practice. Two disgruntled OWI staffers registered their protest by producing, along with their resignation notices, a satirical poster of the Statue of Liberty, with four bottles of Coca-Cola in her up-raised arm, promoting 'The War That Refreshes: The Four Delicious Freedoms!' (Weinberg, 1968, 86). These writers believed the war's integrity was compromised by packaging it like a consumer product, but conversely some companies used the war to sell their wares in an equally demeaning fashion, one truss manufacturer in California apparently advertising: 'To the Four Freedoms Add a Fifth: Freedom from Rupture' (cited by Sherry, 1995, 89).

More often, the relationship between officialdom, the news media and culture industry was fruitfully collaborative, such as the

MOI's Ideas Committee which, as documentarist Paul Rotha described it, 'met round a table over beer and rather lousy sandwiches' (Aldgate and Richards, 1995, 9–10). Even the seemingly 'incompatible couple' – Hollywood and Washington – actually 'worked together fairly smoothly for common ends', concludes Doherty (1993, 39). Generally, the mechanisms and institutions evolved in Britain and America functioned harmoniously in total war, such that both state and citizens approved their media's wartime performance. In part, approval may have depended on people's ignorance of what was being kept from them when the raw stuff of news was censored at source, but a high degree of willingness to accept some censorship undoubtedly existed. With defeating Germany and Japan the over-riding priority, few people insisted on an unrestricted right to information in total war. Patriotism, and an identity of interest between state and media (from which the profit motive was not wholly absent) were the lubricants of the seemingly open but not entirely voluntary systems of media management favoured in Britain and America. When Balfour writes that the MOI's censorship system was 'based on bluff, goodwill (for no editor wanted to help the Germans) and the realisation that, if it broke down, a much more vexatious compulsory scheme would substituted', his words could serve as summation of transatlantic practice as a whole (1979, 60).

3
Media and 'Limited War'

America's military involvement in Vietnam – though it ended over twenty years ago – still casts a long shadow over both countries. The war fought by America in Vietnam also indelibly marked military-media relations, not just in the USA but in much of the Western and non-Western worlds alike. Conflicts since America finally left Vietnam in 1975 have often been conducted – or avoided – with various 'lessons' of Vietnam kept firmly in mind. Americans acrimoniously continue to dispute the rights and wrongs of a war which, in the eyes of some, could have been won, and of others, should never have been fought at all. But for all the controversy surrounding a war which irrevocably changed American society, 'the view that, for better or worse, television turned the American public against the war... probably comes as close as anything to being conventional wisdom' – a shared lesson to which many have subscribed (Hallin, 1989, 105–6).

Many believed – and some continue to hold – that television lost the war in Vietnam by turning American viewers steadily against their country's military commitment in South-East Asia. Vietnam was, it is often repeated, the first 'television war'. Television 'news-reels' having played a rather minor role in reporting the Korean War (1950–3), Vietnam was the first conflict to receive sustained, almost nightly, coverage on the US networks over a period of several years. It was also the first war to benefit from certain technological advances – the use of satellites especially – which made reporting more immediate, and this at a time when American network news first assumed a half-hour format. That more and more Americans regarded television as their primary source of news during the 1960s further confirmed the impression that there *must* be a profound causal connection between television's coverage of the war in Vietnam and declining popular support for it. America's first 'living room war' (as Michael Arlen termed it) was also America's least successful war. For many observers, the latter could only be a direct consequence of the former (Arlen, 1982; Mandelbaum, 1982; Hallin, 1989, 105). The lesson seemed obvious: a war which was nightly screened on television could not be won. Nixon pondered in his 1978 memoirs whether 'America would ever again be able to fight an enemy abroad with unity and strength of purpose at home' (Hallin, 1989, 3). But this worry was not restricted to Americans. The British broadcaster, Robin Day, also famously questioned 'if in future a democracy which has uninhibited television coverage in every home will ever be able to fight a war, however just... The full brutality of the combat will be there in close up and colour and blood looks very red on the colour television screen' (Hooper, 1982, 116).

Day's rhetorical question has never really been tested by subsequent experience, for the simple reason that so many militaries have concurred with his basic hypothesis – unfettered coverage precludes military victory – that they have determined not to prove, at their own cost, the wisdom of his words. The 'Vietnam syndrome' (fear of entangling foreign conflicts and declining popular enthusiasm for them) has meant that one is hard pressed indeed to find a more recent war with 'uninhibited television coverage', no matter who the combatants, be they democratic or otherwise. The belief that 'television wars' and military victories are mutually exclusive certainly had a profound influence over the British Ministry of Defence (MOD). During the conflict over the Falklands/Malvinas islands in 1982, the MOD, aided by logistical circumstances which themselves seriously impeded media coverage, determined not to repeat the American military's perceived mistakes, and duly kept the media on a tight rein. A 'successful' (though not wholly uncontroversial) media war, and quick military victory, ensured that the MOD's experience shaped future Pentagon thinking on military-media relations. The MOD's imprint can thus be detected in the US Department of Defence's attempted total exclusion of reporters during the 1983 Grenada invasion, and its modified media pool system deployed in Panama in 1989 (Adams, 1986; Mercer, Mungham and Williams, 1987; Sharkey, 1991; Young and Jesser, 1997).

Restrictions on reporting in Grenada and Panama in turn influenced controls over the media during the 1991 Gulf War, though the American military also tried to improve its relations with the media to the point where journalists would willingly tolerate wartime infringements. Rather than excluding the media altogether from the scene of military operations – as had been attempted during the Grenada intervention – the Pentagon realised that allowing 'fettered' media access was preferable to an unworkable, and resented, blanket ban. The American military was not alone in attempting to learn from its past mistakes: so too did Saddam Hussein. Also believing that the Vietnam War had been lost in American living rooms, he tried to orchestrate a repeat perform-ance by providing the international (especially US) media with access to scenes of devastation in Iraq. His hope was that American audiences would prove equally sensitive to Iraqi suffering as they had towards their own casualties in Vietnam, and demand a hasty end to the US-led operation. Saddam Hussein miscalculated, but the fact he made the calculation at all is a powerful testament to the enduring legacy of the Vietnam War (P. Taylor, 1992, 10–12).

Although the 'Vietnam Syndrome' still seems alive and well amongst policy-makers (as evidenced, for example, by White House sensitivity in 1993 to media images from Somalia), the con-ventional wisdom concerning the media's role in the original 'living room war' has not gone unchallenged. Indeed much recent scholar-ship raises fundamental questions about the nature of media effects (particularly television's), asking us to scrutinise more closely the presumed correlation between television coverage of Vietnam and declining public support for the war. That American popular sup-port for the war dwindled as it wore on is undeniable: that television instigated this turn-around is more questionable, despite the unshakeable belief in some quarters that this was so. 'Lessons' about the media have certainly been extracted from American experience in Vietnam, but quite possibly inappropriate, misleading or insupportable conclusions have been drawn. Critical scrutiny of media behaviour in 'limited war' suggests that many cherished notions about the media – their antagonistic relations with authority and sway over the audience – may require substantial revision.

Vietnam: The Conventional Wisdom

America became steadily more enmeshed in Vietnam as it increas-ingly shouldered the financial burden of the French attempt to

regain its former colony from Ho Chi Minh's Communist Nationalists after the Second World War, and then assumed primary
responsibility (once Vietnam was partitioned in 1954) for ensuring
that the South did not fall to the Communist North. But if it was
hard to say when America's war in Vietnam started – 'you couldn't
find two people who agreed about when it began', observed Michael
Herr – the North's victorious march into Saigon in April 1975
represented a decisive full-stop (1978, 46). The reunification of
Vietnam under Hanoi's Communist regime left Nixon's 'peace
with honour' looking like nothing but a euphemism for defeat,
with little honourable in televised scenes showing the undignified
scramble of Vietnamese and Americans frantically trying to board
the last US helicopters to leave Saigon. As defeat was not a condition to which Americans were accustomed, the apportioning of
blame became a matter of intense national preoccupation and
dispute.

The First World War generated an influential 'stab-in-the-back'
legend concerning the role of foreign media and propaganda in
Germany's defeat. But after Vietnam, the most compelling 'stab-
in-the-back' theory was yet more alarming: the US military had
been undermined by America's *own* media, who thwarted victory
by 'graphic and unremitting distortion' of the facts, pessimism, and
unvarnished depiction of both America's youthful casualties and
American 'atrocities' inflicted on the Vietnamese (Elegant, 1981,
73–90). Sensational and unbalanced coverage undercut home front
determination to persist with the protracted business of shoring up
the South against Communism, fuelling an increasingly vociferous
peace movement. And, in the eyes of some military critics and
politicians, the media precluded prosecution of the war by the
most appropriate military means. In their opinion, intensive bombing of North Vietnam, Laos and Cambodia (where the North Vietnamese forces re-grouped and re-provisioned themselves), could
have produced an outright military victory, but the media effectively
ruled this out as they would have shown bombardment's human
costs, and these would not have been tolerated by ordinary Americans (Kimball, 1988, 433–58). As Ronald Reagan put it, Vietnam
was a war from which American soldiers 'came home without a
victory, not because they'd been defeated but because they'd been
denied permission to win' (cited in Kimball, 1988, 439). The military
had been forced to fight with one hand tied behind their back.

By harnessing public squeamishness in a time of limited war, the media had served to limit military options to the point at which victory became untenable. Limited war thus ended in unlimited humiliation.

The belief that the media 'lost the war' in Vietnam has many different variants. Not all its exponents blame journalists alone, and neither do all who accept the proposition that media (especially television) destroyed public support for the war bemoan this state of affairs. Some of its champions are to be found within the journalistic profession itself. Correspondents who opposed aspects of the war's prosecution (if not America's involvement *per se*) sometimes proudly represent their role in Vietnam as a classic case of Thomas Paine's 'Fourth Estate' in operation. During the war, according to David Halberstam (at the time a young Saigon-based reporter for the *New York Times*, who famously aroused Kennedy's ire), reporters simply sought out and told 'the story' (cited by Hallin, 1989, 6). In so doing, they revealed the unjust ways in which a war, which may itself have been just, was being fought, ultimately calling a halt to it. Media thus served, as they should in a liberal democracy, as watchdog upon the state: a role which did not always lead to a harmonious relationship been the two. Acrimony between the press corps and government or military officials was indeed evident, on many occasions, in both Saigon and Washington (Wyatt, 1993; Arnett, 1995). But in the eyes of such journalists (and also some peace campaigners), the media's role in Vietnam was creditable not craven, for the war did not ultimately deserve to be won. Other journalists conceive their role more passively, however. Reporters simply showed 'the American people to the American people', as David Brinkley put it, and if the public recoiled accordingly, then one must blame those whose actions repelled, not the mirror itself (Hallin, 1989, 5). More commonly, though, those who argue that the media were responsible for America's 'defeat' in Vietnam do so in a spirit of condemnation, not congratulation.

The journalists who covered the war from the ground in Vietnam have been copiously criticised: by politicians, the military, and certain of their colleagues. Sometimes older versions of the young men who toured Vietnam with notebook in hand have passed highly critical retrospective verdicts on their younger selves. Indeed, 'orthodox' critics often regard youthfulness as one root of media irresponsibility in Vietnam, for cub journalists had something to prove – a name to make – and the easiest way to do so was by being critical of authority. In the early 1960s (when Washington was surreptitiously augmenting its consignment of 'military advisers' to South Vietnam), according to General William C. Westmoreland:

> Saigon...was one of the world's less desirable assignments for newsmen. A faraway, alien place, it had little attraction for American readers, so that nothing short of the sensational was likely to gain space in the newsman's home newspaper. Finding fault was one way to achieve the sensational, and finding fault with an Oriental regime with little background in or respect for Western-style democracy was easy. (cited by Thayer, 1992, 91)

The natural tendency of youth, in other words, was to criticise. Moreover, because in the early days Vietnam was a distant country of which Americans knew nothing, to see their by-line in print at all young reporters had to root out – or invent – something newsworthy.

As far as Westmoreland and others are concerned, a combination of youth (some 51 per cent of reporters were aged under 29, he claimed) and the dictates of a sensation-seeking profession ensured that journalists were adversarial (cited by Hammond, 1989, 313). Vietnam marked the start of an age of investigative journalism – reaching its apogee during the Watergate scandal – in which old habits of journalistic objectivity were abandoned in favour of a deliberately confrontational attitude towards authority. Journalists now saw themselves not as passive mirrors reflecting the world as it was but as active agents in remaking the world as it should be. Westmoreland complained that 'American newsmen in Saigon... confused reporting with influencing policy', and his view was not confined to military ranks. Robert Elegant (a former *Los Angeles Times* reporter) opined, in a famous *Encounter* article of 1981:

> The American press...somehow felt obliged to be less objective than partisan, to take sides, for it was inspired by the *engagé* 'investigative' reporting that burgeoned in the United States in these impassioned years. The press was instinctively 'agin the government' – and, at least reflexively, for Saigon's enemies. (Elegant, 1981, 73)

Youth was also coupled with inexperience. It did not help that many remained 'in country' for a tour of only eighteen months or so (Elegant, 1981, 140). They could never therefore adequately rectify their deficient knowledge of the Vietnamese language and culture (Kaplan, 1982, 47). And their knowledge of military matters was equally woeful: 'few...understood the differences between, say 'a mortar and a howitzer, brigades and divisions, logistics and tactics', complained Braestrup (1994, 12). This ignorance was often compared unfavourably with the informed, empathetic relationship between the military and journalistic old-hands in both the Second World War and Korea, which might suggest that the more worrying deficiency, in military eyes, was less the journalists' prior ignorance than their perceived lack of deference towards the military. No wonder, then, that the Administration offered 'official "gilt-edge" invitations to veteran correspondents of two wars back', who duly rebuked their young colleagues for wanting to see America 'lose the war to prove they're right' (Rigg, 1969, 22; Marguerite Higgins, cited by Arnett, 1995, 34).

While reporters of all types have come under fire, television journalists – and, more generally, television as a medium – have attracted specific criticism for their presumed role in Vietnam, the 'first television war'. Conservative critics have found television an attractive scapegoat for all manner of presumed social ills, such as the breakdown of deference to authority and corresponding upsurge of popular radicalism, witnessed in the civil rights, women's liberation and anti-war movements. But more specific claims about television news and its part in America's Vietnamese downfall have also been frequently mooted.

For a majority of Americans, television became the predominant medium for acquiring news, a development which coincided with the Vietnam War (Hallin, 1989, 106). Television thus gained a quantitative edge over its print media rivals in sheer audience size (newspaper readership additionally being spread widely across numerous different titles). But as a visual medium, television also qualitatively differs from older media in its impact on the individual. Images are naively trusted as the unvarnished truth – the camera's inability to lie being widely believed – whereas newspaper columns are greeted with greater scepticism as the work of fallible and opinionated human columnists. As Schudson puts it: 'the general understanding behind the "television-turned-us-against-the-war" argument is that TV photography comes to us unmediated – it forces itself upon the viewer, who then recoils from war' (1995, 118). Thus Robert Elegant's rueful verdict: 'Television, its thrusting and simplistic character shaping its message, was most shocking because it was most immediate. The Viet Nam War was a presence in homes throughout the world. Who could seriously doubt the veracity of so plausible and so moving a witness in one's own living room?' (1981, 77–8). But being a 'thrusting and simplistic' medium it delivered a grotesquely distorted version of the war. Television news, bemoaned Westmoreland, had to be 'compressed and visually dramatic'. The medium consequently dictated the message with disastrous consequences: 'the war that Americans saw was almost exclusively violent, miserable, or controversial: guns firing, men falling, helicopters crashing, buildings toppling, huts burning, refugees fleeing, women wailing' (cited by Thayer (1992) 93). Gorging on violence and sensation, television had no appetite for *good* news: 'Only scant attention was paid to pacification, civic action, medical assistance, the way life went on in a generally normal way for most the people much of the time' (Thayer, 1992, 93; Elegant, 1981, 78–80).

As far as such critics are concerned, television predominantly played on negative themes – death and destruction – and its images lent themselves to anti-war interpretation alone. Some television journalists concurred. CBS's Morley Safer stated in 1966 that 'on its own every piece of war film takes on a certain antiwar character, simply because it does not glamourise or romanticize. In battle men do not die with a clean shot through the heart; they are blown to pieces. Television tells it that way' (cited by Fox, 1995, 141). To mitigate this negativity, television news required not only more positive images of America's efforts on behalf of South Vietnam but also an interpretative framework to settle disturbing images contextually. Lack of context was singled out by Nixon as a particular problem with Vietnam reportage:

In each night's TV news and each morning's paper the war was reported battle by battle, but little or no sense of the underlying purpose of the fighting was conveyed. Eventually this contributed to the impression that we were fighting in military and moral quicksand, rather than toward an important and worthwhile objective. (Hallin, 1989, 3)

His criticism echoes the remark of US Government information officer, Barry Zorthian, to the press on 7 July 1968: 'Sometimes I think the press has over-covered the war, almost to the point of obfuscation...we are too close to the trees and we forget about the forest' (Rigg, 1969, 24).

Theirs is not the common complaint that American correspondents ceased to be objective. Rather, Nixon and Zorthian seem obliquely to attack objective journalism, with its rigid separation of 'fact' and 'comment', by suggesting that the accretion of numerous facts may add up to a lie – or at least a misleading interpretation of the whole – when 'facts' lack adequate explanation. Conversely, critics of the war also sometimes claim that the media got closer to the larger truth about the war when it got the 'facts' muddled, as in the case of Tet, which television wrongly presented as a US defeat, but rightly interpreted as evidence that the war was a hopeless quagmire (Hallin, 1989, 173; Seib, 1997, 22–3). For Nixon and Zorthian, the missing context was an optimistic spin on events, which would encourage readers or viewers to recognise that, even if the pictures looked grim, the war itself was not going badly, as the nature of the task was inevitably protracted. But television, in particular, was poorly suited to providing this long-term view, and accordingly depressed its viewers with superficially pessimistic daily round-ups (Hooper, 1982, 115).

For many critics, the failings of the media were exemplified by their treatment of the Tet Offensive of February 1968. During the traditional celebrations for the new lunar year, the North Vietnamese and their supporters in the South (whom the Americans termed the Vietcong) launched a series of uprisings in towns and cities across the Southern Vietnam. For the first time, war exploded on to the streets, during daylight. Hitherto, in the words of Michael Herr, 'night was the war's truest medium; night was when it got really interesting in the villages, the TV crews couldn't film at night' (1978, 40). 'Search and destroy' operations, in pursuit of an elusive and usually invisible enemy, did not lend themselves to filming, at night or otherwise. But during Tet, journalists – of whom there were now some 464 as against 20-odd in 1964 – had only to step from their hotels to find themselves 'willy nilly in the midst of bloody fighting' (Epstein cited by Williams, 1993, 310). By its nature, the offensive offered itself to more intensive reporting than war in the jungle. But what to report? The mosaic of country-wide attacks –

and resultant Communist victories and set-backs – was undoubtedly hard to piece together but, according to the critics, the media fitted the pieces in such a way as to create an unrecognisable portrait of Tet. The result of the offensive, in Peter Braestrup's words, was 'a severe military-political setback for Hanoi in the South', but 'the dominant themes of the words and film from Vietnam ... added up to a portrait of defeat for the allies ... a continuous black fog ... a vague, conventional "disaster" image, which few newsmen attempted to re-examine and which few managers at home sought to question' (Braestrup, 1989, 153–4).

What, then, did the (mis)reporting of Tet reveal? For Braestrup (a print journalist, who retrospectively conducted an exhaustive content analysis of press and television coverage of the Offensive), it exposed various in-built limitations of media war-reporting, and the acquired pessimism which had cast a pervasive pall over the press corps by 1968. He did not, however, detect concerted ideological opposition to the war as such (1994). For Westmoreland and Elegant, the tendentious reporting of Tet was more wilful and malicious on the journalists' part, confirming their habitually hostile stance towards America's ally: 'most South Vietnamese units fought well, but it was not the "in thing" in media circles to say anything good about the South Vietnamese. The media misled the American people by their reporting of "Tet", and even a number of officials in Washington were taken in' (Westmoreland, 1979, 38). Arguably, even President Johnson himself was 'taken in'. According to Halberstam, Vietnam was 'the first time in history a war had been declared over by an anchorman' (cited by Hallin, 1989, 168). The man in question was Walter Cronkite, whose verdict on the war, delivered on 27 February 1968 – 'To say that we are mired in stalemate seems the only realistic, yet unsatisfactory conclusion' – allegedly persuaded Johnson to withdraw from the 1968 Presidential race (Hallin, 1989, 170; Seib, 1997, 19). Cronkite was America's 'most trusted man'. Consequently if the Administration had lost Cronkite, it had lost America, and Johnson's press secretary, George Christian, later related that 'shock waves rolled through the government' after the CBS broadcast (Turner, 1985, 232). On 31 March 1968, Johnson duly announced his decision not to run for a second term. In a speech to the National Association of Broadcasters delivered on 1 April, he made clear that they were in many respects responsible for his decision:

As I sat in my office last evening, waiting to speak, I thought of the many times each week when television brings the war into the American home. No one can say exactly what effect those vivid scenes have on American opinion. Historians must only guess at the effect that television would have had during earlier conflicts on the future of this nation: during the Korean war, for example, at that time when our forces were pushed back to Pusan; or World War II, the Battle of the Bulge, or when our men were slugging it out in Europe or when most of our Air Force was shot down that day in June 1942 off Australia. (cited by MacArthur, 1993, 133)

The lesson Johnson clearly culled from this exercise in counter-factual history was that victory in previous wars would have been similarly jeopardised by television's 'daily barrage of bleakness and near panic' (cited by Turner, 1985, 233).

However, for some critics, responsibility for journalistic failings must be more evenly spread. If reporters got important 'facts' – or broader interpretation of the war – wrong, then the fault lay partly with those on whom they relied most heavily for their information: namely, official briefers (whether in the White House, Pentagon, or 'in-country'). Various commentators have accordingly suggested that the emergence of oppositional reporting can be attributed (at least in part) to a failure of official 'spinning': the policy-making and military elite lost the narrative thread, and failed to offer a convincing framework of interpretation for the war (Seib, 1997, 17–18). This shortcoming was particularly evident in the wake of the Tet Offensive, when Johnson more or less resigned himself to negative coverage (as well as to his own resignation) and ceased even trying to manage news presentation on the Capitol (Turner, 1985). With the anti-war Democrat presidential contender Eugene McCarthy doing unexpectedly well in the New Hampshire primaries, the pro-test movement now attracted mainstream media attention and a certain respectability (Hallin, 1989, 197).

The US military also stand accused of inept media management. Writing as early as 1969, Colonel Rigg, for one, acknowledged that the military had not helped journalists to find meaningful ways of reporting a war which defied explanation according to conventional military indices. Feeding the journalists' and public's apparently insatiable appetite for statistics, the military cooked up endless data revealing the 'body count', the 'kill ratio', the areas 'pacified'. But, as Rigg acknowledged, neither such figures nor the ubiquitous maps (showing areas cleansed of, or suffering under, Viet Cong influence) made any sense during a war in which American physical control over territory – in so far as it could be ascertained – was no indicator that America was 'winning'. Neither did statistics of enemy personnel killed provide much illumination, for the North obdu-rately resisted erosion, seemingly able to produce endless new recruits in the face of US 'attrition' (1969, 14–24). Moreover, the 'facts' (for what they were worth) were sometimes distorted so as to bolster the optimistic account of the war's progress which official military briefers unerringly presented to the press corps at the daily briefings known as the 'Five O'clock Follies' (Kaplan, 1982, 43). US Mission information chief, John Mecklin, insisted that 'no respons-ible US official in Saigon ever told a newsman a really big falsehood, instead there were endless little ones' (see Braestrup, 1994, 3.) But in constantly proclaiming that the statistics revealed how well the war was progressing – with light visible at the end of the tunnel – they eventually fell into a trap of their own making (Rigg, 1969, 20). The trap took the form of a 'credibility gap'. Once it became clear that the war was not going swimmingly, journalists ceased to accept the military briefers' word and sought more pessimistic sources which accorded with the evidence of their own eyes. Tet was a notable case where journalists' personal experience directly contra-dicted the military line, unswervingly repeated, however implausi-ble. As a result, Halberstam believes that 'the credibility of the American strategy of attrition died during the Tet Offensive', with Secretary of State Clark Clifford concurring that 'the most serious casualty at Tet was the loss of the public's confidence in its leaders' (see Seib, 1997, 22).

The 'Lessons of Vietnam' in Practice

Those who diagnosed a fatal back-stabbing as the cause of Amer-ica's failure in Vietnam determined to ensure that the media could not lose a war again. For some, such as Rigg, one lesson was that the military themselves needed to become more accurate, and less up-beat, in the news they released to reporters. More commonly, though, officials accentuated the need for tighter control over the media in future wars. Amongst its many stock epithets – 'living room war', 'television war' – Vietnam has also been memorialised as the 'uncensored war', and its loss has often been attributed to this very lack of censorship. Unlike correspondents in the Second World War or Korea, American reporters had unparalleled freedom, even military assistance, to roam South Vietnam; they were helicoptered, more or less on demand, to destinations of their choice, where they could freely interview military personnel and accompany them into action. The stories they subsequently produced were not subjected to routine censorship by the US military, whose generosity and trust many of its members felt the press corps had betrayed.

Given that many 'orthodox' critics ascribe to the media certain endemic flaws and depressant uni-directional effects, it is scarcely surprising that militaries, post-Vietnam, should have repeatedly mooted censorship of copy and control of access as the most appropriate ways to mitigate damaging coverage. If the leopard cannot change it spots, it can nevertheless be kept behind bars, with claws neatly trimmed. Reporters – if they were not to be excluded altogether from the theatre of military operations (as was attempted during the invasion of Grenada in 1983) – accordingly require more effective shackling by the state. Few military planners were minded to allow unfettered journalists a chance to redeem themselves. Vietnam seemed to prove that patriotism alone would not keep journalists 'on side' in time of limited war. And if the media could not simply be entreated to 'show a more convincing sense of responsibility', as Westmoreland put it, then in future conflicts they would have to be compelled to toe the line, by means both positive and negative.

The Falklands/Malvinas Conflict (1982)

Unlike the Vietnam or Gulf Wars, the Falklands/Malvinas conflict is unlikely to contend for the title of history's 'most reported' war. Commentators disagree over the extent to which the journalists' impediments were primarily dictated by the peculiar logistical problems of reporting events while shipbound in the Atlantic and then from dry land 8000 miles from Britain, or by an official reluctance to provide adequate facilities to the media, which compounded an inherently difficult situation. As Derrik Mercer puts it, 'hardly ever have circumstances been more propitious for a censor than they were for the British in the Falklands' (Mercer, 1984, 39). The outcome was a war which, despite being fought in 1982, was not a 'television war'. Indeed for much of its duration it was not even a pictorial war, with despatches on occasion taking longer to reach London than had William Howard Russell's report of the Charge of the Light Brigade in 1854 (Mercer, 1984, 39). In the words of photographer, Martin Cleaver, 'It wasn't a news war, it's as simple as that. It was in the wrong place' (Morrison and Tumber, 1988, 1). In many respects, then, this was an anachronistic conflict: a war fought without the full benefits of late twentieth-century communications technology over the fruits of nineteenth-century imperialism, with Argentina laying physical claim to islands it referred to as the Islas Malvinas, over which Westminster was determined to maintain British sovereignty (Adams, 1986).

Picking the Team

The battle for the Falklands/Malvinas islands was covered 'first hand' by remarkably few correspondents, all of them British, with one lone Reuters representative on board to serve the international press. The circumstances by which the chosen ones came to sail with the Task Force are suggestive of at least as good a measure of cockup as conspiracy on the military's part. Certainly, news of the Argentinian capture of the islands on 2 April 1982 seemed to catch much of Whitehall off-guard. At the Ministry of Defence, there were apparently no current standard guidelines for military-media relations in wartime (despite the British Army's long-standing engagement in Northern Ireland). A 1977 brief on 'Information Policy' was apparently forgotten, or rejected, and the first act of Ian McDonald (the MOD's acting head of Public Relations, who found himself on duty in the hour of need) was to close and lock his door 'trying to think it out for five minutes' (Foster, 1992, 155–6). Preparations for the media's role in the forthcoming – and still only putative – clash with Argentina therefore had to be devised haphazardly. 'Rules' governing who would cover military operations, what they would be allowed to report, and how they would find the technical means for doing, so evolved in an *ad hoc* fashion.

McDonald's own preference was to have correspondents flown out to Ascension Island, joining the armada of Royal Navy vessels comprising the 'Task Force' mid-way through its journey to the

South Atlantic. This would have given the MOD and media organisations two weeks' leave of grace to assemble, and prepare, a press corps. However, the Navy vetoed this plan on the grounds (it later transpired) that journalists might have seen Ascension's lack of air defence (R. Harris, 1983, 17–18). Abandonment of McDonald's scheme meant that if journalists were to fulfil an 'eye witness' role at all, then they would have to sail with the Task Force at only a few hours' notice. Doubtless many in the Navy – mindful of Churchill's First World War dictum that 'a warship in action has no room for a journalist' – would have been more than happy to sail without 'pencil warriors' (Knightley, 1989, 87). Journalists not only were wont to jeopardise military security by constantly searching for 'scoops', but, in naval eyes, were also bulky cargo. As one officer wrote later: 'Space on board ship was very limited and for every war correspondent carried a Marine or Para had to be left behind. This of itself was a risk where the forces engaged were so small' (Le Bailly, 1983, 187). One disgruntled journalist pointed out lack of space did not prevent the Task Force from sailing with thousands of Mars bars for the forces' sustenance, but the unavoidably cramped conditions certainly provided the official explanation (not universally accepted) for the press corps' diminutive size, and the inability of the Task Force to accommodate overseas journalists (R. Harris, 1983, 24).

In the end, 29 British journalists accompanied the Task Force, largely on three different ships. Twenty-nine represented a considerable improvement on McDonald's original plan for ten, of whom five would represent the BBC and Independent Television News (ITN) and five the press in its entirety. Ferocious lobbying of 10 Downing Street by Fleet Street editors, enraged by the shortage of places and unrepresentativeness of those randomly allotted them, led Thatcher's Press Secretary (Bernard Ingham, himself a former columnist) to make a personal intervention on behalf of the press (Ingham, 1991, 285–8). With the Prime Minister's backing, a request for extra places could scarcely be refused by the Navy. But the enlarged team now had to be assembled within hours, making the selection of individual reporters every bit as haphazard as the decision to enlarge the corps.

Some critical commentators insist that the MOD itself hand-picked preferred journalists (notably Max Hastings, then of the London *Standard*, an outspoken champion of the Armed Forces), while denying *personae non grata* places, such as war photographer Donald McCullin, known for his gritty realism (Glasgow University Media Group, 1985; Foster, 1992, 158–9). The MOD later almost corroborated the first charge – Hastings would have been approached but was literally 'on board' in any case – while rejecting the view that McCullin was denied a place for any more sinister reason than lack of space (Morrison and Tumber, 1988, 6). However plausible, or not, one finds these explanations, it does appear that most journalists were selected by their own media organisations, and often for entirely arbitrary reasons: who happened to be available at short notice; who was 'expendable', for what some editors envisaged as little more than a 'boating holiday', as the editor of BBC television news put it (R. Harris, 1983, 22; Morrison and Tumber, 1988, 5–7). Few editors, or the reporters they picked, apparently anticipated a full-blown war (even if never formally declared as such), and many journalists embarked with little more than a toothbrush and change of underwear. With the exception of a few who kitted themselves out almost as thoroughly as Evelyn Waugh's hapless journalist, Boot (the unlikely hero of his satirical novel *Scoop*), most of the 29 were under-equipped in every possible way for the weeks to come: physically unfit; psychologically unprepared for war; and every bit as ignorant of matters military as their counterparts in Vietnam.

Reporting Restrictions

Finding themselves afloat with this motley crew of journalists, the military had to decide how they would regulate reporters' behaviour, check their copy, and transmit it back from the ships to London. As the flotilla set sail, much was still unclear about how 'censorship' would operate. The official position throughout was that none was practised, but as two reporters observed at the time, the system used looked 'remarkably like it' (Robert Low and Patrick Bishop, *The Observer*, 9 May 1982). Logistics enabled the military to regulate almost every aspect of the reporters' lives, and they duly made use of these advantages, adding a number of specific 'dont's' to what was already impracticable. Correspondents were issued with accreditation papers, which were dutifully signed, if not read. On 7 April, Sir Frank Cooper (MOD Permanent Under Secretary of State) laid down various guidelines for editors in

London as to what they could not cover, while officers and crews were briefed on what was they could discuss with their journalist ship-mates. Eight topics were deemed inadmissible: speculation about possible future action; plans for operations; operational capabilities and readiness of individual units; details about military techniques and tactics; logistical details; intelligence about Argentine forces; equipment capabilities and defects; and communications (R. Harris, 1983, 26).

With so much ruled out of bounds, and journalists regarded as belonging to an inherently untrustworthy profession, it fell to the MOD's civilian public relations officers – or 'minders' – to strike offensive passages from their charges' copy. Nicknamed, without much affection, the 'thought police', these rapidly assembled censors were generally unloved by shipbound reporters and sailors alike. As 'non-uniformed "foreign bodies"', the minders were met with hostility by the military, 'keenly aware of rank and insignia, or the lack of them' (Morrison and Tumber, 1988, 14). To the reporters, the minders were failed hacks (former reporters of small-town papers), who lacked sufficient authority to tell them what they could – or could not – report, and were uncomprehending of the pressures imposed by Fleet Street (R. Harris, 1983, 28). To make matters worse, the minders also had responsibility for transmitting copy back to the MOD in London, where it was vetted again by press officers to ensure it did not breach three specially issued D-notices. In the atmosphere of mutual suspicion (and in some cases outright contempt and loathing), which quickly developed between the journalists and their minders, the former tended to attribute difficulties with transmission to deliberate foul-play by the latter, rightly or wrongly. Certainly, there appear to have been many cases where copy construed as critical was 'mislaid', or tardily referred back to its author for further 'fact-checking', and such copy was often useless if delayed.

Officially, no censorship existed. Copy was vetted purely on grounds of security, to ensure that nothing potentially useful to the Argentinians was let slip. However, some journalists not only suspected that certain stories were wilfully 'mislaid' but were equally adamant that the MOD breached its Second World War-style promise not to interfere with matters of tone. *The Observer*'s Patrick Bishop insisted that 'stories that might sap morale' were 'discouraged'. Sensitive to copy or imagery which might reflect poorly on the troops, the MOD withheld certain facts, and tampered with tone. A story written by Independent Radio News' Kim Sabido about British troops spitting on local 'bum-boats' when the *Canberra* docked at Freetown, Sierra Leone, was spiked (Bishop, 1982, 6). Less controversially, the minders were also extremely prickly about the writing up of British losses, most dramatically those incurred by the sinking of *Sir Galahad* (Morrison and Tumber, 1988, 57; Foster, 1992, 161).

By the time the journalists went ashore, according to Bishop:

> it was obvious that anything which reflected badly on the troops, their behaviour or competence, would never get past the censors ... Essentially the journalists were regarded by the MoD as public relations men for the Task Force. Their job was to record good news, look for silver linings if things went wrong, praise the qualities of the fighting men and the equipment they used, and steer clear of anything that could be remotely construed as negative (1982, 7).

Bishop was not alone in his estimation of how the minders regarded their role. The BBC's radio correspondent recalled being told after the Argentinian attack on *Sir Galahad*, 'We only want you to print good news.' Many of the corps consequently felt that they were seen as accessories to a military propaganda effort, not as purveyors of information: a view buttressed by the (alleged) comment of the minder on *Hermes* that journalists were expected to do 'a 1940 propaganda job' (Cockerell, 1988, 270).

Means of transmission

Writing a story which met with the minders' approval was one thing; getting it transmitted back to London was quite another. After three days at sea, radio silence was imposed over the fleet. Two of the ships carrying journalists had secure communications equipment, enabling them to continue filing their stories, but *Sir Lancelot* did not, to the frustration of its consignment of journalists. Utterly reliant on their hosts for facilities to transmit their copy, the journalists found that naval attitudes towards them varied considerably. As a result, being able to despatch stories to London – or not – often depended as much on how favourably disposed the ship's captain was towards journalists as on the communications capability of the vessel concerned.

If transmission was at best difficult on the voyage down to the disputed islands, after landing conditions became even more perilous for the journalists. Daunted by battlefield conditions, reporters had to weigh up the pros and cons of accompanying the troops into action. If they went, they gained eyewitness authority but lacked the means to transmit their copy. If they stayed on board, they had no first-hand material but the ability to transmit second-hand versions. Some chose the latter course, but (to the annoyance of their embattled colleagues who had ventured ashore) tried to pass off poached details, or entirely fictitious battle reports, as stories personally observed. Those who went ashore, on the other hand, were often frustrated that accounts of the battle, entrusted to the hands of helicopter pilots for despatch back to the shipbound minders for onward transmission, subsequently disappeared without trace (Morrison and Tumber, 1988, 187).

Few would dispute, however, that by far the worst logistical problems confronted the television journalists and their crews. Whereas print reporters could, just about, do their job, the television teams found theirs virtually impossible, at least by peacetime standards. Whether the conflict could have been a 'television war', with greater willingness to ensure the facilities for satellite broadcasting on the part of the British military and government, has been much debated. When this contentious issue was raised by the House of Commons Defence Select Committee, in its post-war hearings on the MOD's handling of the media, both the BBC and Independent Television (ITV) insisted that the government lacked the will to televise the war adequately. In his evidence to the Committee, the BBC Assistant Director-General, Alan Protheroe, asserted:

> I have no doubt at all that if the Government had said, "Call in the best brains in the British electronic industry," and locked them up in a hotel for a weekend and said, "Now...let's hack this problem," they would have found a solution. I still believe it was possible. The problem was that it was too low a priority. (cited by Morrison and Tumber, 1988, 164)

It certainly seems that, for at least part of the journey to the South Atlantic, footage could have been screened in black and white on television, with pictures transmitted via the British military satellite, SKYNET, from the larger Naval vessels. But the military were reluctant to relinquish so much of their system's bandwidth, and colour pictures would have exceeded its capabilities altogether (Morrison and Tumber, 1988, 164–6). From South Georgia onwards, use of SKYNET would also have required a ship to be stationed permanently in the satellite's footprint, and this too would have diverted precious resources. While the war itself actually lasted, pictures could have been transmitted from land-based terminals via the American DISCUS satellite, had the American government been willing to tilt the satellite in the direction of the Falklands, but responses to informal soundings of the Pentagon dissuaded the MOD from pursuing the matter further (R. Harris, 1983, 58; Morrison and Tumber, 1988, 167).

In the absence of such initiatives, the television correspondents Brian Hanrahan and Mike Nicholson found themselves reduced virtually to the role of radio correspondents. Piecing together stories from their print colleagues' copy, the two television reporters had to be winched from the *Hermes* to an auxiliary ship, the *Olmeda*, which was equipped with the secure marine satellite phone system, 'Marisat', down which they could relay their voice reports (R. Harris, 1983, 33). Footage *was* shot, but as it could not be beamed homewards by satellite, video reports had to be taken by helicopter, or ship, to Ascension for the onward journey by plane. It was a cumbersome process, though precisely how slow seems to have varied considerably, depending on the sense of urgency attached to getting the footage back – anywhere between nine and twenty-one days, according to ITN's submission to the post-war inquiry. Thus by the time videotape reached London (where it, like print copy, was again reviewed by the MOD), it was almost like the 'Dead Sea scrolls' according to ITN editor, David Nicholas: of historical interest, but hardly the topical stuff of news (R. Harris, 1983, 56). A similar criticism also applied to still photographs: the observable trend whereby 'good news' images arrived expeditiously suggested that something beyond haphazard logistics determined speed of despatch. In short, the MOD appeared to accord preference to heartening images, such as Tom Smith's of villagers offering a Marine a cup of tea ('Cuppa for a Brave Para', as it was captioned in the *Sunday Mirror*), rather than grittier depictions of battle, such as Martin Cleaver's of the

Antelope exploding (Morrison and Tumber, 1988, 181–3; J. Taylor, 1991, 92–6).

To broadcasters, these various anomalies were indicative of wilful interference with the visual representation of the war by the MOD, and it was partly because the absence of television footage became such a vexed issue that a Committee of Inquiry was later constituted. Ultimately, the inquiry refused to adjudicate between state and broadcasters on the issue of deliberate obstructiveness, concluding that the mere existence of a motive for dishonesty (on the government's and military's part) was not proof they *had* behaved dishonestly (Morrison and Tumber, 1988, 164). But in defending themselves against the broadcasters' charges, military, government and civil service representatives were in fact remarkably candid in their acknowledgement that television was regarded as a hindrance, making the Committee's absolution of those eager (from political as much as military motives) to keep 'damaging' footage from the screen perhaps rather generous (Glasgow University Media Group, 1985).

The hearings, if they proved nothing else, certainly demonstrated the potency of Vietnam 'stab-in-the-back' thinking within the British establishment. Sir Frank Cooper was adamant that televised pictures of the war would have caused severe problems for censorship, forcing a reluctant MOD to adjudicate issues of 'taste and tone' (R. Harris, 1983, 59–60). John Nott (Minister of Defence when the crisis began) was equally certain that television's impact in wartime could only be negative: 'I do not think that television would have made our operations any easier to conduct and, after all, we were trying to win a war'. But he insisted that 'We intended that television should go and there were technical obstacles we could not overcome' (Morrison and Tumber, 1988, 170). For their part, the military personnel who appeared before the Committee argued that 'unpleasant scenes' would have damaged military morale, and would have been 'singularly debilitating to our wives and our families', as Brigadier Tony Wilson put it (R. Harris, 1983, 64). The evidence-givers skirted around the issue and dressed up their distaste for television in various guises, but the spectre of Vietnam loomed over the proceedings. As Bernard Ingham made clear in his memoirs, the animus against television derived largely from that war and the effect televised footage was believed to have had, even if nobody – quite – said so directly (Ingham, 1991, 297).

A Successful Information War?

Did the media arrangements evolved during the Falklands/Malvinas conflict offer an appropriate model for the future, even if its specific conditions were unlikely to be replicated? Many media representatives certainly felt not. Alan Protheroe of the BBC complained in June 1982 that the sorry episode had demonstrated the government's 'total failure of perception of the importance of the information war', which had duly been lost, with the public being kept woefully ill-informed of developments. The MOD's performance he judged 'close to disastrous' (1982). Similarly, some journalists on return from 'active service' with the Task Force were wont to complain, along with Patrick Bishop, that 'in times of crisis the perception of a democratic government of the purpose of the media is little different from that of a dictatorship. Both regard it as something to be used and hasten to transmogrify it into an adjunct of state propaganda' (1982, 8). Suppression of bad news and accelerated release of victories – most famously Thatcher's personal announcement, timed to coincide with ITN's 10 p.m. news bulletin, that British troops had landed on South Georgia on 25 April ('Rejoice ... Rejoice!') – strengthened the impression that journalists' professional integrity had been compromised less in the 'national interest' than in the government's own electoral interests (Glasgow University Media Group, 1985; Young and Jesser, 1997).

Dissatisfied that the state had expected too much compliance from them, and exhibited too little confidence in the public's ability to tolerate bad news in limited war (with a General Election looming), journalists also offered more pointed rejoinders. They criticised the MOD's replacement of off-the-record briefings with televised statements read in a dull monotone by Ian ('McDalek') McDonald. So resented was this deviation from the standard 'lobby system' of Westminster reporting that some confidential briefings were resumed by Sir Frank Cooper. But these actually became the source of further controversy: namely, that the MOD used unattributable briefings to misinform journalists with a view to deceiving the Argentinian military. This criticism was at least partially acknowledged in Cooper's revelation that 'there were certainly occasions when we did not tell the whole truth and we did not correct things that were being mistaken or misread', even if the MOD's overall aim, reminiscent of the Second World War, had been 'not to lie' (R. Harris, 1983, 111–14; Morrison and Tumber, 1988, 206–8). Finally, the operation of the pooling system was also attacked. Far from eliminating damaging competition between reporters, depositing all press reports in a pool – into which editors could freely dip – actually exacerbated it. Ignorant of reporters' differential access to communications equipment and information, editors unfairly pressurised their own correspondent to compete with rivals (Morrison and Tumber, 1988, 60–1).

If media organisations were dissatisfied with their treatment during the conflict, however, the military professed themselves reciprocally unhappy with the media. Service personnel were vexed by the amount of armchair punditry engaged in by television news and current affairs programmes, which risked the unwitting disclosure of strategic plans to the Argentinians (Adams, 1986, 157–73). More seriously, the BBC was accused of having prematurely revealed crucial tactical information at vital moments, thus jeopardising operational success and the lives of the military personnel concerned, not to say the safety of journalists accompanying them. When the BBC precipitously announced an imminent attack at Goose Green, Colonel H. Jones, who led and perished in the attack, personally threatened to sue the BBC for manslaughter should he return: or so a story printed in the *Sunday Times* claimed (Morrison and Tumber, 1988, 251–2).

With regard to the print media, military objections related less to matters of life and death than to those of taste and tone. The jingoistic, 'Argy-bashing' tone adopted by some mass circulation tabloids was not to the military taste, though papers such as *The Sun* presented themselves as vocally and vigorously 'behind Our Boys'. Correspondents with the Task Force were not in fact responsible for the headlines under which their stories appeared, which included *The Sun*'s memorably tasteless 'Stick it up your Junta' banner of 20 April, and the notorious 'Gotcha' headline to the news of the sinking of the Argentinian ship, the *General Belgrano*. Neither were the reporters always the inspiration for 'campaigns', such as *The Sun*'s invitation to readers to 'sponsor a sidewinder'. But as their papers' shipbound representatives, reporters such as Tony Snow found themselves unpopular with soldiers and seamen who thought the jingoistic tabloids both frivolous and unchivalrous towards the enemy (R. Harris, 1983, 47–8). Indeed, in response to the 'Gotcha' headline, men on board the *Canberra* wrote to *The Sun* requesting more copies – for toilet paper (Morrison and Tumber, 1988, 35).

On the strength of this evidence of mutual antagonism, the Falklands episode seems to offer little in the way of positive lessons in wartime media-management. But to take such a view, in Philip Knightley's opinion, is to miss the point. Journalists may have complained that governmental secrecy 'lost the information war', but from the government's own perspective it was regulation, not rapid release, of news that was the very essence of the system. Consequently, for the state, the arrangements worked, and in Knightley's view, the MOD's role will 'go down in the history of journalism as a classic example of how to manage the media in wartime' (1989, 434). This, of course, is to ignore certain unique features of that conflict. But certainly, for all the mutual recriminations aired during the 1982 hearings, many aspects of the Falklands system – minders, 'security review' of copy, pooling arrangements – were resurrected by the Pentagon. In May 1983, a US naval officer published an enthusiastic account of the MOD's media handling, concluding that 'the Falklands War shows us how to make certain that government policy is not undermined by the way a war is reported': the key to ensuring 'favourable objectivity' lying in exclusion of certain correspondents from the battle zone (Lieutenant Commander Arthur Humphries, cited by MacArthur, 1993, 138–40). Having been tested and refined in Grenada and Panama by the US military, a system of media management based around pools and minders duly resurfaced in the Gulf conflict of 1990–1.

The Gulf War (1990–1)

Iraq's invasion of Kuwait in August 1990 prompted a huge international military and journalistic mobilisation. The US government, under the aegis of the UN, assembled the largest multi-national coalition since the Second World War. Coalition military forces rapidly amassed in the Saudi desert to thwart an Iraqi attack on Saudi Arabia, and prepare for the armed liberation of Kuwait, should UN sanctions and resolutions prove ineffective. At the same time, an extensive multinational force of journalists also took up residence in the Gulf, and in the months from August to

December, new ground rules evolved to govern relations between the military and the media in this uneasy 'peace' and in the increasingly likely event of war between the Coalition and Iraq.

Conditions in Saudi Arabia raised problems of a different order from those encountered during the Falklands/Malvinas conflict. For a start, although journalists' access to military operations could be almost wholly controlled by the military, far more journalists encamped in Saudi Arabia than travelled with the Task Force. Numbering around 1600, the media presence in the Gulf exceeded the press corps in Vietnam, even at its Tet offensive peak, by some four times (Atkinson, 1994, 159). Furthermore, news organisations now had access to a different generation of technology, despite only eight years having elapsed since the Falklands campaign. Whereas in that conflict, logistics and limited satellite capabilities kept journalists utterly dependent on the military for the transmission of their copy and footage, by 1990, journalists came equipped with lightweight camcorders, portable editing facilities, and satellite uplinks and downlinks. For the military, the problem, therefore, was less how journalists would transmit their reports than what they would report, and how some form of 'review' (or censorship, to use a word they disliked) could be exercised over media output.

The Pentagon was still convinced that media, left to their own devices, were an obstacle to war-winning. President Bush himself, consciously echoing his predecessor Reagan, insisted that American troops would not be asked 'to fight with one hand tied behind their back' – a warning shot to the press, and note of reassurance to the military (P. Taylor, 1992, 4). This time, media organisations would be carefully managed to ensure they discharged 'positive' roles, such as the maintenance of morale and preparation of the public for a potentially longer and costlier war than the Pentagon actually envisaged (Kellner, 1992, 383). Mass media would also be used in the strategic deception of the enemy. But if these functions sound familiar, many critics maintain that the objectives of 'news management' in this conflict far surpassed those conventionally allocated to media by the state in wartime. In short, the military sought completely to reshape public understandings of war itself, so that civilian audiences would see it as an essentially bloodless, hi-tech enterprise, effected with such precision that only infrastructure, not humans, suffered its lethal effects: this point was repeatedly stressed during the air war of January 1991 by both President Bush and General Schwarzkopf (Kellner, 1992, 234). Arguably, then, the Gulf War was the first *real* 'television war': 'our first postmodern war', according to Bruce Cumings, a 'perfect war' in Kellner's ironic labelling (Cumings, 1992, 103; Kellner, 1992, 386). War appeared not as 'blood and guts spilled in living colour on the living room rug' but through a 'radically distanced, technically controlled, eminently "cool" postmodern optic' (Cumings, 1992, 121). Pentagon video footage of the 'real war' merged seamlessly with computer-generated simulations, both appearing as real, unreal or 'hyperreal' as the other: thus Jean Baudrillard's contention that the Gulf War would not, and did not in fact, happen (Baudrillard in *The Guardian*, 11 January 1991; Der Derian, 1992, 173–202; Norris, 1994, 283–300).

The spectre of Vietnam hovered, once again, over the Coalition's preparations for wartime media management (MacArthur, 1993, 112–45). The Coalition's determination to create a hermetically-sealed 'information environment' – one of the war's many euphemisms – was no doubt reinforced by the fact that Saddam Hussein also appeared deeply influenced by certain lessons of Vietnam. He too believed that television coverage of war could destroy morale on the home front. But while the Pentagon was determined to avoid a repeat of Vietnam – this was, after all, to be the war in which America finally 'kicked' Vietnam, as Bush avowed – Iraq was only too keen for a re-run. Casting himself in the role of Ho Chi Minh, Saddam Hussein accordingly invited CNN to be his special guest for the duration of hostilities (even when other organisations were temporarily ordered to leave at the start of the air war). CNN alone was permitted to lease, at the price of $15 000 per week, a four-wire military communications link to the outside world, as the Iraqi regime hoped that footage of civilian casualties of Allied bombing would quickly turn American civilians against the war (Simpson, 1991b, 281–2; Arnett, 1995, 364). To this end, during the air war Hussein also permitted the BBC's John Simpson, ITN's Brent Sadler and various other correspondents to join CNN's Peter Arnett. All consequently found themselves barraged by charges – from their own compatriots (and often most vociferously from fellow journalists) – of treacherous complicity in Iraqi propaganda plans: of Simpson it was claimed that he belonged to the 'Baghdad Broadcasting Corporation', according to the British tabloids; Arnett was the 'Joseph Goebbels of Saddam Hussein's

Hitler-like regime', as Pennsylvania Congressman Lawrence Coughlin put it (Arnett, 1995, 420; Arnett, 1992; Goodman, 1992; Hoagland, 1992). The Commander of British forces in the Gulf, General Sir Peter de la Billière, himself insisted that reporters in Iraq were 'mouthpieces for the enemy, whose aim was to destroy and kill our own servicemen' (de la Billière, 1995, 65).

The Pools

The Coalition military decided to organise the international press corps into news pools as early as August 1990 (MacArthur, 1993, 7). A two-tier system for chaperoning journalists and regulating the information they were either told or could witness first-hand was instituted. The luckiest, or best-connected, were allocated a place with one of the media reporting teams (MRTs). Under close supervision by American military public affairs officers (PAOs) or British public relations officers (PROs) they were allowed access to the troops encamped in the desert. Again, journalists complained that military top brass sometimes interfered in the selection process (Fialka, 1991, 34). Only British, French and American media representatives were eligible for consideration for the coveted 200 places, on the grounds that their respective countries formed the largest military contributors to the Coalition. (British journalists were in fact proportionately best represented, with some six MRTs and four television crews to cover 35 000 British troops: P. Taylor, 1992, 52.) The intention behind these pools, according to Colonel William Mulvey (head of the Coalition's Joint Information Bureau, or JIB), was simply to provide journalists with front-line access, while ensuring that they did not hamper military operations. 'Having reporters running around would overwhelm the battlefield', he informed static journalists (Mould, 1996, 137; P. Williams, 1992, 34). To join an MRT, the journalist was required to sign a set of guidelines, whereby pool members ceded their right to conduct off-the-record interviews with military personnel; agreed to have their reports 'reviewed' for any security breaches; and consented to remain with, and obey, their military escorts at all times (MacArthur, 1993, 19).

Journalists of other nationalities, and less fortunate British, French and American journalists representing smaller, or more critical, outlets were consigned to the second tier (a few rungs lower down the Pentagon-devised journalistic evolutionary ladder). These 'hotel warriors' were billeted in luxury accommodation in Riyadh, the Saudi capital, and Dhahran, home to the Coalition's JIB, where they attended several daily briefings hosted by military public relations officers (nicknamed 'Jiblets'). Purposely to avoid overtones of Vietnam's 'Five O'clock Follies', the main briefing convened at six (P. Taylor, 1992, 64). And unlike the more rambunctious 'follies', the so-called 'Norm and Chuck show' (after its stars, General Norman Schwarzkopf and Lieutenant General Charles Horner) was a slick, televised event.

Many American media outlets greeted these arrangements with audible groans of displeasure. American journalists had less reason than some to complain, not least those completely excluded from the pooling arrangements, of whom some 300 journalists from 23 countries signed an open letter to King Fahd and allied commanders in January 1991, warning that unless access was improved they would attempt to defy restrictions (Mould, 1996, 153). But nevertheless, in comparison with British colleagues, Americans considered themselves ill-treated. Those lucky enough to be assigned one of 159 places with the US MRTs found that their minders sometimes exercised a far more stringent supervision than their British counterparts, invariably denying them the right to use their own satellite uplinks to transmit stories, as was permitted the British MRTs with the 1st Armoured Division (P. Taylor, 1992, 51). Instead, videotape and copy had to be sent back to the JIB by a Forward Transmission Unit (FTU) – tellingly dubbed the 'pony express' – for 'review', and subsequent transmission by satellite (Fialka, 1991, 12). Other organisations were equally dissatisfied that they had been denied a place at all, and that, in America's biggest single military operation since the Second World War, they had no access to front-line service personnel: a situation partly caused by their colleagues from the 'sacred sixteen' (most powerful networks and papers) which, instead of rotating pool places as was intended, refused to surrender theirs (Sharkey, 1991, 125–6; P. Taylor, 1992, 52). Both groups also bridled at military restrictions on what could be reported. Ironically perhaps, some, as Peter Braestrup noted, had recourse to a Vietnam legend of their own in the attempt to force greater official openness (Braestrup in Fialka, 1991, xi). Thus they evoked the late 1960s as a Golden Age of unfettered reportage, when the First Amendment was still respected by government, and journalists without compulsion – under the 'no prior review' system – demonstrated their loyalty by providing supportive copy, with 'very few security breaches of any consequence' as the President of the American Society of Newspaper Editors pointed out (cited by Sharkey, 1991, 121).

The military arrangements did not, therefore, go entirely unopposed. America's major television networks penned a collective letter of protest to Bush on 22 August, complaining that 'Never in American history has this country been faced with as large a commitment of manpower and equipment with as little opportunity for the press to report' (cited by MacArthur, 1993, 10). According to MacArthur, the corporations were largely bought off with the assurance of White House spokesman Marlin Fitzwater that pool arrangements were 'never a desired course', and that the government would do all in its powers to meet the media's needs, including putting pressure on the Saudi government, which the White House blamed for visa shortages and other restrictions. The networks were duly pacified by the announcement that more reporters would be admitted to Saudi Arabia, a promise of free transport to the Gulf once commercial flights into Dhahran ended, and intimation that, as soon as practical, the pools would be disbanded and 'unilateral coverage of activities begin' (MacArthur, 1993, 11–29). Having more reporters on the ground was the government's *quid pro quo* for journalists having little to report, coupled with the promise of Vietnam-style freedom – 'hitch a ride to Da Nang' journalism – once conditions permitted (Sharkey, 1991, 118).

A more formal challenge to the Gulf media management system was launched shortly before the air war began, after the Pentagon issued a series of reporting restrictions which crushed editors' (misplaced) hopes for 'unilateral coverage'. Forbidden areas included: spontaneous or off-the-record interviews with personnel in the Gulf; the filming or photography of soldiers in 'agony or severe shock'; and the transmission of 'imagery of patients suffering from severe disfigurements' (P. Taylor, 1992, 35). However, despite the feeling among many network managers and editors that they had been betrayed by the Pentagon, a law suit against its alleged infringement of the First Amendment – mounted by a clutch of predominantly left-wing weeklies and monthlies, and four prominent writers – was not joined by more powerful organisations (MacArthur, 1993, 34).

Unilaterals

The most sincere form of opposition to the pooling arrangements was to withdraw from them altogether. The MOD insisted, as in previous conflicts, that the media system rested on 'free co-operation and consultation', but, as journalist Philip Knightley darkly warned, 'see how long you last without them' (*Independent on Sunday*, 13 January, 1991). But this was exactly what a number of journalists (from print, radio and television) chose to do, for the only way to evade entirely the 'voluntary' restrictions was to opt out of either tier, and refuse membership of the elite MRTs or the legion of 'hotel warriors' in Dhahran and Riyadh. Portable satellite flyaways and camcorders made reporting from self-imposed exile technologically feasible, and was duly how a number of British, French and American 'unilaterals' operated. Why, then, did so comparatively few of the 1600 or so Gulf-bound journalists opt for this course? American journalists, in particular, posed this precise question in a spirit of post-war self-recrimination. 'I'm embarrassed at how the American press went along with the restrictions. The British and the French media got away from the pool. Why couldn't the Americans?', demanded *Life* reporter Ed Barnes, only to conclude, 'They weren't trying' (MacArthur, 1993, 156).

Mainstream American media were simply too pusillanimous, perhaps. There was, however, a battery of off-putting considerations to deter the faint-hearted. Iraq was not known for its friendliness to free-range Western journalists found within its borders, as attested to by the fate of Farzad Bazhoft, an Iranian reporter for the London *Observer*, hanged by Iraq in March 1990 as a spy. Moreover, as Coalition troops themselves lacked maps, and sometimes, apparently, the ability to read them – and thus were no strangers to getting lost in the desert – it seemed every bit as likely that journalists might stray. If they did inadvertently wander over the Iraqi border, the chances that the unilaterals would be ill-treated were increased by the habit many adopted of cultivating a 'rufty-tufty' para-military look: which ranged from acquiring military haircuts to covering jeeps with camouflage netting, and purloining genuine Coalition uniforms (Fialka, 1991, 45–53; Bishop, 1992, 111–14). And in addition to the risk of running into a hostile enemy, the hapless unilateral might happen upon a hostile ally, if the imposture failed to convince. The Saudis issued a decree that any unescorted journalist found within 100 miles of the war zone faced arrest and deportation. The best reporters could expect, as Patrick Bishop pointed out, was ' "having their credentials removed", a phrase that always carried an unpleasant implication of amputation, or worse' (1992, 111–12). The Saudis were not alone in exhibiting a distinctly chilly attitude to unilaterals: some American correspondents later reported being beaten and harassed by their own troops, though formally the only sanction against unilaterals was that the US military would report them to the Saudi authorities, who could revoke credentials and visas (Fialka, 1991, 47–8; Mould, 1996, 137).

Other considerations also had to be weighed up in the decision to go unilateral. What kind of stories would the freelancer be able to report, given the unlikeliness of the military disclosing anything substantial either about strategy or discontent with desert life? And did readers and viewers back home approve of journalists who stepped beyond the perimeter of the pooling system? The editor of London's *The Independent*, whose experienced correspondent Robert Fisk was one of the most high-profile print 'unilaterals', received aggrieved letters from some readers after publication of Fisk's reports on confusion amongst British forces in the desert (MacArthur, 1991, 113–14). They were dismayed that Fisk's disloyal efforts should be printed, though the editor defended himself – and Fisk – by asserting that 'patriotism does not and should not mean telling lies on behalf of the government of the day', recalling the despatches of William Howard Russell, which had exposed incompetence in the Crimea, thereby helping rectify them (MacArthur, 1991, 114–15). But many other editors took a far less libertarian view than *The Independent*, and insisted that the measure of patriotism in this war was strict abidance by military rules.

An 'Uncensored' War?

No sooner did the 100-hour ground war end in the liberation of Kuwait on 28 February 1991 than recriminations began. Why did Saddam Hussein remain in power when, as many believed, the not-so-hidden agenda of Operation Desert Storm had been to topple him? Why did the Iraqi army, and the notorious 'crack' Republic Guard, not put up a better defence, given that Iraq had been billed during the months of Desert Shield as possessing the world's fourth most powerful military? Was it possible that the Coalition had deliberately exaggerated Iraq's strength – insisting that 545 000 Iraqi troops were in Kuwait, when there were only 300 000 – to prepare domestic audiences for a protracted and costly engagement (which they hoped to avoid), and to legitimise a strategy of intensive aerial bombardment (which they intended to enact)? And if the media had let themselves be misinformed on this issue, what else, spoon-fed by the briefers, had journalists swallowed whole?

Military-media relations during the months of August 1990 to February 1991 may have been reasonably harmonious, as Philip Taylor insists, and certainly for the British MRTs (P. Taylor, 1992, 54). But in the months following the war there was a great deal of hand-wringing by American journalists (and their UK counterparts, to a lesser degree) over the way in which the military had managed the media, and the latter's contributory negligence in lending themselves so pliably to the arrangements. In America, according to MacArthur, 'it was difficult to find anyone who didn't, at least officially, count Desert Storm as a devastating and immoral victory for military censorship and a crushing defeat for the press and the First Amendment' (1993, 8). When Bush proclaimed 'By God, we've finally kicked the Vietnam Syndrome', many journalists no doubt took this to mean that they themselves had been drubbed by their own military. Similarly, when Defense Department spokesman Pete Williams jubilantly proclaimed after the war that the pools 'gave the American people the best war coverage they ever had', many critics took this as corroboration that television had simply become 'Pentavision' for the duration (MacArthur, 1993, 16). For in this war viewers had received saturation television coverage, which offered the illusion of both totality and reality, while remaining ignorant of much of what the war had entailed. One critic bluntly proclaimed, 'the more you watched, the stupider you got' (Cumings, 1992, 117; Morgan, Lewis and Jhally, 1992, 216–33). Who, then, was to blame for this state of affairs: the military for instituting a system which, complained outraged media executives in June 1991, had 'nothing to do with operational security . . . [and] everything to do with sanitizing the nature of war and polishing the image of the military'; or the media, for having, as one *New York Times* columnist put it, 'glorified war and accepted its political premise, forsaking the independence and skepticism that justify freedom of the press' (Sharkey, 1991, 135, 145).

By way of self-defence, the Department of Defense insisted that they had actually withheld very little. Great pains were indeed taken before, during, and after the war to stress that this was a system of *review*, in which copy was checked – referred up to the Pentagon if necessary – but where the ultimate decision rested with editors themselves. Pete Williams evoked 'total war' conditions (without quite doing their 'voluntarism' justice) specifically to insist on the unlikeness of arrangements: 'We did not have authority to get out a blue pen or pencil and change a word or strike something out...as a censor would do back in World War II' (cited by Sharkey, 1991, 133). A number of journalists have concurred that 'military censorship, in the literal sense of the word, was not the problem. Only five reports, 0.03 percent of those filed during and before the war, were sent to Washington for final review. Of those, only one was changed, according to the Pentagon' (Fialka, 1991, 5–6). This is a view echoed by British journalist Nik Gowing (then Diplomatic Editor of ITN), who agreed that 'the active suppression of facts and information by soldiers' (or censorship) 'was not on the scale that many critics believe' (1991, 112).

Others, however, told a different story of reports being altered or stopped on grounds which owed nothing to military security. Robert Fox (a veteran of the Falklands conflict) related that a paragraph from one of his reports – revealing how many British squaddies were ex-prisoners – was discreetly removed (P. Taylor, 1992, 55). Indeed, just as the Falklands conflict had seen the MOD delete a pilot's confession that he had been 'scared fartless', so did the Gulf War offer up many such instances of military sensitivity over matters of self-image rather than security (R. Harris, 1983, 60). The *Detroit Free Press*'s Frank Bruni, for example, was reprimanded for describing returning US pilots as 'giddy': the minders preferred 'proud', but they compromised on 'pumped up' (MacArthur, 1993, 192).

To suggest that there was no real censorship in the Gulf, using purely numerical tallies of stories stopped, is also to ignore the degree to which the media management arrangements as a whole constituted a system of censorship. If, as one detractor remarked, 'security review' was 'still censorship with a censored name', then did not the same apply to a 'controlled information environment' (Christopher Dickey, cited by Norris, 1994, 298)? A number of reporters who covered the war point to 'censorship by lack of access', as ABC network vice-president Walter Porges termed it

(Fialka, 1991, 6). Likewise, a senior colleague opined that 'power to define coverage amounts to censorship of far more dangerous proportions than any "blue pencil" editing', for all Williams's attempts to draw a favourable comparison with the Second World War (Sharkey, 1991, 128–9). Many journalists with the MRTs subsequently claimed that they just did not get to see enough of what was going on in the desert, and were so tightly monitored that they lacked any access to freely expressed opinions (a condition of MRT membership). Journalists were also wont to censure their minders, especially certain US Army PAOs, for having been inadequately briefed, sometimes incompetent, and frequently of too lowly a rank to exercise any compulsion over obstructive commanders in the field who resented reporters' presence altogether. CBS's Martha Teichner put it thus: 'You've got incompetence from the bottom up and you've got resistance from the top down and it met where we were, in the pool. It all came together, and it was disastrous' (Fialka, 1991, 24).

Grievances with the pooling arrangements were exacerbated during the 100 hours of the ground war, when the system for transmission of copy almost completely collapsed. Even after the initial 12-hour news blackout imposed by the military expired, nearly 80 per cent of reports filed took over 12 hours to get back to Dhahran. One in ten took three days or more (P. Taylor, 1992, 246–7). As the ground war only lasted 100 hours, the impact of this breakdown of communications was more muted than it would have been in a longer war, where such newslessness could hardly have been sustained. As it was, the Coalition's pincer movement through the desert into Kuwait, in which Iraqi soldiers were (it was later revealed) buried alive in the sand as trench-fillers bulldozed their way through Iraqi lines, received minimal coverage (Sharkey, 1991, 147–8). Very little was learnt about the ground war as it occurred: the BBC's Martin Bell complained that front-line footage shot by his crew, showing dead bodies, was returned untransmitted. Perhaps the most harrowing visual image of the conflict – showing the charred head of an Iraqi soldier peeping from the burnt-out shell of his tank – did not appear until 3 March in London's *Observer*, by which time the cease-fire was signed.

Footage of cindered Iraqi corpses caught in a procession of vehicles on the main route out of Kuwait by Allied bombardment – the so-called 'Highway of Death' – also surfaced after the cease-fire. Did President Bush call a premature halt to the ground war precisely because he pessimistically anticipated the impact of such grotesque images on American public opinion, as journalist John Simpson alleged (1991b, 7)? Certainly, Schwarzkopf later complained that 'Washington was ready to overreact, as usual, to the slightest ripple in public opinion', but as John Mueller points out, if the administration did 'wobble' it did so reflexively. As in previous wars, the presumed power of images to shatter morale may have been more important than their actual effect. After all, the public had not yet seen the alarming images of which Bush had a private sampling, and there was no polling evidence of weakening public support for the war when he decided to halt it after 100 hours: a decision many commentators attribute less to fear of images than the Administration's fears of a power vacuum in Iraq if Hussein were toppled, and consequent unsettling of the whole Middle Eastern balance of power (Mueller, 1994, 122–3, 134–6; Gowing, 1994, 13–14).

Accident and design together ensured that the ground war went under-reported. While the 'pony express' expired, some MRTs found their units lost in the desert during this brief but crucial phase of the war. Others, deciding finally to throw off the restrictions and make a unilateral dash for Kuwait without their minders, ignored the tactics used in the ground war in their eagerness to cover the 'big story': the liberation of Kuwait. As has often been remarked, CBS and ABC journalists actually spearheaded the entry into Kuwait city, yet having won the race to get there, many were apparently aimless on arrival (MacArthur, 1993, 196). Tony Horwitz of the *Wall Street Journal*, a unilateral, complained of his colleagues who belatedly broke from the pools that, having 'liberated' Kuwait, they had no idea what to do next without their minders: 'Most people ... hung around, reporting on the hotel or something, waiting for briefings' (MacArthur, 1993, 197).

Horwitz's cautionary tale suggests just how successfully the pooling and briefing system had domesticated reporters. The briefers' story was '*the* story'. Indeed, to understand how television became 'Pentavision', it is necessary to consider not just how negative dimensions of the management system prevented news media from reporting certain aspects of the war but how readily reporters succumbed to the positive side of news management, relaying events through the eyes, and in the terminology, of the military.

Undoubtedly, the military attempted to put their spin on events, both in their video presentations and the obfuscatory language they deployed in outlining each day's operations.

Euphemisms were the order of the day. Emitting a stream of 'bovine scatology' (one of Schwarzkopf's more colourful coinages, though applied by him to journalists' stupid questions rather than to the briefings), the briefers used opaque jargon to obscure reality, so that civilian casualties became 'collateral damage', while 'degrading capabilities' was the preferred substitution for bombing. (As a matter of policy, the Pentagon refused to be drawn into the 'game' of body counts of Iraqi casualties: another lesson of Vietnam. 'I'm anti-body count', declared Schwarzkopf; 'Body counts mean nothing, absolutely nothing': Sharkey, 1991, 147). Sometimes the linguistic twisting was less euphemistic than downright tendentious, as when Schwarzkopf and Powell boasted of Coalition airstrikes' 80 per cent effectiveness in the opening days of the air war. The meaning here was surely unambiguous: 80 per cent of bombs had successfully 'degraded' Iraqi capabilities? But apparently not, for on 22 January, Pete Williams explained that 80 per cent of targets had not been destroyed (P. Taylor, 1992, 66). In fact, by military definition, a 'successful' sortie was simply one in which bombs had faultlessly detonated – on something. The US military also acknowledged in March 1991 that, although wartime briefings concentrated on the 'pinpoint accuracy' of the Patriot missiles, the vast majority of bombs rained on Iraq had been conventional explosives, with conventional levels of inaccuracy: of 88 500 tons of missiles, only 5620 tons were precision-guided, and a total of 70 per cent had missed their targets (P. Taylor, 1992, 220). At the time, however, stress was laid upon how the US military was doing everything possible to 'avoid injury or hurting or destroying innocent people' (Schwarzkopf cited by Sharkey, 1991, 148).

Why was the gulf between words and actions not exposed at the time? Many journalists accept some responsibility. Braestrup, for example, criticises journalists for being insufficiently versed in military sleights of tongue, content simply to parrot the briefers' language without interrogating its meaning; just as they had done in Vietnam, where language, as Michael Herr observed, served as 'a cosmetic' (1978, 79). Again, many journalists were too ignorant of the military: 'most did not know a tank from a turd', pronounced one ex-US Army officer (Hackworth, 1992, 187). Their enthralment with military language was heightened by the images which accompanied the misleading words: video footage showing only sorties during which pre-designated targets were eliminated with stunning accuracy, not the 'successful' misses. But whatever the footage omitted, it did offer television one of its pre-requisites: pictures. Indeed some critics attribute the insubstantiality of much television war coverage to the medium's voracious craving for pictures, which left the networks dependent on the hand that fed them this staple. It may not have been a very substantial diet; one journalist likened the daily rations from the JIB to 'candyfloss': 'delicious to consume but devoid of substance' (John Naughton, cited by P. Taylor, 1992, 34). But it looked good, and filled a gap, even if journalists later hungrily bemoaned that 'never in the field of recent conflict has so little been disclosed by so few to so many' (anonymous reporter cited by P. Taylor, 1992, 13).

Whatever the military's sins of omission and commission, however, the news media proved adept at censoring themselves. Where the Pentagon 'jiblets', unsurprisingly, only released images which showed how smoothly operations were progressing, at minimal human cost, Iraqi media minders operated under the diametrically opposed principle of attempting to expose as much human destruction wrought by Coalition bombardment as possible, while preventing Western crews filming strategic targets successfully hit (A. Thomson, 1992, 234). Consequently, those Western journalists who remained in Baghdad were positively encouraged by their Iraqi minders to film such scenes as the wreckage of a 'Baby Milk Factory' on 23 January (which the Coalition claimed was a military installation, duplicitously disguised as a harmless civilian facility), and, more harrowingly, the devastation of a shelter in the Al Amiriya district on 13 February, also alleged to have been a military command centre, in which Saddam had callously and cynically located a shelter (P. Taylor, 1992, 187–218; Arnett, 1995, 396–401).

After two precision-guided bombs smashed through its roof, hundreds of Iraqi civilians died agonising deaths as their 'shelter became their destroyer, an oven' (A. Thomson, 1992, 235). As Iraqi censorship was totally lifted, Western television crews filmed scenes of charred human remains being removed from the ravaged building. CNN broke the story; the BBC and ITN quickly followed with updated stories of their own. The footage was revelatory. As BBC2's *Newsnight* presenter, Jeremy Paxman, put it: 'Until today it had seemed such an uncannily sanitised war: clever bombs that wrecked real estate but somehow appeared to leave people unscathed' (quoted by P. Taylor, 1992, 208–9). The aftermath of Amiriya showed the devastating impact of 'smart' bombs on real people. Yet while the BBC's news footage was unprecedented for the Gulf conflict it was nevertheless sanitised. 'Many of the pictures coming from Baghdad of burned civilian bodies are considered too dreadful to show you', anchor Michael Buerk warned BBC viewers (cited by P. Taylor, 1992, 191). No Coalition official could tell broadcasters not to transmit the most harrowing scenes of grief-stricken survivors unwrapping bundles of molten human flesh for the cameras. Censorship on grounds of 'taste and tone' was undertaken where no official compulsion existed by the broadcasters themselves, judging what their audiences (or, in some cases, commercial sponsors) would, or would not, tolerate. Perhaps paradoxically, given the BBC's discretion, the Corporation's coverage of Amiriya nevertheless earned it the tag 'Baghdad Broadcasting Corporation' from Conservative MPs and newspapers which deemed that *any* coverage of Iraqi civilian casualties was tantamount to treason. The BBC was once again denounced as an 'enemy within', as the *Sun* put it, echoing Churchill's wartime utterance to the same effect (though if the allusion was conscious, it was probably lost on most readers). Other editors drew more explicit parallels with the Second World War, likening the decision to screen such footage to the BBC having reported effects of Allied raids on Dresden and Berlin (A. Thomson, 1992, 238–9). As in the Falklands conflict, then, print journalists often proved the state's firm ally in creating a climate in which only heavy self-censorship was sufficient proof of patriotic intent. Likewise in America, CNN's fiercest critics included outraged press columnists and rival networks.

Vietnam and After: Alternative Lessons

Power elites have clung tenaciously to the notion that media hampered (perhaps fatally) America's war effort in Vietnam. The presumed nexus between television imagery and declining public support for US involvement is seductive but the hypothesis suffers one shortfall: evidence (Schudson, 1995, 22). While militaries and governments seem confident of certain 'lessons', academic research on the Vietnam War has generated a very different set of observations about the role of television in that conflict, and about the relationship between media and the state, suggesting that inappropriate lessons have been extracted. Rather than the media requiring close fettering by the state, one might in fact conclude that the media, censored or uncensored, in 'limited wars' have generally performed a satisfactory job of toeing the official line: good news for the military (although they chose to extract the opposite lesson), but more worrying for those concerned to see vigorous and independent media fulfilling an adversarial or 'watchdog' role.

Vietnam: The 'Guilty Media' Thesis Revisited

Television news came of age in the 1960s; it regularly showed scenes of carnage from a purposeless war, and a television-viewing public increasingly turned against that war, ultimately making its prosecution unsustainable. Put thus, the equation looks obvious. War plus vivid television coverage equals defeat.

However, were television images really as raw and as 'negative' as commonly supposed, feeding viewers a nightly diet of death, injury and wanton destruction, which inevitably made war appear immoral and insupportable? Careful content analysis of US network news coverage suggests that this underlying assumption about footage from Vietnam is in fact misplaced. As Daniel Hallin's seminal work has shown, much of the networks' nightly coverage, for a considerable part of the war, eschewed exposure of war's human costs and certainly of 'atrocities' committed by US forces. Television coverage in fact, until around the time of the Tet offensive, was 'lopsidedly favourable to American policy in Vietnam', often explicitly so (1989, 110). His content analysis reveals that only about 22 per cent of all film reports from Vietnam in the pre-Tet period depicted actual combat; around 24 per cent contained shots of the dead or wounded, but usually only briefly; and less than 10 per cent offered more than one shot of the dead or wounded (Hallin, 1989, 129–30). In 1968, television coverage began to shift, screening more damaging imagery, paying more attention to the peace movement and oppositional views, while passing more critical comment on the South Vietnamese regime and Army. But the networks' initially supportive coverage suggests that the orthodox insistence on television's innate negativism must be flawed. How, then, do we explain media behaviour? And does the apparent slippage towards negativity signify that oppositional media abandoned the practice of objectivity as the war progressed?

The explanation may owe something to technology and logistics. Difficulties of filming a jungle-based war prior to Tet eased as combat took to the streets. The introduction of satellites for transmission in the late 1960s alleviated another problem for television news. Previously, as film had to be physically flown back to the US, with resultant delays of around 48 hours between filming and broadcast, editors requested 'timeless pieces'. Stories from Vietnam consequently contained so little 'hot news' to guard against ageing as frequently to lapse into predictable sameness (Williams in Eldridge, 1993, 310). Michael Arlen characterised the television war, at least until 1968, as 'a nightly stylised, generally distracted, overview of a disjointed conflict which was composed mainly of scenes of helicopters landing, tall grass blowing in helicopter wind, American soldiers fanning out over a hillside on foot' (Eldridge, 1993, 309–10).

News output was informed by something more profound than the solution of practical difficulties, however, for the message was shaped less by the medium itself than by journalistic routines, and the values and norms supporting them. According to Hallin's analysis, the explanation for both television's initially supportive coverage of the war, and its subsequent slow swing towards a somewhat more oppositional (though still by no means anti-war) stance, lies in 'the constant commitment to the ideology and the routines of objective journalism' (Hallin, 1994, 52). Thus television's apparent shift to oppositional journalism is somewhat chimerical. It was not that journalists deviated from customary routines but more that their sources radically reappraised the war, triggering an adjustment in reportorial mode to accommodate dissent.

To elaborate, Hallin suggests that we imagine the television journalist's world as divided into three regions, 'each of which involves the application of different journalistic standards'. The first he terms the 'sphere of consensus' – the 'region of motherhood and apple pie' – wherein lie 'those social objects not regarded by the journalists and most of the society as controversial' (1989, 116). In this sphere, journalists do not feel obliged to act as impartial 'balancers' but can instead celebrate consensual values. After all, there are no – or very few – opposing views for a journalist to balance between. The dissident minority with a distaste for apple-pie or motherhood can be safely banished to the 'sphere of deviance', which lies beyond the purview of routine journalism: a dumping-ground for views discarded by mainstream society (Hallin, 1989, 117). However, between the cosy 'sphere of consensus' and the outer darkness lies an intermediate realm. The 'sphere of legitimate controversy' is where the rules of objectivity reign supreme: 'neutrality' and 'balance' are the prized journalistic virtues, with equilibrium sought amongst contending mainstream voices (Hallin, 1989, 116).

Using this model, Hallin argues that the shifting tenor and content of Vietnam coverage can best be explained by the movement of the war from one sphere to another, not by any counter-cultural jettisoning of 'objectivity' by *engagé* journalists. His analysis bears quoting at some length:

> First, the opposition to the war expanded, moving from the political fringes of the society into its mainstream – into the electoral and legislative arenas, which lie within the sphere of legitimate controversy. As this occurred the normal procedures of objective journalism produced increasing coverage of oppositional viewpoints; when a presidential candidate comes out against the war, as occurred for the first time at the New Hampshire primary in 1968, the opposition becomes not only a respectable but an obligatory subject for news coverage...
>
> Second, the sphere of consensus contracted while the sphere of legitimate controversy expanded. Not only did the media report the growing debate over the war, they were also affected by it. As the parameters of political debate changed, so did the behaviour of the media: stories that previously had been reported within a consensus framework came to be reported as controversies; subjects and points of view that had been beyond the pale in the early years came to be treated as legitimate news stories. (1994, 54–5)

As elite dissatisfaction with US involvement deepened, journalists (both print and television) began reporting as 'atrocities' American actions which had previously received minimal, or no, attention so long as shared anti-communism fixed the war in the 'sphere of consensus'. It is worth recalling that even the 'young Turks' of the print media establishments – Halberstam, Arnett, Browne, Sheehan *et al.* – who provoked such ire in the White House and Saigon, were not originally opposed to the war as such (Arnett, 1995, 91). (Neither were they as young as commonly supposed: in January 1966, of 110 accredited US correspondents in Saigon, 38 were aged below 30, and 72 above: (Hammond, 1989, 314). Indeed, it was perhaps precisely because they concurred that 'democracy' in South Vietnam should be defended against Communism that they wanted to see their government support a more democratic regime.

Some of their dissatisfaction with Diem reached the columns of their newspapers. But stories revealing the war's brutal nature, and the toll it exacted on ordinary Vietnamese villagers, rarely reached the pages of the *Washington Post* or *New York Times* in the pre-Tet years. Martha Gelhorn, for example, found it impossible to persuade an American newspaper to run a series of first-hand accounts written in 1966–7 of what 'winning hearts and minds' actually entailed (Knightley, 1989, 389–90). Similarly, reports about the massacre at My Lai in March 1968 – which became one of the defining horrors of the war – were initially stonewalled by American editors, wary of jeopardising consensus over the justness of America's purposes and practises in Vietnam. Not until November 1968 did My Lai feature prominently in mainstream US media, thanks to the efforts of investigative journalist Seymour Hersh in exhuming buried reports of the massacre; and only in December did the horrific photographs appear which etched My Lai on to the national consciousness, confirming its status as what *Time* called 'an American tragedy' (Knightley, 1989, 390–3).

After 1968, Knightley argues, 'nearly every war correspondent who had been in Vietnam had an atrocity story to tell', and now a ready market for them. Why so belatedly? Hallin suggests that a form of cognitive dissonance prevented Americans, who in the main rigidly adhered to Cold War ideology, from acknowledging American misdeeds throughout most of the 1960s. It seems probable that reporters often did not actually regard such episodes as 'newsworthy', though the grotesque 'Battlefield Gothic' suffuses retrospective, first-hand narratives (Hynes, 1998, 191). When brutality occurred daily, such acts scarcely constituted news, but were rather the backdrop against which 'news' (or the pseudo-news dished out at briefings) happened. Atrocities themselves resisted inclusion in 'the story' for American reporters navigating this unfamiliar terrain with a readjusted moral compass. As Knightley points out, 'it can be argued that My Lai was *not* an atrocity – at least, if it is argued that an atrocity is taken to be something freakish, something quite apart from the normal events coming before and after it' (1989, 393). Similarly, Colonel Nguyen Ngoc Loan's execution of a Vietcong suspect on 1 February 1968 scarcely induced the 'shock of the new' among those familiar with his habitual mode of justice administration, though Eddie Adams's widely reproduced photograph of this particular shooting was later hailed by Harold Evans as the 'instant when Western optimism about the Vietnam War shift[ed] fundamentally' (cited by Brothers, 1997, 204; Culbert, 1988, 253–67).

With war a matter of elite dissension, space opened for the airing of Vietnam's everyday atrocities. Television likewise began to accommodate hitherto marginalised issues which had previously been banished to the sphere of deviance, notably the peace movement. However, as Hallin points out, peace protesters became *domestic* news, not legitimate commentators on the war itself. With violent protests on the streets and campuses of American towns and cities, wide-scale public demonstrations could hardly be ignored: the war was now very visibly a matter of 'legitimate controversy'. That did not mean, however, that the protesters themselves were thoroughly brought in from the cold. While the anti-war movement may have gained increasing airtime, Hallin's content analysis reveals that the protesters themselves remained fringe voices (1989, 191–201; Gitlin, 1980; Small, 1994). Even after Tet, the boundaries of legitimate controversy remained largely defined by the debate raging on the Capitol.

Media coverage of the Vietnam War demonstrates, then, how precisely media are attuned to the fluctuations of their sources, and within what narrow boundaries they operate their balancing mechanisms so that the very practices of 'objectivity' (often taken as a byword for 'impartiality') operate to inscribe a routine bias in favour of power elites. Only when the elite itself is riven with dissent, or an administration loses the will or ability to manage a story after its own fashion – as during Tet – do the mainstream media become discordant. Journalists on the ground in Vietnam were in fact readily domesticated by the military. Although notionally an 'uncensored war', Vietnam saw the US military impose restrictions on certain types of sensitive information: restrictions by which journalists in the main unblinkingly abided (Hallin, 1989, 128, 211). The notion of a feckless, irresponsible and oppositional media is therefore misplaced indeed.

The media's hostile relationship with authority is only one element in the orthodox equation, however: the other is television's presumed negative impact upon public approval of the war. Here too academic research has gone a long way to demolish the notion that television coverage reduced support for the war. Orthodox thinking implicitly subscribes to a particular notion of media effects: namely that audiences receive unambiguous messages from the media which, in osmotic fashion, seep into and transform the viewer's attitudes and beliefs. Media scholars, although they certainly dispute media effects – the relative activity or passivity of audiences – have long modified simplistic 'magic bullet' or 'hypodermic' theories which the Orthodoxy caricatures (Curran, 1990, 135–64). Questions concerning who watches television, how they watch, and with what effect are immensely complex. But on both theoretical and empirical grounds there is little support for the Orthodoxy's insistence that those who watched television news duly became less supportive of the war. Even if such critics had been correct in their assessment of television imagery as relentlessly graphic, the hypothesis could still be challenged, for might not television images diminish, rather than exaggerate, the horror of war by reduction and repetition? Michael Arlen certainly felt that the shrunken three inch-high soldiers who appeared on the television screen were not only reduced in scale but in significance, 'trivialised, or at least tamed, by the cosy alarums of the household' (cited by Williams, 1993, 308).

How people process television news is not easily fathomed. Not every viewer reads a graphic image of war as an anti-war statement (a phenomenon observed with respect to First World War imagery). It is quite possible for different viewers to interpret an identical newscast contrarily, and media scholars have observed that people often tend to read into broadcasts confirmation of pre-existing preferences. Thus researchers found that 'doves' on the war in Vietnam tended to believe that respected anchor, Walter Cronkite, was a dove, while 'hawks' were equally inclined to claim him as one of their own (Hallin, 1989, 107). Such a finding (amongst many other similar studies) may suggest that meanings are not rigidly fixed in news stories but are construed by those watching, or reading, often in support of pre-existing beliefs. With regard to images, however, it is easy to overlook (as the Orthodoxy tends to) the degree to which meanings are cued by context. Newspaper photograph captions and commentary accompanying news footage signal, without dictating, particular readings of visuals whose meaning may be quite unclear were they presented in a void (Schudson, 1995, 113–23). If images are ambiguous, then 'it seems a reasonable hypothesis that most of the time the audience sees what it is told it is seeing': a proposition which makes it problematic to attribute a purely negative effect to a photograph such as Eddie Adams's 'execution', neutralised at the time by uncritical commentary (Hallin, 1989, 131; Hamilton, 1989, 171–83).

Proponents of the 'guilty media' thesis also tend to overlook other influences on opinion-formation besides television. Heralded as the main source of news for a majority of Americans during the war, in fact network news was watched by fewer than half of all television-owning households on any given night, and attentiveness to news has been found to be extremely low (Hallin, 1989, 107; Thayer, 1992, 99). Moreover, television viewers did not – and do not – form opinions solely in response to television reports. As America's involvement in Vietnam lengthened, more and more ordinary citizens had personal experience of the war: whether as parent of a serving GI, as a relative or friend of someone injured, killed, or captured there, as a draftee or draft dodger, or as a payer of the inflated taxes entailed by the protracted commitment. Such factors may have offered powerful reasons for either supporting or becoming disillusioned with the war effort, regardless of how the media reported it. John Mueller's research proposes that the single best explanation for declining public support – from as early as 1966, not simply post-Tet – was the escalating casualty rate. As casualties rose by a factor of 10, public support dropped by 15 percentage points: in other words, when casualties rose from 1000 to 10 000 public support plummeted by 15 per cent; a pattern similar to that observed during the Korean War, when public support had tapered as casualties mounted, but where American media had been censored and generally 'patriotic' in their approach to war-reporting (Mueller, 1973, 42–61).

As the war entered the 'sphere of legitimate controversy', and television news began incorporating more 'negative' stories, television may have confirmed the trend towards disillusion, but many academics are adamant that television did not set it; indeed was, in fact, considerably to its rear. Tet, often viewed as a watershed during which television news first infected the public with unshakeable despair about the war, was actually 'less a turning point than a crossover point, a moment when trends which had been in motion for some time reached balance and began to tip the other way' (Hallin, 1989, 168–9).

The Public and the Media in Limited War

What does the Vietnam War tell us about the relationship between mass media and its audience in 'limited war'? Broadcasters and journalists defending the principle of the public's 'right to know' (which the military invariably poses as directly conflicting with the 'serviceman's right to live – or at least, not to have his life needlessly endangered') have argued keenly that Vietnam demonstrated public eagerness to be fully informed (Mercer, 1987, 39). Shortly after the Falklands conflict, the BBC's Alan Protheroe insisted that, 'Vietnam demonstrated that the public expects, requires, indeed demands, information and pictures, and that such material needs to be distributed throughout the world', a point he used to buttress his claim that 'the civil servants of the United Kingdom chose to learn the wrong lesson' (1982). Similarly, during the conflict itself, the BBC's Chairman, George Howard, had protested, in terms redolent of the MOI: 'One of the greatest virtues, and one of the inescapable consequences of living in a free land like Britain is that our people wish to be told the truth, and can be told it, however unpleasant it may be' (1982). A number of American journalists and academics have been equally adamant in insisting that – in limited war to a degree impossible in total war – the state's censorial impulses must be resisted in the name of the public's 'right to know'.

Do civilians really demand maximum disclosure of their media in times of limited war? As Evelyn Waugh's fictional war correspondent, William Boot, was wont to reply to his press baron boss when he could not muster the courage to disagree: 'Up to a point, Lord Copper.' Worryingly, for those who believe that limited war should not preclude as much press freedom as is consistent with security, research into the Falklands and Gulf conflicts suggests that many Britons and Americans do not cherish their 'right to know': or at any rate regard winning a war as a higher-order 'good' than media freedom (Morrison and Tumber, 1988; Kellner, 1992; Morrison, 1992; P. Taylor, 1997). An anonymous commentator writing shortly after the Falklands War, noted the 'ever-growing avidity of the public for news and their intense, up-to-the-minute awareness of what is going on and the concomitant desire to be involved', but this view was explicitly rejected by the Defence Committee's Inquiry into the MOD's media handling (Anon, naval review, April 1983, 124). In fact, the Committee's report embraced scepticism regarding public eagerness for its own 'right to know':

> Many principles, supposedly regarded as sacred and absolute within the media, are applied in a less rigid and categorical way by the public as a whole when it is judging its government's conduct of a war. In our judgement the public is, in general, quite ready to tolerate being misled to some extent if the enemy is also misled, thereby contributing to the success of the campaign. (cited in Philo, 1995, 98)

One might, of course, ask how the Committee knew what 'the public' thought – whether indeed there was a consensual view – not least as the Report's claim appears to allow the state considerable latitude in misleading the press and suppressing information in future wars (though it urged as full a disclosure of news as tactically viable, in the name of 'public morale': Morrison and Tumber, 1988, 346). This misgiving about the public's desire for 'publicity' finds echoes elsewhere. Immediately after the conflict, and before publication of the Committee's Report, Morrison and Tumber conducted extensive audience research, eliciting attitudes towards censorship and the role of the media in wartime. They concluded that 'the public did not wish the "fourth estate" to become the "fourth service": it expected current affairs to be critical of government policy' (1988, 350). But they held this expectation only up to a point. While three-quarters of those polled were in favour of 'reporting information even though it might reflect unfavourably on British troops', 49 per cent thought that such information should only be published after the war, with just 26 per cent approving wartime publication (1988, 322–3). Morrison and Tumber claim these statistics underline 'a very strong desire on the part of the public for a truthful media', but the public's apparent preference for post-war revelations gives pause for thought. So too do Morrison and Tumber's parallel findings that 34 per cent approved the principle of government issuing false information to the media if it would help the war, and that 21 per cent condoned the media in so doing (1988, 319–22). They attribute these findings not to a disregard for democratic freedoms but to the high level of public support for this particular war: hence, 'the stronger the approval for the Task Force the greater the approval of being lied to' (1988, 322). But the contingency of public approbation of official secrecy and misinformation upon enthusiasm for the war suggests a worrying circularity: if damaging information is withheld from the public then popular support for a war may be more likely, in turn justifying the withholding of information and misleading of the press.

It is possible that the Falklands conflict, which did enjoy consistently high (though far from unanimous) British public support, was *sui generis*. But the Gulf War seems to offer parallel findings on civilians' disinclination to know. Philip Taylor notes that post-Gulf War audience research 'has presented a new challenge: the public's apparent desire *not* to know beyond the sketchiest details what is going on while it is going on'. Audience research in both the US and UK indicated that both publics 'seem prepared to suspend their right to know, provided they believe the war to be just and the anticipated gains worth the price of the deaths of a certain number of professional soldiers' (P. Taylor, 1992, 274–5; Oliver, Mares and Cantor, 1993, 145–64). Partly, this willingness stems from a desire not to harm a war effort, which in the Gulf most (but not all) Americans and Britons thought just. Thus abrogation of the 'right to know' is only a temporary exigency of war, with a majority holding that damaging information should be published after the event (Morrison, 1992, 25). But civilians also rationalise their desire not to know – and, particularly, not to *see* distressing images of war's casualties – on the grounds that everyone knows that soldiers, and sometimes civilians, die in war, and they therefore do not need graphic visual confirmation. Imagination can fill the gap left by legitimate screening out on grounds of 'taste and tone' of what is both unduly distressing and unnecessary. Researchers at Hull found that 67 per cent of their respondents wished to see 'dead bodies' on television (while one American study found 69 per cent and 79 per cent of respondents did *not* wish to see, respectively, wounded or dead soldiers: Oliver, Mares and Cantor 1993, 150). But only 57 per

cent thought it right for the BBC to have shown the shrouded
bodies of the Al Amiriya victims, a finding corroborated by the
Leeds team who uncovered considerable support for BBC self-
censorship of this footage, 23 per cent believing it wrong for television to cover this story at all (Morrison, 1992, 20–2, 28, 34– 8; Shaw
and Carr-Hill, 1992, 144–57).

Of those who did not wish to see the Amiriya footage, 29 per cent
argued that it was 'upsetting for adults' and 24 per cent because it
was 'upsetting for children' (Morrison, 1992, 30). Perhaps viewers
displace their own desire for protection, from scenes the civilian
imagination cannot in fact conjure unaided by images or words, on
to children (Stevenson, 1995, 191). Significantly, however, a further
21 per cent rationalised their disapproval of such images on the
grounds that they 'undermined British morale'. Many of these, one
might hypothesise, had effectively internalised a version of the
'Vietnam syndrome', believing that others (though not necessarily
they themselves) would be distressed or demoralised by footage
which would fuel anti-war feeling. (Thus the *Daily Telegraph* refused
to print pictures of Al Amiriya, arguing that they would only serve
the 'agenda of Saddam': Williams, 1992, 160.) This conforms to a
well-documented phenomenon – the 'third person effect' – whereby
individuals (be they policy-makers or members of the public)
believe that only *others* are negatively influenced by mass media:
'The assumption that gullible others, but not one's own canny self,
are slaves to the media is so widespread that the actions based on it
may be one of the mass media's most powerful creations' (Schudson, 1995, 121). Certainly, it does not appear that audiences in
either Britain or America revolted against the war after witnessing
the aftermath of Al Amiriya, or the 'Highway of Death' despite poll
respondents' fears, like the US Administration's, that viewers are
highly sensitive to such scenes.

Public willingness to suspend its 'right to know' has alarmed civil
libertarians and journalistic opponents of government restrictions
and media self-censorship. Public acquiescence in the contracting
boundaries set on the sayable and showable in limited war lends
encouragement to cautious broadcasters who believe that the imaginative viewer can extrapolate the bigger picture from sanitised
footage without his or her sensibilities being unduly offended. Brian
Barron of the BBC, for example, defended the Corporation's decision not to show mass Iraqi casualties on the 'Highway of Death' on

the grounds that 'It was pretty obvious when you've shown one or two corpses under blankets with their rifles on top of them, what's happened. If you see too much of it, it becomes a casual image on the screen' (cited by A. Thomson, 1992, 259). Experience since Vietnam suggests that, far from the public appetite for news ever increasing, elements of the British and American media – and their publics – are *less* willing for dissent to be aired, or potentially damaging images of suffering to be screened, even in wars where comparatively little is directly at stake for that public. On what grounds, then, to challenge censorship if the public disavows its right to know, and to know by seeing (P. Taylor, 1997, 138)?

Military-Media Relations: Antipathy or Symbiosis?

What clearer statement of traditional wisdom concerning military-media relations than the preface to the MOD's instructions to Task Force-bound correspondents: 'The essence of successful warfare is secrecy; the essence of successful journalism is publicity' (Mercer, Mungham and Williams, 1987, 3)? Both the limited and total wars examined thus far offer numerous examples of tension between military and media personnel, often arising from the military belief that journalists are overwhelmingly governed by their tell-all compulsion and can accordingly only harm a war effort. Indeed, from a military perspective, such innate irresponsibility is likely to be heightened in 'limited war', as it is often imagined that 'a journalist covering a limited conflict finds it easier to sustain a peacetime stance of detachment' (Mercer, 1984, 39). In total war, the palpable consequences of defeat make the costs of waging such a war – including erosion of media freedom – more palatable. But the patriotic self-preservation impulse which suffices in total war to keep journalists' rapacity in check is likely to be diminished or absent altogether in 'limited war', where greater dissent can be expected over military means and the political ends to which they are harnessed. If anything, then, limited war calls for more intense media management.

However, viewed differently, the limited wars analysed in this chapter warrant alternative conclusions. Despite the cherished myths of two professions locked in combat, the routine spats between military and media often resemble a ritualised and symbolic display of shadow-boxing. In Vietnam, the Falklands and the Gulf War, the military and media (vexations with minders and pooling arrangements aside) often appeared to get on remarkably well, despite outward dissimilarities and repeated gripes. Journalists, after all, as they are fond of remarking, are often unkempt, ill-disciplined, and trained largely in bar-rooms in the habits of competition rather than those of co-operation instilled into trainee soldiers. But thrown together, journalists and the military often seem to develop what Kaplan (a military briefer in Vietnam) described as 'an intense loving-hating mutuality and dependency' (1982, 43–5). Others have certainly noted too that many of the American reporters in Vietnam developed close relationships with the military commanders and soldiers on the ground, if not always with press officers. Indeed, some attribute the more critical reports from the field of Halberstam *et al.* to their identification with this level of the military hierarchy: those who daily saw the improbability of ridding South Vietnam of its communists and the unprepared-ness of the Army of the Republic of Vietnam (ARVN) for the job. Thus the pessimism of some of the press corps was in fact acquired from, or corroborated by, the military, and was not an instinctive antagonistic response to those in uniform from a disrespectful younger generation (Arnett, 1995, 95–6).

The phenomenon of military-media 'bonding' was particularly marked during the Falklands conflict, perhaps not surprisingly given the peculiar circumstances of the press corps' long sea voyage to the South Atlantic. What occurred in this conflict was not simply that journalists found they could quite happily enjoy pre-dinner drinks in the mess with their naval travelling companions, but something more profound. As David Morrison puts it:

> If we look at the situation in the Falklands what we see is how journalists can become incorporated into a new reality, indeed make that reality their own which then has consequences for how they see the world and what events and happenings are deemed significant to investigate and report. (1994, 315)

In short, civilian attitudes and values were over-ridden by a new 'social world' in which military norms predominated. The re-oriented journalists accepted matter-of-factly, as the reality of war, acts which in civilian life they might have found unconscionable. As a result, certain aspects of the conflict went unreported, such as the bayoneting of Argentine soldiers while they surrendered (a story which was widely reported, and sometimes contested, several years later).

Morrison and Tumber's post-war interviews with the Task Force press corps found that many journalists had heard rumours at the time of such occurrences, but most were reluctant even to pursue these, let alone attempt to report them. Asked why not, John Shirley of the *Sunday Times* responded revealingly:

> The fact that we became so much participants in the thing affected it. I didn't see so much myself, but [one journalist] told me, that he had seen occasions in which people had shot unarmed men, unarmed Argentinians who were in the process of surrendering. He didn't report it because he said that, although he disapproved of it, he felt he could understand it. In the tension of battle and given what was going on it was an understandable action. That is not a very objective journalistic judgement. That is the judgement of a participant, and to that extent it's wrong. You see, I think that this is an absolutely central problem – this kind of crisis of identity. This problem of participant versus observer. (Morrison, 1994, 316)

Thus identification with the military far exceeded simply sharing the same privations. Civilian journalists, often unwittingly and unselfconsciously, found themselves responding to war as a soldier would, attaching non-civilian meanings and values to military acts.

Despite the Falklands campaign's unique characteristics, the reconstruction of social reality experienced by journalists on that occasion occurs generally in wartime, if sometimes in less intensified forms (Morrison, 1994, 315). That the military can encourage this process of identification, from which they are the beneficiaries, has undoubtedly been recognised since 1982 (though it should have been apparent from as early as the First World War). During Desert Storm, according to BBC correspondent Martin Bell, the British Army operationalised its 'new way of dealing with the press':

> The new way was not only to allow us full access under controlled conditions, with a travelling censorship system operating alongside, but to invite us to share the dangers and hardships of the

front-line soldiers in such a way that we could hardly fail to identify with them. The process was called 'bonding', and – unusually for an army plan – it worked. (1995, 12)

To cement the bond, journalists with the MRTs were set to work digging trenches: more for the amusement of the troops and 'militarisation' of the reporters, one suspects, than for any material advantages of their spade-work. Having shared the military burdens in some small way, the reporters were later 'rewarded' by being briefed – along with the troops – on the full Desert Storm battle plan ('all 120 pages of it'), ten days before it began (Bell, 1995, 13). Of course, given the arrangements for 'security review', even if a journalist had been so minded, he or she could hardly have disclosed Schwarzkopf's 'left hook' manoeuvre into Iraq. But as a symbolic gesture the briefing was a significant reflection of the growing belief within military establishments that 'naturally' adversarial media can be 'tamed', if controlled, massaged and manipulated in certain ways.

Some journalists need little such encouragement. During the Falklands conflict, in which many journalists slipped unconsciously into a military mind-set, some wilfully affected a pro-military disposition, explicitly renouncing peacetime norms of impartiality and detachment. As Max Hastings famously remarked, 'When one's nation is at war, reporting becomes an extension of the war effort. Objectivity only comes back into fashion when the black-out comes down'; these words were borrowed from his father, a celebrated Second World War reporter (cited by Williams 1992, 156). For Hastings junior, it mattered little whether a war was 'total' or 'limited' if it was 'our' war, and it was this sense of patriotic involvement which propelled him to make such a pronouncement.

He has not been alone in adopting the Second World War as a paradigm for later conflicts in which far less has been at stake for the British state, and neither is it simply journalists in close proximity with military personnel who have determined, in limited war, to espouse an uncritically supportive role. During the Falklands conflict, the BBC defended itself from backbench charges of 'almost treasonable behaviour' – in casting doubt on MOD statistics – in terms which were redolent of its Second World War position. Thus, even while the BBC Chairman insisted that the public 'wish[ed] to be told the truth' about the war, he was adamant that 'the BBC is not, and could not be, neutral as between our own country and an aggressor. Our interviewers and newsreaders are not sitting on some kind of lofty Olympian fence, mediating evenhandedly between two equally culpable contestants' (Howard, 1982). The BBC would thus be 'truthful' and avoid blatant identification with 'our boys', but it would not be exactly impartial either, just as it protested in the Second World War that it took sides for Britain but not within it.

The BBC's wartime redefinition of impartiality was, however, insufficient for the tastes of many British newspapers. The *Sun*, most vocally, went much further in abandoning any pretence of neutrality, conceiving its role in the Falklands war primarily as cheerleader for 'our boys'. Thus its ill-advised 'sponsor a sidewinder' campaign; its headlines such as 'Gotcha' and 'Up Yours Galtieri'; its crusade against Argentinian 'bully beef' and so on. That the Task Force did not necessarily approve of the *Sun*'s efforts on its behalf, and that a number of readers deserted the paper for its less jingoistic rival, *The Mirror*, did not prevent the *Sun* from attempting to reprise the role during the Gulf War. During Desert Shield and Desert Storm, the paper was adamant once again that (in the words of its chief leader writer, Ronald Spark): 'Truth is sacred, but a newspaper that tells only part of the truth is a million times preferable to one that tells the truth to harm its country' (quoted by Platt, 1991b, 13). Likewise, some American print journalists were the harshest critics of CNN's reporting from Iraq, and of what they perceived as unacceptable 'neutralism' in television coverage which equivocated morally between Iraq and the Coalition (Aubin, 1992, 359–61).

It is hard to maintain that 'publicity', in the MOD's shorthand, is indeed the undiluted aim of media in limited war. Experience of total and limited war alike might suggest that Gitlin and Hallin are closer to the mark with their generalisation that the media in wartime have habitually acted as patriots and cheerleaders for the military: something the Department of Defense deliberately sought to foster in the Gulf, by offering journalists from local American news outfits 'hometown' tours to see their local boys in action (Sharkey, 1991, 112; Gitlin and Hallin, 1994, 149–63). Throughout the twentieth century, reporters and media organisations have often conceived of their role as celebrants of 'war culture' where war falls into Hallin's 'sphere of consensus'. They enable distant civilians to participate vicariously (or more directly, via patriotic displays and rituals) in an activity esteemed in Western culture. But in so doing, the media may also help obscure the connection between war and death - whether by shying away from showing dead bodies or demurring, as the BBC did during the Gulf War, from playing pop songs which alluded to human mortality – in societies increasingly reluctant to acknowledge their inextricable relationship.

4

Media and Terrorism

Is terrorism a form of war? Many would angrily reject the proposition. An immensely emotive descriptor, 'terrorism' is sometimes regarded not as a continuation of politics by other means – Clausewitz's classic definition of war – but as the illegitimate recourse to particularly reprehensible forms of violence, directed to ends which may have as much to do with gaining publicity as rectifying political grievances. Whereas warfare has developed certain conventions which, at least theoretically, make it possible for war to be fought justly, terrorism is often taken to be the abnegation of these norms (Walzer, 1992).

In classical 'just war' theory, war is conducted between armies (be they states' armed forces or guerrilla organisations) who recognise the legitimacy of targeting their uniformed enemies, but endeavour to limit violence against civilians and, more generally, to keep their use of force proportionate to the ends in question. Terrorism, on the other hand, arouses fierce controversy because it often violates – or appears to violate – just war conventions. Sometimes defined as 'extra-normal' violence, terrorism's norm violation is twofold (allowing that substate actors may legitimately challenge, in certain circumstances, the state's monopoly over the use of force). First, it generally occurs in peacetime, although 'terrorists' often proclaim that their actions constitute a *de facto* state of war. Second, terrorism refuses to offer immunity to civilians, or to engage in open warfare governed by certain agreed conventions. Indeed the distinguishing characteristic of terrorism is frequently taken to be its random selection of 'innocent people' as its particular targets, unlike conventional (and sometimes guerrilla) warfare in which combatants alone are legitimate targets (Walzer, 1992, 197). In tearing at the fabric of peacetime life, and snatching away civilian lives, terrorism is often regarded as a perverse and cowardly crime, and not a form of war at all. Since the first spectacular hijackings of the late 1960s, and the emergence of an apparently new phenomenon of 'international terrorism', the subject has generated intense, emotional responses.

In practice, however, the distinction between terrorism and war is rarely clear-cut. After all, as 'just war' theorist Michael Walzer acknowledges, many twentieth-century wars – however just the recourse to violence – have not been prosecuted with entirely just, or proportionate, means. To take but the most obvious example, the Second World War (whatever justice lay in taking up arms against fascism) saw the deliberate mass bombing of civilians by both sides in the attempt to destroy the opponent's *civilian* morale and productive capacity. If this strategy, which the Allies euphemistically termed 'strategic bombing', violated norms of *jus in bello*, how much more so the American decision to drop atomic bombs on the Japanese cities of Hiroshima and Nagasaki in August 1945? Was such a dramatic departure from convention really necessary to end the war quickly, and was speedy termination of the Pacific war proportionate with unleashing atomic weaponry? By eroding the principle of civilian immunity, Walzer suggests that these wide-scale violations of 'just war' norms during the Second World War encouraged the adoption of terrorism by non-state groups: 'terrorism in the strict sense, the random murder of innocent people, emerged as a strategy of revolutionary struggle only in the period after World War Two, that is, after it had become a feature of conventional war' (1992, 198).

Total war, in Walzer's view, spawned an 'age of terrorism': its illegitimate offspring. However, one could question Walzer's 'strict' definition of terrorism in such a way as to suggest an even closer familial resemblance than he is prepared to concede. In practice, the two phenomena often shade into one another, though many theorists, like Walzer, have tried to erect an impregnable boundary between 'pure terrorism' (an illegitimate resort to norm-violating violence) and war (a legitimate activity, if fought justly and for good cause). Where he highlights the random killing of innocents as terrorism's essence, some insist that coercion through fear, or lack of popular mandate, distinguishes terrorism from forms of unorthodox warfare. Definitions of terrorism abound, and no consensus has emerged – neither is one likely – over this 'essentially contested term' (Schmid and Jongman 1988). As Jennifer Hocking has pointed out: 'Replete with implied moral opprobrium, a socially assigned value and meaning, an imputation of illegitimacy and outrage, "terrorism" can never fit the apparently value-neutral typologies much used in the social sciences' (Hocking, 1992, 86).

The label 'terrorist' does not lend itself to value-free application, having been an 'epithet to fasten on a political enemy' ever since the French Revolution (Walter, 1969, 4). In increasingly common vernacular currency since 1945, the term terrorist has often been applied or avoided in thoroughly partisan ways: a relativism captured in the hackneyed expression, 'one man's terrorist is another man's freedom fighter'. Labelling an opponent 'terrorist', argues Conor Cruise O'Brien approvingly, 'constitutes a declaration of illegality of the political violence referred to' (in Crenshaw, 1983, 93–4). The semantic war over words and definitions forms part of a wider ideological battle over the legitimacy of the resort to force: the label 'terrorist' connotes illegitimacy, while its alternatives – such as 'guerrilla', 'liberation army' or 'freedom fighter' – confer approbation (Peter Taylor, 1986). As the label tells us more about the labeller's stance towards a particular group than it does about the precise nature of that organisation's activities, it is perhaps no surprise that in mainstream Western discourse the term has been most commonly attached to substate groups of a leftist, revolutionary or separatist complexion (Herman, 1982; Walzer, 1992, 197; Schlesinger, 1995, 235). Michael Parenti observes (with particular respect to American media in the 1980s):

> Who is and is not a 'terrorist' in the media is a matter of politics. Leftist guerrillas with a wide popular base are often referred to as 'terrorists'. Right-wing mercenaries, financed by the CIA [Central Intelligence Agency], who attack unarmed villagers, farm cooperatives, clinics, and schools in countries like Nicaragua, Angola, and Mozambique are 'rebels'. 'State terrorism' is what leftist governments do to defend themselves against these rebels, never what the United States does to suppress popular movements in a score of countries. (1993, 202)

In practice, many groups commonly designated 'terrorist' engage in activities which only partially, or occasionally, meet the kind of purist definition offered by Walzer (the 'random murder of innocent people'). Indeed, this is a rather problematic formulation, begging the question 'Innocent according to whom?' After all, those engaged in political violence might well dispute Walzer's notions of both the 'innocence' and randomness of their targets. Terrorism, or what is conventionally defined as terrorism, is not necessarily 'random'. Terrorists may in fact be quite *selective* in their targeting, and might not actually regard their victims as 'innocent people' at all, but rather as having some more or less direct – often symbolic – connection with the particular issue over which they are struggling (Gerrits, 1992, 56–9). (Thus all Americans may appear legitimate targets of hijackings in the eyes of some pro-Palestinian groups, given America's role in supporting Israel.) Often, where the purpose of terror is to have a 're-enforcement' effect, targeting is highly discriminate. For example, the IRA's attacks in Ulster on people who worked in ways, sometimes tangentially, connected with the British state apparatus in Northern Ireland were intended to send a clear message to other 'collaborators' that such behaviour would bring retribution. Terrorism was more 'unpredictable' – in its timing and location – than wholly 'indiscriminate'. And this has been true elsewhere when the aim is to coerce particular categories of people ('collaborators') by engendering a generalised sense of fear, born of the recognition that, to others at least, they are not 'innocent' (Townshend, 1986, 92).

'Terrorism' – a word which, given its contested nature, requires quotation marks in the imagination if not on paper – thus occupies a shadowy area between peace and war. As a special form of warfare, terrorism merits inclusion here. But more particularly, it requires our attention because its specialness is often presumed to lie (at least in part) in terrorists' unorthodox, 'symbiotic', relationship with mass media. When states declare 'emergencies' in order to deal with 'terrorist threats', although still notionally peacetime, such governments often expect considerable – if not total – compliance from national media organisations. As during 'limited wars', states directly confronted by terrorism, though they may begin by trying to deny the terrorists' assertion that a state of war exists, often end by invoking the 'total war' paradigm. The 'war against terrorism' is presented as literally such, by states eager to elicit media support against a 'terrorist threat' construed as severely endangering personal freedoms and shredding the very fabric of civil society (Schlesinger, Murdock and Elliott, 1983, 113). Media organisations may, then, find themselves encouraged, constrained or compelled to adopt a 'counter-terrorist' stance, facing stigmatisation as traitors and possible legal sanctions should they fail to comply. But whether the media do invariably 'aid terrorism', how, and how we can know, are complex issues demanding closer scrutiny.

'Symbiosis': Conventional Wisdom on Terrorism and the Media

Although definitions of terrorism are as divergent as they are numerous, many of them focus on the propagandistic nature of terrorist acts of violence. In the words of Schmid and de Graaf: 'Terrorism cannot be understood only in terms of violence. It has to be understood primarily in terms of propaganda. Violence and propaganda have much in common. Violence aims at behaviour modification by coercion. Propaganda aims at the same through persuasion. Terrorism is a combination of the two' (1982, 14). If the intention of terrorism is, as the term suggests, to induce terror then it follows that the ultimate targets are those watching – not those directly suffering – violent attack. (The US Army definition formulated in 1983, for example, asserts that terrorism involves 'a criminal act that is often symbolic in nature and intended to influence an audience beyond the immediate victims'.) Terrorism is therefore an 'indirect' and largely psychological strategy, which eschews head-on confrontation with a uniformed enemy in favour of 'armed propaganda' calculated to generate maximum response amongst target audiences (Stohl, 1990, 93).

Terrorists, generally unevenly matched militarily with their foe, are less concerned with outright physical victory than with the exertion of pressure (psychological, political, financial) over those from whom they wish to extract concessions. Terrorist strategy, as often understood, aims to generate fear in publics which will then pressurise states to accede to the terrorists' demands. It may have other aims besides: the generation of sympathy for, or conferral of legitimacy upon, the group's aims; a desire to raise the costs of occupation in colonial situations, either financially by attacking infrastructure or security forces' personnel, and/or by provoking state repression which will erode the legitimacy and international standing of that regime to the insurgents' benefit. None of these objectives necessarily requires mass casualties, though they may require spectacular acts to attract attention. Terrorism has thus been likened to a form of theatre, in which 'terrorists want a lot of people watching, not a lot of people dead' (Jenkins, 1988, 253). Violent attacks are choreographed not just for those few with ring-side seats – first-hand witnesses – but for the television cameras which will transmit the spectacle to a wider audience.

Given these prevalent interpretations, it is no wonder that terror-ism is widely perceived as inextricably, symbiotically, linked with mass media. Without media coverage, the argument often goes, terrorism would simply wither away (Szumski, 1986, 70). Acts which garner no publicity may as well not be undertaken. Wide-spread attention alone gives purpose and meaning to terrorist acts, which, in the words of ABC anchorman Ted Koppel, would other-wise resemble the 'philosopher's hypothetical tree falling in the forest – no one hears it fall and therefore it does not exist' (cited by Clawson, 1990, 242). Taking publicity to be the *sine qua non* of terrorism, many writers posit a direct connection between the emer-gence of modern global communications and the explosion, and internationalisation, of terrorism since the late 1960s. Mass jet transportation assisted the mobility of groups which became increasingly multi-national in their organisation and finance, also affording them opportunities for internationalised targeting which would ensure – thanks to mass media – that a dispute was carried far beyond its immediate locus. The French commentator, Gerard Chaliand, for example, asserted in the late 1980s that terrorism's growing impact since 1968 – the year of the first skyjacking of an El Al airliner by the Popular Front for the Liberation of Palestine – could be 'attributed almost exclusively to the development of the mass media' (1987, 13). He is not alone in seeing the late 1960s as a watershed in the development of a form of terrorism that had 'virtually nothing in common with the conventional terrorism long used by such political movements with a specialist armed wing, such as Irgun and the Stern Gang' (Chaliand, 1987, 13; Schmid and de Graaf, 1982, 16).

In fact, states regarded terrorism – including that of Irgun and the Stern Gang (two Zionist organisations fighting for the creation of a state of Israel in the 1940s) – as an essentially publicity-seeking strategy long before the age of television (Carruthers, 1995). British officials in Palestine were quite certain that 'extremist' Zionists' strategy rested on attracting international – and especially American

– attention to that territory (administered by Britain under a 'Mandate' from the League of Nations since the end of the First World War). Terrorism, as amplified by the world's media, was attributed an agenda-setting function. Zionist violence would raise awareness about Zionism's political programme, and possibly garner sympathy, for 'terrorism' simultaneously sought to provoke a repressive response which would demonstrate the illegitimacy of Britain's 'occupation' of Palestine. Menachem Begin later wrote that his organisation's aim had been to make Palestine a 'glass house', into which the world would look 'with ever increasing interest' (1977, 68). Likewise, in other insurgencies British officials feared that *any* reporting of terrorism was likely to favour the 'terrorists'. Typically, one official observed (of Malayan communist activity): 'the BBC is the worst offender in creating the impression that life in Malaya (as in Palestine) consists of a series of incidents. The aim of the grenade thrower is to hit the headlines, and our press and broadcasting do the job for him to his complete satisfaction' (Carruthers, 1995, 90).

The suspicion that media coverage inevitably privileges (and possibly glamorises) terrorist activities, bringing them to the attention of a wider audience who do not necessarily share the government's distinction between 'terrorist' and 'freedom fighter', has long existed in uneasy tension with its opposite: that, left to their own devices, terrorists are their own worst publicists. With sufficient exposure to terrorists' public appearances, audiences would automatically come to distrust such shifty characters. Thus the BBC's Richard Francis mooted that televised interviews with terrorists could be as much 'a scaffold' as 'a platform', when the Corporation came under fire in the 1970s for broadcasting interviews with Irish republicans (Schlesinger, Murdock and Elliott, 1983, 131). Although these colonial counter-insurgencies are often overlooked in the literature on terrorism, official prescriptions – with all their contradictions – for dealing with the media devised in the 1940s and 1950s closely foreshadow more recent media-management techniques for both stigmatisation of 'terrorists' and positive presentation of counter-terrorist measures (Carruthers, 1996, 101–29).

By the mid-1980s the notion of terrorism as publicity-fuelled had become an *idée fixe* (Townshend, 1986, 36). Margaret Thatcher famously proclaimed in 1985 that publicity was the 'oxygen of terrorism'; in fact she borrowed this formulation from Britain's then Chief Rabbi, Lord Jakobovits, and it was shortly followed by a government initiative to starve the IRA, its political wing Sinn Fein, and assorted 'proscribed organisations' in Northern Ireland, of the oxygen which they were believed to crave and require (Thatcher, 1993, 408). At a time when many Western European states faced 'terrorist threats' within their own boundaries, and Middle Eastern groups had 'America held hostage' (as one network famously put it of the Iranian US Embassy siege), this shared transatlantic understanding of terrorism dictated counter-measures which included at their core a 'controlling of the alleged media-terrorism symbiosis' (Hocking, 1992, 87).

If terrorists are believed to be both arch-propagandists in their own right, as well as expert manipulators of the media, then curbing terrorism unavoidably entails severing the terrorists' access to mass media (Schlesinger, 1991, 17–28). Terrorists generally accompany their acts with a flurry of verbal activity; in Segaller's words: 'the violence of terrorism is positively verbose: always accompanied by threats, communiqués and manifestos, and succeeded by historical argument and political reaction' (Segaller, 1987, 62). But more significant than the terrorists' own propaganda is the complicity of the mainstream mass media in terrorist objectives: their own self-generated posters, manifestos, leaflets and broadcasts are unlikely, after all, to reach a wide audience and even less likely to convince any other than the already converted.

According to the orthodoxy which has held sway since the 1980s, news organisations serve terrorist ends in various ways, often unwittingly, and only occasionally as the result of direct pressure by terrorists to publicise their statements, or face unpleasant consequences (as, for example, the 'Unabomber's' successful insistence that US newspapers print his manifesto). Rather, the orthodoxy contends that media 'complicity' is generally not coerced but the result of an unfortunate symbiosis between terrorist and news organisations, whereby the 'super entertainers of our time' (as Walter Laqueur calls terrorists) offer the latter irresistibly dramatic bait which they cannot help but swallow (1977, 223). Terrorists recognise the imperatives of Western broadcast journalism: their acts meet the criteria of 'newsworthiness' (sudden, violent disruptions of normalcy being the very stuff of Western news, not least if the victims are Westerners). As Bowyer Bell puts it: 'There is simply no way that the Western media can ignore an event that has been fashioned specifically for their needs. Television terrorists can no more do without the media than the media can resist the terror-event. The two are in a symbiotic relationship' (Wardlaw, 1989, 76). And as if their violent theatre was not enough in itself to attract attention, terrorists also often tailor the timing of their 'performances' so as to make prime-time newscasts (Gerrits, 1992, 29–61). In short, terrorists offer news organisations every assistance to further the insurgents' own publicity-seeking ends. Furthermore, since the attracting of attention is terrorism's central ambition, it matters to them not at all whether the resultant media interest is hostile or sympathetic towards their objectives: to be centre stage is sufficient of itself (Miller, 1984, 4). Indeed, some orthodox commentators themselves would reason that 'hostile' media coverage is a logical impossibility: the very act of televising terrorism glamorises and confers legitimacy upon actors ill-deserving such recognition, particularly (though not only) when terrorists are called upon to give interviews.

Terrorists, in this interpretation, are therefore uniquely able to disrupt the normal productive processes of news as 'event promoters', in Molotch and Lester's typology (Molotch and Lester, 1997, 201–2; Nacos, 1994). In other words, violent 'spectaculars' enable terrorists figuratively to hijack the news agenda, displacing those political elites who ordinarily set it, and who are held hostage for the duration. George Gerbner postulates: 'Live coverage of terrorists, forced manifestos, extensive publicity of unrest and protest, in other words anything that lets insurgents speak for themselves, risks wresting control of cameras and context, if briefly, from the system' (Gerbner, 1992, 94). The task for states facing such insurgent challenges is consequently to wrest control of the camera back from the terrorists, to sever the presumed 'symbiosis', in the hope that decreased media attention to one terrorist group will also avert a 'copy-cat effect' whereby other such organisations imitate the same, or escalated, tactics (Schmid and de Graaf, 1982, 117–42). Once again, television is the particular target of attention, and sometimes, blame (Clutterbuck, 1981, 147).

Amongst orthodox commentators, television's 'contagion effect' is traced back to the 1970s. Though insistence on violent behaviour being learnt and encouraged by media is often presumptive, one empirical survey from 1980, based on the Rand Corporation's chronology of international terrorism and the output of US television networks and nine newspapers from different countries, concluded that the media had encouraged the spread of terrorist violence from Latin America to Western Europe in two periods, from 1968 to 1971, and 1973 to 1974 (cited by Paletz and Boiney, 1992, 18). Thus, from the orthodoxy's perspective, the purpose of media management is both short and long term: to prevent media furthering the immediate aims of particular terrorist groups, while simultaneously eliminating the 'scourge of terrorism' by disabling television's capacity to accentuate, and thereby promote, terrorism.

'Voluntary Self-Restraint': The US Model

Attempts by states to curb, or otherwise influence, media reporting of terrorism have taken many different forms. In some states, often those not immediately or directly threatened by terrorism, no controls exist, and neither have media organisations generated their own internal guidelines for covering terrorist activity (Paletz and Tawney, 1992, 106). At the other end of the spectrum, certain governments have instituted draconian censorship regimes to constrain, or even eradicate, media reporting of specific terrorist groups, as was the case, for example, in 1980s' South Africa, with respect to the 'terrorist' African National Congress. Here we will focus primarily on two case studies, which exemplify voluntarist and more interventionist state approaches to media management. The American governmental preference for 'voluntary' restraint by US media in reporting terrorism will be contrasted with the movement of British (and other Western European) governments towards more formal controls, particularly as the media reported Northern Ireland's 'troubles' in the 1970s and 1980s.

The American policy-making community became particularly vexed by the issue of terrorism and its mass-mediated transmission at the end of the 1970s. While a number of Western European states had faced leftist and separatist challenges during the late 1960s and 1970s (such as the Red Army Faction, or Baader-Meinhof Gang, in West Germany; the *Brigate Rosse*, or Red Brigades, in Italy; the IRA and Irish National Liberation Army (INLA) in Northern Ireland; and *Euzkadi Ta Akatasuna* (ETA), the Basque separatist movement in Spain), the USA experienced almost no terrorism on its own soil in the corresponding period. Although America continued to experience comparatively few attacks within its own boundaries until the 1990s (with the World Trade Center and Oklahoma bombings), the late 1970s marked the start of a period in which Americans overseas, especially in the Middle East, became the victims of 'international terrorism' (Bremer, 1991, 73).

America's introduction to terrorism was unusually protracted: the hostage-taking of the US Embassy in Tehran by Iranian militants – angered by Washington's offer of sanctuary to the deposed Shah – spanned some 444 days. According to George Ball (President Carter's Under Secretary of State), the networks turned the crisis into a 'television soap opera': one in which not just the Embassy's inmates but America itself was 'held hostage' (as the news show that became ABC's 'Nightline' headlined its nightly updates). According to his own staffers, Carter's inability to draw the episode to a successful conclusion was a major factor in his punishing electoral defeat by Ronald Reagan in 1980, whose inauguration in January 1981 was staged simultaneously with the hostages' release. Carter's Vice-President Walter Mondale later spoke of 'the horror of that evening news guillotine dropping every evening' (Schlesinger, 1995, 250). But for all Reagan's eagerness to present himself as the very antithesis to the dithering Carter, his presidency was by no means immune from terrorist activity. With American targets becoming the increasing object of attack by groups connected with Palestinian liberation (such as the blowing-up of a US marine barracks in Lebanon in October 1983, with 241 fatalities, and the hijacking of TWA flight 847 in June 1985, in which 104 Americans were held hostage), Reagan elevated counter-terrorism to a central plank of his foreign policy. His public stance relied on an uncompromising refusal to deal with terrorists, and the 'blacklisting' of state sponsors of international terrorism, which his advisers ultimately traced back to Moscow, via such channels as Libya and Syria (influenced by journalist Claire Sterling's conspiracist exposé, *The Terror Network: The Secret War of International Terrorism*, 1981). In private, however, as the 'Irangate' hearings later demonstrated, the Administration's stance against terrorism was less than absolute. Attempting to secure the release of American hostages in Lebanon, Washington had covertly entered into arms deals with Iran (then high on the US list of terrorist sponsors, and thought to have some leverage over the hostage-takers), the profits from which were diverted to the Contra 'rebels' in Nicaragua, whom Congress had prevented the President from funding by open means (Chomsky, 1989b).

The 1980s proved a period of intense state anxiety over terrorism, and the media's presumed complicity therein. Some government and academic observers, believing virtually any coverage to be functional to the terrorist cause, advocated sweeping measures to constrain mass media. Others, however, have limited their concern – and practical suggestions – to more specific worries about the ways in which news organisations, 'as a consequence of the journalistic equivalent of the Heisenberg effect', become participants in the 'terrorist drama', often to the detriment of counter-terrorist measures and sometimes at the cost of hostages' lives (Schmid and de Graaf, 1982, 142). These concerns include the high level of attention paid by the media to ongoing 'spectaculars', which accordingly pressurise the government to 'do something', when to do nothing – or act quietly behind the scenes – might be more efficacious. To some commentators, the Iranian hostage crisis highlights the damaging effects of saturation media coverage: the US networks' insatiable interest in the Iranian Embassy siege placed undue pressure on Carter to act resolutely, thereby throwing his subsequent impotence into greater relief. (To others, Carter himself was partially responsible for sustained attention, in a society where the media eye is invariably fixed on the President. By constantly issuing statements on the hostage situation rather than downplaying or doing his best to ignore it, Carter ensured that the hostage situation remained in the public eye. Aimed at training such a powerful media spotlight on the Embassy that the hostages would not be harmed, Carter's 'rose garden' strategy perhaps fulfilled its purpose, though irreparably harming Carter himself in the process: Wallach, 1991, 88).

Journalists have also been indicted for attempting to establish 'informal' communication with the perpetrators during ongoing terrorist 'incidents'. Apart from the questionable wisdom of posing such questions as 'Have any deadlines have been set?', journalistic interventions of this kind also tie up lines of communication at crucial times, possibly hampering official hostage negotiations (Wardlaw, 1989, 79). Intrusive lighting and the jockeying of camera crews for prime positions may also directly compromise imminent rescue bids, even when journalists abide by agreements with officials to leak no prior word of security force operations (Wardlaw, 1989, 80). But perhaps the most vexed question of journalistic 'participation' in the terrorists' theatre is their occasional accession to demands for televised interviews.

This became a matter of pointed governmental concern during the seventeen-day TWA 847 hijacking, from 14 to 30 June 1985. Not only were the networks accused of paying the incident too much attention in general terms – a total of almost 500 reports, totalling some twelve hours of newstime, at a daily cost of some \$100 000 – but they also engaged in forms of coverage particularly irksome to the Administration (Schlesinger, 1995, 251). A news conference was used by hostages, at their captors' instigation, to ask Reagan not to mount a militarised rescue, and to pressure Israel to release the Shi'ite prisoners demanded by the hijackers in exchange for the safe return of the 104 American passengers. Even worse, Nabih Berri, head of the Shi'ite Muslim group *Amal* (who had apparently taken advice from US media studies graduates on the formulation of his tactics) was interviewed several times by the networks (Laqueur and Alexander, 1987, 125). To the chagrin of the White House, the networks treated Berri, in the words of one academic, 'like a po-litical leader, virtually no differently than the President of the Uni-ted States' (Nacos, 1994, 66). Indeed, on one occasion during an ABC 'Good Morning America' broadcast, anchor David Hartman ended his interview with Berri by asking, 'Any final words to Pre-sident Reagan this morning?' (cited in Nacos, 1994, 67). This seemed proof positive of the networks' moral equivalence as between terrorists and the administration, a state of affairs bemoaned by Reagan's Secretary of State Al Haig: 'When TV reporters interview kidnappers it...risks international outlaws seem[ing] like responsible personalities. Television should avoid being used that way' (Nacos, 1994, 67).

How, though, was television to avoid being 'used' by terrorists? Would formal governmental controls over media coverage not imply that terrorism had triumphed, by successfully provoking the state into a repressive erosion of civil liberties? On the other hand, could such a sensation-seeking medium as television be trusted to curb those very excesses which made it such an attractive magnet for publicity-hungry terrorists? The question of what was to be done, and how the rights of citizens to a free press were to be balanced against the responsibility of the state to combat terrorism, caused much agonised debate amongst media and administration elites, and continues to do so, as America (the 'future promised land of terrorism') faces domestic terrorist attacks even when much terrorism in Western Europe has ceased, abated or declined (Zulaika and Douglass, 1996, ix). In general, the preferred solution has been that news organisations act as their own self-regulators in reporting terrorism, albeit with a fair amount of nudging in that direction by official bodies. Certainly for journalists, self-restriction represents a preferable state of affairs to direct state intervention, though media non-observance of 'voluntary' internal guidelines – as during the TWA episode – has provoked repeated governmental moves towards greater regulation.

Media organisations, especially television networks (which, as in wartime proper, often find themselves the primary focus of state anxiety), began to develop guidelines for handling terrorism in the late 1970s. They did so after the US government's Task Force on Disorders and Terrorism published its Report in 1976, recommending that media coverage of terrorist incidents be based on the principles of 'minimum intrusiveness' and 'complete, non inflammatory coverage' (Wardlaw, 1989, 83). Its specific recommendations included: the use of a pool of reporters to cover incidents on behalf of all news organisations (foreshadowing the use of pools in Grenada, Panama and the Gulf, although this would be less practical in an unforeseen terrorist 'episode'); self-imposed restrictions on lighting and use of cameras; limitations on direct interviews with hostage-takers; non-publication of tactical information released by the security forces; delayed reporting of inflammatory details; reliance on official spokespersons; and balancing 'terrorist propaganda' with official statements (Wardlaw, 1989, 83). Such recommendations garnered cross-party support, for although formulated during the Carter presidency, curbs on the media were also championed by Reagan (Terrell and Ross, 1991, 87).

Media organisations' own internal guidelines mirror the concerns of officialdom. For example, CBS's guidelines, having acknowledged the 'dangers of "contagion"' in covering terrorist activities at all, embrace the aspiration not to provide 'an excessive platform for the terrorist/kidnapper': 'it may be better to paraphrase the [terrorists'] demands instead of presenting them directly through the voice or picture of the terrorist/kidnapper'. Moreover, CBS pledged itself not, 'except in the most compelling circumstances, and then only with the approval of the President of CBS or in his absence, the Senior Vice President of News', to broadcast live coverage of the 'terrorist/kidnapper', lest the network unwittingly provide an unedited platform. CBS also expressed its sensitivity to the authorities' prior need for access to the terrorists, and its intention to contact 'experts' on such matters as 'phraseology to be avoided'. Finally, in answer to the charge that television accords terrorism excessive airtime, CBS pledged not to let this type of story 'unduly crowd out other important news of the hour/day' (guidelines reproduced in Wardlaw, 1989, 219–20).

Such guidelines proliferated during the 1980s, but were more often breached than observed, as far as US administrations have been concerned (Gallimore, 1991, 103–18). Certainly the 1985 TWA incident – with its interviews of Berri, and widespread, emotive use of hostages' relatives as 'surrogate correspondents' – did little to suggest that media organisations were restraining themselves in accord with their stated aspirations. Reagan was sufficiently dissatisfied to appoint another Task Force on Terrorism, led by Vice-President George Bush. Media organisations lobbied strongly against the mooted introduction of enforced 'voluntary' guidelines; a rather oxymoronic formulation, with overtones of Second World War censorship practice. Some executives suggested that the Administration's aggressive noises were motivated as much by pique as by constructive counter-terrorist initiative. Ed Joyce, president of CBS News until 1985, remarked of the TWA incident: 'It was obvious that we had access to more information than the US government. A State Department official reacted with horrified disbelief when told by CBS news that hijackers had separated and removed hostages with Jewish-sounding names' (cited by Wallach, 1991, 87). As in the later debate over the 'CNN effect' (examined in Chapter 5), journalists have imagined – perhaps not unreasonably – that officials' animosity often stems from a perception that the media are usurping state prerogatives.

In the face of media criticism, the Task Force ultimately decided against recommending guidelines; instead they identified certain 'media practices that can lead to problems during an incident', such as live interviews, and appealed to the media to formulate their own codes of good conduct (Oakley, 1991, 99). Administration pressure over the media was also maintained in 1986, when Reagan officials threatened media representatives with strict application of existing laws against unauthorised disclosure of classified information (Oakley, 1991, 102). Furthermore, as Reagan escalated his international counter-terrorist campaign to include the bombing of Tripoli in April 1986 (having charged Libya with direct responsibility for the bombing of a disco, frequented by US service personnel, in Berlin), so too were the rhetorical moves intensified. 'Terrorism is war', proclaimed Secretary of State George Schultz in a 1987 statement before the Senate Armed Services Committee. 'It's a shadow war involving direct and brutal assaults on the lives of our citizens, on our national interests overseas, and on our basic values. It's vital that we win that war' (Terrell and Ross, 1991, 75).

In this fervid climate of quasi-war, many major US news organisations – for all their protestations against incipient First Amendment violations – did bow to the Administration's concerns. Stung, perhaps, by charges of insufficient fervour in the 'war against terrorism', news executives no doubt calculated that it was better to agree to introduce 'voluntary guidelines' (albeit under some duress) than have such strictures involuntarily thrust upon them. As one journalist wrote in a trade publication in 1986:

> if newspapers have been lukewarm to suggestions that they consider adopting their own guidelines on covering terrorism and downright cold to the notion of industry-wide action, the idea of talking about the subject – with other media people, with experts in the field of terrorism and with government officials – has hit their button. (Margaret Genovese, cited by Terrell and Ross, 1991, 93)

In practice, unenthusiastically or otherwise, many US media outlets have done both. Thus the late 1980s saw the introduction, or re-drafting, of internal guidelines by a number of major new outlets – such as the *Chicago Sun Times* and CBS News – coupled with a flourishing of conferences and symposia drawing media and state representatives together to discuss their mutual roles (and putative co-operation) in combating terrorism.

Government Intervention: The European experience

In the UK, as elsewhere in Western Europe, the news media have, at times, experienced more direct governmental interference in the reporting of terrorism than their American counterparts. Unlike

Washington, a number of Western European governments have faced protracted separatist/nationalist and/or revolutionary 'terrorist' campaigns on their own soil, beginning in the late 1960s and early 1970s. In America, most discussion has taken the central problem concerning terrorism and the media to be coverage of (usually short-lived) 'spectaculars', or more protracted hostage-takings, often occurring overseas, though sometimes involving US citizens as victims. For some European governments, however, terrorism has posed a more frontal assault on the state itself, and for this reason strict news management has sometimes assumed a central role in counter-terrorist strategy in ways more tangible and direct than those practised in the USA.

Successive British governments, from the early 1970s to the late 1990s, have faced perhaps the most sustained challenge from 'terrorism': in this case from republican groups seeking Irish sovereignty over the whole island of Ireland, and a withdrawal of the British military 'presence' in the North. In turn republican organisations (and the Catholic population as a whole) have been targeted by Protestant para-militaries, determined that Northern Ireland should remain firmly within the UK. The representation of republicanism has, however, been more contentious, with reporting of 'the Troubles' itself constituting one of the most strained areas of state relations with broadcasters in the UK during the 1970s and 1980s (Curtis, 1984; Schlesinger, 1987; Miller, 1994).

Until the late 1980s, British governments generally preferred 'indirect forms of pressure' to 'explicit bans on the transmission of material', or legislative curbs on the media (Schlesinger, 1987, xxi). Loud expressions of government displeasure with broadcasters were – along with other 'positive' and 'negative' news-management techniques – a mainstay of official attempts to ensure a malleable, 'counter-terrorist' media. After all, for the liberal state, managing a counter-insurgency fought within one's own boundaries poses special dilemmas: the contested territory cannot be sealed off from media attention; its citizens will not only be well aware of terrorist 'incidents' (making the sometimes-mooted 'news blackout' an impossibility), but acutely sensitive to how they are reported; and democratic freedoms cannot be wholly disregarded (however eclipsed) in the face of an 'undemocratic' resort to violence.

The 'British way of censorship', as Schlesinger refers to it, was certainly not incompatible with the state spelling out quite unmistakably to broadcasters where it expected their loyalties to lie. Shortly after the emergence of the IRA (or Provisional IRA) in 1970, the government made it clear that British broadcasters, whatever the BBC's Charter commitment to impartiality, were *not* in fact expected to be impartial as between the IRA and the British Army, or between the IRA and the government. As Christopher Chataway, the Minister responsible for broadcasting, put it in November 1971, the BBC's editorial judgements should be exercised 'within the context of the values and objectives of the society they are there to serve' (Schlesinger, Murdock and Elliott, 1983, 122). In other words, if a widespread belief in the IRA's illegitimacy permeated British society as a whole, then the BBC ought to waive its customary impartiality – as it would in wartime – in deference to public sentiment. What Chataway's formulation avoided making explicit was that the government itself well-nigh insisted on the BBC's partiality.

As in other conflicts before and since, the BBC did not find this requirement utterly irreconcilable with its Charter. As Lord Hill (then Chairman of the Governors of the BBC) wrote to the Home Secretary, Reginald Maudling, in November 1971:

> the BBC and its staff abhor the terrorism of the IRA and report their campaign of murder with revulsion... [A]s between the government and the opposition, as between the two communities in Northern Ireland, the BBC has a duty to be impartial no less than in the rest of the United Kingdom. But as between the British Army and the gunmen the BBC is not and cannot be impartial. (Hill, 1974, 209)

Highly redolent of the BBC's defence of its formal independence from government in the Second World War (and anticipating its similar stance during the Falklands/Malvinas conflict in 1982), Hill's response uncovers the BBC's acute sensitivity over its reporting of events in Northern Ireland, and its willingness to redefine impartiality to the exclusion of 'the gunmen'. Caution over the reporting of events in Northern Ireland during a time of civil unrest on a grand scale was also evident in the additional levels of editorial filtration through which all stories on the 'province' had to pass.

As the 1970s progressed, and more notably during the 1980s, this requirement on news reporters and documentarists to seek editorial authorisation for material on Northern Ireland at the highest levels (notably the Director-General himself for permission to interview terrorists) became codified into a formal system of 'reference upwards' (Curtis, 1984, 173–96; Schlesinger, 1987, 205–43). The very existence of this encumbrance, it has been argued, encouraged self-censorship amongst journalists and current affairs programme-makers, for it made matters pertaining to Northern Ireland – almost by definition – contentious, whether they dealt with 'terrorism' or not (Curtis, 1984; Schlesinger, 1987; Miller, 1994). We cannot, of course, quantify the negative impact of the BBC's internal editorial procedures in terms of programmes or news stories not covered for fear of incurring displeasure, if not outright obstruction, amongst the higher management. Neither can we calibrate precisely the degree of cautiousness displayed in news items or documentaries which were successfully referred upwards. We can, however, note the very small number of interviews which the BBC (and indeed ITN) afforded representatives of 'terrorist organisations', which was always one of the most vexed questions concerning media coverage of terrorism, for both broadcasters and governments. The BBC interviewed IRA members once in 1972 and 1974, and not at all between 1974 and 1977, while in the same period ITN interviewed Daniel O'Connell, an IRA leader, twice (Schlesinger, Murdock and Elliott, 1983, 125). And, perhaps yet more tellingly, we can also note the BBC Controller for Northern Ireland's insistence that such individuals, when interviewed (which only occurred with the permission of the BBC Director-General himself), were explicitly treated as hostile witnesses (Curtis, 1984, 183). Indeed, in 1971 the BBC had expressly decided that 'such interviews should only be filmed and transmitted after the most serious consideration, and that the BBC should be seen to be clearly opposed to the indiscriminate methods of the extremists' (Curtis, 1984, 179; Schlesinger, 1987, 207–22). Lord Hill justified this editorial policy on the grounds of necessary self-preservation in a climate where broadcasters faced control and regulation from outside: as in wartime proper, then, it was preferable to make a display of one's loyalty than wait to be forced into a properly 'anti-terrorist' posture.

Caution surrounding interviews was heightened by the introduction, in 1974, of the Prevention of Terrorism (Temporary Provisions) Act. The Act was widely interpreted by broadcasters as outlawing such interviews *de facto*, for it created a new criminal offence of failure to pass to the authorities information relating to terrorist whereabouts or activities, and of course it was scarcely possible to arrange an interview without knowing the proscribed individual's whereabouts (Article 19, 1989, 14–15). Until the BBC interviewed a representative of the INLA (a republican splinter organisation) in 1979, after its assassination of Conservative Northern Ireland spokesman Airey Neave MP, this reading of the Prevention of Terrorism Act went unchallenged. The BBC's decision incensed Thatcher's government, partly because Neave had been her close personal friend, but also because of more generalised worries about the BBC's loyalties. With hindsight, the wisdom of an interview with the INLA looked yet more questionable (to the BBC's critics) when the IRA assassinated Lord Mountbatten in 1980. Contagion theorists readily seized on this action as directly resulting from the BBC interview, which had goaded the IRA into staging a high-profile assassination in order to reclaim the spotlight seized briefly by the rival INLA.

The Thatcher years were thereafter marked by a number of acrimonious disputes between broadcasters and government, many over the subject of televised terrorism, even though the BBC refrained after 1979 from interviews with terrorists within news broadcasts. The BBC *Panorama* team's filming of an IRA roadblock in the village of Carrickmore, though untransmitted, was alleged to have driven the Prime Minister 'scatty with rage'. While the government hinted at the mortality of the BBC's licence fee, the Corporation tightened its 'reference upwards' rules (Curtis, 1984, 165–7; Bolton, 1990, 64–83). Yet more incendiary, in government eyes, was the BBC's 1985 documentary 'At the Edge of the Union' (in the *Real Lives* series), which contained interviews with two leading Republican and Loyalist activists, and drew particular ire for the way in which it represented the Republican, Martin McGuinness, as both 'terrorist' and family man. It was a 'Hitler loved dogs' programme according to one BBC governor (Daphne Park, cited by Milne, 1988, 190). The controversy came in the wake of the TWA episode, during which Thatcher uttered her famous 'oxygen of publicity' remarks (to the American Bar Association in London in July 1985). Although these were made with specific reference to television coverage of that hijacking incident, reporters from the *Sunday Times* deliberately fuelled controversy by eliciting from Thatcher her views on a 'hypothetical' BBC interview with an

IRA figure, which was another case of print and television journalists warring with one another over competing interpretations of loyalty in what increasingly resembled 'wartime' (Moloney, 1991, 36).

Once it became known that a documentary featuring McGuinness was in fact in the pipeline, the Home Secretary, Leon Brittan, put severe pressure on the Corporation to drop it. In a letter to the BBC, he explicitly adopted Thatcher's phraseology:

> Recent events elsewhere in the world have confirmed only too clearly what has long been understood in this country: that terrorism thrives on the oxygen of publicity... Even if the programme and any surrounding material were, as a whole, to present terrorist organisations in a wholly unfavourable light, I would still ask you not to permit it to be broadcast. (quoted by Leapman, 1987, 304)

Any publicity, in short, is good publicity. Whereas Thatcher seemingly favoured a voluntarist approach – 'Ought we not to ask the media to agree among themselves to a voluntary code of conduct, under which they would not say or show anything which could assist the terrorists' morale or their cause while the hijack lasted?', she rhetorically interrogated her American audience – her Cabinet's actual behaviour towards the media far exceeded this somewhat anodyne prescription (Terrell and Ross, 1991, 92). Ultimately, in the *Real Lives* dispute, the BBC refused to shelve the programme, despite intensive pressure from both Brittan and a Board of Governors packed with political appointees. The then Director-General (to whom the programme had not in fact been referred) insisted that the BBC had 'not and will not provide unchallenged opportunities for the advocacy of terrorism', but simultaneously affirmed its right to explore and explain 'the views and motives of those who avow terrorist activity – and their associates. It includes, on occasion, the use of broadcast interviews' (Milne, 1988, 194). The programme was duly broadcast but delayed until October, and with some changes to highlight the illegitimacy of IRA violence.

It was a bruising encounter between government and Corporation, only exceeded in ferocity by the clash between Westminster and Thames Television over the screening of *Death on the Rock* in 1988. Thames's *This Week* documentary (directed by Roger Bolton, also responsible for the 'Carrickmore' episode) cast doubt over the official account of the circumstances in which three unarmed IRA members had been shot on Gibraltar by the Special Air Service. The documentary accordingly re-animated a long-standing controversy over whether British security forces operated a 'shoot to kill' policy concerning IRA suspects. Thatcher herself was said to be 'beyond rage', and railed against the programme for prejudicing the outcome of the forthcoming inquest into the deaths of the three shot dead in Gibraltar: 'Trial by television or guilt by accusation is the day that freedom dies' (cited by Henderson, Miller and Reilly, 1990, 2).

The episode aggravated an already tense relationship between Thatcher and British broadcasters, whose industry was undergoing a fundamental restructuring (which arguably made broadcasters – fearful of losing their franchises, as Thames later did – more deferential towards the government's undisguised proclivities). The nadir in the relationship, however, was undoubtedly the introduction of 1988's 'Broadcasting Ban' on the *direct* broadcasting of representatives of certain Northern Irish organisations, or the views of those soliciting support for them (or whose words could be construed thus). This highly unusual and sweeping move against radio and television reporters had been a long time in the making, and was inspired in part by the government's escalated sense of grievance over television coverage of terrorism and Thatcher's mistrust of television people generally. Moreover, faced with both an upsurge of IRA activity (as seen, for example, in the Enniskillen Remembrance Day bombing of 1987, and by attacks on British bases in Germany) and an increase in Sinn Fein's share of the Northern Irish vote (especially in 1982–3, in the wake of the Long Kesh hunger strikes), the government was searching for a means to stigmatise the IRA's political wing without resorting to such a measure of dubious profit (and legality) as internment without trial (Moloney, 1991, 8–50).

That the Ban's central target was Sinn Fein, a legal political party, was at any rate one interpretation of the extraordinary move's underlying motivation (Moloney, 1991; Schlesinger, 1991, 58; Miller, 1994, 54–7). This was not, of course, how the government publicly rationalised the measure. When the Home Secretary, Douglas Hurd, announced the Ban in the House of Commons on 19 October 1988 he couched it in terms of denying terrorists the 'support and sustenance' which they drew from access to radio and television.

Although there had in fact been very few interviews, Hurd opined that 'such appearances have caused widespread offence to viewers and listeners throughout the United Kingdom, particularly just after a terrorist outrage'; broadcasters themselves later disputed this assertion (Henderson, Miller and Reilly, 1990, 43). He further explained that the Ban followed 'very closely' similar provisions in the Republic of Ireland – which had indeed been in existence since the 1970s – but he was adamant that the restrictions did not amount to censorship, and neither did they imply censure of the broadcasters (Curtis, 1984, 189–96):

> Broadcasters have a dangerous and unenviable task in reporting events in Northern Ireland. This step is no criticism of them. What concerns us is the use made of broadcasting facilities by supporters of terrorism. This is not a restriction on reporting. It is a restriction on direct appearances by those who use or support violence. (House of Commons Debates 138, 19 October 1988, c.885)

Yet when Thatcher herself justified the Ban, her words suggested a more serious censorial intent on the government's part, in recognition of an extant state of war which she had hitherto adamantly insisted did not pertain: 'To beat off your enemy in a war you have to suspend some of your civil liberties for a time' (cited by Article 19, 1989, 25). This re-formulation of course begs the question of precisely what measures such a 'war' legitimises (Gilbert, 1992). But many British newspapers welcomed the move regardless, and even criticism from broadcasters was somewhat muted, loth, as many were, to be seen as 'soft on IRA terrorism' (Article 19, 1989, 26–7).

Initially, broadcasters were thrown into confusion by the vaguely-worded, but seemingly all-inclusive, nature of 'the Ban', in another echo of the imposition of wide but nebulous reporting restrictions at the start of both world wars. What were the retro-active penalties for non-compliance? Did it apply to fictional historical dramas and documentaries dealing with Irish history and politics, as well as current affairs and news programmes? Who was to decide which words might be construed as supportive of the proscribed organisations? Although the government introduced some clarifications, it seems likely that the Ban's terms were deliberately vague so as to encourage the maximum self-censorship amongst broadcasters when dealing with Northern Ireland. The government could, after all, have banned the offensive 'terrorist interviews' outright, under its powers contained within the BBC's Licence and Agreement, and under Section 29(3) of the 1981 Broadcasting Act regulating the government's relationship with independent television.

If the encouragement of caution was the Ban's intended effect, then it could perhaps be said to have worked. Many broadcasters predicted increased self-censorship after October 1988, and according to Paul Hamann, Executive Producer of BBC documentaries, a number of programmes were immediately shelved (Moloney, 1991, 46–7; Curtis and Jempson, 1993, 67–91). In some cases, broadcasters' discretion probably surpassed even government expectations, such as the Independent Broadcasting Authority's ruling that The Pogues' song, 'Streets of Sorrow', concerning the Birmingham Six, should not be broadcast as it indicated a 'general disagreement with the way the government responds to, and the courts deal with, the terrorist threat' (cited by Article 19, 1989, 65). More unequivocally, the Ban ruled out live discussions (whether with studio audiences or 'vox pops' on the street) on Northern Ireland (Article 19, 1989, 31). Soon after its introduction, Sinn Fein pointed out that the Ban was duly stigmatising them as a source of news. Not only was it clear that, whenever its representatives appeared on television, they were not accorded the same treatment as members of other legitimate parties, but also the number of such appearances was dramatically reduced after October 1988 (Henderson, Miller and Reilly, 1990, 55–63). This state of affairs was hardly surprising (and hardly unintentional) given, as one senior BBC journalist put it, 'the time-consuming rigmarole that has to be gone through if a Sinn Fein... extremist is to be brought to the microphone' (John Simpson in *The Guardian*, 18 October 1993).

However, the benefits the government accrued from the Ban are also open to question, not least because the broadcasters quickly discovered an apparent loophole: although the direct transmission of proscribed persons' voices was disallowed, these individuals could still appear, soundlessly, on television with their words subtitled or spoken by an actor. Increasingly, broadcasters 'lip-synched' actors' voices over the words of Sinn Fein leader Gerry Adams and others whose own speech was debarred, with a 'health warning' to viewers that government reporting restrictions were in place (a concession to BBC journalists' anger at the government measure which the Corporation's management made). To many, these circumventions made a mockery of the Ban, which was shown to fetishise mere voices while doing nothing about the supposedly offensive views they uttered. The government was, in this reading, made to look ridiculous by the broadcasters' ever more audacious circumventions. 'There is no more ludicrous sight on television', opined the BBC's Foreign Editor John Simpson, 'than the lip-synched soundbite' (*The Guardian*, 18 October 1993). Furthermore, this governmental 'gag' was also attacked for having given Sinn Fein an easy propaganda victory, not least in America, where Republican sympathy could be garnered for an organisation silenced (literally) by the British government (Moloney, 1991, 37). The South African apartheid regime, on the other hand, used the Ban to justify its own draconian censorship on reporting of African National Congress 'terrorism', warning South African journalists that they should not complain when the government 'adopt[ed] measures similar to those used by the British government in the fight against terrorism' (cited in Moloney, 1991, 31–2).

The Ban was not lifted until 16 September 1994, a fortnight after the IRA announced a cease-fire, and amid widespread press reports of long-standing Cabinet dissatisfaction with it. However, its introduction – and longevity – are revealing about the degree of sensitivity felt by British governments both to 'terrorism' *per se* (and the electoral success of Sinn Fein in particular), and the presumed nexus between television and terrorism. Although the Ban may well have increased broadcasters' (already considerable) caution in dealing with Northern Irish matters, it is, however, extremely doubtful whether the measure could be judged an outright success for the government.

Similarly, other Western European governments which have also resorted to censorship of the media when faced by terrorism have found that while media coverage can sometimes be controlled, terrorism itself is not necessarily thwarted by so doing. Both the Italian and West German states in the 1970s aimed to draw mass media centrally into their strategies for countering media-savvy terrorist organisations. The West German Red Army Faction was believed to be expert in manipulating mass media to its own ends: for example, by transmitting images of its imprisoned members in prison, where they claimed to be victims of state torture and martyrs of their own hunger-strikes (Schmid and de Graaf, 1982, 47–50). Similarly, the Italian government was irked by the readiness with which Italian newspapers carried the manifestos and communiqués of the *Brigate Rosse* in the 1970s. In both countries, a clamp-down on the media was mooted, especially in relation to two high-profile kidnappings: of West German industrialist Hanns Martin Schleyer by the Red Army Faction in September 1977, and of Aldo Moro, president of Italy's Christian Democratic party, by the Red Brigades in March 1978.

Only in West Germany, however, was such a blackout actually instituted. For a month, the German media agreed not only to desist from publishing any communications from the kidnappers themselves but also to report the story solely on the basis of official briefings, some of which were actually false. Despite the Red Army Faction bombarding three dozen news media outlets with almost 140 communications over the 45-day kidnapping, the government secured media silence (Schmid and de Graaf, 1982, 49). A similar news-management strategy was likewise advocated in Italy – by such unlikely proponents as Marshall McLuhan – as the Red Brigades deluged Italian newspapers and television with communiqués, photographs of the kidnapped Moro, letters, tape recordings, statements and so on (Wagner-Pacifici, 1986, 59–60). In the end, no blackout was imposed, possibly because Italy's rich network of 'counter-information' sources meant that such a blanket ban would be unsustainable in a country where national newspapers had achieved far less social penetration than elsewhere, and where a left-wing counter-culture, through which news would 'unofficially' spread, flourished. Thus novelist and philosopher Umberto Eco pointed out, of his own country, that 'to invoke silence and censorship regarding certain news items becomes beyond immoral, technically impossible' (Wagner-Pacifici, 1986, 60).

Morality and technicality aside, the imposition of 'blackouts' is also of questionable efficacy. True, the German media demurred from granting the terrorists direct access to the airwaves or press columns, but in so doing they – and the state which gagged them thus – did not save the life of Schleyer, who was duly killed when the state refused to release a number of prominent Red Army Faction prisoners in exchange for his safe release. On the other hand, although Italian media acceded to a number of the Red Brigades' demands, the group did not spare Moro, which may suggest that terrorism is not easily curtailed, however the media behave (Harper, 1991, 203–18). Correspondingly, one should be cautious in suggesting that censorship has played a significant part in ridding Western Europe of terrorism. German media's enforced strategic silence over the Red Army Faction did not play a decisive role in the organisation's later demise (Schlesinger, 1991, 24–5). Similarly, few commentators on politics in Northern Ireland would attribute the IRA's August 1994 cease-fire in any way to the cumulative, stigmatising effect of the Broadcasting Ban of 1988. Indeed the years between 1988 and 1994 saw some of the most intensive IRA activity in England since the 1970s.

Questioning the Orthodoxy

Governmental attempts to curb the media have generally been more successful in doing just that than in eliminating or reducing terrorism, the goals which (at least ostensibly) animate restrictive measures. Drawing on empirical case studies, it is hard to sustain the thesis that denial of 'oxygen' does indeed stifle publicity-dependent terrorists. But much 'orthodox' thinking rests on articles of faith, not irrefutable evidence. And what has made such thinking so entrenched is, at least in part, the impossibility of categorically proving either what terrorists (so called) *do* want from mass media, or what forms of media attention are in fact functional to their cause, perhaps irrespective of the group's objectives (McQuail, 1992, 248). So, for example, while terrorists might *say* that they seek media attention to disseminate their political grievances, and are affronted by sensationalist coverage which focuses on their actions at the expense of their motivations, it could be argued – and is, by the Orthodoxy – that such reportage nevertheless serves to generate fear, to the terrorists' own advantage.

Central to dominant interpretations has been the belief that terrorists seek publicity (good or bad) as a primary aim, and consequently, without it, they have no real *raison d'être*; hence Walter Laqueur's insistence: 'The success of a terrorist operation depends almost entirely on the amount of publicity it receives' (1977, 109). Such reasoning, however, ignores the many motivations of groups labelled 'terrorist', in which political grievances are normally uppermost. It is also, perhaps, fundamentally to confuse tactics with strategy, means with ends. As Schlesinger points out, 'political violence is not reducible to communicative behaviour alone' (Schlesinger, Murdock and Elliott, 1983, 158). Terrorism generally arises in 'blocked societies': the result of 'unpalatable political problems whose solution, in effect, is too low a priority' to the state, or states, concerned (Segaller, 1987, 5). In such immobile situations, groups sometimes representing a demographic minority in the legislative arrangements which claim jurisdiction over them (as with Catholics in Northern Ireland or Basques in Spain), or displaced from the state whose claim to sovereignty is disputed (Palestinians vis-à-vis Israel, or Africans confined to 'Independent Homelands' in apartheid South Africa), resort to violence in the attempt to 'unblock' situations which defy remedy via constitutional channels (Hocking, 1992, 100–2). In pursuit of political ends, the gaining of publicity may be an intermediate objective: tactical stunts can fulfil various short-term aims, such as highlighting the cause, creating fear in some onlookers and reassurance in others. But the gaining of publicity is rarely the ultimate end in its own right: publicity is useful only in so far as it furthers the rectification of deep-rooted political grievances. In follows, then, that terrorism is unlikely to disappear unless this 'blockage' is eased. Withholding the 'oxygen of publicity' may suppress some outward manifestations of terrorism, although such repressive measures may also, it has been argued, force 'terrorists' to resort to yet more spectacular atrocities in order to pierce the veil of censorship (Martin, 1990, 161). But bans on media reportage are most unlikely to suffocate terrorism altogether, for this prescription tackles only symptoms, not the underlying malady, and treats terrorism as essentially a problem for journalists, not for politicians.

Even were one to accept that terrorists are essentially publicity-seekers, it is still highly questionable whether the type of publicity accorded by most mainstream media is indeed functional to them, as the orthodoxy also commonly holds. Although much of this literature leaves unspecified the ends to which publicity is sought (suggesting, implicitly or explicitly, that media attention is its own reward), a number of critical empirical studies propose that media coverage does not confer legitimacy upon the organisation in question, and neither does it generally raise public awareness of the political issues at stake: two of the objectives commonly attributed to terrorists, in which the media have been regarded as complicit (Gerrits, 1992, 29–61). Media reporting usually does neither.

Although terrorist 'spectaculars' can hijack media attention, this is not to say that the insurgents themselves actually control the news agenda, or determine the way in which their activities are framed. A number of studies conclude that, even where terrorists gain 'disruptive access', media reports still often rely on official sources, and dominant understandings of where legitimacy lies, in their re-packaging of the drama (Dobkin, 1992; Paletz and Schmid, 1992, 19). Press and television news reports often replicate – or exceed – the language of the state in stigmatising 'terrorist' groups: thus, for example, the British tabloids' customary headline references to the IRA as 'scum', 'cowardly murderers', 'bastards' and so on.

Similarly, those characterised as 'terrorists' are rarely accepted as legitimate sources of news – or commentators upon the political situation which has given rise to violence – in their own right, just as Daniel Hallin found that, even when the anti-Vietnam War protesters ceased to inhabit the sphere of deviance, they were scarcely treated as authoritative sources (1989). Certainly, on the few occasions when the BBC or ITV interviewed Republican para-militaries in the 1970s and 1980s, they were emphatically not, as a matter of policy, treated as individuals whose opinions could be accorded the same respect and due consideration as others'. Interviews need not necessarily, then, confer legitimacy.

Moreover, by concentrating almost exclusively on the violent dimension of terrorism – with little or no attempt to contextualise its causes – media reports often leave readers, listeners or viewers ignorant as to the motivations of acts which, of themselves, may seem simply the senseless, inexplicable behaviour of lunatic extremists. So it is quite possible for public awareness of a terrorist group's existence to be raised by media attention, without that audience being any better informed as to the organisation's objectives. If the purpose of violence is (sympathetic) awareness of political grievances, then it fails. One social scientist, for example, found after the intensively-reported TWA hijacking episode that while more Americans now recognised the name Nabih Berri, television news largely ignored the history of Lebanon and situation in the Middle East which inspired the hijacking, focusing overwhelmingly on the US hostages and American government reaction: domesticating the story, in effect, so that its 'victims' – Americans – were its primary, objectified subjects (Atwater, 1991, 63–72).

Devoid of the necessary historical and political context which would make sense of violent actions, terrorism often appears to the public as little more than psychotic behaviour. As Gerbner comments: 'Typically isolated from their historical and social context, denied legitimacy of conditions or cause, and portrayed as unpredictable and irrational, if not insane, those labelled terrorists symbolise a menace that rational and humane means cannot reach or control' (Gerbner, 1992, 96). Violence appears to be its own justification: the terrorist is 'simply another kind of pornographer', proposes novelist John Irving in *The Hotel New Hampshire*. 'The pornographer pretends he is disgusted by his work; the terrorist pretends he is uninterested in the *means*. The *ends*, they say, are what they care about. But both are lying... The terrorist and the pornographer are in it *for* the means' (1986, 412). But while the view can readily be found (in academic literature as in popular culture) that terrorists fetishise violence, and that their stated political objectives are mere self-justificatory froth, more thoughtful social scientists reject this characterisation of terrorism as psychosis (Reich, 1990).

What is the result of de-contextualised reportage which concentrates on the violent, not the political, dimensions of terrorism? Exaggerated and sensationalist coverage of terrorism may put at least some spectators in a state of fear. However, whether such fearfulness (even if a terrorist group has deliberately sought to engender it) actually furthers that organisation's cause remains debatable. On the contrary, by privileging a relatively uncommon form of activity and elevating it to a major threat, media exaggeration has served to justify extra-legal and/or disproportionate state responses to terrorism. Thus Gerbner proposes we look beyond the 'one or two in a thousand who imitate violence and threaten society' to the 'large majority of people who become more fearful, insecure and dependent on authority, and who may grow up demanding protection and even welcoming repression in the name of security' (cited by Schlesinger, Murdock and Elliott, 1983, 160). One could even suggest that some Western states have encouraged the aggrandisement, if not necessarily of specific acts of terrorism directed against their own citizens, then of 'terrorism' as threat: a 'cancer of the modern world'. The very features of media coverage of terrorism which are so often deemed favourable to the terrorist may in fact have more utility to the state. As Hocking observes, the

'ultimate impact of terrorism has been to provide a ready legitima-
tion of... increased security control', even in states – such as Australia – which have not themselves experienced terrorism, but where
modes of subservient interaction between media and state have
nevertheless been formulated to deal with putative instances of
terrorism, or more common 'law and order' reporting (1984, 109;
Hocking, 1992, 91–6). In the words of Philip Cerny: 'terrorism
becomes a myth that can be used for the purposes of social control... it fulfils the function of war-in-microcosm, increasing social
solidarity' (in Lodge, 1981, 111).

Reagan's 'war against terrorism' offers a fitting illustration. While
it may be true that his administration was keen to avoid paying
excessive attention to incidents such as the TWA hijacking, lest the
President appear impotent and irresolute like his predecessor, the
White House did nevertheless build up terrorism *per se* into a major
international security threat. Carter's concern with 'human rights'
as the central plank of American foreign policy was over-ridden by
vigilance against international terrorism because, in Al Haig's
words, terrorism was 'the ultimate abuse of human rights'. In the
eyes of some commentators, the 'terrorist' had 'displaced Communism as public enemy number one', though the White House was
eager to suggest their indivisibility: all 'international terrorism'
could be traced back ultimately to the Kremlin (Said and Hitchens,
1988, 149).

In elevating terrorism thus, the Administration was (it could
plausibly be argued) well served by the US media. In the first
place, mainstream media duplicated the state's own (highly partial)
allocation of labels, 'in such a way as to associate an identification of
"terrorist" practice exclusively with the foreign other, and correspondingly to endow the self (and allies) with the identity of a victim
of terrorism'. The media's semantic complicity, argues Richard
Falk, served to disguise 'the more pervasive embrace of terrorist
attitudes and practices by "our side"', as seen in Nicaragua, Angola,
and other countries where the 'Second Cold War' was vigorously
prosecuted (Falk, 1991, 109). Playing on a sense of American victimhood, sensational, high-profile reporting of terrorism also served
to build consensus – and sometimes more active popular enthusiasm for – extraordinary counter-terrorist measures, which might
have been questioned had the enemy not seemed both so threatening and so impervious to less forceful treatment. Consequently

Americans were overwhelmingly supportive of the Reagan administration's bombing of Tripoli in 1986: a move presented as pre-
emptive self-defence against Colonel Gaddafi, a leader likened to
Hitler (before that resemblance was transferred to Saddam Hussein), and whose sponsorship of terrorism was presented as 'a form
of warfare' (Shultz cited by Dobkin, 1992, 78–80, 101). A large
number of Americans were pessimistic that Gaddafi would be
deterred, but they nevertheless approved the strike, and the proliferation of T-shirts bearing legends such as 'Nuke Gaddafi' attested
to a certain level of active endorsement, not just passive toleration,
of this approach to combating terrorism (Dobkin, 1992, 1).

The experience of the last 30 years suggests that 'counter-terrorist' Western states have simultaneously wished the media to down-
play specific acts of terrorism directed against their own institutions
or personnel, while also recognising that extraordinary counter-
terrorist measures may require the inflation of the 'terrorist threat'.
Mass media have often been berated for aiding terrorism, but those
same governments, militaries and police forces which make such
criticisms have themselves recognised that media can play a positive
role in combating terrorism. As the British counter-insurgency
'expert' Richard Clutterbuck wrote in the early 1980s:

> the television camera is like a weapon lying in the street. Either
> side can pick it up and use it. If governments use it in this way
> encouraging their officials, policemen and soldiers to help the
> media-men, and to answer their questions – it is far more effect-
> ive than any kind of censorship or government control. (Clutter-
> buck, 1981, 147)

For this reason, states beset by terrorism within their own borders
will often attempt via the media not only to delegitimise their
opponents but also to emphasise their own legitimacy. The aim
here, then, is to offer a 'good news' alternative to the media's
fixation on terrorist violence: a strategy attempted by successive
British governments *vis-à-vis* Northern Ireland, and by P.W. Botha's
apartheid regime in South Africa during the protracted 'state of
emergency'. Not wishing the national and, especially perhaps, international press to focus exclusively on violence, which might emphasise injustices or suggest the 'ungovernability' of the contested
territory, governments encourage journalists to show significant

areas of 'peace and progress' and the marginal impact of, and support for, 'terrorism' (Windrich, 1989, 51–60; Miller, 1994, 150–9).

While this 'good news' strategy sometimes founders on the rock of news values – where uplifting stories lack newsworthiness – it is nevertheless striking how many broadcasters and journalists have enlisted for active service in the 'war against terrorism' (Schmid, 1992, 111–36). Some may feel that they are conscripted at the barrel of the recruiting sergeant's gun. For others, the powerful connotations of the term 'terrorist' suffice to make them fall in line, for fear of being branded – by the public, as much as the state – terrorist sympathiser or 'fellow traveller'. One journalist from Northern Ireland put the point rather well: 'Broadcasters are more afraid than most of Mrs Thatcher – and in Northern Ireland they are even more afraid of being thought soft on the IRA' (Moloney, 1991, 24).

This is not to say, however, that journalistic efforts to combat terrorism – by exposing its methods and practitioners – have always met with state approval. Broadcast interviews with terrorists, rationalised by reporters on the grounds that these reveal terrorists for what they are, form a case in point. But in combating an 'enemy' so shadowy, whose objectives are so ill understood, and for whom any publicity is often construed as beneficial, it is scarcely surprising that interpretations of good counter-terrorist practice should sometimes clash. Media organisations have sometimes fought shy of state control. Much heated debate has occurred over the question of 'voluntary guidelines', not to mention more overt forms of government interference such as the Broadcasting Ban. But acrimonious exchanges between state and news media can obscure the more significant point: that, in arguing against repressive measures, the media have often advanced the superior wisdom of their own particular forms of counter-terrorism. Thus Moloney points out that the BBC's response to the Ban barely mentioned freedom of speech, but was instead 'defensive, apologetic and almost indignant that the government had thought local journalists anything but hostile in their treatment of terrorist sympathisers' (Moloney, 1991, 34).

In what is often not, in fact, a state of war, many Western news organisations have often seemed all too willing to present arms against terrorism, encouraged or bullied by governments which regard any dissent as tantamount to treason. 'Either one is on the side of justice... or one is on the side of terrorism', Thatcher warned the British media in March 1988 (Henderson, Miller and Reilly, 1990, 1). Insufficient displays of 'patriotism' in the war against terrorism have resulted in formal restrictions being imposed on the media. But generally overt censorship has been an infrequent – because unnecessary – last resort of dubious effectiveness.

5

Media, Globalisation and 'Other People's Wars'

'Our wars' are different. Or so journalists often claim in justifying
the jettisoning of vaunted peacetime norms of objectivity, detachment and neutrality, and redefining their self-image to permit open
partisanship when their own country is at war. If their 'boys' are
fighting, and their readers or viewers are presumed to identify
closely with the interests at stake in the conflict, then media organisations – as we have seen – often adopt supportive or more out-
spokenly patriotic roles in reporting 'their' wars (whether 'total' or
'limited'). But what happens when media are confronted with 'other
people's wars'? And what results if media organisations lack a
simple identification with one particular nation, and owe allegiance
to no single state? Arguably, both of these conditions increasingly
prevail. For many journalists in industrialised and stable areas of the
'North', most contemporary – and foreseeable – wars are and will
remain essentially 'other people's' in a world where mass media,
other corporations and social, economic and cultural processes
generally, are ever more 'globalised' (Waters, 1995; Holton,1998).

Since the 1980s, and especially since the end of the Cold War, a
number of commentators have hailed the obsolescence of 'major
war' between industrialised liberal democracies which, especially
in our enmeshed and globalised world, do not fight with other
states sharing the same political complexion and economic disin-
centives to waging disruptive war (Mueller, 1989). The 'democratic
peace' thesis has not gone unchallenged. But certainly the demise of
the USSR in 1991 would seem to rule out Cold War scenarios of
large-scale conventional warfare being staged in Central Europe,
along with the threat of nuclear war between the superpowers.

Moreover, the stability of the EU makes it hard to envisage a reprise of the century's two 'total wars' between Britain, France and Germany. For many West Europeans, even as the prospect of war on 'our' soil has receded, it has been necessary to look no further than the Former Yugoslavia or Chechnya for evidence that the end of the Cold War has not spelt the end of war itself. Indeed, within Europe and beyond, the 1990s have offered ample evidence that various forms of violent conflict have not become obsolescent, whatever the prospects of another 'major' war. Cold War bipolarity has seemingly given way to a 'New World Disorder', of disputed boundaries, of failed states, of 'ethnic' conflicts between peoples who in the face of globalising processes show a greater propensity for fissiparous fragmentation (Barber, 1996; I. Clark, 1997).

War certainly still occurs, then, and small-scale conflict has perhaps become more widespread precisely because the prospect of major war – nuclearised and fought between the superpowers – has evaporated. (The Cold War, in this view, threatened a nuclear war to end all wars but it also kept nationalist secessionism and other fragmentary tendencies in check.) For many comfortable Northerners or Westerners, then, genocide in Rwanda, 'ethnic cleansing' in Bosnia or Kosovo, the implosion of Somalia and other manifestations of post-Cold War disorder are essentially 'other people's wars'. They become 'our wars' only if our states – or the international organisations to which they cede some of their sovereignty – actively choose to entangle themselves therein.

That such interventions in cases of distant conflict or catastrophe have been primarily instigated by news media, not by politicians, has been much debated in the 1990s. The case that mandarins' decision-making autonomy has been ended by (if not lost to) the media rests on various claims which will shortly be examined, but central to the argument is the notion that media organisations are increasingly globalised in nature: no longer bound to one particular territory or beholden to any one state. In that sense, no war is 'theirs' but potentially they may make any conflict around the globe 'ours'. Internationalised media, it has thus been claimed, play a central role in the constitution of 'global crises', in selecting which of the many wars ongoing around the world at any one time will receive global attention and, with it, a place at the top of policy-makers' agendas. 'If a humanitarian emergency is not featured in the media', suggests Lionel Rosenblatt (flippantly but aptly, in his own estimation), 'it does not become an emergency for political leaders and policy-makers' (1996, 138). Tellingly, the agenda-setting power of international media is often labelled 'the CNN effect', which is testimony to the 'totemic status' accorded to Ted Turner's Atlanta-based network in the post-Cold War, and especially post-Gulf War, world (Shaw, 1994, 647).

Undoubtedly, media organisations have been subject to processes of globalisation. Even nationally-based television companies increasingly rely on international agencies (such as Visnews), or regional exchanges (such as Eurovision), to provide them with satellite 'feeds' of foreign news stories which their own crews are not 'on the ground' to cover. In that sense, the 'global newsroom' is a reality. But of perhaps yet greater significance has been the emergence since the 1980s of global media corporations with extensive transnational and cross-media interests. Thanks in part to deregulatory policies favoured in the 1980s, Rupert Murdoch's News Corporation, for example, now not only controls newspapers in America, Australia and Britain but also the satellite broadcaster BSkyB (and its offshoots in Asia), Hollywood's Twentieth Century Fox studio, and the publishing giant HarperCollins, amongst other interests. It is not uncommon for the tentacles of such corporations to reach into all aspects of communications. Their provision of television programming, newspapers and movies (often now 'synergistically' accompanied by CDs, books and sundry tie-in merchandising) runs parallel with supply of the very fibre optic cables which, in the digital age, simultaneously link homes and businesses to television, telephone and internet services. Clearly, such powerful and de-territorialised communications empires lie beyond the scope of regulation by any one government.

Internationalised news media, however, have been much discussed for their content, not just their ownership. After all, the emergence of satellite and cable 'rolling news' channels (such as CNN and BBC World) has made news a constantly available commodity, no longer rationed to 22 minute or half-hour slots at pre-determined intervals during the day's television schedule. Some commentators believe that CNN and its imitators have supplanted conventional diplomatic and intelligence channels for policy-makers, now constantly updated on foreign events by the televisual 'wallpaper' in their offices. President Bush seemed to prove the point when he claimed to learn more from CNN than from the

CIA (cited by Stech, 1994, 236). The alleged upshot is a compression of policy-makers' response times during crises. Where before decision-makers usually had occasion for leisurely consideration of diplomatic dispatches and intelligence estimates, they are now compelled to respond instantly to fast-breaking foreign stories (Gowing, 1994, 1996). Thanks to global media, the hitherto closed world of diplomacy has been exposed to the full force of international indignity in times of crisis, and the resultant pressure on policy-makers to 'do something' – even if just to engage in symbolic politics for the cameras – may be irresistible.

Whence the power of 'global' television to exert such pressure? To proponents of this view, television's suasion over governments and international organisations is partly a function of audience size: the constitution of 'macropublics of hundreds of millions of citizens... nurturing public controversies beyond the boundaries of the nation-state' (J. Keane, 1996, 172–3). Both CNN International (CNNI) and BBC World boast impressive totals of countries which lie under the footprint of their satellite transmitters. But besides membership of an international audience, these networks also offer their global viewers 'real-time' news coverage. Instantaneous satellite transmission – on a constantly running news channel – means that compelling pictures do not have to wait until 9 p.m. or the next scheduled news cast. Images are beamed into homes almost as the very events under the camera's gaze actually occur. And this immediacy, it is often supposed, lends television heightened emotive power. Instantaneous images of suffering intensify the viewer's identification with those whose plight they witness: 'crying cries out to be indefinitely heard, to be understood, to be remedied', insists John Keane. And for him this means that media preoccupation with 'virtually all forms of violence', deplorable though some of its manifestations may be, contains a 'hidden, potentially civilizing dialectic' (1996, 172–3, 182–3).

Some commentators thus propose that the television industry has not just been subject to globalising forces but is itself an agent of globalisation. For if globalisation creates a world in which 'the constraints of geography on social and cultural arrangements recede and in which people become increasingly aware that they are receding', then media (including, increasingly, the Internet) clearly play a vital role in making real that shrinkage (Waters, 1995, 3). 'What we are seeing', proposes Ted Turner, 'is not just the globalization of television but also, through television, the globalization of the globe ... How else to explain Kenyans who lined up six-deep in front of electronics stores to watch footage of a war they had no soldiers fighting in?' (cited in Alleyne, 1997, 10–11). The architect of CNN is not alone in believing that, through global media, people are becoming gradually detached from national allegiances and identities rooted in their particular locales, instead regarding themselves more as members of Marshall McLuhan's celebrated 'global village'. Increasingly, a sense of community springs from empathy and not merely from geography; television is helping to transform the whole world into a single 'imagined community' where shared humanity replaces nationality as the primary point of identification (Hannerz, 1996, 121; Ignatieff, 1998, 27). Thus Martin Shaw suggests that whereas in the past 'people responded to local or national events and to epochal world conflicts which – once or twice in a lifetime – engulfed national societies', today they are 'faced with a constant stream of wars, each of which is represented to us and demands, in a sense, our response' (1995, 2). Following Anthony Giddens, he implies that globalisation, by introducing new forms of interconnectedness, is creating a world where 'once again there are no "Others"' (Giddens, 1990, 175).

The degree to which internationalised media, by moulding a cosmopolitan global consciousness, have usurped policy-makers' ability to decide when and whether to make 'other people's' wars their own business is explored below; but first some words of caution. It is easy to exaggerate the extent to which television – or the world itself – has indeed been globalised. The ubiquity of 'globe speak' in the 1990s has fuelled the rather fanciful notion that 'for the first time in history, the rich and the poor, literate and illiterate, city worker and peasant farmer are linked together by shared images of global life' (Michael J. O'Neill, cited by Stech, 1994, 237). Globe-trotting Westerners may be impressed by the ubiquity of CNN and the BBC (or alternately bemoan the erosion of local cultures by homogenising global forces), but beyond their air-conditioned and multinationally-owned hotels neither the Internet nor satellite television plays a part in the lives of many ordinary citizens in much of the developing world. A huge swathe of the globe has as yet been by-passed not just by CNN but by the 'communications revolution' itself. As Parker points out, 'despite the global technological "availability" of the telephone, radio, airplane, and automobile, well over half the planet's population enjoys no routine access to any of them' (Parker, 1995, 432–3). Their consumption requires money, and the globalisation of capital has done nothing to eliminate (and has arguably exaggerated) global inequalities in the distribution of wealth. An estimated 1.2 billion television sets in the world, even allowing for multiple users of many sets, still leaves a huge number of television-less homes and communities, particularly in Africa (Parker 1995, 432). The global 'information imbalance' decried by the developing world, most vociferously via the UN Educational, Scientific and Cultural Organization in the 1970s, has certainly not disappeared (Hamelink, 1994; Mowlana, 1996; Alleyne, 1997; Schiller, 1996). Thus while it may be true that a latent global audience exists – thanks to over 100 communications satellites – and that CNNI broadcasts can be picked up in 209 countries and territories, those who currently watch satellite and cable television remain a tiny minority. 'In a world with more than 5 billion inhabitants, the actual number of viewers claimed by CNNI is less than 65 million', which perhaps makes CNN less a global mass medium than 'the office intercom of global elites' (Parker, 1995, 440). As Hamid Mowlana reminds us, 'what is global is not universal ... global communication does not mean universal communication. Although the distribution of information might be universal in nature, the capacity for distributing messages is severely limited and centralized' (1996, 199).

In other words, the content of the 'globalised' media broadly reflects the interests, concerns, and values of elites, and generally of First World elites (Alleyne, 1997). But if we examine the news media *within* many industrialised Northern states, we find contradictory forces at work in news provision. While some social theorists proclaim the emergence of a cosmopolitan global consciousness, others point to the stubborn preference of many audiences for national, regional or more local news. Many countries have seen a decline of foreign news in their national media, even as 'globalised' media have emerged, and partly because of their emergence. In 1994 one study found that America's national television networks (CBS, ABC, NBC) were presenting barely half the amount of international news broadcast ten years ago, with local commercial stations generally offering even less (Pedelty, 1995, 189). Even CNN, the totemic global player, offers its home audience in the USA a decidedly parochial news diet, based on distinctly national news values, and often featuring few foreign stories (Wallis and Baran, 1990, 6, 174). Meanwhile, in the UK, a number of prominent BBC journalists have complained that BBC World has been fattened on financial rations poached from the BBC's domestic news budget, in the Corporation's bid to compete with CNN globally and meet the further challenge to terrestrial news broadcasting posed by the increasing availability of on-line Internet news services, many established by print media competitors.

The result, in the critics' eyes, is a poorer news service all round. Domestically-provided news becomes more parochial in focus as leaner budgets allow for less foreign news, with an increased dependency on agency 'feeds', and a paring down of the number of correspondents permanently based abroad to cover specific geographical 'news-beats' (Wallis and Baran, 1990, 33–4, 65). Contrary to optimistic expectations, electronic news-gathering has not reduced the cost of news production. Keeping up with rapidly changing technology has raised costs, even if recording and editing equipment is more mobile and requires fewer operators. Covering foreign wars still does not lend itself to minimalism. In reporting the wars in Former Yugoslavia, Martin Bell cautions that the minimum television crew still numbers seven: 'a newsgathering unit of cameraman, interpreter and reporter, a producer or "fixer" at the heart of the operation, and at the transmission end a videotape editor (sometimes doubling as a sound recordist) and two engineers with the satellite dish' (1995, 113). This is a far remove from the vision sometimes touted of a near-future in which the single 'backpacking' war-tourist/journalist, toting video recorder and mobile dish, will wander at will around the most inhospitable war zones, in an echo of the golden days of the indefatigable war correspondent armed with only notebook and pencil, but whose pencil was nevertheless mightier than the sword.

As for rolling news, a number of journalists complain that having to be constantly 'on-call' eliminates the time required for thorough news-gathering, for the amassing of information from different sources, and for weighing and evaluating evidence. Martin Bell thus concluded from his experience in Bosnia (where he daily had to file frequent television and radio reports for the BBC) that: 'More means worse. The multiplication of deadlines takes us away from the real world, and drives us back into our offices and edit rooms. It is safer there, and we may find reasons to stay.' This view has been echoed across the Atlantic by ABC's Ted Koppel: 'putting someone on the air while an event is unfolding is clearly a techno-logical *tour de force*, but it is an impediment, not an aid, to good journalism' (Bell, 1995, 28; Koppel, cited by Gowing, 1994, 4). Pressure of rolling-news deadlines is likely to increase levels of 'puppetry' in journalism. The highly-paid star foreign correspond-ent is 'parachuted' into a trouble zone to provide constant 'on-the-spot' news-verité (Pedelty, 1995, 109–12). Paradoxically, if pre-dictably, the reporter – whose 'eye-witness' status is intended to lend authority to the news – may in fact have little idea of what is happening in the location from which they are being bounced back live into the studio. On some occasions, their lines are actually fed by earpiece from HQ in Atlanta, New York or London, based on incoming agency reports (a phenomenon much in evidence during the Gulf War in 1991).

Much news, then, remains stubbornly local, and a fair amount of foreign news – whether provided terrestrially by national broad-casters or via satellite from CNN – rests on the shaky foundations of parachute journalism. What, though, of the 'global newsroom'? To the extent that regional/global satellite exchange services do provide local, national and international news-programmers with much of their raw footage, this notion is useful. But there is con-siderable divergence in the use to which such satellite feeds are put. Empirical research carried out by Gurevitch, Levy and Roeh into 36 European participators in the Eurovision News Exchange found some convergence over news stories featured in national broadcasts but considerable diversity of news values and styles (Gurevitch, Levy and Roeh, 1991, 200–2). As footage is generally delivered 'raw' (without a narrated commentary), news media retain consid-erable scope for 'framing' material in distinctive ways. Often they will 'domesticate' stories to render them comprehensible, appealing and 'relevant' to local audiences who – globalisation not withstand-ing – are still presumed to take an interest in proximate events, which often means those physically close at hand (Gurevitch, Levy and Roeh, 1991, 206–7). Thus the researchers concluded that:

> while the images may have global currency, the meanings given to them may not necessarily be shared globally. Television news in different countries, feeding on an increasingly similar global diet, facilitated by a global system of distribution and exchange of news

materials, still speaks in many different voices. The Global News-room is still confronted by a Tower of Babel. (Gurevitch, Levy and Roeh, 1991, 214–15).

An analogous verdict was reached after a more recent compara-tive survey of thirteen countries' coverage of the war in Former Yugoslavia (Preston, 1996, 119–25).

There are, then, very real limits to the 'globalisation' of the media. Beneficiaries of the communications revolution undoubtedly enjoy access to technology which has indeed collapsed time and space, but the quality of information that flows instantaneously around the connected world is open to question. Foreign correspondent Edward Girardet is not alone in suggesting that: 'Despite having far greater access to an overwhelming surfeit of information sources than ever before, the public (and policy-makers for that matter) may not really have a more enlightened command of the humanitarian state of affairs in Angola, Afghanistan, or even the Bronx' (Girardet, 1996, 45). Moreover, residents of Angola and Afghanistan may not enjoy access to this 'surfeit' of imperfect information sources at all.

Outside Intervention in 'Other People's Wars': The 'CNN effect' Considered

The dispute over the impact of 'real-time' television, although not exclusively American, in many respects resembles the post-Vietnam controversy over the media's alleged role in 'losing' that war. Both debates have been played out against a backdrop of technological innovation in mass communications. By the time of the Tet Offensive in 1968, satellites were starting to relay footage from Vietnam back to the USA, more rapidly offering television news casts fresher, and sometimes more dramatic, material. The post-Gulf War debate about 'real-time' television is similarly linked to uncertainty over, if not outright hostility towards, the political ramifications of techno-logical progress (Neuman, 1996; Robinson, 1999). Immediacy was then as now equated with greater impact, though such hypothesised media effects lack convincing, non-anecdotal validation.

In addition, both debates have shadowed re-appraisal of America's world role, and whether it can, or should, act as 'global policeman'. America's inability to prevail in Vietnam led to much agonised discussion of the wisdom of interventionism in pursuit of such nebulous international goals as 'containment'. Similarly, in the fluid post-Cold War environment, American policy-making elites have divided over whether to intervene in distant conflicts and humanitarian disasters, or retreat into neo-isolationism. Chastening reversals of fortune – such as that suffered by US forces involved in Operation Restore Hope in Somalia – have shown that America, contrary to George Bush's immediate post-Gulf War euphoric assertion, has not finally 'kicked the Vietnam syndrome'. At any rate, the Gulf War does not seem to have augured an age when Washington could send troops abroad unhindered by the fear that public support would melt away at the sight of returning body bags displayed by the media. US fortunes in Somalia serve for some commentators as the paradigmatic case of real time's alleged 'push-me-pull-me' effects: television images catalysing intervention, and equally quixotically insisting on withdrawal. In the words of one US congressman, 'pictures of starving children, not policy objectives, got us into Somalia in 1992. Pictures of US casualties, not the completion of our objectives, led us to exit Somalia' (Minear, Scott and Weiss, 1996, 46).

In the eyes of some of CNN's detractors, this 'fickleness' retrospectively vindicated the draconian press management of the Gulf War, for Somalia seemed to prove that, unless heavily constrained, neither 'global' nor national media lend sustained support to national policy objectives (even in support of international, humanitarian goals). Indeed, in the opinion of a former Chair of the US Joint Chiefs of Staff, Colonel Bill Smullen, the presence of satellite television in a crisis zone will henceforth 'be a definite factor in decision making', with General Colin Powell going so far as to suggest that 'real-time' television 'could now be a factor in *not* going to war' (both cited by Gowing, 1994, 15). Certainly, in the wake of the Somalia débâcle, the US Government dramatically redefined the circumstances in which it would contribute to UN 'humanitarian interventions', setting out (in Presidential Decision Directive No. 25 of 5 May 1994) much more stringent conditions on US assistance, and emphasising the scale of emergency which would be required to invoke it (Gowing, 1994, 86).

Contending voices in the CNN debate do not, however, fall into camps neatly delineated by professional or political affiliation. In other words, journalists have not lined up squarely against policy-makers and the military to 'defend' television from charges of undue influence over the political process (which some journalists would regard, in any case, as a welcome development), and neither are the positions clearly associated with left/right, or interventionist/isolationist schisms. Indeed some points of consensus are shared by many contributors to the debate: first, that new communications technology has compressed policy-makers' 'response times' (Gowing, 1994, 1; Neuman, 1996, 7; Rotberg and Weiss, 1996, 2), conceivably because 'public opinion which used to take weeks or months to form can now be galvanised on some issues in hours' (Everett Dennis cited by Boccardi, 1995, 50). Second, most agree that television coverage of foreign events has *some* impact on policy-making. The dispute is over when, why and to what degree.

In its most extreme form, proponents of the 'CNN effect' thesis hold that 'foreign policy decision making has become epiphenomenal to news decision making': that the presence of graphic television images from a crisis zone demands that policy-makers respond to this particular issue, rather than others which may be equally or even more serious (Livingston and Eachus, 1995, 415). Moreover, they must respond instantly in order to appease an emotional public demanding action. In this scenario, television distorts the policy-agenda, re-arranging priorities, and leading to ill-considered action, and hasty – possibly inappropriate – interventions in other people's wars and crises. Some such emergencies would arguably be better served by outside agencies (be they governments or inter-governmental organisations such as the UN or NATO) resisting the guilt-stricken or panicked temptation to interfere, and from intervening in ways seemingly choreographed for the television cameras.

Such arguments have sometimes been deployed by print journalists, who, according to CBS anchor Dan Rather, habitually 'like to accuse television of irresponsibility' (Rather, 1995, 29). More frequently they emanate from the pens or lips of diplomats, especially those who disfavour intervention, notably George Kennan in the USA and Douglas Hurd in the UK (Seib, 1997, 44–5). Martin Bell explains their revulsion for 'real time' thus: 'The mandarins' objection is not just to the power but to the impertinence of the upstart medium, which challenges their monopoly of wisdom, and rushes in where the pinstripes fear to tread' (1995, 137–8). In other words, statespeople resent being made to address distant suffering (which, without television, they could otherwise have ignored) by an emotional, ill-informed public mobilised by images which have 'a way of touching the heart without reaching the brain' (Walter Goodman, cited by Seib, 1997, 45). Bell's position suggests that some journalists themselves hope to arouse a 'CNN effect' of sorts, shaking diplomats from their torpor. Other commentators too point to television's 'democratising' potential: permitting public pressure to permeate the traditionally cloistered world of foreign policy-making where 'pinstripes' fear that others, more emotional and ignorant than they, might blithely tread (Seaver, 1998, 78–9).

However, a number of journalists, Bell amongst them, have reached a fairly modest estimation of their own *actual* influence. This 'revisionism' about the ramifications of 'real time' has been pioneered by Nik Gowing (formerly Diplomatic Editor of ITN, and currently with BBC World), and has perhaps now acquired the status of a neo-orthodoxy. His position, in short, is that television's impact is limited. In general, policy is not swayed by images: only when policy is unclear are politicians liable to be pressurised into making 'pseudo responses' to media-manufactured crises: 'Real-time pictures compress response times in a crisis. They put pressure on choice and priorities in crisis management. They skew responses. They shape the policy agenda but do not dictate responses. They highlight policy dilemmas but do not resolve them' (Gowing, 1996, 83). Similarly, Bell concurs that only when governments lack purpose do television images 'have a jolting effect' (1995, 142). But his insistence that the media has 'no political agenda', that journalists are merely 'messengers, and partly lamplighters...cast[ing] some light on those dark places', may strike some as a rather naive, if not disingenuous, borrowing from Walter Lippmann, who likened the press to 'the beam of a searchlight that moves restlessly about, bringing one episode and then another out of darkness into vision' (Bell, 1995, 138, 141; Lippmann, 1922, 226).

Because the debate about the impact of television during humanitarian disasters eludes empirical verification, Gowing's conclusions – now so widely echoed – are based largely on personal interviews with policy-makers. While this methodology sheds interesting anecdotal light on media effects, it does beg the question as to whether we can trust policy-makers to respond forthrightly to inquiries about the impact of television on them, and, indeed, how far any individual (however trustworthy) can adequately quantify television's effects on their own opinions, let alone reach estimations of its impact on others (Minear, Scott and Weiss, 1996, 45). After all, as many of the latter acknowledged to Gowing, they felt under tremendous pressure to be *seen* to be doing the right thing. For that reason, they may exaggerate television's – or its viewers' – effect on their actions, 'hiding behind public opinion' as a justification for their decisions (Seaver, 1998, 77). However, as policy-makers also commonly like to protest their immunity from transient influences, it is equally plausible that the desire to project an image of steadfastness leads to an under-emphasis on television reporting and public pressure.

Moreover, Gowing's research methodology will not tell us anything about how the public actually responds to footage of 'distant violence': it can only tell us how politicians presume the public reacts. When policy-makers chose to act, Gowing suggests, they imputed to television a particular 'do-something' response in the audience, or read into press 'op-ed' columns a generalised public desire for action. Equally, on other occasions, the opposite 'third person effect' – presumed disinclination for intervention – formed justification for inaction. What members of the public themselves feel about intervening in 'other people's' crises may be almost totally irrelevant to policy-makers. By way of illustration, Gowing quotes a Downing Street official's view that 'public opinion' and 'national interest' are 'two cant phrases that have been around for 200 years', and a Clinton aide who attests that 'public opinion is not that important' (1994, 11). Few policy-makers, Gowing found, watched television themselves, or garnered opinion polling-data to tell them slightly more reliably how their citizens did feel about interventionism (Gowing, 1994, 21–9). Extrapolation of public opinion from print and broadcast media, Richard Sobel suggests, may in fact lead politicians to under-estimate the strength of feeling in support of intervention overseas, as, he argues, was the case with the Clinton administration over Bosnia (1998, 16–33). Thus, although public opinion is often posited as a crucial component of the 'CNN effect' equation – television pressures politicians via the audience – it is generally a significant absence in studies of, or generalised assertions about, television and intervention, featuring only as refracted through the eyes of the media or policy-makers. No wonder, then, that a social scientist should recently conclude that 'the media's effects on the public's foreign policy attitudes requires more systematic investigation' (Seaver, 1998, 79).

One less impressionistic approach to trying to establish the inter-play between media coverage and policy-making lies in quantitative research into the amount of television attention devoted to parti-cular foreign crises. From this the researcher attempts to deduce whether high levels of media interest precede – and implicitly provoke – intervention. However, this methodology too is open to the objection that it is interested only in uni-linear media impact (not in more complex relationships of mutual influence, preferred by some theorists), and that its conclusions about causality are ultimately somewhat conjectural (O'Heffernan, 1994, 231–49). A more fruitful approach, as adopted by Steven Livingston and Todd Eachus's study of the Somalia case, is to undertake both quantitat-ive research and interviews, and to ground these in a more general theoretical understanding of how the media function (1995, 413–29). It is also helpful, as shown in the work of Minear, Scott and Weiss, to look at the interplay of media, policy-makers and non-governmental organisations (NGOs) (another often neglected ele-ment of the equation) in different *phases* of complex emergencies: from recognition of a problem by all the above actors, to policy formation, its implementation, and the long-term aftermath.

In the following case studies, we survey the interactions between media institutions, humanitarian agencies and policy-makers, in an effort to establish patterns of influence in their mutual interactions, and to understand how some 'other people's wars' become 'global crises', and the conditions under which outside governments and inter-governmental organisations (IGOs) may intervene.

The Kurdish Crisis (1991)

Occurring in the wake of the Gulf War, and to a considerable extent because of it, the Kurdish rebellion in Northern Iraq was instantly seized upon as an example of the new power of unfettered media to instigate humanitarian interventionism. In the months following the UN Coalition's victorious ground war against Iraq, Kurdish resist-ance groups rebelled against Saddam Hussein. In this they were implicitly, and more directly, encouraged by the American-led Coa-lition, which had done more than insinuate a desire to see Hussein removed from power. The niceties of international law ensured that the US-led Coalition could not make the toppling of another state's leader a formal war aim, but Allied psychological warfare operations nevertheless targeted the Kurds and Shias, inciting rebellion, while the CIA covertly channelled funds to groups with the potential to destabilise Hussein's regime (M. Shaw, 1996, 22–3; P. Taylor, 1997, 172–9). The ensuing rebellions both foundered as they met repression from Baghdad.

There were, however, cameras present (most of which arrived via Turkey) to record the plight of the Kurds. The visibility of this 'global crisis' was in marked contrast to the largely overlooked rebellion of the Shia population of Iraq's southern marshes, which in fact cost far more lives (M. Shaw, 1996, 80–3). The Shia rebellion, certainly for British television, occurred largely beyond the reach of its crews and tended to be framed in sound-only reports as a 'fundamentalist' uprising (Gowing, 1994, 39). In contrast, the displaced Kurds (numbering around two million) were more easily filmable, and, as homeless refugees in a snowy wasteland, were susceptible to being cast as pitiable victims rather than fanatical Muslims. In addition, according to Martin Shaw's qualitative analysis of British television coverage of the crisis, reporters went beyond merely showing Kurdish suffering – the Lippmann/Bell 'lamplighting' role – to actual advocacy of Western intervention of the Kurds' behalf: 'television was putting world leaders on the spot, linking them directly to the visible plight of the miserable refugees, putting the victims' accusations [of abandonment] against the powerful' (M. Shaw, 1996, 87–97).

The result was that on 8 April 1991, Prime Minister John Major, who had initially abjured any responsibility for the rebellion – 'I don't recall asking the Kurds to mount this particular insurrection' – retracted (cited in M. Shaw, 1996, 89). 'Safe havens' were to be established for the Kurds, and Westminster's policy lead was followed by the White House two days later. In April 1991, a multinational coalition of Western troops entered Northern Iraq from Turkey, reclaiming land occupied by the Iraqi army north of the thirty-sixth parallel, establishing the so-called 'safe havens' (Minear, Scott and Weiss, 1996, 51).

The Kurdish crisis therefore appears as a classic case of television-led intervention to serve humanitarian ends. Gowing himself made the point in a *World Today* piece which saw him argue television's power. Although he subsequently moderated his position,

Gowing's analysis retains the Kurdish crisis as one example when policy-makers – caught on the hop by real-time images – did make *ad hoc* responses under media pressure. John Major himself, playing up to his Pooterish image, confirmed as much to Gowing. He had been moved by footage of the Kurdish refugees 'as he was putting his socks on in his flat', and had, against diplomatic advice, devised the 'safe havens' scheme 'on the back of an envelope' flying to an EC summit in Luxembourg (1994, 38). In this tableau, Major projects himself as the personification of outraged British opinion: the little-man hero who rushes in 'where pinstripes fear to tread'.

However, Major's account of his response to televised suffering omits much that might help to explain why the apparent power of the media in this instance was not clearly replicated in other humanitarian crises of the 1990s (including those heavily televised). First, as Shaw acknowledges, the Kurdish crisis was exceptional in that responsibility could be easily attributed to Western leaders, particularly Bush and Major, who obviously encouraged Iraqi dissidence during the Gulf War. BBC and ITN television reporters did not necessarily spell out America's and Britain's duty to help the Kurdish refugees directly but by interviewing Kurds – who made the linkage between their rebellion and the West's desire to be rid of Saddam Hussein – they implicitly urged intervention. Reporters based in Washington were more forceful in attributing accountability to President Bush, in so doing (Shaw suggests) implicating Prime Minister Major. This sense of responsibility for others' suffering – aroused in Major by *national* media, it seems – was less easily evoked in later humanitarian crises (M. Shaw, 1996, 156).

Second, as Minear, Scott and Weiss note (but Gowing conspicuously does not) there were 'domestic political factors' at work in Major's about-turn: 'Sources close to the decisionmaking process noted that Prime Minister John Major feared criticism for inaction from his predecessor Margaret Thatcher, who had taken it upon herself to meet with Kurdish refugee leaders in an effort to goad her government to act' (1996, 51). While Thatcher went on to make similar protestations of solidarity with the Bosnians, which were largely ignored by Major, it should be remembered that in April 1991, Major had only occupied Number 10 Downing Street for some five months (since November 1990). Moreover, he had assumed the premiership in a bitter Conservative Party leadership contest following Thatcher's deposition, in which he presented himself as the moderate 'unity' candidate, capable of healing the party's self-inflicted wounds. The following April, he had not yet been elected Prime Minister by the British public, but merely by the Conservative parliamentary membership. Still anxious to appease both wings of his party, he was therefore perhaps particularly vulnerable to pressure from his predecessor, not least if her views seemed to chime with those of the public. Neither of these factors remained such powerful incentives to action when Major faced conflict in Former Yugoslavia.

The Wars in Former Yugoslavia (1991–5)

The series of wars in Former Yugoslavia have not wanted for media attention, though the coverage has been criticised (as we will see) for its selective concentration on some geographical locales, and its preoccupation with certain interpretative frameworks, at the expense of others. Bell goes so far as to suggest that: 'No other war – not even the Gulf War, which took on the character of a made-for-television CNN special event – has been fought so much in public, under the eye of the camera' (1995, 137). However, despite the volume of coverage, for those minded to debunk the 'CNN effect', Former Yugoslavia offers the best illustration of the *absence* of an automatic link between media images of suffering and decisive intervention to alleviate it. In the words of Minear, Scott and Weiss, the Balkan wars are a case of 'blanket coverage, selective action' (1996, 57).

According to a number of commentators, the foremost objective of most EU states and the USA was to avoid a commitment of ground troops to Former Yugoslavia charged with enforcing a separation of warring parties who repeatedly failed to adhere to cease-fires or to concur over a repartition of territory. There was certainly no commitment to upholding the territorial sovereignty of Bosnia, or to promoting the ideal of an ethnically heterogeneous polity on which it was based. If this avoidance of commitment is deemed 'policy' or 'strategy', then Western governments successfully steered a more or less straight path; a 'triumph of the lack of will' in James Gow's formulation (1997). Determined to set clear limits on their interventionism, key members of the UN Security Council ensured that its Resolutions allowed only the dispatch of a 'protection force' (UNPROFOR), whose job was essentially to provide safe passage for 'humanitarian' supplies of food and medicine in areas cut off by fighting. UNPROFOR forces had an extremely narrow mandate, which did not extend to firing upon those who shelled the beleaguered areas to which UNPROFOR delivered aid. Only later were airstrikes enacted against Serb soldiers who refused to stop shelling predominantly Muslim Bosnian towns, and frequently the UN backed down from its threats to use force. Moreover, it was only to implement a peace plan (which recognised the *de facto* fruits of 'ethnic cleansing' by breaking Bosnia into ethnic cantons), that Clinton was prepared to pledge 25 000 US troops. Bosnia's break-up – to which Clinton had previously professed his aversion – was thus to be policed by US ground forces whom Clinton had refused to deploy in defence of Bosnia's ethnic heterogeneity.

Despite much media attention to the plight of some besieged areas (though notably not all), on only a few occasions did Western policy-makers feel their minimal-intervention policy in Bosnia come under serious threat, and on even fewer did they appear to respond to media images. These occasions, enumerated by Gowing, suggest that intermittently the media could shift politicians' resolve. But these shifts were largely at the level of tactics, not overall strategy:

> Security Council Resolution 770 of 1992 supported humanitarian aid. Subsequent US aid-drops of aid, emergency medical evacuations from Sarajevo by the UK, and even NATO's protection measures for the Bosnian capital were all responses to well-televised predicaments. In retrospect, these actions appear to have been exercises in damage control in response to public exposure of governmental impotence instead of key elements in established or evolving policy. (Minear, Scott and Weiss, 1996, 57–8)

Indeed, Douglas Hurd, UK Foreign Secretary for much of the period – and renowned for suggesting that 'real time' was unduly distorting policy-making – made a virtue of *not* being deflected from his government's preferred path, remarking in September 1993 that Her Majesty's Government would not be propelled into military intervention 'simply because of day-to-day pressure from the media' (cited by Minear, Scott and Weiss, 1996, 58). In other words, if a 'CNN effect' existed, it was resistible.

On what occasions, then, did news produce tactical shifts over Former Yugoslavia? Gowing suggests that the first occasion was in the wake of American and British press and television reports uncovering Serb concentration camps at Omarska and Trnopolje in August 1992 (1994, 40–5). Images of emaciated Bosnian prisoners, which shockingly recalled images of the Holocaust as Nazi camps were liberated at the end of the Second World War, put the treatment of prisoners on the policy-makers' agenda. There is some controversy as to whether Western capitals had already been alerted by the UN High Commission for Refugees to the camps' existence. If they had, they certainly failed to act decisively in advance of the reporters' exposés (Gutman, 1993, xiii; Gowing, 1994, 43–5). Thereafter, at the London UN/EU Conference on Yugoslavia in late August, the camps were a major issue, and a commitment was extracted from the Bosnian Serb leader, Radovan Karadžić, to close the death camps. On this occasion, one could consequently argue that the media had an effect but not the effect which some journalists, such as Pulitzer Prize-winning US correspondent Roy Gutman (who first 'discovered' the camps) had hoped. In his opinion, inadequate attempts were made to investigate the camps, and their existence did not shake the West from its spectator's seat at the ring-side of genocide (1993, xxxii).

A similar argument could be made concerning UN Resolution 819 of April 1993, which authorised the creation of 'safe areas' in besieged Bosnian towns (Srebrenica and Zepa initially, and later Gorazde) around which the Bosnian Serbs had almost completed their task of 'ethnic cleansing'. This tactical shift was also largely the product of television imagery from Srebrenica (shot by cameraman Tony Birtley, who had smuggled himself and his camcorder into the town), coupled with the defiance of the UN's General Morillon, who pledged personally to 'save' Srebrenica whatever Headquarters in New York might advise to the contrary. According to Gowing, the footage from the beleaguered town so moved the Third World non-permanent members of the UN Security Council (particularly the Muslim states), that they pushed through the 'safe area' plan in the teeth of permanent member opposition (1994, 49). However, whether the 'safe areas' did in fact make safe the endangered Bosnians (in the absence of a UN mandate authorising UNPROFOR to target the towns' attackers), or were conducive to a just settlement in the longer term (since they did nothing to reverse the ethnic cleansing of the surrounding areas) looks highly doubtful (Gowing, 1994, 54). Ultimately, when television cameras were absent, the 'safe' town of Srebrenica and other 'enclaves' in Eastern Bosnia were allowed to fall into Serb hands virtually unopposed.

In 1994, a more forceful approach was espoused – albeit with vacillations – by NATO and President Clinton. Airstrikes against the recalcitrant Bosnian Serbs were now being mooted seriously, and later actually enacted on a few occasions. This too was apparently the result of television footage which depicted (almost in 'real time') the gruesome consequences of a mortar bomb attack on a Sarajevo market in February 1994. For Martin Bell, coverage of this episode produced a media-generated policy shift, though he concedes that:

> the timing may also have had much to do with it. A new take-charge commander, Lieutenant-General Sir Michael Rose, was on the scene. The UN was fulfilling its mandate for the first time in months, and had embarked on a policy of threatening force against the Serbs...but the TV images certainly made a difference. Among other effects, they brought about a change of policy by the British and Canadian governments about the use of airpower. (1995, 143–4)

Gowing, as we might expect, argues an even more 'limited effects' case. Clinton, though purportedly 'outraged' at the televised scenes of the Serb atrocity, in fact reacted tentatively at first, holding an inconclusive impromptu Oval Office meeting. The real pressure for airstrikes, Gowing postulates, came from the French government, which had been agitating in favour of airstrikes for some time. Scenes of carnage amongst Sarajevan civilians thus came at an opportune moment for the French (1994, 70–2). The combination of diplomatic and media pressure – again with a largely presumed public stiffening of opinion behind airstrikes – explains why these images, not others of similar atrocities, prompted action. However, the transitory nature of media influence, when it is not supported by sustained evidence of public strength of feeling (or a sustained interpretation by officials of public will), was demonstrated by Clinton's wavering over airstrikes after the decision to bomb Serb positions but before their enactment.

To conclude, then, the clearest cases of governmental response to media coverage of Former Yugoslavia are those where the subsequent action was itself most obviously designed for the television cameras, and least capable of being labelled a shift in policy. The (in)famous response of John Major's government to television coverage of 'little Irma' – a five-year old Sarajevan girl, with shrapnel wounds to her spine – exemplifies this. Irma's anguish was brought to British audience's attention by the BBC one weekend in early August 1993. Her case became an overnight *cause célèbre*, as various London-based tabloids competed to evacuate her from Bosnia and bring her to London for specialist medical treatment (Gowing, 1994, 80–2). However, they were outstripped by the British government, which itself organised a military airlift for 'little Irma' and 40 other Sarajevan casualties, arguably for motives every bit as self-serving as the tabloids' own. The desire to be seen to be doing *something* – making an Instant Response to Media Attention, in UN Commander Brigadier Hayes' punning acronym – with a staged 'pseudo-event', whether to woo readers or voters, appears the common denominator (Bell, 1995, 143). However, Douglas Hurd shrugged off accusations of cynicism, claiming his government had simply realised that just 'because you can't help everybody doesn't mean you shouldn't help somebody' (Gowing, 1994, 81).

Although the British government's decision to airlift Irma and 40 others from Sarajevo led to more willingness amongst some other West European states to free up hospital beds for Bosnian casualties, the episode raises a number of unsettling questions about the nature of reporting 'other people's wars' and governments' responses to such mediation. Whatever one might think about the personalisation and sentimentalisation of reportage epitomised by the Irma story, it is by no means certain that such emotionally-manipulative journalism invariably produces the policy responses which it aims to provoke. Indeed, Irma's story might not have gained such enormous media prominence – let alone have evinced Whitehall action – had it occurred during a busier news period. As it was, Irma's wounding in early August coincided with a traditionally 'slow' season for British news organisations, corresponding to the parliamentary recess, which allowed her story to run for several days (Gowing, 1994, 80).

The Yugoslav case thus provides considerable support for the view that television's impact is, borrowing Gowing's preferred epithet, 'fickle': narrowly, in its capricious selection of a few individual tragedies from the mass, and broadly, in its focus on one or two embattled areas at the expense of other sites of extreme suffering. The 'unfair' attention given to Irma amongst so many Bosnian victims replicated, in microcosm, television's elevation of only certain crises into global 'events'. Furthermore, the fickleness is demonstrated in the media's failure to instil a genuine will amongst governments and international governmental organisations to tackle the roots of conflict rather than merely to bandage its consequences.

In the Yugoslav case – unlike its Kurdish predecessor – Western media (themselves still primarily national in both their organisation and news values) failed to penetrate the armoury of 'national interest' which continues to shield foreign policy-making from appeals to humanitarianism or, as Ignatieff puts it, 'to pierce the carapace of self-absorption and estrangement that separates us from the moral worlds of others' (1998, 29). 'When journalists argued that the West should save victims in Bosnia, they were appealing to a general sense of responsibility which went with power rather than a specific sense connected to prior Western actions', remarks Shaw (M. 1996, 162). They largely failed. If peoples around the world are developing a cosmopolitan sense of global citizenship in which responsibility for alleviating suffering arises from a shared humanity – not because of any narrowly national interest served by aiding distant endangered communities – then Yugoslavia suggests that leaders are as yet impervious to it, or determined to resist its lure.

Somalia (1992–3)

While the attention of many Western foreign correspondents was focused on Former Yugoslavia, starvation decimated east African populations in Somalia and the southern Sudan in the early 1990s. Neither case was a wholly natural disaster (in so far as any famine is purely the result of climatic conditions leading to crop failure): rather these severe shortages of food were functions of civil war and disintegrating state structures. One received a massive amount of media attention, and was the subject of a UN humanitarian intervention. The other was at best intermittently covered, though some Western NGO and governmental efforts were made to relieve Sudan's suffering (Livingston, 1996; Neuman, 1996, 229).

For some time, relief workers and Western governmental aid officials feared that Somalia's famine might go similarly ignored. In July 1992, UN Secretary General Boutros Boutros Ghali famously opined that Somalia was the victim of the highly-publicised 'rich man's war' in Former Yugoslavia (cited in Minear, Scott and Weiss, 1996, 54). Contrary to the common belief, however, Western media did not 'discover' starvation in anarchic Somalia and bring it to the attention of hitherto ignorant, distant governments. The sudden, but overwhelming, descent of Western news crews upon Somalia in the autumn of 1992 may well have fuelled a collective impression of television acting as both Western governments' intelligence service and their conscience, but the impression is seriously misleading.

In fact, it appears that US media began to take an interest in Somalia *after* American government officials and aid organisations encouraged them to do so, and only after an estimated 300 000–500 000 Somalis had died of starvation by mid-summer 1992 (Livingston and Eachus, 1995, 417). Livingston and Eachus contend that US officials within the government's specialised relief agencies worked to put Somalia at the top of the policy-making agenda, attempting to awaken American media to the story, partly as a means of overcoming bureaucratic obstacles and military resistance within Bush's administration to a large-scale humanitarian intervention (1995, 418). According to Andrew Natsios of the Office of Foreign Disaster Assistance, initial efforts to this end were notably unsuccessful, as had been Red Cross press briefings and tours for journalists in the autumn of 1991 (Gassman, 1995, 155). Little media attention was paid to a US Congressional Hunger Caucus, at which Natsios testified, or to 'sparsely attended media briefings on Somalia in January and February 1992' (Natsios, 1996, 159). Gradually, however, Natsios' attempts to frame the Somalia famine as 'the worst humanitarian crisis in the world today' – in the words of his testimony – began to take effect. Livingston and Eachus report 50 usages of a similar phraseology by the media over the next few months (1995, 424). But what really brought a decisive shift towards *military* intervention by the US government was a more conventional piece of diplomatic traffic: a strongly worded telegram from the US ambassador to Kenya, describing his visit to Somali refugee camps along Kenya's border. The so-called 'day in hell' cable was ultimately brought to President Bush's attention by national security adviser

Brent Scowcroft, himself an opponent of military involvement (Livingston and Eachus, 1995, 425). However, Bush reportedly wanted to be 'as forward leaning as possible', and was encouraged by various officials, as well as vocal members of Congress (425–6).

Having decided to 'do something', the Bush administration took action which was itself designed to secure media attention: a US military airlift of food into Somalia:

It was this announcement [on 14 August 1992] that finally sparked the sort of intense media attention usually associated with the CNN effect. Following the President's announcement, media attention – in terms of story frequency – increased more than fivefold, to 26 pieces per week. When the airlift commenced on August 28, the Somalia story was established. (Livingston and Eachus, 1995, 426)

So why did Bush take action, over-riding opponents of 'doing something'? While media attention to Somalia after August 1992 may have encouraged him to launch the more far-reaching Operation Restore Hope, as is commonly suggested, it appears that more complex motivations were also at work (Natsios, 1996, 163). Some of those who knew the President attest to his humanitarian engagement with the Somali issue. The 'Day in Hell' telegram apparently stirred memories of a trip Mr and Mrs Bush had made to a CARE shelter in the Sudan during the Sahelian famine of the mid-1980s. Bush claimed that memories of what he had witnessed there had 'clearly affected his decision to send troops into Somalia' (Natsios, 1996, 161, 168).

Less charitably, it has been suggested that Bush 'had some personal wish to leave office a humanitarian', having been stung by Clinton's charges during the 1992 Presidential election campaign that he was doing too little about starvation in Somalia (Minear, Scott and Weiss, 1996, 54; Neuman, 1996, 229). Perhaps Bush (who had not responded vigorously to Southern Sudan's famine, despite his moving visit there the previous decade) saw the utility of a militarised intervention, which might reanimate memories of America's victory in the Gulf War, allowing the departing 'Foreign Policy President' to go out 'in a blaze of glory' (Rather, 1995, 33; Dowden, 1995, 94–5). Lawrence Eagleburger, then Secretary of State, asserts that he recommended action to Bush not only because of Congressional pressure but because of his 'honest belief that we could do this...*at not too great a cost* and, certainly, without any great danger of body bags coming home' (emphasis added, cited in Minear, Scott and Weiss, 1996, 55). While detractors claim that Bush was not overly concerned with establishing a clear 'exit strategy' for disengagement from Somalia – since his successor would be exiting – others argue that the decision to 'Restore Hope' was driven by the conviction that food aid could rapidly be delivered without loss of American life. (Indeed, Powell is reported to have made his consent conditional on a strict time-limit being set on the operation, ensuring its completion before, or very soon after, Clinton took office in January 1993: Mayall, 1996, 111.)

That the Somali intervention was conceived in many respects as a public relations stunt is further suggested by the manner of the US Navy SEALs' (Sea, Air and Land units) dramatic arrival in Mogadishu during the pre-dawn hours of 9 December 1996. According to Thomas Keenan, the US military's Somalia strategy was:

from the start...oriented toward the production of images... conceptualised, practised, and evaluated – by all parties – strictly in terms of the publicity value of the images and headlines it might produce. Comprehensive media coverage has not just changed the conduct of military operations – images and publicity have become military operations themselves, and the military outcome cannot easily be distinguished from the images of that operation. (Keenan, 1994, 142–3)

Thus when the SEALs arrived in (anticipated) darkness on the beach in Mogadishu, they were met by around 600 members of the international press corps, including anchors from the four US networks. Military commanders might complain that the unseemly media scrum created the wrong effect – that television lights dazzled the troops in their night-vision goggles – but in fact US officials had invited cameramen to attend the SEALs' 'invasion' of Somalia (Keenan, 1994, 147). According to one British journalist who was present, from the moment of the televised landing he knew 'that Somalia would become a disaster for the United States...To invade Somalia as if it were a military objective and treat all Somalis as potential enemies was worse than a mistake. It was to lead to catastrophe' (Dowden, 1995, 93).

Staging the landing was easy. Providing the international 'media circus' with an ongoing stream of positive images of the US/UN humanitarian forces delivering the Somalis from one another, and delivering humanitarian assistance to the needy, proved more difficult. US military commanders failed to understand the complexities of the situation on the ground, finding themselves in the midst of a civil war in a 'failed state' whose structures of central government and administration had totally collapsed. A process of 'mission creep' occurred, with the objectives of the US-led UN operation successively widening. The initial humanitarian purposes of the United Task Force (UNITAF) mission gave way to UNOSOM (UN Operation in Somalia) II's attempt to disarm warring Somali factions, hunt down General Aideed, and restore order and authority, not merely hope:

> What had begun as a US-led humanitarian mission had come to include, through a process of 'mission creep', disarming the warlords and gunmen, restoring the police forces, reviving of regional leadership, and transitioning to a multi-national UN operation. 'Mission-creep' became 'mission gallop' as larger numbers of nations sent UN forces which tried to satisfy increasingly conflicting objectives. Command and control of the multitude of forces and non-governmental humanitarian agencies became increasingly uncoordinated. The tense but functioning *modus vivende* worked out between US military forces and Somali warlords broke down as UN forces tried to conduct nation-building, security of feeding stations, peace enforcement, and peacekeeping operations. After Aidid's forces retaliated to what they perceived as an attack on their radio station, and killed UN/Pakistani troops, the UN placed a bounty on Aidid. What had been professional became personal, as one senior US officer observed, 'manhood was on the line', a sentiment inconsistent with an even-handed peacekeeping dialogue with all parties. (Stech, 1994, note 37, 266)

As the Somali situation spiralled out of UN control so too did the US briefers' 'spin' lose its lustre. The narrative now was less one of US forces saving innocent victims of famine than an inconclusive manhunt which had 'got personal', and in which journalists, as well as UN blue berets, were being killed. Indeed, the security situation in the summer and early autumn of 1993 had deteriorated to the point where US forces were no longer able to guarantee the safety of the diminished number of journalists who still remained. In July, three Western journalists were beaten to death by Somalis after 60 Somalis had been killed in a US helicopter attack on an Aideed stronghold (Lyman, 1995, 126). Some journalists, however, even found themselves under attack from the US military: in an incident in September 1993, the military lobbed stun grenades at three photographers and reporters in an effort to keep them away from the scene of a military operation (Keenan, 1994, 156).

The dénouement was perhaps predictable: Operation Restore Hope was shot down by a powerful image of a dead US ranger being dragged through the streets of Mogadishu. In many accounts, this single image ended the Operation – the classic 'CNN effect' thesis propounded by George Kennan – by whipping up an instant public reaction against its continuation. There were apparently thousands of enraged calls to the White House (Minear, Scott and Weiss, 1996, 55). Clinton proclaimed himself to be 'very angry': it was the 'worst day of my life' (Gowing, 1994, 67). And his National Security Adviser, Anthony Lake, admitted that on this occasion television had brought home what conventional intelligence had failed to make clear: 'the pictures helped make us recognise that the military situation in Mogadishu had deteriorated in a way that we had not frankly recognised' (Gowing, 1994, 67). An announcement of withdrawal was hastily made.

However, this account again irons out several complexities, and appears to exaggerate the effect of that notorious image. First, it should be noted that the footage itself – powerful though it undoubtedly was – did not derive any of its impact from being delivered 'real-time'. By the time of the attack, the international press corps had dwindled from its peak of 600 (to watch the 'invasion'), to a mere six to eight individuals, none of them American (Pilkington in *The Guardian*, 11 October 1993). None of these recorded the footage. Instead, it was shot by a Somali driver, who had been left a Hi-8 camcorder by the departing Reuters crew for whom he was now acting as 'stringer'. His shots of the US ranger were relayed by CNN and quickly re-broadcast by other channels, but they were not simultaneous with the attack itself.

Second, it has been suggested that the Clinton administration – contrary to Lake's claims that they were caught unawares by the footage – had been considering scaling down and then abandoning Operation Restore Hope for some time: the news, paradoxically, gave them the pretext. Even then, as Gowing points out, Clinton resisted the temptation to make an instant withdrawal, initially strengthening the US presence while announcing that the operation would terminate on 31 March 1994. Perhaps public pressure to withdraw was not insurmountable after all? Certainly, Andrew Natsios claims that there was 'a high level of support from the American public…for the US to remain in Somalia to finish its work after the killing of American soldiers in October 1993' (Natsios, 1996, 163). This suggests that the failure was not one of public confidence so much as of leadership, and certainly a number of commentators propose that if Clinton's administration had wanted to persist in Somalia, it could have moulded public opinion accordingly. Stech implies that the failure in Somalia was partially due to poor news management, and an absence of positive news frames when things went wrong in October 1993 (1994, 244). Similarly, Gowing cites US officials who point out that Clinton might have made a rapid assertion of US determination to proceed with Operation Restore Hope after the incident, just as he had done after 'friendly fire' casualties were incurred in northern Iraq (1994, 69). Perhaps not coincidentally, those who dissent from the view that better public communication could have saved the Operation are two former White House communications directors, Marlin Fitzwater and Mark Gearan, who may have personal reasons for arguing the limits of the spin doctor's healing powers.

Rwanda (1994)

Media responsibility for inspiring the massive relief operation to assist the refugees who fled from Rwanda in the wake of 1994's genocide has been less discussed than the other cases reviewed, though one could argue that television's impact on (inter-)governmental and NGO policy was 'more important and direct than elsewhere' (Minear, Scott and Weiss, 1996, 62–3). Certainly Martin Shaw contends that Rwanda 'appears closest of all to a "pure" media-defined crisis, as in Kurdistan': 'the coverage of the refugees was highly reminiscent of the plight of the Kurds…television commentary was often of the "something must be done" kind, an implicit call for action by the west' (1996, 171–2). The 'west' responded with not only huge levels of non-governmental aid but also with another UN humanitarian intervention.

However, many commentators (including journalists themselves) have pointed out that praise for the media in alerting the world to Rwanda's plight is scarcely warranted. After all, most of the world's media missed the 'big story' in Rwanda: the genocide of over half a million Tutsis and moderate Hutus by Hutu *interahamwe* militia. The media arrived *en masse* only once the killing was over, and a massive outpouring of refugees was under way, many of whom were complicit in the massacre. This crucial point was missed by some journalists who confused the (mainly Tutsi) victims of the genocide with the (mainly Hutu) refugees in the camps, seeing only an undifferentiated mass of 'victims'. By and large, however, the refugees were Hutu fleeing Rwanda in the face of the victorious Tutsi RPF, fearing that vengeance would be exacted upon them for their part in the genocide.

So why did the media largely ignore the genocide whilst in progress? Journalist Lyndsey Hilsum notes that Rwanda was off the beaten track for Nairobi-based East Africa correspondents, and that in the 1980s it had been regarded as 'boring – a place where farmers farmed and the government governed' (1995, 148). That this was a woefully inadequate picture should have been obvious, given the clear preparations for genocide which were in train. If nothing else, a massacre in Burundi in October 1993 ought to have alerted reporters to a disturbed situation in Central Africa, but this too was ignored (Lorch, 1995, 102).

In their defence, journalists might well point to several logistical and organisation obstacles confronting them. Nairobi-based correspondents are expected to cover a huge geographical news-beat. They cannot be everywhere at once, and their attention is likely to be directed to those locations where they can gain fairly easy access (thanks to co-operative authorities and available transport), and in which they think their news organisation will have an interest, often dictated – still – by where their state takes an interest. For many of the same reasons that Sudan's famine was under-reported – poor transport coupled with Sudanese government visa restrictions – so too was the initial stage of Rwanda's genocide (Livingston, 1996, 68–89). American reporter Donatella Lorch, who visited shortly after President Habyarimana's plane crashed, after which the genocide was unleashed, paints a vivid picture of dangers confronting reporters who attempted to cover it:

> In April 1994, six days after the plane crash, I entered Kigali in a Red Cross medical convoy driving in from Burundi. With the airports closed, it was the only way in. The roads were clogged with fleeing refugees, but the terror started on the outskirts of the city. At each checkpoint, drunken, armed men threatened us, banging grenades on our windows, demanding money and passports. There was no law, no sense that anyone was in command. Bodies lay everywhere. Several truckloads of frenzied screaming men waving machetes and screwdrivers drove by. At night, screams followed by automatic gunfire could be heard from the churches in Kigali. (Lorch, 1995, 104)

In such a situation, journalists could not necessarily expect 'immunity'. Lorch reports that some of her colleagues encountered organisational resistance from New York to their covering this dangerous assignment (Lorch, 1995, 101). And if Western editors were sometimes motivated primarily by a desire to protect their own people, they were only following the lead set by the UN, whose minimal presence in Rwanda was withdrawn (not strengthened) when the genocide began, and whose final act was to evacuate Westerners, but not Rwandan UN staffers, to safety (de Waal, 1994, 29; Hilsum, 1995, 158–9). Rwanda thus seemed, initially, to be a case of media attention calibrated not to the magnitude of the genocide but to the level of (un)interest it was arousing in Washington or London.

Furthermore, a compelling 'good news' story was concurrently being played out in South Africa, which monopolised media and diplomatic attention as the genocide reached its conclusion: namely the inauguration of Nelson Mandela as President of the new 'multiracial' South Africa on 10 May 1994. Some media organisations apparently felt unable to cover both stories simultaneously. Pierre Gassman, head of media at the International Committee of the Red Cross's Geneva headquarters, recounts his visit to the CNN's Atlanta base in early April 1994 to discuss CNN coverage of 'underreported conflicts':

> I tried to persuade its assignment editors to cover Rwanda immediately. Yes, of course, they said, they knew about Rwanda, but all

their available crews and satellite uplinks were in South Africa. The editors also expressed doubt about the possibility of showing two African topics at the same time as this might confuse their audience. (Gassman, 1995, 157)

The latter remark is hardly encouraging for those who see the 'global media' as agents of an enlightened humanitarian awareness, revealing CNN's own parochialism and its disparaging view of an audience which (under CNN's tutelage) would be confused by simultaneous 'good' and 'bad' news from Africa. The confusion would presumably arise from the unexpectedness of the 'good news' – Mandela's inauguration against a backdrop of far less inter-racial tension than some anticipated – in a continent where the routine 'bad news' narrative is generally framed in terms of 'acts of God' (such as drought) or 'ancient tribal hatreds'. As the BBC's then Southern Africa correspondent pointed out, 'African news is generally only big news when it involves lots of dead bodies' (F. Keane, 1996, 7). Rwanda thus became 'big news' not only after there were indisputably 'lots of dead bodies' but after the international press corps departed from South Africa and parachuted into Rwanda on the way home (Lorch, 1995, 104). Live satellite broadcasting facilities were not established in the border town of Kigali until late May (Minear, Scott and Weiss, 1996, 64).

However, it seems fair to assert that mass media attention preceded any concerted international intervention at the inter-governmental level. The gathering of heads of state in Johannesburg might have provided a useful opportunity for a co-ordinated multinational intervention force to have been mustered but, in Natsios's words, 'American efforts to recruit African troops were lethargic' (Natsios, 1996, 162). The Clinton administration was particularly dilatory in its response, suffering (one ex-official suggests) from 'Vietnam and Somalia syndrome', namely 'a fear of losing' which had been given tangible expression in Presidential Decision Directive No. 25 (Shattuck, 1996, 173). The narrow criteria set out therein for a US intervention provided either an obstacle to action or a convenient cover for inaction, depending on one's perception of Clinton's willingness to avert genocide and deal with its consequences. When the US did contribute to a UN relief effort, it was aimed purely at helping the refugees, now beset by an outbreak of cholera in Goma, where a makeshift refugee city had formed:

perhaps because television pictures impressed upon the administration the necessity of once again 'doing something' (Minear, Scott and Weiss, 1996, 65). It would be hard, though, to insist that the compressed response times of the 'real-time' age had produced an 'instant response' in this case.

The more important point about television's impact on the situation in Rwanda is not whether it provoked intervention but how news media framing of events – and indeed reporters' very presence in such droves – shaped the humanitarian operation in Rwanda. The media have been accused of distorting the NGOs' work in the camps in Tanzania and Zaire to which refugees had flooded. For one thing, camera crews' very presence encouraged inter-agency duplication of efforts, discouraging co-ordination (always a problem in such massive operations): 'only a limited number of agencies were prepared to work in the sanitation sector ... a situation that contrasted starkly with the number of agencies working in the higher-profile activities, such as establishing cholera treatment centres and centres for unaccompanied children' (Minear, Scott and Weiss, 1996, 66). In other words, the media encouraged NGOs to practice more telegenic forms of humanitarianism, and NGOs, anxious to capitalise on the public awareness afforded them by television, colluded in the projection of stereotypical images of 'suffering Africa', in contravention of their own codes of conduct relating to the non-exploitative use of images (Benthall, 1993, 182–3).

The media's framing of Rwanda as a refugee crisis – rather than as a 'genocide and its aftermath' story – had other distorting effects. It meant that the NGOs and subsequent UN operation concentrated their efforts on those who had left Rwanda, neglecting to assist the internally displaced, or to aid the new RPF government in restoring stability to the country (Lorch, 1995, 105–6; Minear, Scott and Weiss, 1996, 66). As Feargal Keane remarks, overwhelming though the mass exodus of refugees was, dealing with over a million people was nevertheless:

> something relatively easy, something the world was used to: masses of people needing food and shelter. In responding to the refugee crisis the bureaucrats in New York were able to salve the consciences of member nations. Having failed pitifully to act during the genocide, food drops, refugee camps and pious

words were used to give the impression that something was being done about Rwanda ... It was as if the genocide was being swept to one side, something regrettable that happened in the past, an African 'thing' that would be sorted out in an African way later on. (1996, 109)

As the UN and NGOs made no real attempt to undertake the much less tractable task of separating the perpetrators of the genocide from 'innocent' Hutus who had been encouraged to flee, the camps became, in the words of a *Médecins sans Frontières* official, 'humanitarian havens' for the killers (cited by F. Keane, 1996, 186). Indeed, to make the work of food distribution easier and to bring some semblance of order to the massive camps around Goma in Zaire, aid workers permitted the social structures of Hutu Rwanda to be re-constituted in the camps (de Waal, 1994, 25; F. Keane, 1996, *passim*). Consequently the camps fell under effective *interahamwe* control, and the militia encouraged Hutu refugees to remain in them semi-permanently, whipping up fresh fears of a 'genocide' enacted by the now ruling RPF should the refugees return (a grip only broken in November 1996 by an uprising of Zairean rebels with Rwandan army support). As Keane suggests, encouraged by the media to view Rwanda through the simplifying lens of 'refugee crisis', external 'humanitarian agencies' doubly delayed the process of reconstruction and reconciliation in Rwanda by allowing the camps to operate indefinitely under *interahamwe* control, and failing to assist the process of indicting those responsible for the genocide so that they could be dealt with at the Tanzania-based international tribunal: a process which (at least in theory) aids reconciliation by individualising guilt (Dworkin, 1996, 137–44).

Why Some 'Others' Wars' and Not Others?

Not every occurrence of human suffering on a grand scale is transformed into an epic media spectacle, or 'global crisis' in Martin Shaw's phrase, despite the availability of technology which potentially allows the coverage of a greater number of 'other people's wars'. Consider news-editor Nik Gowing's analogy of news film with 'supermarket war video':

Editorially, we can pick and choose – just like walking down shelves of breakfast cereal. One day Nagorno Karabakh. The next day Tajikistan, or perhaps Georgia or Afghanistan, then a bit of Angola, Liberia or Yemen and perhaps Algeria if we are lucky. All of it streams relentlessly into our news machines. Much of it is never transmitted. (Gowing, 1996, 81)

For him, what determines whether somebody else's war is placed in the news editor's shopping basket on any given day is the availability of footage: 'the main principle is: no pictures, no serious coverage of a conflict' (Gowing, 1996, 81). But while television news undoubtedly requires pictures for its storytelling, more determines whose wars become 'our wars' – if only temporarily – than pictures alone, since, as Gowing concedes, footage shot by local 'stringers' piles high in cold storage. The crucial question, then, is how decisions are reached about the positioning of 'our' journalists. After all, though people often blithely imagine that 'journalists are where the news is', in fact, as Bell points out, 'the news is where journalists are'; thus sending our reporters to others' wars is crucial to their constitution as global crises (1995, 59). It is hardly surprising that many people labour under this misapprehension, as journalists and media organisations themselves like to perpetuate the notion that they provide a digest of all the day's important events, giving us 'all the news that counts', or taking us 'around the world in thirty minutes'. But if we reject the implication that the news agenda is self-selecting, then we must ask why some war-stories for which footage is accessible pass muster as news while others do not: in short, how the world-map according to the news is constructed.

Many processes of filtration occur which ensure that some events are reported as 'news' while other long-term phenomenona or more ephemeral incidents are discarded as un-newsworthy, or overlooked entirely. Some of this selection results from conscious decisions taken by news 'gate-keepers', who fish usable items from the stream of wire service reports, 'supermarket war-video', press releases, briefings, and copy from reporters on various 'news-beats', which flows into the newsroom. In guarding the gate, news editors are guided (some claim intuitively) by 'news values': criteria which enable them to judge a story's newsworthiness. Is it topical, proximate, timely, or relevant (Shoemaker and Reese, 1996, 110–12)? Various practical calculations may also have to be factored in, especially when it comes to reporting foreign news, and war news most particularly. What financial and personnel commitments are required to cover 'somebody else's war'? Do the costs – financial and potentially human, if the war is unlikely to afford immunity to the outside reporter – outweigh the public interest served by reporting the story? (Sometimes the dangers may be considered simply too great: hence the paucity of coverage of the war in Algeria by many Western news agencies, fearing for their reporters' lives in a conflict which has targeted non-Islamic outsiders.)

However, other processes of filtration are more deeply embedded in broad social and cultural values which shape what is deemed newsworthy in different polities. After all, judgements about newsworthiness do not just occur after the fact of newsgathering: some *a priori* notion of what constitutes news determines the location of foreign correspondents and the 'news-beats' covered by domestic reporters (such as crime, health, parliament, education). These pre-existing conceptions – some below the consciousness of news editors themselves – obviously vary from one political system to another, and, perhaps to a lesser degree, from one news medium to the next within the same state. News in the Soviet Union, for example, was accorded an overt ideological function by the state: its job was to reveal the 'correctness' of Marxist-Leninism, and its superiority as a political and socio-economic system over its capitalist competitors. With this remit, news focused much more on long-term trends and phenomena, with an emphasis on explaining – with one clear model – underlying processes of causality (McNair, 1991).

In many Western democracies, however, 'news' is construed in episodic terms: dramatic, (often) short-term, and sometimes violent, occurrences which disrupt the surface of everyday life, and are newsworthy because of their disruptiveness, or their 'discreteness' as bounded events. On the one hand, then, much Western news comprises such 'pseudo-events': staged-for-the-media briefings, press conferences, speeches, summits, spectacles. However, these are coupled with a fair dose of more disturbing, and seemingly less predictable, 'bad news' stories, though even the unpredictable, disruptive 'bad news' (wars, famines, floods and hijackings often in physically distant locations) may take on a familiar and predictable quality. As Walter Lippmann recognised back in 1922: 'without standardisation, without stereotypes, without routine judgements, without a fairly ruthless disregard of subtlety, the editor would soon die of excitement' (cited in McQuail, 1994, 213). Arguably, though, the routinisation of 'bad news' – as it is often 'other people's news' – serves a veiled ideological function. For Johan Galtung and Richard Vincent, Western news (including the content of the 'globalised' media) is the carrier of 'occidental cosmology', serving to confirm 'to people in the centre countries what a miserable life people have in those periphery countries, and consequently how fortunate people in the centre countries really are for not being there or being members of periphery countries' (cited by Alleyne, 1997, 40).

Such a view would suggest that, globalisation notwithstanding, Giddens's vision of a world no longer with 'Others' is far from a reality. Indeed, news values often implicitly rely on the audience sharing notions of 'us' and 'them', with the presumption that 'we' are only 'naturally' interested in ourselves or those close to, or like, us. As news values are commonly shaped according to the audience's presumed 'common interest', criteria such as 'proximity' and 'relevance' recur in news judgements. By 'proximity' something more than mere geographical nearness is involved. As Shaw argues, we may be 'distant' from those who are physically close to us but nevertheless alien from mainstream society, such as the homeless and the mentally ill, who are often confined to Hallin's 'sphere of deviance' (M. Shaw 1996, 9; Hallin, 1989). Evaluating 'proximity' thus involves the gate-keeper in weighing the audience's likely interest in the subjects of a story: Rousseau's notion of the 'general will' providing the 'philosophical basis for assumptions about what is in the common interest' (McQuail, 1992, 23). Perhaps not coincidentally, Rousseau believed that 'natural commiseration' – or what we might call an empathetic concern – such as experienced between individuals at first-hand could hardly exist between one society and another, except amongst a few *'grandes Ames Cosmopolites'*, (great cosmopolitan spirits: Benthall, 1993, 215). What Rousseau believed true in the eighteenth century still appears to colour news editors' instinct that audiences draw a very narrow circle of 'we', and hence can stomach only so many 'other people's wars', and even then, only if framed in ways which hook the reader/viewer, without necessarily redrawing a wider circle.

Thus in order to become news, distant events often have to involve suffering on a huge scale or have to endanger or involve citizens 'proximate' to the media organisation: the fate of one or two of 'us' caught up in 'their' conflict – in Kashmir, say – may absorb domestic media for days. Van Ginneken proposes a rule of thumb for assessing when death reaches tragic proportions: '10 000 deaths on another continent equal 1000 in another country equal 100 deaths in an outpost equal ten deaths in the centre of the capital equal one celebrity' (1998, 24). But even a quantitative measure of disaster alone is not sufficient condition to assure international news media attention, and certainly humanitarian agencies often complain that *forecasts* of mass deaths are insufficient to draw media attention to those areas of imminent disaster. As Lionel Rosenblatt has pointed out, the media are not interested in 'anticipated events' because the anticipated is unfilmable (Rosenblatt, 1996, 141). Television reporters are therefore only likely to be interested in human suffering after the event, or after thousands of lives have already been lost, as was the case during the early stages of the Ethiopian famine in 1984 (Philo, 1993). And a news organisation is often more likely to be interested if its competitors – the 'media circus' – are pursuing the story, for, as Italian reporter Furio Colombo notes, news media 'provoke an effect directly proportionate to the number of reporters present. Each one acts as an alibi for the others' (Colombo, 1995, 86). For these reasons, as a number of writers concerned with building more effective humanitarian responses have pointed out, mass media cannot be relied upon as an 'early warning system' to alert governments to human catastrophes, potential wars or genocides, even where advance signals are clear.

A lack of media interest in imminent or current emergencies is especially likely to prevail, as during the southern Sudanese famine, where an area presents logistical difficulties for film crews and where the media's own state fails to take an interest. With respect to Somalia, American television networks made a serious commitment to covering that story only after the US government had decided upon a military-assisted airdrop of food aid, even though this was after the worst of the famine. Again, globalisation notwithstanding, many Western news media exhibit an enduring trend to 'index' their coverage to the preoccupations of national policy-making elites, calibrating their attention to those with most power over the decision-making process. Indeed, some media scholars contend that the most pervasive but least visible form of gate-keeping is structural, embedded in the worldview of those sources on whom news most crucially depends, which it then replicates. 'Gates', proposes Steven Livingston, are thus not 'simply naturally occurring phenomena, but rather are established and controlled by politically powerful actors (usually in government) and not by editors and reporters' (Livingston, 1996, 86).

Representing 'Others'

The distant audience's presumed lack of interest in 'other people's wars', and the degree to which those others are still regarded as Other, is suggested by the frames and narrative devices employed by Western media in covering conflict, genocide and complex emergencies in the 1990s. A pronounced tendency to 'domesticate' news prevails (Gassman, 1995, 149). The boundary-blurring process of domestication – whereby foreign news is hung on a domestic peg – may sometimes explain the reporters' very presence in a distant war zone or emergency in the first place. For example, the presence of troops from the reporter's country is likely to ensure ongoing attention to that location, as the audience is imagined to share a 'common interest' with their armed representatives, if not necessarily with those whom they are going to defend or aid (thus, in part, the ongoing commitment of the BBC to covering the Former Yugoslavia where British troops formed an important contingent of UNPROFOR). Foreign news therefore often appears an extension of the domestic. Not surprisingly, then, American reports on Somalia frequently focused on the activities of US troops there, while Irish media tended to concentrate on stories concerning Irish aid workers (Hammock and Charny, 1996, 115). Similarly, the US intervention in Haiti, 'Operation Uphold Democracy', was 'domesticated' twice over by American media as, first, a story about US forces and endangered US citizens in the island and, second, a putative 'threat' to America from an influx of Haitian refugees (Minear, Scott and Weiss, 1996, 59–62).

In addition, the phenomenon of 'celebrity journalism' has given rise to a tendency for foreign news stories to be framed effectively around, and about, the star (Girardet, 1996, 60). Where news editors anticipate a lack of interest among their audience in distant suffering, the star reporter serves as the audience's primary point of identification and empathy. Anthropologist Ulf Hannerz explains the function of foreign correspondents thus:

in the contemporary cultural market-place, some news correspondents become commodities in their own right. Their reporting is imbued with their own personal authority, and in the end the places where they go, and the events they report on, may be marked as more important by their presence. They are the people you can trust to give you trouble. (1996, 122)

But how misplaced this trust may be! The emergence of highly-paid stars has proceeded hand-in-hand with the growth of parachute 'journalism': the latter, to a degree, a product of the former. As with inflated 'star' salaries in other arenas (think of Hollywood, or professional football), the consequences for the profession as a whole tend to be deleterious, as money is siphoned from the lower organisational reaches and underling support staff in order to recruit and retain 'stars'. For news media, this skewing of the budget at the top has led to cost-cutting below, and a reduction of permanent 'staffers' overseas. When a foreign story 'breaks', the star is thus despatched to the trouble zone, fortuitously making the star the story, but with damaging effects on news quality overall. The consequences of such 'parachuting' were particularly acute in the case of Rwanda, where many reporters' lack of background expertise produced extremely formulaic stories, often, in this case, framed around notions of 'tribal' bloodletting and 'ancient hatreds' (Minear, Scott and Weiss, 1996, 64; Girardet, 1996, 64; Wall, 1997, 121–34; Allen and Seaton, 1999).

The pre-scripted nature of much news reporting of 'other people's wars' is easily discernible. (For a particularly frank insider's account of setting up such a story in Afghanistan, Kevin Toolis's 'The Angel Angle' in the *Weekend Guardian* of 9 November 1996 is highly instructive.) A number of commentators point to the prevalence of narratives framed around the 'victim and rescuer' – 'the totems of our age' – which differ little from one location to the next (Brauman, 1993, 154; Benthall, 1993, 189–90). Hammock and Charny also observe a 'strong tendency to view all emergencies as if they were the equivalents of natural disasters, beyond the control of people' (Hammock and Charny, 1996, 117). Although none of the 'humanitarian emergencies' in Kurdistan, Rwanda and Somalia was 'natural' – free from human agency – the inattention (or inability?) of television news to explaining the causes of human suffering they depicted was apparent. Instead television news often focused on refugees, apparently happier to treat people as passive 'victims', the objects not the subjects of history; or, in the words of one US journalist, 'good people to whom bad things happen' (Minear, Scott and Weiss, 1996, 64). Not only, then, are the distant 'Others' depicted as powerless to improve their future situation, and in need of 'rescue' by outside humanitarians (one of the stereotypes of a Third World dependent on First World charity which NGOs have been trying to demolish), but they may also be effectively absolved of responsibility for the past. Indeed, with respect to those Hutu refugees who had hitherto participated in Rwanda's genocide before fleeing to camps in Goma and elsewhere, it is hard to think of a less apt designation than 'good people to whom bad things happen'.

Television news thus seems to insist on the 'innocence' of those suffering as a precondition for its attention. As Ignatieff regretfully observes, 'the ethics of victimhood generate empathy only where victims are obviously blameless' (1998, 24). Even where television finds 'blameless victims', they are often not allowed to speak for themselves (Brauman, 1993, 154). Their suffering is mediated through the person of the reporter or aid worker who speaks on their behalf (Brauman, 1993, 150; M. Shaw, 1996, *passim*). Correspondingly, the heroic figure of the 'rescuer' is elevated: be it the reporter her- or himself, the humanitarian volunteer – 'a new, newsworthy figure, neither statesman nor guerrilla, but half-amateur and half-expert' – or the UN blue berets in 'humanitarian interventions' which have increasingly been conceived as military operations (Brauman, 1993, 153; de Waal, 1994, 26).

Concentrating on individual acts of heroism or suffering, television news (or more feature-style press coverage) often produces essentially 'human interest' reporting from distant war and crisis zones. The use of a human interest 'hook' can be defended as a device for fostering empathy: a means of drawing an audience into a story which they might not otherwise see as 'relevant'. Sensitively done, human interest stories of 'other people's wars' may involve allowing 'victims' to speak for themselves. Interviews, Martin Bell suggests, referring to his own experience in Former Yugoslavia, 'personalised the conflict, so that people elsewhere could relate to it more easily, as if it were their homes and families being targeted, and not some foreign conflict of no consequence' (1995, 99). However, personalised stories often do not take the form Bell suggests, possibly because Yugoslavia was a very different conflict from those beyond Europe. Both its location and duration perhaps fostered Western media and audience identification with Yugoslavia's victims: 'people who could have been us', as Gowing puts it (1994, 8).

The problem with an unleavened diet of human interest reporting is that paradoxically – in singling out seemingly unique, individual stories – it may ultimately have the reductive effect of suggesting the essential sameness of all suffering. And while the creation of a 'cosmopolitan' global civic consciousness may rely on people understanding their essential sameness as fellow humans, it is unlikely to be served by reporting which ignores the specific causes of very different cases of suffering, or implies they are all at root inexplicable. Where the roots of the Kurdish rebellion, or the Somali famine, or genocide in Rwanda are largely left unexplained, the audience may indeed become fatigued by the 'sameness' of news of distant victims, and unable repeatedly to feel 'pity' (the emotion which television news often seems most keen to evoke). Television news has been charged with producing 'compassion without understanding', and without understanding, compassion is unlikely to endure or to solidify into something more meaningful than mere pity (J. Keane, 1996, 7). Perhaps, as novelist James Hamilton-Paterson writes, 'at some point charity has to shade into commitment or else turn away and reward other victims for their pitiability' (1996, 29–30). Worse, suggests Michael Ignatieff, television news may foster a 'generalized misanthropy, that irritable resignation toward the criminal folly of fanatics and assassins, which legitimizes one of the dangerous cultural moods of our time – the feeling that the world has become too crazy to deserve our serious attention' (1998, 25).

Whether the often-diagnosed condition of 'compassion fatigue' actually exists in more than just the eyes of its beholders is a moot point. And if it does, it is debatable whether fatigue testifies to the audience's 'innate' disinterest in 'others' wars' and crises, or whether media reporting itself, by encouraging viewers to make short-term emotional investments, has produced ever-diminishing compassionate returns for the 'single banalized commodity of horror' (Ignatieff, 1998, 29). Mort Rosenblum of Associated Press tends to the former position: media try to counter 'compassion burnout' by repackaging each new humanitarian disaster in a new frame. Hammock and

Charny, on the other hand, argue that 'to the extent that it exists, [compassion fatigue] is a rational response by the public to the constant repetition of the same story in the same places. Hope – generated from real understanding... is a more sustainable motive for giving than pity' (Hammock and Charny, 1996, 124; Minear, Scott and Weiss, 1996, 23). Whether we should automatically conflate charitable giving – generosity – with compassion, though, bears some consideration. Is it not possible that charitable giving may derive from the desire to assuage guilt (not shame) as much as from empathetic concern: a desire to displace thought through a simple action? The measure of real compassion, William Shawcross and others suggest, may lie more in questioning our desire to provide 'charity' and to mount 'humanitarian interventions'; recognising the ambivalence of 'giving', which, inappropriately framed, can serve to reinforce dependency while doing nothing to tackle the structural causes of 'others'' poverty and insecurity.

Whether or not the audience experiences fatigue, certainly television news seems quickly to tire of 'other people's wars'; Yugoslavia was an exception, as it was both geographically nearer to home for Western media and involved people much more 'like us' (Gowing, 1994, 8). Many commentators note how short an attention span television news has, its generic conventions militating against 'the minimum moral requirement of engagement with another person's suffering: that one spends time with them' (Ignatieff, 1998, 29). Television's 'shifting agenda syndrome' means that a distant crisis is likely to remain as headline news for a few weeks – at most – before the 'circus' moves on, though the story may be sporadically returned to, should new developments regenerate an interest, as did the pictures of the US ranger in Somalia (Pedelty, 1995, 188). As Livingston notes, having 'discovered' the story, the media draw the audience into an euphoric initial phase of intensive coverage, which quickly subsides as the 'problem' proves less tractable than initially imagined (Livingston, 1996, 83). This restlessness derives not only from editorial decisions concerning the audience's saturation point with a story but also from the financial costs of maintaining a crew overseas for prolonged periods. (Gowing notes that in January 1994, a ten-day stint for an ITN team in Bosnia, based in only one location, was costed at £23 000: 1994, 93.) One result is that the long-term consequences of humanitarian interventions are rarely plumbed, and neither (some critics suggest) are NGO activities and impact sufficiently scrutinised. As Alex de Waal writes, 'Humanitarianism, it seems, is its own justification' (1994, 21).

Television's uneasiness in covering foreign news is also discernible in its seeming incapacity to deal meaningfully with more than one foreign issue at a time. 'This means', Girardet suggests, 'that while the Rwandas of today will be covered on a massive scale before they too fade into oblivion, other crises (such as Angola, the southern Sudan, and Afghanistan) will continue to be ignored' (Girardet, 1996, 57). Why so? To the extent that the media *do* 'package' distant crises differently, as Rosenblum argues, they may accordingly justify covering fewer of them. In other words, whatever their underlying narrative similarities (as stories of 'victims and rescuers'), the outer packaging of Somalia as 'famine in a failed state', of Rwanda as 'resurgent tribalism', or Bosnia as 'perils of nationalism', permits these stories to function as representative allegories of what the 'New World Disorder' entails. It consequently becomes superfluous to deal extensively with 'ethnic violence' and 'resurgent nationalism' elsewhere. A Danziger cartoon in the *Christian Science Monitor* illustrates this point nicely, with the Bosnian desk editor on the telephone, telling a colleague: 'Tadjikistan? Sorry, we've already got an ethnic war story' (reproduced in Minear, Scott and Weiss, 1996, 39).

Conclusion: Objectivity and 'Other People's Wars'

The news media's 'shifting agenda syndrome' and 'parachute journalism' often mean that reporters despatched to cover distant crises and wars scarcely have time to develop an emotional bond with the subjects of their stories (Bosnia being an obvious exception). Does this, and the very fact of these wars being 'other people's', consequently make reporting by 'our' agencies more objective? If truth is the 'first casualty' when our own country is at war, is it equally a casualty when patriotic attachment to a shared cause does not thicken the 'fog of war'? The proposition that distance lends itself to detachment and hence to greater objectivity seems commonsensical. After all, interviewing British journalists about the Falklands/ Malvinas conflict, Morrison and Tumber found many reporters (not just Max Hastings) ready to testify that this war – as 'ours' – was different. One sound recordist, for example, confessed to them:

We did an absolutely horrendous massacre in Uganda; we actually fell upon it just [after it happened], hours before in the middle of nowhere, children mutilated and everything. [That's] no problem at all – it's not pleasant, but you do it without feeling. And Beirut the same; it's not your problem. It becomes different when it's people you're involved with. (1988, 103)

Similarly, more recent events provide evidence of Western journalists and their crews remaining emotionally detached – cynical, or possibly just self-protective – in covering distant violence. For example, Mort Rosenblum writes of cameramen, keen to film emaciated children in the UN International Children's Emergency Fund compound in Mogadishu, asking aid-workers where they might find some 'stick action' (Rosenblum, 1995, 79). Freelance journalist Richard Dowden also describes television crews, restless with filming merely terminal sickness, requesting relief workers' assistance in capturing Somalis actually dying in front of the camera (Dowden, 1995, 122–3).

However, this kind of 'detachment' and objectivity should not perhaps be taken as synonymous. Conversely, whether commitment (or 'attachment') and objectivity may co-exist has been the subject of much recent discussion, stirred especially by Martin Bell's interventions (1995, 1996, 1998). The BBC reporter (now an MP) who spent considerable time covering the Balkan wars was accused by some, notably Douglas Hurd, of belonging to the 'something must be done' brigade: a group including journalists such as *The Guardian*'s Maggie O'Kane who openly espoused pro-Bosnian interventionism. While Bell distances himself from crusading journalism, he has nevertheless openly stated his distaste for neutrality in war reports: 'I do not believe that we should stand neutrally between good and evil, right and wrong, aggressor and victim', he told the News World conference in November 1996. He called instead for a 'journalism of attachment, journalism which cares as well as knows', a call he has repeated in print and in radio broadcasts, and which has been widely debated (1995, 1997, 1998; Ward, 1998, 121–5).

While Bell's position contains clear tensions – it is hard to see, for example, how one can reconcile his insistence that 'attached' journalists should not take sides with his injunction that they should not stand neutrally between good and evil – his views certainly suggest a discrepancy between the 'truthfulness' of news reports and the procedures of 'objectivity' as widely practised in Western news media. As we have seen illustrated before, 'objectivity' frequently does not lead to an absence of bias. The practices themselves, suggest some media scholars, sprang more from a desire to protect journalists from occupational hazards such as libel suits and accusations of partisanship, than from a desire to uncover 'the truth' in stories (Shoemaker and Reese, 1996, 113). Consequently, 'balance' is one of objective journalism's central precepts but, in seeking 'balance' between all parties to a dispute, reporting may convey a concomitant implication of their moral equivalence. Some critics of Western media coverage of the Balkan wars suggest that (where it existed) the tendency to represent all sides as being 'as bad as each other' was seriously misleading: balancing every incident of, say, Serbs 'ethnically cleansing' Croats with footage showing Croats shelling Serbs produced a distorted understanding of where preponderant culpability lay (Sadkovich in Meštrović, 1996, 113–57). In other words, Serbian aggression was primarily responsible for the chain of conflicts of the early 1990s, even though Croatian forces may also have engaged in 'ethnic cleansing' and the Bosnian government may have deliberately provoked Serb shelling in Sarajevo. None was entirely blameless, then, but some were more culpable than others, and objective journalism – construed as strictly balanced neutrality between warring factions – could not convey such complexities.

Some commentators, journalists amongst them, bemoan the perceived decline in objective reporting which Bell welcomes (so long as a scrupulous attitude to 'the facts' is nevertheless maintained). Both Bell and his critics, however, suggest that such scruples are harder to come by in the age of 'real time' television and of feature-led print journalism. One British freelancer, for example, notes an increasing tendency for journalists not to check facts, partly through pressure of constant deadlines: 'It is also a result of a shift in emphasis in journalism, away from objective reporting of events and towards more personalised, opinionated, and sensationalist reporting' (Weaver, 1995, 211). Some went further, maligning the Sarajevo international press corps for abandoning objectivity, and positioning themselves too squarely with the Bosnian government side, to the extent of becoming virtual propagandists on its behalf, and ignoring atrocities perpetrated by Bosnian government forces (Burns, 1996, 92–100).

However, whether to the detriment of 'objectivity' or not (and whether indeed 'objectivity' as frequently practised is devoutly to be wished for), recent journalistic experience in Bosnia clearly demonstrates that just as those geographically close may nevertheless remain alien, so conversely distance does not preclude closeness. Such 'involvement' has taken many forms, wilful or otherwise. Indeed, to suggest that a clear choice arises between 'attachment' and 'neutrality' may be somewhat misleading as it implies that journalists may, should they so choose, remain utterly aloof from their surroundings, producing reports that coolly mirror the world as it is, not invariably a world as refracted through the journalist. In that sense, one might suggest that journalists are always a part of what they report and thus can never be totally apart – neutral or detached – from events (Bell, 1997, 8). This is not to deny, of course, that journalists may choose to become more or less knowingly engaged or committed. Some reporters (especially print journalists) consciously espoused advocacy roles, Maggie O'Kane and Pulitzer Prize-winning reporter Roy Gutman amongst them. Some got caught up in 'somebody else's war' in more intimate ways, like the British reporter Michael Nicholson, whose real-life adoption of a Bosnian girl forms the basis of Michael Winterton's film *Welcome to Sarajevo* (1997). Others found that, without prior intent, they became participants in events they hoped simply to observe and report.

Wars change reporters, but reporters change war. The modified Heisenberg principle which Benjamin Netanyahu advanced during the Gulf War – 'as you observe a phenomenon with television, instantly you modify it somewhat' – was surely ever thus (cited by P. Taylor, 1992, xiv). Not only does the televisual eye invariably distort what it sees – 'little men three inches high', as Arlen put it – but, conscious of its gaze falling on their activities, those same men may modify their own behaviour accordingly. Recognising this, UN forces charged with mounting interventions in Former Yugoslavia (and elsewhere) have tried to harness the activities of the international press corps to their own ends. (Again, not perhaps such a surprising development as some suggest: after all, the history of military-media relations throughout the century is largely one of militaries re-learning techniques of co-optation.) In the case of Bosnia, former UN commanders and journalists alike have related how valuable a role television cameras could fulfil as unofficial monitors of cease-fires and prisoner of war exchanges; how military and media were now 'partners' not 'antagonists' (Bell, 1995, 29). The military's hope was thus that television cameras would not so much 'hold a mirror to events' as hold – or attempt to hold – a mirror up to the warring parties, which would reflect indisputable visual evidence of broken promises should the camera's mere presence be insufficient to deter breaches of formal commitments.

The presence of television in this respect, as in others, may not always be positive. Canadian Major General Lewis MacKenzie, at the end of his term as commander of UNPROFOR in July 1992 regretted his inability to extract a cease-fire, because he could not 'keep the two sides from firing on their own positions for the benefit of CNN' (1993, 308). Combatants' propensity to play up for the cameras may raise troubling ethical questions for reporters about what purpose reporting war serves and to whom, if anyone, they owe humanitarian obligations. The 'war tourist', after all, generally enjoys the luxury of being able to leave at any time (P. Harris, 1992, 23). Others are less fortunate, and their plight may be aggravated by the mere presence of tourists casually visiting their war. Bell recounts an episode about a reporter interviewing a sniper in Sarajevo which, apocryphal or not, could certainly serve as an allegory for war correspondents' ambivalent position in 'other people's wars':

The sniper was peering out from between two bricks in his forward defence. The reporter asked, 'What do you see?' The sniper replied, 'I see two people walking in the street: which of them do you want me to shoot?' It was at this point that the reporter realised, too late, that he had embarked on a project which was inherently lethal and which he should not even have considered. So he urged the sniper to shoot neither of them, made his excuses and turned to leave. As he did so he heard two shots of rapid fire from the position just behind him. He turned and looked, questioning. 'That was a pity,' said the sniper, 'you could have saved one of their lives'. (1997, 9; 1995, 173).

6
Media After War

Wars never end when the shooting stops. States sometimes attempt to encourage collective amnesia by suppressing memorialisation, but more commonly past wars are endlessly recycled in different guises: victories restaged, defeats rendered palatable, historical grievances nurtured, new enemies substituted for old. No wonder, then, that wars bulk large in the 'usable past' of many nations. In the twentieth century, while war has continued to be evoked in traditional ways – be that through poetry, painting or the construction of memorials – its most wide-reaching representations have generally been those circulated by mass media, cinema and television most particularly. From the birth of cinema, historical films have been staple fare, in countries as diverse as India, Japan, France, Russia and China (Rosenstone, 1995, 8), and of historical themes, war has proved one of the most potent. Fittingly, the first classic of American film-making was an epic re-working of the Civil War: D. W. Griffith's *Birth of a Nation* (1915).

Television has likewise plundered past wars for programming of varied kinds. War figures prominently in historical documentaries, some of them collaborative international productions, and many transmitted (sometimes in quite different forms) to diverse national audiences: the American Civil War, the First and Second World Wars, Korea, Vietnam, the Gulf War and former Yugoslavia have all had their television histories, to name but a few. War has also been the subject of – or backdrop to – numerous drama series, of divergent degrees of seriousness. The Second World War, given its centrality to Western understandings of war since 1945, has perhaps seen the most frequent appropriation, from the American prisoner of war camp comedy *Hogan's Heroes* to the gentle nostalgia of the BBC's *Dad's Army*; from the internationally syndicated American

mini-series *Holocaust*, to the British 'Resistance' farce, set in occupied France, *'Allo, 'Allo*. The 'home front', the Resistance, Axis
prisoner of war camps and Nazi concentration camps, have all
returned in television drama, whether as serious drama about the
camps, or as camp comedy. Diverse images of past conflicts thus
pulse through popular culture, shaping consciousness about historical events and colouring perceptions of war.

Mass media, then, play a central role in helping both to disinter
and to bury past wars: sometimes enabling people to make sense of
fragmented and traumatic experience, even as media muffling of
uncomfortable aspects may hasten viewers towards forgetfulness
(Winter, 1989, 328). This chapter, by way of an epilogue to the
examination of the media at war, explores some of the many ways
in which – and purposes for which – visual media (cinema, especially)
revisit conflicts that have formally ended. Whether media valorise
war, or solemnly warn against it, attentive spectators are liable to
discern 'a view of the present embedded within a picture of the past'
(Sorlin, 1980, 19). Present needs generally frame the uses of the past.

Dealing with Defeat

All wars leave their scars. Shattered buildings can be readily reconstructed, but damaged bodies and minds are less easily restored to
pre-war form, and death is not only the inevitable consequence of
war but its uniquely irreversible feature. For war's victors, these
material and human costs are likely to be more readily assimilated –
and transmuted into the 'usable past' – than for the vanquished
(though what it really means to 'win' or 'lose' a war is in many ways
imponderable). It is perhaps no wonder that for American and
British cinematographers the Second World War should have
exerted a lasting appeal, especially in the first two post-war decades:
'the magnetic pull of the war years wasn't merely the attraction of
adventure, romance or high melodrama but the consolation of
closure and the serenity of moral certainty' (Doherty, 1993, 271;
Sherry, 1995, 88–100). This was war as monochrome morality play:
good against evil, concluding with the requisite, and decisive, triumph of the forces of light over dark. Moreover, the 'people's war'
also represented an era of growing material prosperity and greater
racial inclusiveness for many Americans: a time when the 'melting

pot' ideal perhaps seemed something more than rhetorical flourish, and when social problems were less squeamishly confronted, in Hollywood as on the Capitol itself.

Hollywood's retrospective depictions of the Second World War have tended to foreground the gains of war rather than the costs. Despite the victors' moral certainties in total war, its greatest atrocities have been somewhat diminished in the filmic and televisual memory. *Schindler's List* and *Holocaust* notwithstanding, American representations of the Holocaust remain comparatively few, given the enormity (in every sense) of the Nazi genocide. Whether cinema or television can or should try to depict – let alone 'recreate' – the unthinkable is, of course, profoundly contentious as illustrated by recent controversy surrounding Roberto Benigni's Italian concentration camp 'comedy', *Life is Beautiful* (1998) (Insdorf, 1989; Bartov, 1996; Loshitzky, 1997). That the war's victors can hold Nazi Germany directly to account for the deaths of six million Jews (assuming they do not prefer to indict modernity itself, or themselves for failing to rescue European Jewry) scarcely dilutes the difficulty and sensitivity of the representational task.

Dealing with morally unsettling aspects of Allied wartime strategy has posed special, if quite distinct, dilemmas for American media. For the most part, mainstream American media have dealt with the atomic bombing of Hiroshima and Nagasaki – the apocalyptic culmination of the Pacific War – by avoidance (Barnouw, 1982, 91–100). Once the Soviets exploded an atomic 'device' in 1949, Hollywood was quick to reflect Americans' fears of their own nuclear annihilation, albeit often behind a flimsy veil of science fiction (Broderick, 1996, 2–3). But American cinema has fought shy of dealing with Japan's atomic experience (let alone America's role as nuclear nemesis), with the exception of a few anodyne references in contemporaneous features such as RKO's *First Yank in Tokyo* (1945) or films, such as *The Beginning of the End* (1957), in which the historical record is deliberately falsified to suggest that the *Enola Gay* dropped warning leaflets for 10 days over Japan before delivering its pestilent cargo over Hiroshima (Broderick, 1991, 5–10).

Germany and Japan after the Second World War

How much more problematic, though, for defeated countries to come to terms both with the fact of defeat itself and with crimes committed for a lost – and perhaps now discredited – cause? For the vanquished of the Second World War, the old dictum that history is written by the victors took quite literal form in the early post-war years. The Allied attempts to 'de-Nazify' Germany and to expunge Japan of its imperialist ambitions and feudal traditions entailed the wholesale re-writing of their national histories: to emphasise – or invent, as was sometimes thought necessary – long-standing, if recently submerged, democratic and pacific tendencies. And if history proved infertile soil, such attitudes would simply be grafted on to the stunted trunks of post-war German and Japanese society.

To root out dangerous ideological impulses, the British, French and American occupiers of divided post-war Germany made an attempt (quickly abandoned and not wholly successful) to remove Nazis from public life, to reconstruct school curricula with re-written textbooks, and to remodel German media along democratic lines, while the Soviets simultaneously 'communised' their zone. Press, radio and cinema were to be at once 'impartial' *and* in favour of the Occupiers (Welch, 1989, 227). Meanwhile, the evils of Nazism were to be brought home to Germans, as was the totality of their defeat: a task particularly suited to visual media. To the Western Occupiers, footage shot by Allied cameramen during the 'liberation' of concentration camps would confront any Germans for whom unconditional surrender was not confirmation enough of the Third Reich's bankruptcy with irrefutable visual evidence of Nazi barbarity. As part of the policy of 'de-Nazification', many Germans watched a special issue of the Anglo-American newsreel for occupied Germany, *Welt im Film*, which included the most horrifying footage of the death camps (Culbert, 1985, 177). A more elaborate film about the camps, Hanus Burger's *Todesmühlen* (*Death Mills*) was put into production, with the intention that every German civilian should see it. Although this policy was in fact abandoned before the film was finished, certainly all German prisoners of war in Allied camps were compelled to view concentration camp footage (Faulk, 1977, 121–5).

In Hollywood films depicting this process of disbelievers being confronted with visual proof of their crimes (Orson Welles's *The Stranger*, 1946, Samuel Fuller's *Verboten*, 1958; Stanley Kramer's *Judgement at Nuremberg*, 1961), hitherto unreconstructed Nazis are shown flinching in terrible recognition. But in reality, German viewers' reactions were not always as straightforwardly repentant as the Allies anticipated. For those vestigial Nazis who remained unshaken by mere military defeat, the footage was not necessarily accepted as an unimpeachable witness to SS atrocities. Indeed, some prisoners when shown the film insisted that the skeletal forms, of those barely living and the dead, belonged to German soldiers imprisoned by the Allies (Faulk, 1977, 122). Refusing to acknowledge the Jewish victims of the Holocaust, or to confront their own culpability, such Germans transformed themselves into the victims of the piece: regarding the Allies as exacting unjust retribution for crimes other Germans – the Nazi leadership – had instigated (a sense of victimisation which the process of de-Nazification as a whole perhaps encouraged: Herf, 1997).

For Germany, reckoning with the Nazi past – the whole *Hitlerzeit* (the National Socialist era from 1933–45) as well as the war – has been protracted and painful. In the early post-war years, many Germans on both sides of the divide seemed rather keener to repress this history than acknowledge it as their own. As far as some West Germans were concerned, discussion of the *Hitlerzeit* and war was an unnecessary obstacle to national reconstruction under a democratic constitution certain to thwart any future recrudescence of Nazism. For its part, in mirror-imaging fashion, the East German regime denounced, then disowned, Nazism as a particularly virulent strain of capitalism, against which Communism was sure inoculation. Some Germans, however, have sought a more forthright confrontation with the past in a spirit of acknowledgement, not of 'remembering to forget', or of 'normalisation' (a historical relativism which pits Nazi crimes against those of the USSR and finds German history not to have been uniquely evil). Controversy ranges beyond issues of interpretation of the past to questions about its very preservation. Are cultural artefacts of the *Hitlerzeit*, formerly in 'quarantine', now sufficiently innocuous for public consumption? Some of the more noxious products of the UFA studios (such as *Jud Süß* and *Der Ewige Jude*) were immediately outlawed under the Occupation, preserved as testimony to the evils of Nazi anti-Semitism but hidden from public view. (The Allies initially banned 700 films; by 1954, the list had been reduced to 275, and by 1995, to a mere 30–35 feature films: Rentschler, 1996, 271; Short, 1996, ix–xli.) Implicitly concurring with Goebbels' own estimation that most UFA films were not overtly 'political' as such, a number of German television stations and cinemas have regularly screened movies from the *Hitlerzeit*, billing them as products of a 'golden age of German cinema'. They are, claims Rentschler, 'an integral part of everyday entertainment fare throughout Germany', though their ideological innocence has been contested by some (1996, 2).

For German media, as for German people, coming to terms with an 'unmasterable' Nazi past has been traumatic (Maier, 1988). Although the Western occupiers encouraged West Germans to remember, confront and re-invent their past in such a way that Nazism was no longer the inevitable *telos* of German tradition, many Germans, suggests Ian Buruma, initially suffered from a 'moral anaesthesia', numbed by a defeat which blocked remembrance (1995, 21). Such amnesia has not completely vanished: Michael Verhoeven's film *The Nasty Girl* (1990) tellingly portrays a German schoolgirl's attempts to research her town's past in the face of abusive obstruction from those who wilfully misremember their *Hitlerzeit* as innocent of Nazi collusion. However, since the late 1970s, German novelists and film-makers have certainly made greater attempts to confront the burden of the past, in ways both more or less direct.

Ironically, perhaps, it took a somewhat sentimental American television mini-series, *Holocaust*, to pierce 30 years of silence surrounding the concentration camps (Kaes, 1989, x). First shown in West Germany in January 1979, the series was watched by some 20 million people: every other adult in the Federal Republic (Kaes, 1989, 30). Broadcasting stations were overwhelmed with positive feedback, though many German intellectuals (of both left and right) bemoaned the fact that a trivial American 'soap opera' had, in film-maker Edgar Reitz's words, 'stolen our history', preventing Germans from 'taking narrative possession of our past, from breaking free of the world of judgements' (cited in Buruma, 1995, 88). However, as some critics point out, when German directors (including Reitz himself in his sixteen-hour epic, *Heimat*) *have* reclaimed the past, they often tend to depict (Aryan) Germans as the subjects – not infrequently the victims – of that past. By ignoring or underplaying the Holocaust, they relativise the Nazi era so that *all* Germans, Aryans and Jews alike, blandly emerge as its casualties in a shared suffering which diminishes any sense of collective responsibility for, or agency in, the genocide (Bartov, 1996, 128, 150–1). Whatever its defects, then, *Holocaust* certainly stirred its German viewers, and encouraged German media to resist an appropriation of their country's past by the war's victors. Thus Günter Rohrbach (of German television station WDR, the man largely responsible for bringing the mini-series to German screens) claimed that, 'After *Holocaust* television can no longer be what it was before' (cited by Kaes, 1989, 31).

If some Germans have been minded to paint themselves as victims of Nazism and the war, the sense of victimisation has undoubtedly been stronger in post-war Japan. That Japan surrendered after America dropped atomic bombs on Hiroshima and Nagasaki – their first and only use 'in anger' – has bestowed a unique sense of 'victimhood' on some Japanese (Buruma, 1995, 104). The neo-nationalist right, especially, represents America's atomic atrocities at Hiroshima and Nagasaki as the (im)moral equivalents to Auschwitz and Belsen, displacing any need for Japan to accept its own war crimes. The victims of Nanking, Bataan, the Burma–Siam railway and Manila are thus trampled in the rush for moral high ground (Buruma, 1995, 104; Dower, 1996, 123).

Under the American occupation which began in September 1945, the bomb was very much a subject *non grata*. One Japanese writer wryly noted later, 'We were not allowed to write about the atomic bomb during the Occupation. We were not even allowed to say that we were not allowed to write about the atomic bomb' (Sadako Kurihara, cited by Braw, 1991, 7). As in Germany, American occupation authorities set about reconstructing Japan's media along democratic lines, with the recurrent irony that freedom of speech was tolerated so long as the American occupiers approved the speech in question. So much for 'demokurashee'. Along with Hollywood movies which cast – or threatened to cast – an unfavourable glow on America (including *Mr Smith Goes to Washington*, with its 'misleading and unfavourable' depiction of corruption on the Capitol), Japanese criticism of the occupation was disallowed (Hirano, 1992, 246). Correspondingly, the censors regarded any mention of the fate of Hiroshima and Nagasaki as likely to incite anti-American sentiment, and possibly undermine the Tokyo War Crimes Tribunals by suggesting precisely that 'immoral equivalence' between America and Japan which some Japanese did indeed assert (Dower, 1996, 116–17; Dower, 1999).

The American occupiers busily encouraged the six main Japanese film studios to produce suitably pro-democratic fare, offering guidance rather along the lines of the wartime OWI's 'poynters' to Hollywood (Hirano, 1992, 34–41). The long list of 'don'ts', essentially anything which evoked Japan's imperial and feudal past or indicted America and the Supreme Commander of the Occupation, was supplemented by an equally eclectic set of 'do's', including the injunction that Japanese films *should* show men and women publicly kissing. American censors did not read the prior absence from Japanese screens of public displays of affection as cultural aversion to such indelicacy, but rather as evidence of Japanese 'sneakiness': the very national characteristic which had produced Pearl Harbor, and which was earmarked for replacement by American-style openness (Hirano, 1992, 155–6).

Matters atomic topped the list of cinematic 'don'ts', and even the most oblique references were promptly deleted. As Kyoko Hyoto points out, 'conversations referring to war devastation without mentioning "the Japanese responsibility for the war" were also judged problematic' (in Hirano, 1992, 54). But the Occupation's attitude towards the bomb was more ambivalent than either pure denial of America's actions or insistence on Japan's ultimate responsibility for its irradiated fate. An American censor, for example, recommended in September 1945 that a Japanese newsreel on 'The Atomic Bomb' feature more scenes of the devastation of Tokyo after 'conventional' American bombing, because 'Japan was actually militarily beaten' before the atomic bombings, which the uncut film duly exaggerated. Such an attitude seems almost certain to have increased a widespread view in Japan that America cynically regarded the citizens of Hiroshima and Nagasaki as guinea pigs in two 'test blasts'. Certainly the censor's line was utterly at odds with President Truman's own insistence that the bombs were necessary to shorten the war – and save lives – by effecting an immediate Japanese surrender which was not otherwise forthcoming (Hirano, 1992, 59–60). A reprehensible dual standard also operated whereby Japanese camera crews who had filmed scenes of the bombings' aftermath, exposing themselves to considerable radiation in so doing, found their documentary footage (*The Effects of the Atomic Bomb on Hiroshima and Nagasaki*) confiscated by Occupation forces, keen to maintain private scientific records but not so eager for their public display (Barnouw, 1982, 91–100; Hirano, 1992, 60–1; Nornes, 1996, 120–59).

After the Occupation, films – from Japan and elsewhere – appeared which combined sexual frisson with atomic fission (Alain

Resnais's *Hiroshima Mon Amour* (1958) for example, or the Japanese film, *I'll Not Forget the Song of Nagasaki* (1952), in which a returning American GI falls in love with a blind victim of the bombing). Yet although the ending of the Occupation did make it possible for Japanese film-makers to approach the most sensitive subject of Hiroshima and Nagasaki, the resultant treatments rarely excoriated the Americans for their decision to drop the infelicitously named 'Fat Man' and 'Little Boy' on the two Japanese cities. Many of the earliest films exhibited a sense of resigned fatalism, of 'sympathetic sadness' (or *mono no aware*), towards an event which was treated more as natural disaster – an 'act of God' – than as a deliberate act of war (Richie, 1996, 20–3). Hiroshima (as ultimate anti-war emblem) has not been immune from polemical film treatment, but Japanese cinema, like its American counterpart, has nevertheless frequently dealt with atomic apocalypse in allegorical guise. The popular series of *Godzilla* movies, the first of which appeared after the Occupation in 1954, plausibly represents the return of the repressed (the bomb? radiation? the American occupation?) in monster form (Noriega, 1996, 55–71).

If America's atomic visitation of Japan is often allegorised, atrocities committed by the Japanese in the course of the 'Great East Asian War' are often shunned altogether. Amongst the victims (Korean 'comfort women' pressing the Japanese government for compensation, or former British prisoners of war protesting at their Queen's honouring the Japanese Emperor in London in May 1998) memories of Japanese war crimes remain keen, but unwelcome in Japan. Thus many Japanese cinemas have demurred from screening a China-Hong Kong co-production, *Don't Cry Nanjing* (1995), which depicts in graphic detail the slaughter of thousands of Chinese prisoners of war, and mass rape of women and girls, in the city formerly known as Nanking. Although the film has not been formally banned, 'there has been a great deal of self-censorship', according to one cinema owner in Nagoya who showed the film to an almost empty house (*The Guardian*, 10 December 1997, 15).

America post-Vietnam

By virtue of physical occupation, as by cultural colonisation, America has played a key role in how its Second World War antagonists have come to terms with (or avoided) the war, their wartime behaviour, and the meaning and manner of their defeat. More recently, however, America has had to confront loss itself: the 'peace with honour' in Vietnam, a defeat by any other name. Painful as this reversal of military fortune and moral purpose has undoubtedly been, America itself has still retained considerable power over representation of the war. If 'Vietnam' signifies a war more often than a country, the perceptions of 'Vietnam' which prevail – at least in North America and Europe – remain those of the ostensibly vanquished. America's conventional military superiority did not guarantee it victory over the Vietcong and the North Vietnamese Army in South Vietnam, but its international cultural supremacy – the hegemony of Hollywood – has ensured the triumph of the American image over a much wider mental terrain (Baudrillard, cited in Kroes, 1996, note 1, 188). Whatever else it lost, 'America has won when it comes to the imaginative representation of the Vietnam War', claims Dutch scholar Rob Kroes (1996, 137). If Hollywood has managed – where Washington failed – to sell the war to the American public, surely the greatest irony is that the Vietnamese themselves now repackage their country for American consumption on the tourists' own terms, with an eye more to the auditorium witness than the battlefield veteran. Thus bars in downtown Hanoi bear names such as 'Apocalypse Now' and 'Good Morning Vietnam', as the government seeks to lure Americans back to Vietnam, the country, through perverse nostalgia for Vietnam, the war.

Vietnam itself has succumbed to the American image, but the image of the war in Hollywood film is deeply ambiguous. Some of the most high-minded Vietnam movies lend themselves (at least superficially) to anti-war readings: Michael Cimino's *The Deer Hunter* (1978) with its 'Russian roulette' motif as a striking (if spurious) metaphor for the war as a whole; Francis Coppola's *Apocalypse Now* (1979), with pyrotechnic visions of violence; Oliver Stone's *Platoon* (1986), with combat verisimilitude on self-conscious display. But few fall unmistakably into 'pro-war' or 'anti-war' camps (Sherry, 1995, 361). The films' messages have been fought over in the same way as has the meaning of the event they seek to depict, transcend or recast: hence Gilbert Adair's suggestion that such movies are 'less about the Vietnam War than a part of it', albeit a part which tells us rather more about America than Vietnam (1989, 142, 5). And where commentators divided over the impact of news footage (inherently anti-war, or trivialising and desensitising?), critical opinion on Hollywood's Vietnam cleaves over 'hyper-realistic' combat scenes. Is realistic recreation intrinsically repellent or, as Jean-Luc Godard insists, does it invariably redeem war as thrilling enterprise, irrespective of the film-makers' intentions?

Initially, however, Vietnam threatened not to be a Hollywood war at all. Perhaps precisely because Vietnam was a 'television war', Hollywood long delayed replicating on the big screen what was nightly offered by its living-room rival. But the war in Asia was not dodged simply because an upstart medium seemed to have it covered. Unlike the clear-cut confrontations of the Second World War and Korea, with their easily identifiable heroes and villains, Vietnam was not susceptible to conventional Hollywood treatment, with its preference for straightforward story-telling. The war in Vietnam 'was a lousy narrative with a vague beginning, an ungainly middle, and no end in sight' (Doherty, 1993, 282; Adair, 1989, 3). America's purposes were too vague, its allies too indistinguishable from its foes, its methods too questionable and their outcome too uncertain, to lend themselves to easy cinematic translation. As early as 1965, the war was sufficiently divisive that trade journal *Variety* proclaimed it 'too hot for Hollywood' (cited by Doherty, 1993, 283). To anxious studio executives, John Wayne's ill-judged attempt to make a movie about Vietnam with the moral certainty of the Second World War, *The Green Berets* (1968), did not augur well: picketed at the theatres, panned by the critics, and only slowly recouping its costs (largely, it has been claimed, thanks to loyal Wayne fans rather than war enthusiasts, since, as Herr pointed out, the film 'wasn't really about Vietnam, it was about Santa Monica': 1978, 153).

The war's sole contemporaneous feature film, and still Hollywood's one uncomplicatedly pro-war statement, *The Green Berets* exhibits an outmoded sensibility which most post-war treatments of Vietnam decisively rejected. Only in its hostile depiction of rival media does *The Green Berets* bear comparison with the products of Hollywood's later Vietnam cycles in the 1970s and 1980s. The Wayne film presents a journalist as liberal hate-figure who must – like the viewer – be made to see the war 'as it really is', for, according to the film's naive epistemology, to see is to know, and to know is to believe in America's cause in Vietnam. The journalist's progression from opposition to support for the war is as predictable as it is thorough (he finally volunteers to relinquish his pen for the sword, could he but wield the latter more adeptly) although it is utterly at odds with the trajectory of most journalistic careers in Vietnam, where initial support for 'containment' was punctured by experience which slowly deflated official optimism. Later films too, despite greater embitterment towards the war, are similarly jaundiced against journalists – and television in particular – with Hollywood effectively lending credence to variants of the 'stab-in-the-back' myth. *Apocalypse Now* catches a television crew in the act of staging phoney war sequences, while in *Hamburger Hill* (1987) the American GIs have greater respect for the North Vietnamese than the newsmen: 'At least they take sides, you just take pictures', rebukes one grunt (Williams, 1991, 121). Likewise, in Stanley Kubrick's *Full Metal Jacket* (1987), the grunts jeer at a television crew, with a mocking 'Hey, start the cameras. This is "Vietnam – the Movie!"'.

However, if Hollywood was ready to implicate (and sometimes castigate) the news media in the Vietnam imbroglio, many American soldiers who actually fought there were equally prepared to censure *Hollywood* for its part in the war. The venom of veteran memoirists and novelists was not aimed at Hollywood's depiction of the war as it progressed – since it had signally failed to do so, the lamentable *Green Berets* aside – but was reserved for the industry's role in entangling America in Vietnam in the first place. 'World War Two – the Movie' offered young American boys an unrelieved diet of 'guts and glory', which made war seem heroic, death appear noble, and any wounds less than fatal, bearable. Kids, muses Herr, got 'wiped out by seventeen years of war movies before coming to Vietnam to get wiped out for good' (1978, 169). For many veterans, the process of disillusionment in Vietnam was, at least in part, occasioned by the cinematic conventions of Hollywood combat movies blowing up in their faces: the discovery that war was not a movie, and certainly not one in which they wanted starring roles (Doherty, 1991, 258). In veterans' memoirs, one of the chief culprits for the deception perpetrated against a generation of young Americans was Hollywood. But, unsurprisingly, Hollywood displaced the grunts' bitterness on to television in re-staging their war.

Perhaps by way of oblique atonement for glamorisation of wars past, Hollywood's post-war Vietnam movies often deliberately undermine the cherished fictions of Second World War films. The compensatory camaraderie of the combat unit is exposed as a sham: American grunts as often turn on one another, and on themselves, as on the Vietnamese enemy, in *Full Metal Jacket*, *Platoon* and Brian De Palma's *Casualties of War* (1989), to name but a few. (Indeed, the theme is explicitly vocalised by *Platoon*'s hero, Chris Taylor: 'I think now, looking back, we did not fight the enemy, we fought ourselves. And the enemy was in us.') Combat and its physical effects are also more unflinchingly observed than hitherto, aided by advances in special effects generation. But technology aside, the moral ambiguity shrouding America's whole enterprise in South-East Asia made the Vietnam War less susceptible to airbrush treatment than past wars, in which the certainty of fighting a just war by just means had made the costs palatable but also less in need of vivid depiction.

When the ends only questionably justified the means (or failed to do so altogether), Hollywood acquired a sharper taste for combat realism. By the late 1970s and into the 1980s, Vietnam movies ostentatiously promised to show war 'as it really was': a claim made on the cover of *Time* magazine with the 1987 release of Oliver Stone's *Platoon*. As Hollywood's first 'veteran auteur', Stone's credentials for the task seemed unimpeachable, and were indeed attested to by no less an authority than JFK's press-pack *bête noire*, David Halberstam, who asserted that '*Platoon* is the first real Viet Nam film' (cited by Adair, 1989, 145). While *The Green Berets* (like Rambo in his debut sortie, *First Blood*, in 1982) insisted that first-hand experience 'in country' was the prerequisite to sympathetic appreciation of America's endeavours in Vietnam, *Platoon* seemed to some critics to suggest the precise opposite: seeing for oneself was to guarantee revulsion against the war, against war itself. Such verisimilitude apparently betokened an anti-war aesthetic. But hyper-realism can equally be seen as approbation of the war (after a, perhaps unintentional, fashion). 'Meticulously aping an atrocity *is* an atrocity', insists Gilbert Adair; 'the hyperrealistic depiction of an obscenity cannot avoid being contaminated with that atrocity' (Adair, 1989, 159; for a similar critique of *Apocalypse Now* see Hagen in Rollins, 1983, 244). Directors themselves sometimes insist, as Michael Cimino did of *The Deer Hunter*, that 'any good picture about war is an anti-war picture' (cited by Christensen, 1987, 152). Those unconvinced, however, worry that the 'anti-war war film' is an inescapably oxymoronic endeavour, perhaps recalling the question rhapsodically posed by photographer Tim Page to Michael Herr (who collaborated on the screenplays of ambiguous anti-war war movies, *Full Metal Jacket* and *Apocalypse Now*): 'Take the glamour out of war! I mean how the bloody hell can you do *that*? . . . It's like trying to take the glamour out of sex, trying to take the glamour out of the Rolling Stones' (1978, 199).

Hollywood's apparent attempts to redeem itself for glorifying wars past thus look compromised and confused. Less ambiguous, however, was the cinematic bid to redeem America's defeat in Vietnam, as exemplified in a number of Hollywood's later treatments. Such films, not content that American cinema should have broadly determined the war's imagistic afterlife, strove more literally to win the war for America in the re-writing and re-fighting. *The Deer Hunter*, for example, despite its memorable roulette metaphor for war's arbitrary and meaningless cruelty, nevertheless elevates the male warrior figure, the nobility of killing 'cleanly', and the irredeemable 'otherness' of Vietnam's population, in seeming affirmation of America's frontier tradition. Much cruder efforts to salvage something positive from the Vietnam experience – achieving not only closure but victory – have been made by a subgenre of films dealing with the rescue of American soldiers still Missing in Action (MIA) in Asia, most notably the Rambo series.

As a whole, Vietnam movies have tended to avoid making themselves historically specific. 'Hollywood', Gilbert Adair notes, 'has portrayed Vietnam as a kind of phantasmagoric limbo, untrammelled by dates or place names, all 'middle' with no real, definable beginning or end' (1989, 83). The MIA subgenre, however, locates itself – indistinctly – in a post-war future, 'avoid[ing] the past to achieve a mythical victory years after the conflict's historical resolution' (Williams, 1991, 117). In its best-known exemplar, *Rambo: First Blood Part II* (a film which earnt over $100 million in the USA alone), America's national defeat is avenged by one individual, John Rambo. Awarding Rambo a covert assignment to return to Vietnam in search of MIAs, his superiors intend Rambo to corroborate their claim that no Americans remain in captivity. On the contrary, however, Rambo wages war not only against Communist villains but against these duplicitous bureaucrats who are ignorant of how combat must be waged in Vietnam and who, having effectively thwarted America's victory, now wish to declare the war over. In the Rambo movies, however, the absence of an American victory – along with the missing men – means that the war cannot be permitted to end. Significantly, in perpetuating the conflict, Rambo finds himself captured and tortured by Russians, who constitute a more menacing enemy than the Vietnamese. On-screen action thus reflected the broader political climate, in which Rambo's targets – the dual evils of the Reds and of Big Government – were also Reagan's. In answer to Rambo's embittered inquiry, 'Are they going to let us win this time?', Reagan offered a ringing affirmative. America's involvement in Vietnam had been a 'noble cause', thwarted because one hand had been tied behind the American military back. The binding error would not be repeated, Reagan asserted on the 1980 campaign trail: 'Let us tell those who fought in that war that we will never again ask young men to fight and die in a war our government is afraid to let them win' (cited by Vlastos, 1991, 69).

Consequently by the mid-1980s, Hollywood and Washington joined in suggesting that the war had not been lost in Vietnam: victory was only missing, and could be recovered, along with the MIAs (Berg, 1991, 116). Reagan's words at the dedication of the Tomb of the Unknown Soldier for the Vietnam War – 'We write no final chapter. We close no books, until we have achieved the fullest accounting of those missing in action' – echoed those of the publicity posters for *Missing in Action*, 'The war's not over until the last man comes home!' (Jeffords, 1986, 187). As ever, it was hard to judge whether Reagan was mimicking the movies, or the movies mimicking the former actor. In effect, though, such films *did* present themselves as fitting epilogue to America's sorry Vietnam chapter, so that the book could indeed be shut, as Americans prepared to fight new wars: with both hands and in different locations.

Using Past Wars to Fight Present Battles

Strikingly, many of the Hollywood movies with a Vietnam setting in fact appear more concerned to explain shifts in American culture and society than to understand Vietnam, the war or the country. (Arguably, for example, *Platoon*, *The Deer Hunter* and *Full Metal Jacket* all take far greater interest in the dichotomised American psyche than in the war as a multi-sided, and cross-cultural, encounter.) Certainly many of the films are more or less mute on Vietnam and the Vietnamese, who rarely appear as fully realised characters, whether friend or foe, and generally (notably in *The Deer Hunter*) as vicious stereotypes. As a consequence of this self-absorption, even the more liberal films (such as *Apocalypse Now*) end up presenting *Americans* as the war's primary victims, psychologically broken by the physical destruction which they themselves have meted out. Moreover, films which pretend to the most vivid reconstruction of Vietnamese scenes may appear ultimately to borrow the war as metaphor for more generalised American experience, while some films located squarely in America (Martin Scorsese's *Taxi Driver* (1976), for example) can reveal as much about the war's effect on those who fought it, even though they promise to tell us nothing in particular, and certainly not to 'show it as it was'. John Hellmann has even suggested that the most telling film about the Vietnam war was *Star Wars*, ostensibly about neither America nor Vietnam (1986, 205–20).

To understand the prevalence of war as a cultural mainstay is thus to grasp the utility of past wars as allegories for present or future conflicts. Sometimes film-makers resurrect past wars with a specific view to *averting* future confrontations which loom perilously. During the 1930s, the Great War was often enlisted cinematically to this anti-war end, in the hope that 1914–18 would not duly become merely a *First* World War: curtain-raiser to a more devastating sequel. In the decade following the war, as Modris Eksteins points out, 'publishers, theatre directors, and film makers had treated war material gingerly, viewing it as a poor commercial proposition, on the assumption that the public wished, contrary to annual remembrance day exhortations, to forget the war' (1980, 345). But by 1929–30, the audiences had become receptive to representations of war. Erich Maria Remarque's novel *All Quiet on the Western Front* (*Im Westen nichts Neues*), published in 1929, met with unprecedented commercial success, both in its native Germany and far beyond. Capitalising on the popularity of the novel, Lewis Milestone's *All Quiet on the Western Front* (1930) was, and remains, undoubtedly the best known film of the belated Great War cycle, remarkable both for the clarity of its anti-war message, and the fact that American cinema should have forged this transcendent pacifism from *German* wartime experience.

All Quiet on the Western Front may be the most enduring of the First World War films but it was not, however, the first (Kelly, 1997). Its lineage was both European and American, for its predecessors included Abel Gance's *J'accuse* (1919), arguably 'the first great cry of protest in cinema' against war, and a popular success at the time, with a conservatively estimated 1–2 million viewers in Europe and North America (Winter, 1995, 137–8), as well as a cycle of American Great War films which began in the 1920s. These, notably King Vidor's *Big Parade* (1925), a commercial success widely praised for its realism, encouraged the process of exhumation of the war in Europe (Isenberg, 1988, 27). Indeed, as Pierre Sorlin demonstrates, during the 1930s European cinematographers made more films about the Great War than did Hollywood. Some of them, including Pabst's *Westfront 1918* (1930) and Renoir's *La Grande Illusion* (1937), were bigger box office draws than *All Quiet* itself (1991, 24–7).

Many such films apparently struck contemporary audiences as remarkably realistic (and partly for that reason were often read as pacifistic). But the flimsiness of the film-makers' pretensions to battlefield accuracy has subsequently been exposed. Unlike Oliver Stone, who promoted *Platoon* on the back of his year's experience 'in country', Lewis Milestone claimed that the authenticity of *All Quiet*'s trenches derived from twelve months spent in Washington, DC, with the US Army Signal Corps during the First World War. There, he said in a later interview, 'having examined thousands of feet of actual war footage', he 'knew precisely what it was supposed to look like'. 'Supposed' is very much the operative word, for the Signal Corps photographers were able to photograph battlefields only after the actual fighting. They were, of necessity, not above reconstructing what they could not spontaneously capture. Thus Milestone's own recreation of the western front in southern California was based on second-hand scrutiny of the Signal Corps' first-hand efforts to shoot war after the shooting had stopped (Chambers, 1996, 19). But *All Quiet* certainly bore a close enough resemblance to how war was *supposed* to look that its realism was viewed as a deterrent against war: 'greater than mere entertainment', announced Carl Laemmle, President of Universal Pictures, the film waged 'a war against war itself' (cited by Kelly, 1989, 141). Possibly for fear that Germans would be contaminated with anti-war sentiments, though ostensibly for a rather different reason – that this 'Jewish propaganda' film impugned German bravery – Goebbels spearheaded Nazi brownshirt agitation against *All Quiet*'s screening in Weimar Germany. It was duly banned, cut and re-released, only to be censored again once Hitler assumed power in 1933 (Chambers, 1996, 21–3).

Anti-war films of the 1920s and 1930s were rooted in war-weariness born from past experience. Not surprisingly, some film-makers hoped to avert future conflict in Europe (or America's renewed entanglement therein) by unsentimental revelation of the recent war's consequences. Protesting against war while one's country is actually engaged in combat is a more delicate business, often necessitating oblique borrowings from the past. Cinematographers take refuge in allegory because it is easier – and possibly more effective – to adopt critical postures towards past conflicts than contentious current ones. Anti-war commentary during Vietnam decamped to a number of historical locations, since, as Linda Dittmar and Gene Michaud observe, 'policymakers' determination to escalate the fighting allowed for only covert, highly mediated, and murky expressions of concern' (1990, 2). Mike Nichols's *Catch-22* (1970) made unusually subversive use of the Second World War to highlight the absurd logic of war, in which insanity appears the only sane response, and accordingly feigned madness, far from buying a passage home, only confirms the impostor's fitness for service. Some viewers also read *Patton* (1970), an epic bio-pic of the Second World War general, as an anti-war minded exposé of 'the worst kind of red-blooded American who loves to fight and whose crude talk is straight talk', even as Nixon apparently drew from the film encouragement to bomb Cambodia (Toplin, 1996, 156–75). Less ambiguously, Robert Altman's film *M*A*S*H* (1969), and the television series it spawned about a US army mobile surgical unit in Korea, bore so amply suggestive a relationship to events still ongoing in Vietnam as to leave no one in any doubt as to which war was the real target of its black comedy. As if the geographical and geopolitical parallels were not striking enough (a stalemated war in an East Asian country divided between a communist north and US-backed south), the substitution of Korea for Vietnam was heightened by the popular series's wilful anachronisms: characters supposedly of the early 1950s who spoke, dressed, and behaved with the sensibility and style of the late 1960s.

The First World War remains the *locus classicus* of on-screen pacifism, continuing to inspire indictments of militarism from Bernard Tavernier's *La Vie et Rien d'Autre (Life and Nothing But*, 1989) to Gillies Mackinnon's *Regeneration* (1997), but it has not invariably been used to discredit the very enterprise of war. Past wars are as frequently appropriated to *fuel* militarism as to discredit it, and the

First World War is no exception. Jay Winter argues that many films of the Great War, along with other forms of popular, inter-war art, in fact offered a 'sanitization of the worst features of the war and its presentation as a mythical or romantic adventure' (1995, 132; Isenberg, 1975). They exemplified what George Mosse refers to as 'the Myth of the War Experience', by which 'the memory of the war was refashioned into a sacred experience which provided the nation with a new depth of religious feeling, putting at its disposal ever present saints and martyrs, places of worship, and a heritage to emulate' (1990, 7). Film played a leading role in the process of mystification. So while from our distant vantage-point we might reconstruct that war solely from the anti-war genre it spawned (*All Quiet, Westfront 1918, La Grande Illusion*), more often than not, inter-war years' cinema actually lent sustenance to the 'Myth of the War Experience'. Scenes of despoiled landscapes, calculated to instil feelings of nostalgia, patriotism and vengeance, outnumbered sequences showing the dead and dying, whose depiction threatened to engender, or reanimate, revulsion against war (Mosse, 1990, 188). And just as war lends itself as metaphor for other social processes, so non-martial subjects may form suggestive allegories for competition, combat and military triumph. Thus, in the fractious inter-war years, those who sought to undermine the prevailing sentiment of 'never again', found inspiring surrogates in seemingly innocent pursuits and places. In 1930s Germany, 'mountain films' and depictions of sporting prowess and aerial derring-do proliferated, with German mastery over the human physique and over nature prefiguring more sinister bids for mastery (Mosse, 1990, 151–2).

During the Second World War, film-makers turned to the First World War (as the Great War had now indisputably become) for inspiring promotional material for a new war, not alarums against war in general. Mindful of its own pacifistic treatments of the First World War, Hollywood's most significant revisitation, *Sergeant York* (1941), dealt with the necessity of overcoming such scruples in the interests of a higher cause, at a time when many Americans questioned the need to enter the fray. The story of Alvin York, a real-life American Great War hero who had surmounted biblically-inspired conscientious objection to fight the good fight in 1917, was clearly intended to address American audiences more about the current war in Europe than the now patriotically rehabilitated events of 1917 (Doherty, 1993, 100–3). Playing to divided audiences, the film stood as a 'powerful metaphor ... for a nation that did not wish to engage in another foreign war but needed to convince itself that freedom was endangered and intervention necessary' (Toplin, 1996, 83). Small wonder, then, that *Sergeant York* was one of those films against which isolationist senators Nye and Clark took exception as 'vicious' interventionist propaganda: 'a picture ... rousing the American people ... to be killed on a real battlefield' (cited by Leab, 1995, 230). However, after Pearl Harbor legitimised this task of rallying Americans for battle, with President Roosevelt leading the charge, Hollywood specifically extolled *Sergeant York* in support of its bid for 'Essential War Industry' status.

For all the major combatants of the Second World War, past conflict provided serviceable material for wartime cinema. It was quite acceptable to get history muddled – if not plain wrong – so long as the message was clear. The purpose of historical film, after all, was not to provide accurate reconstructions of the past but object lessons for the present, although their creators were sometimes wont to take refuge from charges of blatant propaganda behind a shield of 'historical veracity'. Consequently, Harry Warner had defended *Sergeant York* from the isolationist senators' assault by stressing that the film was a 'factual portrait of one of the great heroes of the last war', as though 'facticity' alone were sufficient refutation of the slur upon his studio. Indeed, so confident was Warner that the case was accordingly shut, that he added a triumphant flourish: 'If that is propaganda, we plead guilty' (cited by Doherty, 1993, 41).

Of course, the 'plausible deniability' of propaganda in representations of the past was a significant part of the attraction of historical themes. As Chapter 2 has already demonstrated, Nazi cinema particularly favoured resonant scenarios from German history, often involving conflict (if not war) between the Aryan German *Volk* and their internal and external enemies. Hitler himself, after all, was adamant that 'we do not learn history only in order to know the past; we learn history in order to find an instructor for the future and for the continued existence of our own nationality' (cited by Rentschler, 1996, 171). Historical parallels were thus deployed in the promotion of genocidal anti-Semitism. Contemporary audiences judged as 'frighteningly real' Veit Harlan's *Jud Süß*, which claimed that its depiction of the Jewish money-lender, Joseph Süss Oppenheimer, was 'based on historical occurrences'. Viewers easily transposed the lesson that the Jew incarnated Evil – and consequently required extermination – from eighteenth-century Württemberg to the present, as was the intention (Rentschler, 1996, 151–5). Past war also offered fertile soil in which to cultivate anti-British animosity. Hans Steinhoff's *Ohm Krüger* (1941) chose the Boer War as setting for another exercise in transference. Where *Jud Süß* projected on to its eponymous anti-hero many of the Nazis' own traits, *Krüger* suggested that concentration camps were the exclusive invention – by implication, the preserve – of the English, whose national character expressed itself 'in violence, murder, and the exploitation of enslaved peoples' (Welch, 1983b, 271). Intended to prepare Germans for the forthcoming invasion of Britain, the film attempted to mobilise hatred against a country which (according to *Krüger*'s accompanying illustrated booklet) had started the war, and was now inhumanely bombing Germany cities (Welch, 1983b, 273). The origins of the current war were, then, as susceptible to revision as events of more distant ones. And when current events failed to promise imminent victory, as the Nazis invariably had, the past was used to bridge the chasm between optimistic expectation and grim reality.

Kolberg, first screened on the very day (30 January 1945) that Hitler made his final radio broadcast, depicted the heroic resistance in 1807 of beleaguered Prussian townsfolk against Napoleon's surrounding troops. The French might have won the war but the Kolbergers retained their town, and as Peter Paret points out, the siege's 'relevance to Germany in retreat is obvious' (Paret, 1996, 51). For Kolberg, read Hamburg, Berlin and Dresden; for French artillery, Allied bombers. The message, however, may be less clear than the parallel. Was the film intended to recast defeat as a form of victory: a triumph of the will, if nothing more material? Or was *Kolberg* meant to imply that, by unyielding resistance, ultimate salvation could yet be won? And were the intended – presumably inspiring – surface messages of the film not in danger of being overshadowed by its defeatist subtext? Harlan's falsification of the historical record, which portrayed Kolberg as more heavily besieged and intensively attacked than had actually been the case, threatened to reinforce, not transcend, the depressive effects of off-screen bombardment (Paret, 1996, 60).

British wartime cinema, on the other hand, tended to plunder the past for more harmonious depictions of (predominantly English) landscape and 'national character': a character which was not, in the manner of Nazi film, invariably counterpoised to its negative correlative. Thus it was enough, sometimes, for 'heritage films' simply to purvey nostalgic images of a pastoral – largely fictive – past (Richards, 1997, 97–104). But the MOI was also keen, however, that the rural idyll for which Britons fought be pitted against encroachments: that cinema project 'Britain's role as defender of freedom and a bulwark against foreign tyrants' (Chapman, 1998, 235). The finest – and certainly costliest – fulfilment of this injunction was Laurence Olivier's *Henry V*: a film which clearly attempted to reinforce a belief in victory, and a sense of deep-rooted patriotism (England substituting again for the UK as a whole, with Shakespeare's reference to Scotland as a separate kingdom being excised; Chapman, 1998, 244). The imprecision of *Henry V*'s historical analogue was scarcely material. By 1945, only the most incorrigible literalists – and the French – were likely to quibble that the film tendentiously identifies France as Britain's enemy (Chapman, 1998, 248). The same was also true of a number of wartime historical features, including Carol Reed's *The Young Mr Pitt* (1942), in which a clearly Churchillian Pitt sees off the Napoleonic challenge (Aldgate and Richards, 1995, 138–67). But the broader parallels – British troops massing, under inspired leadership, to cross the Channel and rout a continental adversary – were quite apparent in both films.

In its cinematic afterlife, the Second World War has generally figured – in American cinema at least – as an uncomplicated tribute to martial values in the service of democratic ideals: and in its Soviet counterpart, the cult of the 'Great Patriotic War' buttressed the entire regime, under Stalin and beyond (Youngblood, 1996, 85). *Catch-22* and a few other films aside, the Second World War has infrequently formed the backdrop to pacifistic sentiment in Western cinema (Pronay, 1988, 41; Adair, 1989, 11). And attempts to characterise Spielberg's *Saving Private Ryan* (1998) as 'anti-war' rest largely (and unconvincingly) on the presumed pacifistic impact of its gut-wrenching realism on queasy viewers in the absence of 'blustery pro-American anti-Nazi rhetoric' alerting them to the war's necessity (Doherty, 1998, 70). Strikingly, unlike the Great War, or indeed Vietnam, the Second World War did not lie dormant for some years before enjoying cinematic resurrection. Perhaps for the victors, the war was sufficiently clear-cut in its purposes and outcome that it did not require instant burial and forgetting (other than those troubling aspects which were suppressed with unseemly haste: the bomb, most notably, for America). Or maybe the rapid shading of total war into Cold War – one 'totalitarian' enemy seamlessly merging with another, seemingly in the same image – meant that the Second World War was simply too useful, too pertinent, to go into abeyance. The war against Hitler was such a serviceable allegory for the West's looming confrontation with Stalin that it could scarcely retire from the screens. (And in the USSR, the war offered such heroic narratives of self-sacrifice, resistance and endurance – and such telling illustrations of capitalist perfidy – that there was no question of Stalin commanding Soviet cinema to demobilise what had been its sole war-years' subject.)

In America, far from war being 'box office poison', as conventional wisdom held, Hollywood's nine Second World War themed features of 1949 grossed the 'whopping figure' of $25 million, as *Variety* approvingly noted (Doherty, 1993, 272). Their success surely owed much to the backdrop against which they played: sentimentalised recollection of the recent war, combined with fear of a (possibly imminent) sequel. 'Though these films were putatively concerned with World War II', suggests Gary Wills, 'the real unseen enemy was Communism, and the real battle was to impose the psychological conditioning necessary for a new kind of "war"' (1997, 154). That the movies succeeded (at least initially) in the task of mental mobilisation was proved by those embittered young Americans who fought a new kind of war in Vietnam. Reared on an unbalanced diet of fare such as *Sands of Iwo Jima* and *To Hell and Back*, their palates revolted on finding the experience of war less appetising than Hollywood's ersatz concoction.

The function of British post-war cinema's recycling of the Second World War, on the other hand, was perhaps less to perpetuate warlike attitudes and instil preparedness than to mask Britain's decline, though doubtless the effect was not always, or even often, intentional. To evoke the war, however, was sometimes to engage in nostalgic self-aggrandisement: reliving the days when Britain retained an empire, and one, moreover, which fought alongside the Mother Country against Nazi and Japanese aggression rather than for independence from Britain itself; when the 'special relationship' with America resembled a partnership of equals, not an asymmetrical relationship of dependence; when the UK exhibited (at least cinematically) a unity of nations, classes, races and sexes which peacetime failed to preserve. The war, as Britain's 'finest hour', certainly offered suitable material for a 'usable past' (as 83 war-themed films between 1945 and 1960 attest), and according to Nicholas Pronay the post-bellum cinema offered Britons 'the opportunity of a weekly spiritual/emotional experience to help them cope with their lives ... to lay the ghosts of the war' (1988, 51).

Conclusion: an expensively purchased metaphor

Focusing specifically on feature film as perhaps the most significant purveyor of historical images and interpretations for the better part of the twentieth century, this chapter has explored how and why past wars often continue to be repackaged long after their formal conclusions. The television age notwithstanding, Hollywood's revisionings of history often themselves become news events (think of the fanfare accompanying *Apocalypse Now* or *Saving Private Ryan*), and still reach a wider global audience than most historically-based television documentaries can hope to attract.

This is not to say that since the 1960s television documentary and drama series have not sought to explain, and sometimes draw a line under, conflicts whose meanings are still disputed and socially divisive. Thus have US network documentary histories of the war in Vietnam tended to reach anodyne conclusions about the purpose and meaning of the experience, and concerning America's, or specific Americans', culpability therein (if they did not reflect, especially in the Reagan years, more partisan 'revisionist' conclusions: Vlastos, 1991, 68). Like feature films, however, documentaries may also seek to animate discussion and controversy surrounding past events, with a view to jolting mass amnesia rather than encouraging an easy resolution and collective forgetting.

Rich in metaphoric potential, ancient (or more recent) conflicts often tellingly refract images of – or lessons for – the present. Without exhausting the possibilities, the dramatic or documentary evocation of war past can serve as a collective act of memory or forgetting, or remembrance in order to forget; as a warning against war in general, or conversely as stimulus to current (or future) conflict; or as an analogue for quite distinct phenomena, be they other wars or peacetime processes. Thus David Kennedy suggests that for many young literary figures of the 1920s (Hemingway, Dos Passos, e.e. cummings) the Great War was a subject of interest not only in its own right but as 'a fabulously useful, if expensively purchased, metaphor for the corruption of the culture they had under siege' (1980, 227).

Past war has likewise been 'fabulously useful' for political leaders in seeking to rationalise current conduct, and sometimes in structuring the analogical reasoning by which they reach decisions about appropriate action during international crises. 'The lessons of Munich', for example, have long reverberated: in escalating US commitment in Vietnam under Lyndon B. Johnson, as in validating Bush's decision to place a 'desert shield' in Saudi Arabia to thwart the ambitions of the new Hitler, Hussein (Khong, 1992). At this point, then, our analysis swings full circle: we end where we began. The media's treatment of wars past – whether directly cued by politicians or broadly reflecting a prevailing climate – may well be synonymous with the media's preparation for future war, intentionally so or otherwise. And once at war, as we have seen, the media frequently find their activities governed by rules which themselves derive from the 'lessons' of wars past.

Conclusion

War isn't what it used to be. As large-scale war seemingly fades into obsolescence, many war-watchers anticipate an era perhaps of more devastatingly one-sided knockout blows – such as the Gulf War – but certainly of recurrent smaller-scale skirmishes between 'other people', for whom the prospect of war was never over-ridden by the superpowers' mass stockpiling of nuclear missiles, or erased by the conclusion of the Cold War. Strategists dispute whether the prospect of another 'total war' was defused as soon as nuclear missiles made war between their possessors unthinkable, and thus impossible, or concluded only after superpowers stopped threatening their use and began dismantling their warheads. But most seem agreed that the twentieth century has outlived the 'Age of Total War', which is now categorically over. For 'us', the prospect of all-out war has vanished. For the technological 'haves', current speculation buzzes around the concept of 'infowar'. In such projections, conflict of the future will turn on the disabling of enemies' informational systems, with cyberspace itself the battlefield: a type of warfare waged by hackers and software viruses in which a heavily computerised military (notably the USA's) would be particularly vulnerable (Gray, 1997, 24).

However, it is inconceivable that all warfare will in future be conducted via fibre optic superhighways. Although 'netwar' raises the prospect of technological have-nots spectacularly sabotaging the micro-chip rich, it is plausible that most wars will continue to be fought – along more conventional lines – between more evenly matched foes. Chris Hables Gray thus suggests that we live in an age of 'imperfect' (though he prefers 'postmodern') war: 'the actual battles are not decisive or heroic; they are confusing, distant, and squalid' (1997, 22). Moreover, they are often fought by 'others'. Besides fretting over 'infowar' scenarios, many Western militaries therefore anticipate that their future terrestrial engagements are likely to resemble those of the 1990s, in which peacekeeping and

269

delivery of humanitarian assistance superseded actual war-fighting as such.

That being so, a number of military commentators envisage a future of more harmonious media relations. After all, in 'peace-keeping' operations, the peacekeepers' imperatives are quite distinct from those of combatants. In particular, the overwhelming concern with informational 'security' – protecting operational secrets from the prying eyes of journalists – dissolves, while the requirement for positive publicity for the peacekeepers' activities is heightened. Colonel Bob Stewart derived these lessons from his experience commanding UN forces in Bosnia:

> It is...vital that UN troops are seen to be effective both inter-nationally and at home, which is where the media enter the equation. Surely there are no real secrets when working on a humanitarian or indeed peacekeeping mandate. This is a funda-mental difference between general war and peacekeeping... Therefore the press can have almost unlimited access with the proviso that they do not get in the way too much. The media can be used as a form of weapon and to inform people in the theatre. (Stewart, 1993, 322)

Of course, peacekeeping operations are not unique in their requirement that mass media enhance the military's reputation and profile. Historical experience suggests that states generally encourage, or otherwise coerce, their media into performing this function in wartime. But in peacekeeping operations media appro-bation may be vital to sustain popular support for the contribution of national forces to an international operation – in the absence of narrow 'national interest', as a glue binding contributor states' citizens to their military contingents – and in attaching peace-keepers themselves to their mission (Nash, 1998, 133). Less con-ventionally, media, as Stewart argues, are also vital *within* a theatre of operations to build warring parties' confidence in the neutrality, competence, and the 'firmness of purpose' of peacekeepers deployed there (Nash 1998, 133). UN commanders in former Yugo-slavia (and elsewhere) have often come to regard the media as a positive tool. Indeed, to Lewis MacKenzie, media were 'the only major weapons system' at his disposal: not, as sometimes in con-ventional warfare, to mislead others as to military capabilities or plans (since the notion of an 'enemy' vanishes in such operations), but to offer reassurance to civilians as to the peacekeepers' reliability, and to encourage warring militaries to abide by international agreements (1993, 21–4; Nash, 1998, 131–5). Such operations have also witnessed the increasing development by UN forces of their *own* channels of communication: thus the use of radio broadcasting in Cambodia, Somalia and Former Yugoslavia (P. Taylor, 1997, 199–200; Adam, 1995, 179–90).

Optimistic forecasts of future team-playing between humanitarian international forces and 'embedded' journalists committed to furthering their objectives have engendered, in some quarters, greater sanguinity about military-media relations than has been apparent since the early 1960s (Nash, 1998). Throughout the 1970s and 1980s, the shadow of Vietnam – with its infectious belief that the media fundamentally undermined America's war effort – was such that many journalistic and military observers alike could perceive only antagonism between their two professions. However, at the century's end, Vietnam (understood as the nadir of military-media relations) looks increasingly anomalous: the single outstanding example of media 'disloyalty', now safely neutralised by subsequent experience (Rowe, 1991).

However, to foresee uniformly harmonious military-media relations is perhaps to ignore the very different requirements of peacekeeping operations and 'conventional' war, neglecting the new dynamics which the absence of an enemy lends peacekeepers' interactions with journalists. In a different type of war (one of 'our' wars), the old 'irritations' between military and media would doubtless resurface although, as this book has argued, these are often largely superficial disagreements, since most journalists *do* align themselves with 'their' military (thus their resentment of being compelled to protect military security which they would not knowingly jeopardise in any case). In short, to describe the trajectory of twentieth-century military-media relations as an upwards arc – with Vietnam as aberrant blip on the learning curve – is to ignore the overwhelmingly supportive roles which the media have performed *throughout* its many wars. The alleged antagonism between the two professions in the Vietnam War was more a matter of mutually serviceable mythology than incontrovertible fact. Indeed, even where interpersonal relations have been strained (and as often as not these have been companionable), as *institutions*, the media have generally served the military rather well. From a statist perspective, then, there have long been grounds for optimism about military-media relations, although precisely the reverse has often been feared and proclaimed.

When journalists, on the other hand, look ahead they tend to predict mixed outcomes for the future of war reporting. Broadcast journalists ponder the impact of rolling, 24-hour news on 'conventional' formats and journalistic standards, while print media wonder how the increasing provision of on-line news services might erode their readerships (and increasingly they attempt to dampen this threat by pumping resources into their own Internet sites). Some war correspondents anticipate – or more actively advocate – a change in their professional rules of engagement. In reporting 'other people's wars', some journalists have argued for a redefinition of their relationship not so much with the military as with those whose humanitarian plight they report. Hence the recent calls from Martin Bell and others for a 'journalism of attachment', challenging the interpretation of 'objectivity' which has reporters attempting to stand above the events they report (Bell, 1995, 1997, 1998; Tumber, 1997).

Reporting war can often confront journalists with the problematic nature of this enterprise. The war zone may jolt correspondents into an awareness that they themselves are a part of the proceedings and thus can never satisfactorily be apart from them in the manner 'objective journalism' prescribes. War does (or may do) this in different ways. For one thing, the war reporter often observes, first hand, the way in which a media presence alters the very nature of the phenomenon under observation. People 'act up' for the cameras, as Michael Herr observed in Vietnam:

> You don't know what a media freak is until you've seen the way a few of those grunts would run around during a fight when they knew that there was a television crew nearby; they were actually making war movies in their heads, doing little guts-and-glory Leatherneck tap dances under fire, getting their pimples shot off for the networks...A lot of correspondents weren't much better. We'd all seen too many movies, stayed too long in Television City. (Herr, 1978, 169)

Soldiers and journalists alike, then, may act out for the cameras the 'war-in-the-head' they have acquired from exposure to the conventions of media representation (as embedded in war movies or news film), matching their behaviour with what war on the big or small screen *should* look like (Hynes, 1998, 202–3). Not infrequently, journalists and photographers return from war with the confession that they ceased to be mere observers and became 'participants'. As Herr memorably averred: 'I went to cover the war and the war covered me' (1978, 24).

This awareness of their own transformative impact upon others' behaviour sometimes shatters journalists' conception of their professional role as a mere 'mirror' to reality (though it may leave intact the entrenched notion that in peacetime it is still possible to report from a 'place of greater safety' and, once again, from 'no one's point of view'). But whether or not war fully alerts journalists to their own constitutive role in shaping social reality, it certainly often confronts reporters with stark choices about where their moral responsibility lies. While most reporters have little difficulty (in many cases) in answering their state's appeal for loyalty, as 'responsible' citizens of their country at war, some grapple with altogether more personal dilemmas of involvement and attachment: perhaps most acutely in 'other people's wars'. Do they answer the desperate calls for help of war's victims? Is it enough to record suffering and refuse to intervene? Is photography itself, as Susan Sontag insists, 'essentially an act of non-intervention' (1979, 11)? Can the journalist satisfactorily fall back on the 'mirror' analogy, confronted with cries for assistance, by responding to the sufferer that circulating verbal or visual portraits of their plight is the best form of journalistic assistance possible, and the only one professionally sanctioned? Certainly not all journalists have found that response adequate, whether their infringement of 'objectivity' has taken the form of impassioned pleas for outside intervention, or private acts of rescue, such as the adoption of war orphans. Offered a choice between a life and a photograph, photojournalists do not invariably, *pace* Sontag, choose the photograph (1979, 12).

These dilemmas, although current, are not in fact particularly new (Tumber, 1997, 7). News values and professional practices are not fixed and unchanging over time or across cultures. And even at any one time and in any one place, different sections of the media interpret their own professional standards and roles quite differently. As Hallin shows with respect to American media during the Vietnam War, print and television journalists did not observe the same procedures where 'objectivity' was concerned (1989). Indeed many of the internecine media clashes documented in this book have sprung from the divergent roles espoused by news organisations, and journalists' own disagreements over quite how much latitude wartime permits for 'dissent'. Clearly, the tabloid end of print journalism does not regard detachment as part of its war- or peacetime repertoire at all. Partisanship in newspapers having a long history, perhaps the fetishisation of 'objectivity' will come to appear as a peculiarity of a particular (and particularly positivistic) phase of the twentieth century.

Where technology, not changing professional standards, may differentiate future wars from those of the past is in making journalists less readily 'censorable'. The prospect that miniaturised, lightweight equipment, less susceptible to surveillance, will enable reporters to evade censorship remains, however, a debatable hypothesis. Technology certainly did not free journalists thus in the Gulf War of 1991. Depending on where future wars are fought and the disposition of those fighting them, militaries might yet find ways of scrutinising journalists' activities, preventing them from enjoying the unfettered fruits of technological progress by tightly proscribing access – to 'the story' and its important players – as in the Gulf. Finding herself expelled from Kosovo by the Yugoslav authorities at the onset of NATO airstrikes in March 1999, journalist Maggie O'Kane pessimistically concluded that: 'The very technology that liberated journalists has now, by its very efficiency, changed our status in wars... We have become players, and therefore participants, and have to be controlled – ruthlessly' (*The Observer*, 28 March 1999, 20). In short, states' inability to censor the medium has resulted in yet greater hostility towards the messenger, such that journalists find themselves forcibly 'cleansed' from warzones. Whether such draconian denial of access will become a recurrent phenomenon remains to be seen. But should military censorship become obsolescent, it is, in any case, questionable whether a different kind of 'antagonistic' war reportage would always or necessarily ensue. If news output is also shaped by self-censorship and pressures other than those emanating from the state, then the absence of formal controls might have relatively little effect where media perceive future wars to be widely supported by their audience.

As a number of journalists and others have pointed out, self-censorship is as real a threat to the free circulation of opinion and images in wartime as anything enacted by the state. Hence one increasingly visible anomaly, for 'consumers' of news, is that our visual experience of war appears to be contracting even as the technological capacity to convey higher-definition images with greater immediacy expands. One former BBC war correspondent ruminates thus on his profession's growing desire to avoid coupling death with war:

> We film the outgoing ordnance, but not the incoming. We show soldiers blazing away amid the ruins, and even the ruins can seem picturesque in the altered state of television. What we do not show is what happens at the other end – the killing, the maiming, the wounding, and the suffering, the irredeemable waste of young lives, which is what war is . . . [television news] prettifies and sanitizes. Taken over the months and years of a conflict, it promotes the idea of warfare as a costfree enterprise, not even shocking anymore but almost an acceptable means of settling differences. (Bell, 1998, 105; see also P. Harris, 1992, 35)

As far as some cultural critics are concerned, what the late twentieth century has witnessed in effect is at once a distancing of individuals from war and simultaneous divorce of death from war in the mediated public consciousness. Some postulate that this severance is a direct outgrowth of the increasing 'remoteness' of industrialised 'techno-warfare' from those who conduct it. 'Killing is done at a distance, and if the victims are optically separated from their killers the insulation of combatants and viewers from the action is likely to be enhanced' (J. Taylor, 1998, 157). But it would be misleading to think that war fighting and imaging technology itself dictates war's visual record. Modern technology *potentially* permits us to see more than ever: the guns and bombs, after all, as Margot Norris notes, 'have eyes':

> Guns with camera 'eyes' could reverse the 'blind', impersonal, anonymous and nonhuman killing made possible by the telekinesis of the big guns, missiles and bombs in modern mass warfare. Giving guns 'eyes' so that we see what they 'see' makes it possible to reintroduce a 'witness' into mass warfare, that obliges those who pull the trigger to 'see', literally and visually, those human beings they kill. By extension, if such video clips of close-up kills

were shown on television, the viewer would find himself or herself
ocularly in the position of the gun and its operator and would
have to recognize himself or herself as occupying the position of
the agency of killing. (Norris, 1994, 289)

That soldiers and civilians alike are allowed to dissociate themselves from war's materiality – denying that war involves humans
harming one another – results from human decisions to withhold
what the bombs witness, or, as in the Gulf War, to release only
images which confirm that late twentieth-century bombing is not
only smart but 'clean'.

How do we account for this evasion? Does post-Vietnam US
military sensitivity to the impact of dead bodies – photographed
and daily tallied – account for this negatory impulse? It may in part.
But these particular scruples do not wholly explain a refusal to
expose civilian audiences to the full impact of war on fellow
humans. The instinct to sanitise transcends cultural boundaries:
thus, for religious reasons, some Islamic journalists were equally
reluctant to broadcast the satellite feeds of the victims of Al Amiriya
during the Gulf War, believing that 'the humanity of the individual,
the dignity, cannot be defiled' (Wolfsfeld, 1997, 189). Neither is the
Western military aversion to acknowledging killing as a central fact
of war as historically specific to the post-Vietnam era as some
analyses of the mediated Gulf War imply. Militaries have long
found distancing mechanisms – visual but also linguistic (the use
of 'words that had no currency left as words', as Herr observed in
Vietnam) – to confound understanding of what war actually means
(Herr, 1978, 173). Denial of injury as war's central purpose and
consequence has deep roots, as Elaine Scarry and others have
argued (Scarry, 1987; Hüppauf, 1995). This evasion derives from
complex witting and unwitting – 'malevolent' or 'relatively benign' –
motivations: the omission of what appears 'too self-evident to
require articulation'; a 'failure of perception on the part of the
describer', or 'an active desire to misrepresent the central content
of war's activity', sometimes by conscious 'redescription' of events in
the euphemistic vocabulary of war (Scarry, 1987, 64–81).

How much injury civilians are permitted to see (or otherwise
learn of) is, then, largely a matter of human, not technological,
determination, broad cultural mores in part informing specific
choices. In so far as general trends are observable, however, it

appears that states and reporters alike over the course of the twentieth century inclined to show less, even as technology permitted more accurate imagistic capturing of moving subjects in motion. Ironically, perhaps, the nineteenth-century dawn of the photographic age exposed American civilians to unflinching portraits of the Civil War dead – immobile corpses forming the best subjects for early battlefield photography – of a starkness rarely encountered now (certainly not during one of 'our wars'). Then their effect was mesmerising: the *New York Times* related, in October 1862, how hushed and reverent crowds gazed 'in the pale faces of the dead', captured by Mathew Brady, 'chained by the strange spell of that dwells in the dead men's eyes' (cited by Franklin, 1994, 29). But as the technologisation of twentieth-century warfare spawned new forms of mass killing, militaries seemingly became keener to avoid advertising (to their own publics) the devastating effects of their weaponry, seeking instead to amputate human bodies from representations of modern industrial war. Thus the aestheticised imagery of both total wars was generally less graphic than Brady's 'Dead of Antietam'. But as strategic commodities in wartime, images – even those displaying a certain measure of realism – have not invariably been regarded by the state as damaging to civilian morale. As George Roeder demonstrates, American 'officials perceived pictures of the American dead as extremely hazardous material during the war's early years. Before it ended they considered them the most powerful weapons in their motivational arsenal' (1993, 25). Fearing that American civilians might otherwise grow complaisant with a geographically distant war, and remain emotionally unprepared for the return home of the wounded, a certain amount of injury was restored to the depiction of war.

When the state refuses to circulate such images, do media then have a responsibility to confront citizens of democracies with what their uniformed representatives experience on the battlefield, and with what soldiers themselves suffer and what they inflict on others? Some academics and journalists think so. 'If the public supports a war then it has a responsibility for the consequences ... surely one of the responsibilities [of citizens in wartime] is to see – or at least be provided with the opportunity to see – the price being paid to prosecute the war, whether this is the body of your neighbour's son or innocent civilians killed in the crossfire', insists Kevin

Williams (Williams, 1992, 161; J. Taylor, 1998). The media's responsibility, in short, is to force civilians to accept their *duty* to know: to throw the reality of war in 'terrible handfuls' into the eyes of audiences. For if civilians are prepared to forgo, or substantially curtail, their 'right to know', then journalists' own championship of freedom of information in wartime becomes problematic (Morrison and Tumber, 1988; P. Taylor, 1997). Whether this full exposure need necessarily be *visual* in the most literal sense, however, is a moot point. Arguably, powerfully realised verbal description can fulfil this visceral function just as effectively as photography (Hallin, 1989, 130). The common insistence on seeing may, then, derive less from a belief in the visual image's epistemological superiority as a way of knowing than simple acknowledgement that television is the commonest medium through which people acquire news.

Those who champion full exposure of war to civilians must, however, confront a recurrent phenomenon in twentieth-century war (whether total or limited): namely, the apparent disinclination of audiences to be shown too much, too vividly, of what war actually entails. This distaste for undue verisimilitude in wartime imagery derives from different, sometimes contradictory, and certainly ambivalent, impulses. T.S. Eliot noted that 'human kind cannot bear very much reality', and that may be part of it. But the distaste is often rationalised (by civilians, not just the military or media) on sundry other grounds: that imagination can join the dots left by sanitised imagery; that such sanitisation is required in order to maintain support for a war effort because realistic portrayal of war is likely to have an anti-war impact; that close-up photography of the dead and wounded is a violation of their dignity; or that in 'total war' the primary function of visual media especially is to entertain and distract, not to show the wounded boy next door, or the deaths of those who could be (potentially or actually) our loved ones.

This same 'squeamishness' – if such it is – does not seem to apply to fictionalised representations of violence, however. Paradoxically, the seeming propensity to shy away from war's consequences has grown even as many Western cultures have become saturated with fictional simulations of death. While technology has made it possible for 'real' war to be filmed and transmitted in 'real time', so too have computer-generated special effects in the motion picture industry also made it possible to reconstruct war on screen with ever greater battlefield verisimilitude. Thus Steven Spielberg's

Saving Private Ryan promotes itself as, in effect, a war movie to end all war movies, such is the stomach-churning realism of its special effects, although similar promotional claims were made of *Platoon*, and the long lineage of 'realistic' combat movies preceding it (Doherty, 1998, 68). Why, then, will Western audiences accept cinematic depictions of war which emulate the real thing with ever growing graphic realism, while apparently preferring their television news coverage not to project such images on the small screen in wartime?

What does this seemingly radical disjunction between news and entertainment media's propensity for realism tell us? The paradox is suggestive of the way that media, throughout the twentieth century, have served equally to distance civilians from war as to transform them into its eye-witness spectators. The act of watching can itself be distancing. Elaine Scarry describes this paradox, with reference to the television Gulf War: 'The nighttime spectacle enthralled and captured: it suspended, rather than incited, the population's capacity for deliberation and debate' (Scarry 1993, 64). For their part, fictionalised war movies (even if based on 'true life') are likely to be able to show more than actuality footage, though possibly with no greater illumination. After all, audiences can suspend their suspension of disbelief should the actors' wounds be felt as too disturbingly 'real'. In other words, if war's effects are too upsetting, we have the consolation of reminding ourselves that this is 'just a film', not real life, however convincingly recreated. Moreover, the reconstructed real events lie safely in the past. If they did not, they would doubtless not have been translated on to the big screen with quite so much unsettling verisimilitude.

Some critics suggest that war films invariably, irrespective of directorial intent, serve to glamorise war. One does not need wholly to accept that proposition (only to reject its negative counterpart, that realistic war movies are inevitably anti-war), to argue that many of Hollywood's offerings in that genre appear more as valorisation than condemnation of war. Prompted to enlist, in part, by cinematic eulogies to war, generations of young men during twentieth-century conflicts have found their direct encounter with combat mediated by its on-screen counterpart. Some soldiers in the First World War, for example, experienced trench warfare as a distanced and disjointed phenomenon, as though watching a film. Thus one British soldier who had been at Gommecourt later wrote: 'The other men were like figures on a cinematograph screen – an old film that flickered violently – everybody in a desperate hurry' (cited by Eksteins, 1990, 302). Many American GIs in Vietnam, on the other hand, discovered, even as they played to the ubiquitous cameras, that if war was a movie, then this particular one 'sucked': 'I *hate* this movie' a grunt emphatically informs Michael Herr in *Dispatches* (1978, 153).

The study of war and the media is replete with such paradoxes: of media simultaneously drawing some aspects of conflict into focus while keeping others resolutely out of frame; of fictional films reinstating death in war where news footage often avoids it, sometimes in promotion of pacifism, though only questionably able to do so without perversely adding to war's mystique. More frequently, perhaps, endless media recyclings of wars past have served over the century to encourage participation in a field of human endeavour which, as John Mueller reminds us, 'unlike breathing, eating, or sex...is not something that is somehow required by the human condition' (1989, ix). Mass media do less to mirror the world as it is than to shape a world as it should *not* be: a world where war too readily appears an inevitable outgrowth of 'human nature' and still, after a long century of conflict, an appropriate form of dispute resolution.

Select Bibliography

Adair, G. (1989) *Hollywood's Vietnam: From the 'Green Berets' to 'Full Metal Jacket'*. London: Heinemann.

Adam, G. (1995) 'Radio's Peacekeeping Potential in Humanitarian Crises' in Girardet.

Adams, V. (1986) *The Media and the Falklands Campaign*. London: Macmillan.

African Rights, (1994) *Rwanda: Death, Despair and Defiance*. London: African Rights.

Alali, O. and Eke, K. (1991) *Media Coverage of Terrorism: Methods of Diffusion*. Newbury Park, CA: Sage.

Aldgate, A. and Richards, J. (1995) *Britain Can Take It: The British Cinema in the Second World War*. Edinburgh: Edinburgh University Press.

Aldridge, M. and Hewitt, N. (eds) (1994) *Controlling Broadcasting. Access Policy and Practice in North America and Europe*. Manchester: Manchester University Press.

Alexander, Y. and Latter, R. (eds) (1990) *Terrorism and the Media: Dilemmas for Government, Journalists and the Public*. Washington, DC: Brassey's.

Alexander, Y. and O'Day, A. (eds) (1984) *Terrorism in Ireland*. London: Croom Helm.

Alexander, Y. and Picard, R. (eds) (1991) *In the Camera's Eye: News Coverage of Terrorist Events*. Washington, DC: Brassey's.

Allen, T. and Seaton, J. (eds) (1999) *The Media of Conflict: War Reporting and Representations of Ethnic Violence*. London: Zed Books.

Alleyne, M. (1995) *International Power and International Communication*. London: Macmillan.

Alleyne, M. (1997) *News Revolution: Political and Economic Decisions about Global Information*. London: Macmillan.

Anderegg, M. (ed.) (1991) *Inventing Vietnam: The War in Film and Television*. Philadelphia: Temple University Press.

Ang, I. (1985) *Watching 'Dallas': Soap Opera and the Melodramatic Imagination*. New York: Methuen.

Ang, I. (1991) *Desperately Seeking the Audience*. London: Routledge.

Arendt, H. (1958) *The Origins of Totalitarianism*. Cleveland: Meridian Books.

Arlen, M. (1982) *Living-Room War*. New York: Penguin.

Arnett, P. (1992) 'Why I Stayed Behind' in Smith.

Arnett, P. (1995) *Live from the Battlefield*. London: Corgi.

Article 19. (1989) *No Comment: Censorship, Secrecy and the Irish Troubles*. London: Article 19.

Article 19 (1992) *Stop Press: The Gulf War and Censorship*. London: Article 19.

Atkinson, R. (1994) *Crusade. The Untold Story of the Gulf War*. London: HarperCollins.

Atwater, T. (1991) 'Network Evening News Coverage of the TWA Hostage Crisis' in Alali and Eke.

Aubin, S. (1992) 'Bashing the Media: Why the Public Outrage' in Smith.

Aulich, J. (1992) *Framing the Falklands War: Nationhood, Culture and Identity*. Milton Keynes: Open University Press.

Badsey, S. (1983) '*Battle of the Somme*: British War Propaganda', *Historical Journal of Film, Radio and Television*, 3, iii, 99–115.

Badsey, S. (1994) 'Modern Military Operations and the Media', Camberley: Strategic & Combat Studies Institute Paper, No. 8.

Baird, J. (1974) *The Mythical World of Nazi War Propaganda, 1939–45*. Minneapolis: University of Minnesota Press.

Baldwin, T., McVoy, D. and Steinfield, C. (1996) *Convergence: Integrating Media, Information and Communication*. London: Sage.

Balfour, M. (1979) *Propaganda in War, 1939–45*. London: Routledge & Kegan Paul.

Barber, B. (1996) *Jihad vs McWorld: How Globalism and Tribalism are Reshaping the World*. New York: Ballantine Books.

Barnouw, E. (1982) 'The Hiroshima–Nagasaki Footage: a report', *Historical Journal of Film, Radio and Television*, 2, i, 91–9.

Bartov, O. (1996) *Murder in Our Midst: the Holocaust, Industrial Killing and Representation*. New York: Oxford University Press.

Basinger, J. (1986) *The World War Two Combat Movie: Anatomy of a Genre*. New York: Columbia University Press.

Beckett, I. (1988) 'Total War' in McInnes and Sheffield.

Begin, M. (1977) *The Revolt*. New York: Nash Publishing.

Behr, E. (1992) *Anyone Here Been Raped and Speaks English? A Correspondent's Life Behind the Lines*. Harmondsworth: Penguin.

Bell, M. (1995) *In Harm's Way: Reflections of a War Zone Thug*. London: Hamish Hamilton.

Bell, M. (1997) 'TV news: how far should we go?', *British Journalism Review*, 8, i, 6–16.

Bell, M. (1998) 'The Truth is Our Currency', *Press/Politics*, 3, i, 102–9.

Belsey, A. and Chadwick, R. (eds) (1992) *Ethical Issues in Journalism and the Media*. London: Routledge.

Bennett, W. (1990) 'Toward a Theory of Press-State Relations in the United States', *Journal of Communication*, 40, 103–25.

Bennett, W. and Paletz, D. (eds) (1994) *Taken by Storm: the Media, Public Opinion and US Foreign Policy in the Gulf War*. Chicago: University of Chicago Press.

Benthall, J. (1993) *Disasters, Relief and the Media*. London: I.B. Tauris.

Berg, R. (1991) 'Losing Vietnam: Covering the War in an Age of Technology' in Rowe and Berg.

Bergmeier, H. and Lotz, R. (1997) *Hitler's Airwaves: The Inside Story of Nazi Radio Broadcasting and Propaganda Swing*. New Haven, NJ: Yale University Press.

Berkowitz, D. (1997) *Social Meanings of News: A Text-Reader*. London: Sage.

Bishop, P. (1982) 'Reporting the Falklands', *Index on Censorship*, 11, vi, 6–8.

Bishop, P. (1993) *Famous Victory: the Gulf War*. London: Sinclair-Stevenson.

Boccardi, L. (1995) 'Let the Reporters Report' in Girardet.

Boelke, W. (1970) *The Secret Conferences of Dr. Goebbels: The Nazi Propaganda War, 1939–43*. New York: E.P. Dutton.

Bolton, R. (1990) *Death on the Rock and Other Stories*. London: W.H. Allen.

Bond, B. and Roy, I. (1975) (eds) *War and Society: A Yearbook of Military History*. NY: Holmes & Meier.

Bonham-Carter, M. (1989) 'Broadcasting and Terrorism', *Index on Censorship*, 18, ii, 7–8.

Boorstin, D. (1961) *The Image: or What Happened to the American Dream?* Harmondsworth: Penguin.

Borden, A. (1993) 'War of Words and Pictures' in Scott and Jones.

Bourdieu, P. (1998) *On Television and Journalism*. London: Pluto Press.

Boyer, P. (1996) 'Exotic Resonances: Hiroshima in American Memory' in Hogan.

Braestrup, P. (1989) 'An Extreme Case' in Sevy.

Braestrup, P. (1994) *Big Story: How the American Press and Television Reported and Interpreted the Crisis of Tet 1968 in Vietnam and Washington*. Novato, CA: Presidio.

Bramsted, E. (1965) *Goebbels and National Socialist Propaganda, 1925–45*. London: Cresset Press.

Brauman, R. (1993) 'When Suffering Makes A Good Story' in *Médecins sans Frontières*.

Braw, M. (1991) *The Atomic Bomb Suppressed: American Censorship in Occupied Japan*. New York: Armonk.

Breed, W. (1955) 'Social Control in the Newsroom', *Social Forces*, 33, 326–35.

Bremer, L. (1991) 'Terrorism, the Media and the Government' in Matthews.

Briggs, A. (1985) *The BBC: The First Fifty Years*. Oxford: Oxford University Press.

Briggs, A. (1995) *The War of Words, 1939–45*. Oxford: Oxford University Press.

Broderick, M. (1991) *Nuclear Movies: A Critical Analysis and Filmography of International Feature Length Films Dealing with Experimentation, Aliens, Terrorism, Holocaust and Other Disaster Scenarios, 1914–1989*. Jefferson, NC: McFarland.

Broderick, M. (ed.) (1996) *Hibakusha Cinema: Hiroshima, Nagasaki and the Nuclear Image in Japanese Film*. London: Kegan Paul International.

Brothers, C. (1997) *War and Photography: A Cultural History*. London: Routledge.

Brough-Williams, I. (1996) 'War Without End?: The *Bloody Bosnia* Season on Channel Four' in Gow, Paterson and Preston.

Brown, J. (1963) *Techniques of Persuasion: From Propaganda to Brainwashing*. Harmondsworth, Penguin.

Brownlow, K. (1979) *The War, the West, and the Wilderness*. London: Secker & Warburg.

Buitenhuis, P. (1989) *The Great War of Words: Literature as Propaganda, 1914–18 and After*. London: Batsford.

Burns, J. (1996) 'The Media as Impartial Observers or Protagonists – Conflict Reporting or Conflict Encouragement in Former Yugoslavia' in Gow, Paterson and Preston.

Buruma, I. (1995) *The Wages of Guilt: Memories of War in Germany and Japan*. London: Vintage.

Buruma, I. (1996) *The Missionary and the Libertine: Love and War in East and West*. London: Faber & Faber.

Calder, A. (1969) *The People's War: Britain, 1939–45*. London: Panther.

Campbell, D. (1993) *Politics Without Principle: Sovereignty, Ethics and Narratives of the Gulf War*. London: Lynne Reinner.

Carruthers, S. (1995) *Winning Hearts and Minds: British Governments, the Media and Colonial Counterinsurgency, 1944–60*. London: Leicester University Press.

Carruthers, S. (1996) 'Reporting Terrorism: The British State and the Media, 1919–94' in Stewart and Carruthers.

Chaliand, G. (1987) *Terrorism: From Popular Struggle to Media Spectacle*. London: Saqi Books.

Chambers, J. (1996) '*All Quiet on the Western Front* (US, 1930): The Antiwar Film and the Image of Modern War' in Chambers and Culbert.

Chambers, J. and Culbert, D. (1996) *World War II: Film and History*. New York: Oxford University Press.

Chapman, J. (1998) *The British at War: Cinema, State and Propaganda, 1939–45*. London: IB Tauris.

Chomsky, N. (1989a) *Necessary Illusions: Thought Control in Democratic Societies*. London: Pluto Press.

Chomsky, N. (1989b) *The Culture of Terrorism*. London: Pluto Press.

Christensen, T. (1987) *Reel Politics: American Political Movies from 'Birth of a Nation' to 'Platoon'*. Oxford: Blackwell.

Cigar, N. (1995) *Genocide in Bosnia: The Politics of 'Ethnic Cleansing'*. College Station: Texas A&M University Press.

Clark, I. (1997) *Globalization and Fragmentation: International Relations in the Twentieth Century*. Oxford: Oxford University Press.

Clark, M. (1985) 'Vietnam: Representations of Self and War', *Wide Angle*, 7, iv, 4–11.

Clawson, P. (1990) 'Why We Need More but Better Coverage of Terrorism' in Kegley.

Cline, R. and Alexander, Y. (1986) *Terrorism as State-Sponsored Covert Warfare*. Fairfax, VA: Hero Books.

Clutterbuck, R. (1981) *The Media and Political Violence*. London: Macmillan.

Cockburn, A. (1991) 'The TV War', *New Statesman and Society*, 8 March, 14–15.

Cockerell, M. (1984) *Sources Close to the Prime Minister: Inside the Hidden World of the News Manipulators*. London: Macmillan.

Cockerell, M. (1988) *Live From Number 10: The Inside Story of Prime Ministers and Television*. London: Faber.

Cohen, L. (1995) *Broken Bonds: Yugoslavia's Disintegration and Balkan Politics in Transition*. Boulder, CO: Westview Press.

Coker, C. (1994) *War and the Twentieth Century: a study of war and modern consciousness*. London: Brassey's.

Collins, R., Hennessey, P. and Walker, D. (1986) *Media, Culture and Society: A Critical Reader*. London: Sage.

Colombo, F. (1995) 'The Media and Operation Restore Hope in Somalia' in Girardet.

Conners, J. (1998) 'Hussein as Enemy: The Persian Gulf War in Political Cartoons', *Press/Politics*, 3, iii, 96–114.

Cook, E. (1920) *The Press in Wartime*. London: Macmillan.

Cook, T. (1994) 'Washington Newsbeats and Network News after the Iraq Invasion of Kuwait' in Bennett and Paletz.

Cordingley, P. (1996) *In the Eye of the Storm. Commanding the Desert Rats in the Gulf War*. London: Hodder & Stoughton.

Corner, J., Schlesinger, P. and Silverstone, R. (eds) (1997) *International Media Research: A Critical Survey*. London: Routledge.

Costello, J. (1986) *Love, Sex and War, 1939–45*. London: Pan.

Coultass, C. (1984) 'British Feature Films and the Second World War', *Journal of Contemporary History*, 19, i, 7–22.

Crenshaw, M. (ed.) (1983) *Terrorism, Legitimacy, and Power: The Consequences of Political Violence*. Middleton, Conn.: Wesleyan University Press.

Cripps, T. (1983) 'Racial Ambiguities in American Propaganda Movies' in Short.

Cripps, T. (1997) *Hollywood's High Noon: Moviemaking and Society before Television*. Baltimore: Johns Hopkins University Press.

Cruikshank, C. (1977) *The Fourth Arm: Psychological Warfare 1938–45*. Oxford: Oxford University Press.

Culbert, D. (1983) '*Why We Fight*: Social Engineering for a Democratic Society at War' in Short.

Culbert, D. (1985) 'American Film Policy in the Re-education of Germany after 1945' in Pronay and Wilson.

Culbert, D. (1988) 'Television's Vietnam and Historical Revisionism in the United States', *Historical Journal of Film, Radio and Television*, 8, iii, 253–67.

Culbert, D. (ed.) (1990) *Film and Propaganda in America: A Documentary History, Vols II & III, World War II*. Westport, CT: Greenwood Press.

Cull, N. (1995) *Propaganda for War: The British Propaganda Campaign against American 'Neutrality' in World War II*. New York: Oxford University Press.

Cumings, B. (1992) *War and Television*. London: Verso.

Curran, C. (1990) 'The New Revisionism in Mass Communication Research: A Reappraisal', *European Journal of Communication*, 5, ii–iii, 135–64.

Curran, C. and Porter, V. (1983) *British Cinema History*. London: Weiden-feld & Nicolson.

Curry, R. (1995) 'How Early German Film Stars Helped Sell the War(es)' in Dibbets and Hogenkamp.

Curtis, L. (1984) *Ireland: The Propaganda War. The British Media and the Battle for Hearts and Minds*. London: Pluto Press.

Curtis, L. and Jempson, P. (1993) *Interference on the Airwaves: Ireland, the Media and the Broadcasting Ban*. London: Campaign for Press and Broadcasting Freedom.

Dahlgren, P. and Sparks, C. (eds) (1991) *Communication and Citizenship: Journalism and the Public Sphere*. London: Routledge.

DeBauche, L. (1997) *Reel Patriotism: The Movies and World War I*. Madison: University of Wisconsin Press.

de la Billière, P. (1995) *Storm Command: A Personal Account of the Gulf War*. London: HarperCollins.

Demm, E. (1993) 'Propaganda and Caricature in the First World War', *Journal of Contemporary History*, 28, i, 163–92.

Denton, R. (ed.) (1993) *The Media and the Persian Gulf War*. Westport, CT: Praeger.

Déotte, J.-L., *et al.* (eds) (1994) *Visites aux armées: tourismes de guerre. (Back to the Front. Tourisms of War)*. Basse-Normandie: FRAC.

Der Derian, J. (1992) *Antidiplomacy: Spies, Terror, Speed and War*. Oxford: Blackwell.

Destexhe, A. (1995) *Rwanda and Genocide in the Twentieth Century*. London: Pluto Press.

Devereaux, L. and Hillman, R. (eds) (1995) *Fields of Vision: Essays in Film Studies, Visual Anthropology and Photography*. Berkeley: University of California Press.

de Waal, A. (1994) 'African Encounters', *Index on Censorship*, 6, 14–31.

Dibbets, K. and Hogenkamp, B. (1995) *Film and the First World War*. Amsterdam: Amsterdam University Press.

Dittmar, L. and Michaud, G. (eds) (1990) *From Hanoi to Hollywood: The Vietnam War in American Film*. New Brunswick, NJ: Rutgers University Press.

Dobkin, B. (1992) *Tales of Terror. Television News and the Construction of the Terrorist Threat*. Westport, CT: Praeger.

Doherty, T. (1988–9) 'Full Metal Genre: Stanley Kubrick's Vietnam Combat Movie', *Film Quarterly*, 42, ii, 24–30.

Doherty, T. (1991) 'Witness to War: Oliver Stone, Ron Kovic and *Born on the Fourth of July*' in Anderegg.

Doherty, T. (1993) *Projections of War: Hollywood, American Culture and World War II*. New York: Columbia University Press.

Doherty, T. (1998) '*Saving Private Ryan*', *Cineaste*, XXIV, i, 68–71.

Doob, L. (1995) 'Goebbels' Principles of Propaganda' in Jackall.

Dorman, W. and Livingston, S. (1994) 'The Establishing Phase of the Persian Gulf Policy Debate' in Bennett and Paletz.

Dowden, R. (1995) 'Covering Somalia – Recipe for Disaster' in Girardet.

Dower, J. (1986) *War Without Mercy: Race and Power in the Pacific War*. New York: Pantheon.

Dower, J. (1996) *Japan in War and Peace: Essays on History, Culture and Race*. London: Fontana.

Dower, J. (1996) 'The Bombed: Hiroshimas and Nagasakis in Japanese Memory' in Hogan.

Dower, J. (1999) *Embracing Defeat: Japan in the Wake of World War II*. New York: W.W. Norton & Company.

Downing, J., Mohammadi, A. and Sreberny-Mohammadi, A. (eds) (1995) *Questioning the Media: A Critical Introduction*. London: Sage.

Dworkin, A. (1996) 'The World in Judgement', *Index on Censorship*, 25, v, 137–44.

Eckstein, H. (ed.) (1964) *Internal War: Problems and Approaches*. New York: Free Press.

Eksteins, M. (1980) '*All Quiet on the Western Front* and the Fate of a War', *Journal of Contemporary History*, 15, 345–66.

Eksteins, M. (1990) *Rites of Spring: The Great War and the Birth of the Modern Age*. London: Black Swan.

Eldridge, J. (1993) *Getting the Message: News, Truth and Power*. London: Routledge.

Elegant, R. (1981) 'How to Lose a War', *Encounter*, 57, ii, 73–89.

Ellul, J. (1972) *Propaganda: The Formation of Men's Attitudes*. New York: Alfred A. Knopf.

Elsaesser, T. (1996) (ed.) *A Second Life: German Cinema's First Decades*. Amsterdam: Amsterdam University Press.

Entman, R. and Page, B. (1994) 'The News Before the Storm' in Bennett and Paletz.

Ettema, J. (1994) 'Discourse That is Closer to Silence Than to Talk: The Politics and Possibilities of Reporting on Victims of War', *Critical Studies in Mass Communication*, 11, 1–21.

Falk, R. (1991) 'The Terrorist Foundations of Recent US Foreign Policy' in George.

Farrar, M. (1998) *News From the Front: War Correspondents on the Western Front, 1914–18*. Stroud: Sutton Publishing.

Faulk, H. (1977) *Group Captives: The Re-education of German Prisoners of War in Britain, 1945–1948*. London: Chatto & Windus.

Ferguson, M. (1992) 'The Mythology about Globalization', *European Journal of Communication*, 7, 69–93.

Fialka, J. (1991) *Hotel Warriors: Covering the Gulf*. Washington, DC: The Woodrow Wilson Center.

Fishman, M. (1980) *Manufacturing the News*. Austin, TX: University of Texas Press.

Fiske, J. (1987) *Television Culture*. London: Methuen.

Flichy, P. (1995) *Dynamics of Modern Communications: The Shaping and Impact of New Communication Technologies*. London: Sage.

Foster, K. (1992) 'The Falklands War: A Critical View of Information Policy' in Young.

Fox, T. (1995) 'The Media and the Military: An Historical Perspective on the Gulf War' in Walsh.

Franklin, H.B., (1994) 'From Realism to Virtual Reality: Images of America's Wars' in Jeffords and Rabinovitz.

Fraser, L. (1957) *Propaganda*. Oxford: Oxford University Press.

Frey, R. and Norris, C. (eds) (1991) *Violence, Terrorism, and Justice*. Cambridge: Cambridge University Press.

Friedlander, S. (1992) *Probing the Limits of Representation: Nazism and the 'Final Solution'*. London: Harvard University Press.

Fussell, P. (1989) *Wartime: Understanding and Behavior in the Second World War*. New York: Oxford University Press.

Fyne, R. (1994) *The Hollywood Propaganda of World War II*. Metuchen, NJ: Scarecrow Press.

Gallimore, T. (1991) 'Media Compliance with Voluntary Press Guidelines for Covering Terrorism' in Alexander and Picard.

Gans, H. (1979) *Deciding What's News*. New York: Pantheon.

Garber, M., Matlock, J. and Walkowitz, R. (1993) *Media Spectacles*. London: Routledge.

Gassman, P. (1991) 'TV Without Government: The New World Order?' in Girardet.

George, A. (ed.) (1991) *Western State Terrorism*. Cambridge: Polity Press.

Gerbner, G. (1992) 'Violence and Terror in and by the Media' in Raboy and Dagenais.

Gerrits, R. (1992) 'Terrorists' Perspectives: Memoirs' in Paletz and Schmid.

Giddens, A. (1990) *The Consequences of Modernity*. Cambridge: Polity Press.

Gilbert, P. (1992) 'The oxygen of publicity: terrorism and reporting restrictions' in Belsey and Chadwick.

Girardet, E. (1996) 'Reporting Humanitarianism: Are the New Electronic Media Making a Difference?' in Rotberg and Weiss.

Girardet, E. (ed.) (1995) *Somalia, Rwanda and Beyond: The Role of the International Media in Wars and Humanitarian Crises*. Dublin: Crosslines Global Report.

Gitlin, T. (1980) *The Whole World is Watching: The Mass Media in the Making and Unmaking of the New Left*. Berkeley: University of California Press.

Glasgow University Media Group. (1985) *War and Peace News*. Milton Keynes: Open University Press.

Gledhill, C. and Swanson, G. (1996) (eds) *Nationalising Femininity: Culture, Sexuality and Cinema in Britain in World War II*. Manchester: Manchester University Press.

Glenny, M. (1993) *The Fall of Yugoslavia*. Harmondsworth: Penguin.

Goldhagen, D. (1996) *Hitler's Willing Executioners: Ordinary Germans and the Holocaust*. New York: Alfred Knopf.

Golding, P., Murdock, G. and Schlesinger, P. (1986) *Communicating Politics: Mass Communications and the Political Process*. Leicester: Leicester University Press.

Gombrich, E. (1970) *Myth and Reality in German War-Time Broadcasts*. London: Athlone Press.

Gow, J. (1997) *Triumph of the Lack of Will: International Diplomacy and the Yugoslav War.* London: Hurst & Co.

Gow, J., Paterson, R. and Preston, A. (eds) (1996) *Bosnia by Television.* London: BFI Publishing.

Gowing, N. (1991) 'The Media Dimension 1: TV and the Kurds', *World Today*, 47, vii, 111–12.

Gowing, N. (1994) 'Real-Time Television Coverage of Armed Conflicts and Diplomatic Crises: Does it Pressure or Distort Foreign Policy Decisions', Harvard: Joan Shorenstein Barone Center, Working Paper 94–1.

Gowing, N. (1996) 'Real-Time TV Coverage from War: Does it Make or Break Government Policy?' in Gow, Paterson and Preston.

Gray, C. (1997) *Postmodern War: The New Politics of Conflict.* London: Routledge.

Greenberg, B. and Gantz, W. (eds) (1993) *Desert Storm and the Mass Media.* Creeskill, NJ: Hampton Press.

Gurevitch, M., Levy, M. and Roeh, I. (1991) 'The Global Newsroom: Convergences and Diversities in the Globalization of Television News' in Dahlgren and Sparks.

Gutman, R. (1993) *A Witness to Genocide: The First Inside Account of the Horrors of 'Ethnic Cleansing' in Bosnia.* Shaftesbury: Element.

Hackworth, D. (1992) 'The Gulf Crisis: The Media Point of View' in Young.

Hale, O. (1964) *The Captive Press in the Third Reich.* Princeton, NJ: Princeton University Press.

Hall, T. (1993) 'Why the broadcasting ban should go', *Index on Censorship*, 8/9, 4–6.

Hallin, D. (1989) *The 'Uncensored War': The Media and Vietnam.* New York: Oxford University Press.

Hallin, D. (1994) *We Keep America on Top of the World: Television Journalism and the Public Sphere.* London: Routledge.

Hallin, D. (1994) 'Images of Vietnam and the Persian Gulf Wars in US Television' in Jeffords and Rabinovitz.

Hallin, D. (1997) 'The Media and War' in Corner, Schlesinger and Silverstone.

Hallin, D. and Gitlin, T. (1994) 'The Gulf War as Popular Culture and Television Drama' in Bennett and Paletz.

Hamelink, C. (1994) *The Politics of World Communication: A human rights perspective.* London: Sage.

Hamilton, R. (1989) 'Image and Context: The Production and Reproduction of *The Execution of a VC Suspect* by Eddie Adams' in Walsh and Aulich.

Hamilton-Paterson, J. (1996) *The Music.* London: Vintage.

Hammock, J. and Charny, J. (1996) 'Emergency Response as Morality Play: The Media, the Relief Agencies and the Need for Capacity Building' in Rotberg and Weiss.

Hammond, W. (1989) 'The Press in Vietnam as Agent of Defeat: A Critical Examination', *Reviews in American History*, 17, ii, 312–23.

Hammond, W. (1998) *Reporting Vietnam: Media and Military at War.* Lawrence, KA: University of Kansas Press.

Hannerz, U. (1996) *Transnational Connections: Culture, People, Places.* London: Routledge.

Harper, J. (1991) 'The Italian Press and the Moro Affair' in Serfaty.

Harper, S. (1988) 'The Representation of Women in British Feature Films, 1939–45' in Taylor.

Harris, P. (1992) *Somebody Else's War: Frontline Reports From the Balkan Wars, 1991–2*. Stevenage: Spa Books.

Harris, R. (1983) *Gotcha! The Media, the Government and the Falklands Crisis*. London: Faber & Faber.

Haste, C. (1977) *Keep the Home Fires Burning: Propaganda in the First World War*. London: Allen Lane.

Henderson, L., Miller, D. and Reilly, J. (1990) *Speak No Evil: The British Broadcasting Ban, the Media and the Conflict in Ireland*. Glasgow: Glasgow University Media Group.

Herf, J. (1997) *Divided Memory: The Nazi Past in the Two Germanies*. Cambridge, MA: Harvard University Press.

Herman, E. (1982) *The Real Terror Network: Terror in Fact and Propaganda*. Boston, MA: South End Press.

Herman, E. and Chomsky, N. (1988) *Manufacturing Consent: The Political Economy of the Mass Media*. New York: Pantheon.

Herr, M. (1978) *Dispatches*. London: Pan.

Herzstein, R. (1979) *The War That Hitler Won: The Most Infamous Propaganda Campaign in History*. London: Hamish Hamilton.

Hill, C. (1974) *Behind the Screen: the Broadcasting Memoirs of Lord Hill of Luton*. London: Sidgwick & Jackson.

Hill, C. (1996) 'World opinion and the empire of circumstance', *International Affairs*, 72, i, 109–32.

Hilsum, L. (1995) 'Where is Kigali?', *Granta*, 51, 145–79.

Hirano, K. (1992) *Mr. Smith Goes to Tokyo: Japanese Cinema Under the American Occupation, 1945–52*. Washington, DC: Smithsonian Institution Press.

Hitler, A. (1992) *Mein Kampf*. (Translated by Ralph Mannheim.) London: Pimlico.

Hoagland, J. (1992) 'Simpson's Scud Attack' in Smith.

Hobsbawm, E. (1995) *Age of Extremes: The Short Twentieth Century, 1914–1991*. London: Abacus.

Hocking, J. (1984) 'Orthodox Theories of "Terrorism": the Power of Politicised Terminology', *Politics*, 19, ii, 103–10.

Hocking, J. (1992) 'Governments' Perspectives' in Paletz and Schmid.

Hoffmann, H. (1996) *The Triumph of Propaganda: Film and National Socialism, 1933–45*. Providence, RI: Berghahn Books.

Hofstetter, C. and Moore, D. (1979) 'Watching TV News and Supporting the Military, A Surprising Impact of the News Media', *Armed Forces and Society*, 5, i, 261–9.

Hogan, M. (ed.) (1996) *Hiroshima in History and Memory*. Cambridge: Cambridge University Press.

Hollinger, D. (1993) 'How Wide the Circle of "We"? American Intellectuals and the Problem of Ethnos since World War II', *American Historical Review*, 98, 317–37.

Holton, R. (1998) *Globalization and the Nation-State*. London: Macmillan.

Hooper, A. (1982) *The Military and the Media*. Aldershot: Gower.

Hopkin, D. (1970) 'Domestic Censorship in the First World War', *Journal of Contemporary History*, V, iv, 151–70.

Howard, G. 'A speech given to the Chartered Building Societies Institute, 6 May 1982', BBC Press Release (PR/12/82).

Howe, E. (1982) *The Black Game: British Subversive Operations Against the Germans During the Second World War*. London: Futura.

Hüppauf, B. (1995) 'Modernism and the Photographic Representation of War and Destruction' in Devereaux and Hillman.

Hull, D. (1969) *Film in the Third Reich: A Study of the German Cinema, 1933–45*. Berkeley: University of California Press.

Huntington, S. (1996) *The Clash of Civilizations and the Remaking of World Order*. New York: Simon & Schuster.

Hynes, S. (1998) *The Soldiers' Tale: Bearing Witness to Modern War*. London: Pimlico.

Ignatieff, M. (1998) *The Warrior's Honor: Ethnic War and the Modern Conscience*. London: Chatto & Windus.

Ingham, B. (1991) *Kill the Messenger*. London: HarperCollins.

Insdorf, A. (1989) *Indelible Shadows: Film and the Holocaust*. Cambridge: Cambridge University Press.

Irving, J. (1986) *The Hotel New Hampshire*. London: Black Swan.

Isenberg, M. (1975) 'An Ambiguous Pacifism: A Retrospective on World War I Films, 1930–38', *Journal of Popular Film and Television*, 4, ii, 99–115.

Isenberg, M. (1988) 'The Great War Viewed from the Twenties: *The Big Parade* (1925)' in O'Connor and Jackson.

Jackall, R. (ed.) (1995) *Propaganda*. London: Macmillan.

Jeffords, S. (1986) 'The New Vietnam Films: Is the Movie Over?', *Journal of Popular Film and Television*, 13, 186–94.

Jeffords, S. and Rabinowitz, L. (eds) (1994) *Seeing Through the Media: the Persian Gulf War*. New Brunswick, NJ: Rutgers University Press.

Jenkins, B. (1988) 'Future Trends in International Terrorism' in Slater and Stohl.

Jensen, R. (1992) 'Fighting Objectivity: The Illusion of Journalistic Neutrality in Coverage of the Persian Gulf War', *Journal of Communication Inquiry*, 16, i, 20–32.

Jowett, G. and O'Donnell, V. (1992) *Propaganda and Persuasion*. London: Sage.

Kaes, A. (1989) *From 'Hitler' to 'Heimat': The Return of History as Film*. Cambridge, MA: Harvard University Press.

Kaplan, H. (1982) 'With the American Press in Vietnam', *Commentary*, 73, v, 42–9.

Keane, F. (1996) *Season of Blood: A Rwandan Journey*. Harmondsworth: Penguin.

Keane, J. (1991) 'Democracy and the media', *International Social Science Journal*, 129, 523–40.

Keane, J. (1996) *Reflections on Violence*. London: Verso.

Keen, S. (1986) *Faces of the Enemy: Reflections of the Hostile Imagination*. San Francisco: Harper & Row.

Keenan, T. (1994) 'Live From...' in Déotte *et al.*
Kegley, C. (1990) *International Terrorism: Characteristics, Causes, Controls.* New York: St Martin's Press.
Kellner, D. (1992) 'Television, the Crisis of Democracy and the Persian Gulf War' in Raboy and Dagenais.
Kellner, D. (1992) *The Persian Gulf TV War.* Boulder, CO: Westview Press.
Kelly, A. (1989) '"All Quiet on the Western Front": Brutal Cutting, Stupid Censors and Bigoted Politicos, 1930–1984', *Historical Journal of Film, Radio and Television*, 9, ii, 135–50.
Kelly, A. (1997) *Cinema and the Great War.* London: Routledge.
Kenez, P. (1995) 'Russian Patriotic Films' in Dibbets and Hogenkamp.
Kennedy, D. (1980) *Over Here: The First World War and American Society.* Oxford: Oxford University Press.
Kershaw, I. (1983) 'How Effective was Nazi Propaganda?' in Welch.
Kershaw, I. (1987) *The 'Hitler Myth': Image and Reality in the Third Reich.* Oxford: Clarendon Press.
Kershaw, I. and Lewin, M. (eds) (1997) *Stalinism and Nazism: Dictatorships in Comparison.* Cambridge: Cambridge University Press.
Khong, Y. (1992) *Analogies at War: Korea, Munich, Dien Bien Phu and the Vietnam Decisions of 1965.* Oxford: Princeton University Press.
Kimball, J. (1988) 'The Stab-in-the-Back Legend and the Vietnam War', *Armed Forces and Society*, 14, iii, 433–58.
Klinghoffer, A. (1998) *The International Dimension of Genocide in Rwanda.* London: Macmillan.
Knightley, P. (1989) *The First Casualty.* London: Pan.
Knightley, P. (1991) 'Lies, Damned Lies and Military Briefings', *New Statesman and Society*, 8 February, 26–7.
Koppes, C. and Black, G. (1977) 'What to Show the World: the Office of War Information and Hollywood, 1942–45', *Journal of American History*, LXIV, i, 87–105.
Koppes, C. and Black, G. (1987) *Hollywood Goes to War. How Politics, Profits and Propaganda Shaped World War II Movies.* New York: Free Press.
Kracauer, S. (1947) *From Caligari to Hitler: A Psychological History of the German Film.* Princeton, NJ: Princeton University Press.
Kroes, R. (1996) *If You've Seen One You've Seen the Mall: Europeans and American Mass Culture.* Urbana: University of Illinois Press.
Lang, G. and Lang, K. (1994) 'The Press as Prologue' in Bennett and Paletz.
Lant, A. (1991) *Blackout: Reinventing Women for Wartime British Cinema.* Princeton, NJ: Princeton University Press.
Laqueur, W. (1977) *Terrorism.* London: Weidenfeld & Nicolson.
Laqueur, W. and Alexander, Y. (eds) (1987) *The Terrorist Reader: An Historical Anthology.* New York: Meridian.
Lasswell, H. (1927) *Propaganda Technique in the World War.* London: Kegan Paul.
Leab, D. (1995) 'Viewing the War with the Brothers Warner' in Dibbets and Hogenkamp.
Leapman, M. (1987) *The Last Days of the Beeb.* London: Coronet.
Le Bailly, L. (1983) 'The Navy and the Media', *Naval Review*, 71, 3, 184–8.

Leiser, E. (1975) *Nazi Cinema*. New York: Macmillan.
Lichty, L. & Carroll, R. (1988) 'Fragments of War: *Platoon* (1986)' in O'Connor and Jackson.
Lippmann, W. (1922) *Public Opinion*. London: George Allen and Unwin.
Livingston, S. (1996) 'Suffering in Silence: Media Coverage of War and Famine in the Sudan' in Rotberg and Weiss.
Livingston, S. and Eachus, T. (1995) 'Humanitarian Crises and US Foreign Policy: Somalia and the CNN effect reconsidered', *Political Communication*, 12, 413–29.
Lodge, J. (ed.) (1981) *Terrorism: A Challenge to the State*. Oxford: Martin Robertson.
Lorch, D. (1995) 'Genocide versus Heartstrings' in Girardet.
Loshitzky, Y. (1997) *Spielberg's Holocaust: Critical Perspectives on 'Schindler's List'*. Bloomington: Indiana University Press.
Louvre, A. and Walsh, J. (1988) *Tell Me Lies About Vietnam: Cultural Battles for the Meaning of the War*. Milton Keynes: Open University Press.
Lyman, R. (1995) 'Occupational Hazards' in Girardet.
MacArthur, J. (ed.) (1991) *Despatches from the Gulf War*. London: Bloomsbury.
MacArthur, J. (1993) *Second Front: Censorship and Propaganda in the Gulf War*. Berkeley, CA: University of California Press.
MacKenzie, L. (1993) *Peacekeeper: The Road to Sarajevo*. Toronto: Douglas & McIntyre.
Mackinnon, S. (1995) 'Remembering the Nanjing Massacre: *In the Name of the Emperor (1995)*', *Historical Journal of Film, Radio and Television*, 15, iii, 431–3.
Magaš, B. (1993) *The Destruction of Yugoslavia: Tracking the Break-Up, 1980–92*. London: Verso.
Maier, C. (1988) *The Unmasterable Past: History, Holocaust and German National Identity*. Cambridge, MA: Harvard University Press.
Malcolm, N. (1996) *Bosnia: A Short History*. London: Papermac.
Mamdani, M. (1996) 'From Conquest to Consent as the Basis of State Formation: Reflections on Rwanda', *New Left Review*, 216, 3–36.
Mandelbaum, M. (1982) 'Vietnam: The Television War', *Daedalus*, 3, iv, 157–69.
Manheim, J. (1994) 'Strategic Public Diplomacy' in Bennett and Paletz.
Manvell, R. (1974) *Films and the Second World War*. Cranbury, NJ: AS Barnes.
Marling, K. and Wetenhall, J. (1991) *Iwo Jima: Monuments, Memories and the American Hero*. Cambridge, MA: Harvard University Press.
Marquis, A. (1978) 'Words as Weapons: Propaganda in Britain and Germany during the First World War', *Journal of Contemporary History*, 13, 467–98.
Martin, L. (1990) 'The Media's Role in Terrorism' in Kegley.
Matthews, L. (1991) *Newsmen and National Defense: Is Conflict Inevitable?* Washington, DC: Brassey's.
Mayall, J. (ed.) (1996) *The New Interventionism 1991–1994: United Nations Experience in Cambodia, former Yugoslavia and Somalia*. Cambridge: Cambridge University Press.

McCullin, D. (1992) *Unreasonable Behaviour: An Autobiography*. London: Vintage.

McEwen, J. (1982) 'The National Press during the First World War: Ownership and Circulation', *Journal of Contemporary History*, 17, iii, 459–86.

McInnes, C. and Sheffield, G. (eds) (1988) *Warfare in the Twentieth Century: Theory and Practice*. London: Unwin Hyman.

McLaine, I. (1979) *Ministry of Morale: Homefront Morale and the Ministry of Information in World War II*. London: Allen & Unwin.

McNair, B. (1991) *Glasnost, Perestroika, and the Soviet Media*. London: Routledge.

McQuail, D. (1992) *Media Performance: Mass Communication and the Public Interest*. London: Sage.

McQuail, D. (1994) *Mass Communication Theory: An Introduction*. London: Sage.

Médecins Sans Frontières, (1993) *Life, Death and Aid*. London: Routledge.

Mercer, D. (1984) 'Is press freedom a threat during national crises?', *Royal United Services Institute Journal*, 129, iii, 38–42.

Mercer, D., Mungham, G. and Williams, K. (1987) *The Fog of War: The Media on the Battlefield*. London: Heinemann.

Messinger, G. (1992) *Propaganda and the State in the First World War*. Manchester: Manchester University Press.

Messinger, G. (1993) 'An Inheritance Worth Remembering: the British approach to official propaganda during the First World War', *Historical Journal of Film, Radio and Television*, 13, ii, 117–27.

Meštrović, S. (1996) *Genocide After Emotion: The Postemotional Balkan War*. London: Routledge.

Meyerson, J. (1995) 'Theater of War: American Propaganda Films During the Second World War' in Jackall.

Miller, A. (ed.) (1982) *Terrorism, the Media and the Law*. New York: Transnational.

Miller, D. (1993) 'Official Sources and "Primary Definition": the case of Northern Ireland', *Media, Culture and Society*, 15, iii, 385–406.

Miller, D. (1994) *Don't Mention the War: Northern Ireland, Propaganda and the Media*. London: Pluto Press.

Milne, A. (1988) *DG: The Memoirs of a British Broadcaster*. London: Coronet.

Minear, L., Scott, C. and Weiss, T. (1996) *The News Media, Civil War and Humanitarian Action*. Boulder, CO: Lynne Reinner.

Moloney, E. (1991) 'Closing Down the Airwaves: the story of the Broadcasting Ban' in Rolston.

Molotch, H. and Lester, M. (1997) 'News as Purposive Behaviour: On the Strategic Use of Routine Events, Accidents and Scandals' in Berkowitz.

Morgan, M., Lewis, J. and Jhally, S. (1992) 'More Viewing, Less Knowing' in Mowlana, Gerbner and Schiller.

Morrison, D. (1992) *Television and the Gulf War*. London: John Libbey.

Morrison, D. (1994) 'Journalists and the Social Construction of War', *Contemporary Record*, 8, ii, 305–20.

Morrison, D. and Tumber, H. (1988) *Journalists at War: The Dynamics of News Reporting During the Falklands Conflict.* London: Sage.

Mosco, V. (1996) *The Political Economy of Communication: Rethinking and Renewal.* London: Sage.

Mosse, G. (1990) *Fallen Soldiers: Reshaping the Memory of the World Wars.* Oxford: Oxford University Press.

Mould, D. (1996) 'Press Pools and Military-Media Relations in the Gulf War: a case study of the Battle of Khafji, January 1991', *Historical Journal of Film, Radio and Television,* 16, ii, 133–59.

Mowlana, H. (1996) *Global Communication in Transition: The End of Diversity?* London: Sage.

Mowlana, H., Gerbner, G. and Schiller, H. (eds) (1992) *Triumph of the Image: The Media's War in the Gulf, a Global Perspective.* Boulder, CO: Westview Press.

Mueller, J. (1973) *War, Presidents and Public Opinion.* New York: John Wiley.

Mueller, J. (1989) *Retreat from Doomsday: The Obsolescence of Major War.* New York: Basic Books.

Mueller, J. (1994) *Policy and Opinion in the Gulf War.* Chicago: University of Chicago Press.

Mühl-Benninghaus, W. (1996) 'Newsreel Images of the Military and War, 1914–1918' in Elsaesser.

Mungham, G. (1985) 'The Eternal Triangle: Relations Between Governments, Armed Services and the Media', *Army Quarterly,* 115, i, 7–21.

Nacos, B. (1994) *Terrorism and the Media: From the Iran Hostage Crisis to the World Trade Center Bombing.* New York: Columbia University Press.

Nash, W. (1998) 'The Military and the Media in Bosnia', *Press/Politics,* 3, iv, 131–5.

Nathan, J. and Oliver, J. (1975) 'Public Opinion and US Security Policy', *Armed Forces and Society,* 2, i, 58–9.

Natsios, A. (1996) 'Illusions of Influence: The CNN Effect in Complex Emergencies' in Rotberg and Weiss.

Neuman, J. (1996) *Lights, Camera, War. Is Media Technology Driving International Politics?* New York: St. Martin's Press.

Nicholas, S. (1996) *The Echo of War: Home Front Propaganda and Wartime BBC, 1939–45.* Manchester: Manchester University Press.

Nicholson, M. (1992) *A Measure of Danger: Memoirs of a British War Correspondent.* London: Fontana.

Noriega, C. (1996) 'Godzilla and the Japanese Nightmare: When *Them!* is U.S.' in Broderick.

Nornes, M. (1996) 'The Body at the Center – *The Effects of the Atomic Bomb on Hiroshima and Nagasaki*' in Broderick.

Norris, C. (1992) *Uncritical Theory: Postmodernism, Intellectuals and the Gulf War.* London: Lawrence and Wishart.

Norris, M. (1994) 'Only the Guns Have Eyes: Military Censorship and the Body Count' in Jeffords and Rabinowitz.

Oakley, R. (1991) 'Terrorism, Media Coverage and Government Response' in Serfaty.

O'Connor, J. and Jackson, M. (eds) (1988) *American History/American Film: Interpreting the Hollywood Image*. New York: Ungar Publishing.

O'Heffernan, P. (1994) 'A Mutual Exploitation Model of Media Influence in US Foreign Policy' in Bennett and Paletz.

Oliver, M., Mares, M.L., and Cantor, J. (1993) 'News Viewing, Authoritarianism, and Attitudes Toward the Gulf War' in Denton.

O'Sullivan, N. (ed.) (1986) *Terrorism, Ideology and Revolution: The Origins of Modern Political Violence*. Brighton: Wheatsheaf Books.

Orwell, G. (1995) 'Politics and the English Language' in Jackall.

Page, C. (1996) *US Official Propaganda during the Vietnam War, 1965–73*. London: Cassell.

Paletz, D. and Boiney, J. (1992) 'Researchers' Perspectives' in Paletz and Schmid.

Paletz, D. and Schmid, A. (1992) *Terrorism and the Media: How Researchers, Terrorists, Government, Press, Public, Victims View and Use the Media*. Newbury Park, CA: Sage.

Paletz, D. and Tawney, L. (1992) 'Broadcasting Organizations' Perspectives' in Paletz and Schmid.

Parenti, M. (1993) *Inventing Reality: The Politics of News Media*. New York: St Martin's Press.

Paret, P. (1996) '*Kolberg* (Germany, 1945): As Historical Film and Historical Document' in Chambers and Culbert.

Parker, R. (1995) 'The Future of "Global" Television News: An Economic Perspective', *Political Communication*, 12, iv, 431–46.

Pedelty, M. (1995) *War Stories: the Culture of Foreign Correspondents*. London: Routledge.

Peer, L. and Chestnut, B. (1995) 'Deciphering Media Independence: The Gulf War Debate in Television and Newspaper News', *Political Communication*, 12, 81–95.

Peterson, H. (1939) *Propaganda for War: The Campaign Against American Neutrality, 1914–17*. Norman: University of Oklahoma Press.

Petrie, J. (ed.) (1994) *Essays on Strategy XII*. Washington, DC: National Defense University Press.

Philo. G, (1995) *Glasgow Media Group Reader, Volume 2: Industry, Economy, War and Politics*. London: Routledge.

Philo, G. (1993) 'From Buerk to Band Aid: the media and the 1984 Ethiopian Famine' in Eldridge.

Pilger, J. (1991) 'Video Nasties', *New Statesman and Society*, 25 January, 6–7.

Pilger, J. (1994) *Distant Voices*. London: Vintage.

Platt, S. (1991a) 'Paper Flags', *New Statesman and Society*, 25 January, 13–14.

Platt, S. (1991b) 'Casualties of War', *New Statesman and Society*, 22 February, 12–13.

Ponsonby, A. (1928) *Falsehood in Wartime*. London: George Allen & Unwin.

Ponting, C. (1998) *Progress and Barbarism: The World in the Twentieth Century*. London: Chatto & Windus.

Postman, N. (1987) *Amusing Ourselves to Death: Public Discourse in the Age of Show Business*. London: Methuen.

Pratkansis, A. and Aronson, E. (1992) *Age of Propaganda: The Everyday Use and Abuse of Persuasion*. New York: W.H. Freeman.

Preston, A. (1996) 'Television News and the Bosnian Conflict: Distance, Proximity, Impact' in Gow, Paterson and Preston.

Primoratz, G. (1996) 'Israel and Genocide in Croatia' in Meštrović.

Pronay, N. (1982) 'The News Media at War' in Pronay and Spring.

Pronay, N. (1988) 'The British Post-bellum Cinema: a survey of the films relating to World War II made in Britain between 1945 and 1960', *Historical Journal of Film, Radio and Television*, 8, i, 39–54.

Pronay, N. and Croft, J. (1983) 'British film censorship and propaganda policy during the Second World War', in Curran and Porter.

Pronay, N. and Spring, (1982) *Propaganda, Politics and Film, 1918–45*. London: Macmillan.

Pronay, N. and Wilson, K. (1985) *The Political Re-education of Germany and her Allies after World War II*. London: Croom Helm.

Protheroe, A. (1982) 'Why we have lost the information war', *The Listener*, 3 June, 2–3.

Prunier, G. (1997) *The Rwanda Crisis: History of a Genocide*. London: Hurst.

Raboy, M. and Dagenais, B. (eds) (1992) *Media, Crisis and Democracy: Mass Communication and the Disruption of Social Order*. London: Sage.

Ramet, P. (1992) *Balkan Babel*. Boulder, CO: Westview Press.

Rather, D. (1995) 'The United States and Somalia: assessing responsibility for the intervention' in Girardet.

Read, D. (1992) *The Power of News: The History of Reuters*. Oxford: Oxford University Press.

Reeves, N. (1983) 'Film Propaganda and its Audience: the example of Britain's Official Films during the First World War', *Journal of Contemporary History*, 18, iii, 463–94.

Reeves, N. (1986) *Official British Film Propaganda in the First World War*. London: Croom Helm.

Reeves, N. (1993) 'The Power of Film Propaganda – Myth or Reality?', *Historical Journal of Film, Radio and Television*, 13, ii, 181–201.

Reeves, N. (1997) 'Cinema, Spectatorship and Propaganda: "Battle of the Somme" and its contemporary audience', *Historical Journal of Film, Radio and Television*, 17, i, 5–28.

Reich, W. (ed.) (1990) *Origins of Terrorism: Psychologies, Ideologies, Theologies, States of Mind*. Cambridge: Cambridge University Press.

Reid, J. (1941) *Atrocity Propaganda, 1914–19*. New Haven, NJ: Yale University Press.

Renshon, S. (ed.) (1993) *The Political Psychology of the Gulf War: Leaders, Publics and the Process of Conflict*. London: University of Pittsburgh Press.

Rentschler, E. (1996) *The Ministry of Illusion. Nazi Cinema and its Afterlife*. Cambridge, MA: Harvard University Press.

Reuth, R. (1993) *Goebbels*. London: Constable.

Richards, J. (1988) 'National Identity in British Wartime Films' in Taylor.

Richards, J. (1997) *Films and British National Identity, from Dickens to Dad's Army*. Manchester: Manchester University Press.

Richards, J. and Sheridan, D. (1987) *Mass-Observation at the Movies*. London: Routledge and Kegan Paul.

Richie, D. (1996) '*Mono no aware*: Hiroshima in Film' in Broderick.

Rigg, R. (1969) 'How Not to Report a War', *Military Review*, 49, vi, 14–24.

Roach, C (ed.) (1993) *Communication and Culture in War and Peace*. London: Sage.

Robertson, J. (1982) 'British Film Censorship Goes to War', *Historical Journal of Film, Radio and Television*, 2, i, 49–64.

Robinson, P. (1999) 'The CNN Effect: Can the News Media Drive Foreign Policy?', *Review of International Studies*, 25, i, 301–9.

Roeder, G. (1985) 'A Note on US Photo Censorship in WWII', *Historical Journal of Film, Radio and Television*, 5, ii, 191–8.

Roeder, G. (1993) *The Censored War: American Visual Experience During World War Two*. London: Yale University Press.

Roetter, C. (1974) *Psychological Warfare*. London: Batsford.

Rollings, P. (ed.) (1983) *Hollywood as Historian: American Film in a Cultural Context*. Lexington: University of Kentucky Press.

Rolston, B. (eds) (1991) *The Media and Northern Ireland: Covering the Troubles.* London: Macmillan.

Rolston, B. and Miller D. (eds) (1996) *War and Words: The Northern Ireland Media Reader*. Belfast: Beyond the Pale Publications.

Rose, M. (1998) *Fighting for Peace: Bosnia, 1994*. London: Harvill.

Rose, T. (1995) *Aspects of Political Censorship, 1914–18*. Hull: Hull University Press.

Rosenblatt, L. (1996) 'The Media and the Refugee' in Rotberg and Weiss.

Rosenblum, M. (1993) *Who Stole the News? Why We Can't Keep Up With What Happens in the World and What We Can Do About It*. New York: John Wiley.

Rosenblum, M. (1995) 'Lack of Information or Lack of Will?' in Girardet.

Rosenstone, R. (1995) *Revisioning History: Film and the Construction of a New Past*. Princeton, NJ: Princeton University Press.

Ross, A. (1992) 'The Ecology of Images', *The South Atlantic Quarterly*, 91, i, 215–38.

Ross, S. (1996) *Propaganda for War: How the US was Conditioned to Fight the Great War of 1914–18*. Jefferson, NC: McFarland.

Rotberg, R. and Weiss, T. (eds) (1996) *From Massacres to Genocide: the Media, Public Policy and Humanitarian Crises*. Washington, DC: Brookings Institution.

Röther, R. (1996) 'Learning From the Enemy: German Film Propaganda in World War I' in Elsaesser.

Rowe, C. (1991) 'The "Vietnam Effect" in the Persian Gulf War', *Cultural Critique*, 19, 124.

Rowe, C. and Berg, R. (1991) *The Vietnam War and American Culture*. New York: Columbia University Press.

Royle, T. (1989) *War Report*. London: Grafton.

Said, E. (1996) *Covering Islam: How the Media and Experts Determine how we see the Rest of the World*. London: Vintage.

Said, E. and Hitchens, C. (eds) (1988) *Blaming the Victims: Spurious Scholarship and the Palestinian Question*. London: Verso.

Sakmyster, T. (1996) 'Nazi Documentaries of Intimidation: *Felzug in Polen* (1940), *Feuertaufe* (1940) and *Sieg im Westen* (1941)', *Historical Journal of Film, Radio and Television*, 16, iv, 485–514.

Sanders, M. and Taylor, P. (1982) *British Propaganda during the First World War*. London: Macmillan.

Scarry, E. (1987) *The Body in Pain: The Making and Unmaking of the World*. New York: Oxford.

Scarry, E. (1993) 'Watching and Authorizing the Gulf War' in Garber, Matlock and Walkowitz.

Schiller, H. (1996) *Information Inequality: the deepening social crisis in America*. New York: Routledge.

Schlesinger, P. (1987) *Putting 'Reality' Together: BBC News*. London: Methuen.

Schlesinger, P. (1991) *Media, State and Nation: Political Violence and Collective Identities*. London: Sage.

Schlesinger, P. (1995) 'Terrorism' in Smith.

Schlesinger, P., Murdock, G. and Elliott, P. (1983) *Televising 'Terrorism': Political Violence in Popular Culture*. London: Comedia.

Schmid, A. (1992) 'Editors' Perspectives' in Paletz and Schmid.

Schmid, A. and de Graaf, J. (1982) *Violence as Communication: Insurgent Terrorism and the Western News Media*. London: Sage.

Schmid, A. and Jongman, A. (1988) *Political Terrorism: A New Guide to Actors, Authors, Concepts, Data Bases, Theories and Literature*. Amsterdam: North Holland Publishing.

Schudson, M. (1995) *The Power of News*. Cambridge, MA: Harvard University Press.

Schudson, M. (1997) 'The Sociology of News Production' in Berkowitz.

Schull, M. and Wilt, D. (1996) *Hollywood War Films, 1937–1945: An Exhaustive Filmography of American Feature-Length Motion Pictures Relating to World War II*. Jefferson, NC: McFarland.

Scott, N. and Jones, D. (eds) (1993) *Bloody Bosnia: A European Tragedy*. London: The Guardian/Channel 4 publications.

Seaver, B. (1998) 'The Public Dimension of Foreign Policy', *Press/Politics*, 3, i, 65–91.

Segaller, S. (1987) *Invisible Armies: Terrorism into the 1990s*. Orlando, FL: Harcourt Brace Jovanovich.

Seib, P. (1998) *Headline Diplomacy: How News Coverage Affects Foreign Policy*. Westport, CO: Praeger.

Serfaty, S. (ed.) (1991) *The Media and Foreign Policy*. New York: St Martin's Press.

Sevy, G. (ed.) (1989) *The American Experience in Vietnam: A Reader*. London: University of Oklahoma Press.

Shafer, D. (ed.) (1990) *The Legacy: The Vietnam War in the American Imagination*. Boston, MA: Beacon Press.

Shao, T. (1995) 'John Magee's Documentary Footage of the Massacre in Nanjing, China, 1937–1938', *Historical Journal of Film, Radio and Television*, 15, iii, 425–29.

Sharkey, J. (1991) *Under Fire: US Military Restrictions on the Media from Grenada to the Persian Gulf*. Washington, DC: Center for Public Integrity.

Shattuck, J. (1996) 'Human Rights and Humanitarian Crises: Policy-Making and the Media' in Rotberg and Weiss.

Shaw, M. (1992) 'Global Society and Global Responsibility: The Theoretical, Historical and Political Limits of "International Society"', *Millennium: Journal of International Studies*, 21, iii, 421–34.

Shaw, M. (1994) 'Civil Society and Global Politics: Beyond a Social Movements Approach', *Millennium: Journal of International Studies*, 23, iii, 647–67.

Shaw, M. (1996) *Civil Society and Media in Global Crises: Representing Distant Violence*. London: Pinter.

Shaw, M. and Carr-Hill, R. (1992) 'Public Opinion and Media War Coverage in Britain' in Mowlana, Gerbner and Schiller.

Shaw, T. (1996) *Eden, Suez and the Mass Media: propaganda and persuasion during the Suez Crisis*. London: I.B. Tauris.

Sherry, M. (1995) *In the Shadow of War: the United States Since the 1930s*. New Haven, CT: Yale University Press.

Shindler, C. (1979) *Hollywood Goes to War: Films and American Society, 1939–52*. London: Routledge & Kegan Paul.

Shoemaker, P. (1991) *Gatekeeping*. London: Sage.

Shoemaker, P. and Reese, S. (1996) *Mediating the Message: Theories of Influence on Mass Media Content*. White Plains, NY: Longman.

Short, K. (ed.) (1983a) *Film and Radio Propaganda in World War Two*. Knocksville: University of Tennessee Press.

Short, K. (ed.) (1983b) *Washington's Information Manual for Hollywood*, *Historical Journal of Film, Radio and Television*, 3, i, 171–80.

Short, K. (ed.) (1985) *Hollywood: An Essential War Industry*, *Historical Journal of Film, Radio and Television*, 5, i, 90–9.

Short, K. (ed.) (1996) *Catalogue of Forbidden German Feature and Short Film Productions held in Zonal Film Archives of Film Section, Information Services Division, Control Commission for Germany*. Westport, CT: Greenwood Press.

Sifry, M. and Cerf, C. (eds.) (1991) *The Gulf War Reader: History, Documents, Opinions*. New York: Times Books.

Simpson, J. (1991a) 'Enemies Within', *The Spectator*, 23 February, 11–12.

Simpson, J. (1991b) *From the House of War: John Simpson in the Gulf*. London: Arrow.

Simpson, J. (1991c) 'Worse than Saddam', *The Spectator*, 9 February, 17–19.

Sinclair, J., Jacka, E. and Cunningham, S. (1996) *New Patterns in Global Television: Peripheral Vision*. Oxford: Oxford University Press.

Sklar, R. (1975) *Movie-Made America: A Cultural History of American Movies*. New York: Random House.

Slater, R. and Stohl, M. (eds) (1998) *Current Perspectives on International Terrorism*. London: Macmillan.

Small, M. (1994) *Covering Dissent: the Media and the Anti-Vietnam War Movement*. Brunswick, NJ: Rutgers University Press.

Smith, A. (1990) 'Towards a Global Culture?' *Theory, Culture and Society*, 7, 171–91.

Smith, A. (1995) *Television: An International History*. Oxford: Oxford University Press.

Smith, H. (ed.) (1992) *The Media and the Gulf War: The Press and Democracy in Wartime*. Washington DC: Seven Locks Press.

Smither, R. (1993) ' "A Wonderful Idea of the Fighting": the question of fakes in *The Battle of the Somme*', *Historical Journal of Film, Radio and Television*, 13, ii, 149–68.

Sobchack, V. (ed.) (1996) *The Persistence of History: Cinema, Television, and the Modern Event*. New York: Routledge.

Sobel, R. (1998) 'Portraying American Public Opinion toward the Bosnia Crisis', *Press/Politics*, 3, ii, 16–33.

Sontag, S. (1979) *On Photography*. Harmondsworth: Penguin.

Sorlin, P. (1980) *The Film in History: Restaging the Past*. Oxford: Blackwell.

Sorlin, P. (1991) *European Cinemas, European Societies, 1939–1990*. London: Routledge.

Sorlin, P. (1994) 'War and Cinema: Interpreting the Relationship', *Historical Journal of Film, Radio and Television*, 14, iv, 357–66.

Spillman, K. and Spillman, K. (1991) 'On enemy images and conflict escalation', *International Social Science Journal*, 127, 57–76.

Squires, J. (1935) *British Propaganda at Home and in the United States from 1914 to 1917*. Cambridge, MA: Harvard University Press.

Stead, P. (1988) 'The People as Stars' in Taylor.

Stech, F. (1994) 'Preparing for More CNN Wars', in Petrie.

Sterling, C. (1981) *The Terror Network: The Secret War of International Terrorism*. London: Weidenfeld & Nicolson.

Stern, J. (1975) *Hitler: The Führer and the People*. London: Fontana.

Stevenson, N. (1995) *Understanding Media Cultures: Social Theory and Mass Communication*. London: Sage.

Stewart, B. (1993) *Broken Lives: A Personal View of the Bosnian Conflict*. London: Harper/Collins.

Stewart, I. and Carruthers, S. (eds) (1996) *War, Culture and the Media: Representations of the Military in Twentieth Century Britain*. Trowbridge: Flicks Books.

Stites, R. (ed.) (1995) *Culture and Entertainment in Wartime Russia*. Bloomington: Indiana University Press.

Stohl, M. (1990) 'Demystifying the Mystery of International Terrorism' in Kegley.

Szumski, B. (ed.) (1986) *Terrorism: Opposing Viewpoints*. St Paul, Minnesota: Greenhaven Press.

Taylor, J. (1991) *War Photography: Realism in the Press*. London: Routledge.

Taylor, J. (1998) *Body Horror: Photojournalism, Catastrophe and War*. Manchester: Manchester University Press.

Taylor, P. (1981) 'Techniques of Persuasion: Basic Ground Rules of British Propaganda during the Second World War', *Historical Journal of Film, Radio and Television*, 1, i, 57–65.

Taylor, P. (1983) 'Propaganda in International Politics, 1919–1939' in Short.
Taylor, P. (1988) *British and the Cinema during the Second World War.* London: Macmillan.
Taylor, P. (1992) *War and the Media: Propaganda and Persuasion in the Gulf War.* Manchester: Manchester University Press.
Taylor, P. (1995) *Munitions of the Mind: War Propaganda from the Ancient World to the Nuclear Age.* Manchester: Manchester University Press.
Taylor, P. (1997) *Global Communications, International Affairs and the Media since 1945.* London: Routledge.
Taylor, Peter, (1986) 'The Semantics of Political Violence' in Golding, Murdock and Schlesinger.
Taylor, R. (1983) 'Goebbels and the Function of Propaganda' in Welch.
Taylor, R. (1998) *Film Propaganda: Soviet Russia and Nazi Germany.* London: IB Tauris.
Terrell, R and Ross, K. (1991) 'The Voluntary Guidelines' Threat to US Press Freedom' in Alexander and Picard.
Tester, K. (1994) *Media, Culture and Morality.* London: Routledge.
Thatcher, M. (1993) *The Downing Street Years.* London: HarperCollins.
Thayer, C. (1992) 'Vietnam: A Critical Analysis' in Young.
Thies, J. (1983) 'Nazi Architecture – A Blueprint for World Domination: the Last Aims of Adolf Hitler' in Welch.
Thompson, M. (1992) *A Paper House: The Ending of Yugoslavia.* London: Vintage.
Thompson, M. (1994) *Forging War: The Media in Serbia, Croatia and Bosnia-Hercegovina.* London: Article 19.
Thomson, A. (1992) *Smokescreen: The Media, the Censors, the Gulf.* Tunbridge Wells: Laburnham & Spellmount.
Thomson, G. (1947) *Blue Pencil Admiral: the Inside Story of Press Censorship.* London: Sampson Low, Marston & Co.
Thorpe, F. and Pronay, N. (1980) *British Official Films in the Second World War.* Oxford: Oxford University Press.
Toplin, R. (1996) *History by Hollywood: The Use and Abuse of the American Past.* Urbana: University of Illinois Press.
Towle, P. (1975) 'The Debate on Wartime Censorship in Britain, 1902–14' in Bond and Roy.
Townshend, C. (1986a) *Britain's Civil Wars: Counterinsurgency in the Twentieth Century.* London: Faber & Faber.
Townshend, C. (1986b) 'The Process of Terror in Irish Politics' in O'Sullivan.
Trevor-Roper, H. (ed.) (1978) *The Goebbels Diaries: The Last Days.* London: Secker & Warburg.
Tuchman, G. (1978) *Making News: A Study in the Construction of Reality.* New York: Free Press.
Tuchman, G. (1997) 'Making News by Doing Work: Routinizing the Unexpected' in Berkowitz.
Tumber, H. (1997) 'Bystander journalism, or the journalism of attachment?', *Intermedia*, 25, i, 4–7.
Tunstall, J. (1996) *Newspaper Power: The New National Press in Britain.* Oxford: Clarendon Press.

Turner, I. (ed.) (1989) *Reconstruction in Post-War Germany: British Occupation Policy and the Western Zones, 1944–55.* Oxford: Berg.

Turner, K. (1985) *Lyndon Johnson's Dual War: Vietnam and the Press.* Chicago: University of Chicago Press.

Van Ginneken, J. (1998) *Understanding Global News: A Critical Introduction.* London: Sage.

Viereck, G. (1931) *Spreading Germs of Hate.* London: Duckworth.

Virilio, P. (1989) *War and Cinema: The Logistics of Perception.* London: Verso.

Vlastos, S. (1991) 'Revisionist Vietnam History' in Rowe and Berg.

Voss, F. (1994) *Reporting the War: The Journalistic Coverage of World War II.* Washington, DC: Smithsonian Institution Press.

Vulliamy, E. (1994) *Seasons in Hell: Understanding Bosnia's War.* London: Simon & Schuster.

Wagner-Pacifici, R. (1986) *The Moro Morality Play: Terrorism as Social Drama.* Chicago: University of Chicago Press.

Wall, M. (1997) 'A "Pernicious New Strain of the Old Nazi Virus" and an "Orgy of Tribal Slaughter": A Comparison of US News Magazine Coverage of the Crises in Bosnia and Rwanda', *Gazette: The International Journal for Communications Studies,* 59, vi, 411–28.

Wallach, J. (1991) 'Leakers, Terrorists, Policy Makers and the Press' in Serfaty.

Wallis, R. and Baran, S. (1990) *The Known World of Broadcast News: International News and the Electronic Media.* London: Routledge.

Walsh, J. (1995) *The Gulf War did not happen: politics, culture and warfare post-Vietnam.* Aldershot: Arena.

Walsh, J. and Aulich, J. (eds) (1989) *Vietnam Images: war and representation.* Basingstoke: Macmillan.

Walter, E. (1969) *Terror and Resistance: A Study of Political Violence with Case Studies of Some Primitive African Communities.* Oxford: Oxford University Press.

Walzer, M. (1992) *Just and Unjust Wars: A Moral Argument with Historical Illustrations.* New York: Basic Books.

Ward, S. (1998) 'An Answer to Martin Bell: Objectivity and Attachment in Journalism', *Press/Politics,* 3, iii, 121–5.

Wardlaw, G. (1989) *Political Terrorism: Theory, Tactics, and Counter-Measures.* Cambridge: Cambridge University Press.

Waters, M. (1995) *Globalization.* London: Routledge.

Waugh, E. (1943) *Scoop: A Novel About Journalists.* Harmondsworth: Penguin.

Weart, S. (1988) *Nuclear Fear. A History of Images.* Cambridge, MA: Harvard University Press.

Weaver, T. (1995) 'Prostituting the Facts in Time of War and Humanitarian Crisis' in Girardet.

Weinberg, S. (1968) 'What to tell America: the Writers' Quarrel in the OWI', *Journal of American History,* LV, i, 73–89.

Weinberg, S. (1984) 'Approaches to the Study of Film in the Third Reich: A Critical Appraisal', *Journal of Contemporary History,* 19, i, 105–26.

304   *Select Bibliography*

Welch, D. (1983a) *Nazi Propaganda: The Power and the Limitations*. London: Croom Helm.

Welch, D. (1983b) *Propaganda and German Cinema, 1933–45*. Oxford: Clarendon Press.

Welch, D. (1983c) 'Nazi Wartime Newsreel Propaganda' in Short.

Welch, D. (1989) 'Priming the Pump of German Democracy: British "Re-Education" Policy in Germany after the Second World War' in Turner.

Welch, D. (1993) *The Third Reich: Politics and Propaganda*. London: Routledge.

West, W. (ed.) (1987a) *Orwell: The War Broadcasts*. Harmondsworth: Penguin.

West, W. (1987b) *Truth Betrayed*. London: Duckworth.

Westmoreland, W. (1979) 'Vietnam in Perspective', *Military Review*, 59, i, 34–43.

Wilkinson, P. (1986) *Terrorism and the Liberal State*. New York: New York University Press.

Wilkinson, P. (1997) 'The Media and Terrorism: A Reassessment', *Terrorism and Political Violence*, 9, ii, 51–64.

Wilkinson, P. and Stewart, A. (eds) (1987) *Contemporary Research on Terrorism*. Aberdeen: Aberdeen University Press.

Willcox, T. (1983) 'Projection or Publicity? Rival Concepts in the Pre-War Planning of the British Ministry of Information', *Journal of Contemporary History*, 18, i, 97–116.

Williams, K. (1992) 'Something more important than truth: ethical issues in war reporting' in Belsey and Chadwick.

Williams, K. (1993) 'The light at the end of the tunnel. The mass media, public opinion and the Vietnam War' in Eldridge.

Williams, P. (1992) 'Statement Before the US Senate Committee on Governmental Affairs' in Smith.

Williams, T. (1991) 'Narrative Patterns and Mythic Trajectories in Mid-1980s Vietnam Movies' in Anderegg.

Williams, V. (1994) *Warworks: Women, Photography and the Iconography of War*. London: Virago.

Wills, G. (1997) *John Wayne: The Politics of Celebrity*. London: Faber & Faber.

Wilson, T. (1979) 'Lord Bryce's Investigation into Alleged German Atrocities in Belgium, 1914–15', *Journal of Contemporary History*, 14, iii, 369–83.

Windrich, E. (1989) 'South Africa's Propaganda War', *Africa Today*, 36, i, 51–60.

Winkler, A. (1978) *The Politics of Propaganda: the Office of War Information, 1942–45*. New Haven, NJ: Yale University Press.

Winter, J. (1989) *The Experience of World War One*. New York: Oxford University Press.

Winter, J. (1995) *Sites of Memory, Sites of Mourning: The Great War in European Cultural History*. Cambridge: Cambridge University Press.

Wolfsfeld, G. (1997) *Media and Political Conflict: News from the Middle East*. Cambridge: Cambridge University Press.

Woodward, B. (1992) *The Commanders*. London: Simon & Schuster.

Wyatt, C. (1993) *Paper Soldiers: The American Press and the Vietnam War*. New York: W.W. Norton.

Young, P. (ed.) (1992) *Defence and the Media in Time of Limited War*. London: Cassell.

Young, P. and Jesser, P. (1997) *The Media and the Military: From the Crimea to Desert Strike*. London: Macmillan.

Youngblood, D. (1996) '*Ivan's Childhood* (USSR, 1962) and *Come and See* (USSR, 1985): Post-Stalinist Cinema and the Myth of World War II' in Chambers and Culbert.

Zaller, J. (1992) *The Nature and Origins of Mass Opinion*. Cambridge: Cambridge University Press.

Zeman, Z. (1973) *Nazi Propaganda*. London: Oxford University Press.

Zulaika, J. and Douglass, W. (1996) *Terror and Taboo: the follies, fables and faces of terrorism*. London: Routledge.

Index